# Husserl's Phenomenology
# of Natural Language

# Husserl's Phenomenology of Natural Language

*Intersubjectivity and Communality in the Nachlass*

Horst Ruthrof

BLOOMSBURY ACADEMIC
LONDON · NEW YORK · OXFORD · NEW DELHI · SYDNEY

BLOOMSBURY ACADEMIC
Bloomsbury Publishing Plc
50 Bedford Square, London, WC1B 3DP, UK
1385 Broadway, New York, NY 10018, USA
29 Earlsfort Terrace, Dublin 2, Ireland

BLOOMSBURY, BLOOMSBURY ACADEMIC and the Diana logo are trademarks of
Bloomsbury Publishing Plc

First published in Great Britain 2021
This paperback edition published 2023

Copyright © Horst Ruthrof, 2021

Horst Ruthrof has asserted his right under the Copyright, Designs and Patents Act, 1988, to be identified as Author of this work.

For legal purposes the Acknowledgments on pp. viii–ix constitute an extension of this copyright page.

Cover design by Charlotte Daniels
Cover image © SuperStock / Alamy Stock Photo

All rights reserved. No part of this publication may be reproduced or transmitted in any form or by any means, electronic or mechanical, including photocopying, recording, or any information storage or retrieval system, without prior permission in writing from the publishers.

Bloomsbury Publishing Plc does not have any control over, or responsibility for, any third-party websites referred to or in this book. All internet addresses given in this book were correct at the time of going to press. The author and publisher regret any inconvenience caused if addresses have changed or sites have ceased to exist, but can accept no responsibility for any such changes.

A catalogue record for this book is available from the British Library.

Library of Congress Cataloging-in-Publication Data
Names: Ruthrof, Horst, author.
Title: Husserl's phenomenology of natural language: intersubjectivity and communality in the Nachlass / Horst Ruthrof.
Description: London; New York: Bloomsbury Academic, 2021. | Includes bibliographical references and index. |
Identifiers: LCCN 2021004561 (print) | LCCN 2021004562 (ebook) | ISBN 9781350230873 (hardback) | ISBN 9781350230880 (ebook) | ISBN 9781350230897 (epub)
Subjects: LCSH: Husserl, Edmund, 1859-1938. | Language and languages–Philosophy. | Phenomenology. | Intersubjectivity.
Classification: LCC B3279.H94 R88 2021 (print) | LCC B3279.H94 (ebook) | DDC 121/.68–dc23
LC record available at https://lccn.loc.gov/2021004561
LC ebook record available at https://lccn.loc.gov/2021004562

ISBN: HB: 978-1-3502-3087-3
PB: 978-1-3502-3091-0
ePDF: 978-1-3502-3088-0
eBook: 978-1-3502-3089-7

Typeset by Deanta Global Publishing Services, Chennai, India

To find out more about our authors and books visit www.bloomsbury.com and sign up for our newsletters.

*For Yingchi, my wife*

# Contents

| | |
|---|---|
| Acknowledgments | viii |
| List of Abbreviations | x |
| Preface | xii |

1  Introduction: Language and Intersubjective Intentionality — 1

## Part I  Two Husserlian Points of Departure

2  Husserl's Philosophy of Language and Its Revisions — 21
3  Language *as* Eidetic Reduction: The Fuzzy *Eidos* — 39

## Part II  Intersubjective Intentionality *in* Language

4  Introjective Reciprocity: Meaning as Communal, Cognitive Event — 61
5  From Husserl's *Tone* to *Implicit Deixis* — 81
6  From Meaning Sufficiency to Communal Control — 101
7  A Phenomenological Redefinition of Linguistic Meaning — 118

## Part III  Implications for the Theorization of Language

8  Why Language Is Not Simply a "Symbolic" System — 137
9  Displacement, Mental Time Travel, and Protosyntax — 160
10  Conclusion: The Social Mode of Being of Language — 178

| | |
|---|---|
| References | 197 |
| Index | 218 |

# Acknowledgments

Foremost, I want to acknowledge the professional support I have received from the Geoffrey Bolton Library at Murdoch University while writing this book. I want to thank especially our humanities librarian Helen Gibson and her staff who have gone out of their way to fill the gaps in our research resources with interlibrary loans and especially texts from Germany. For much of what I wanted to say depended on access to Husserl's *Nachlass*, two volumes on his revisions of the *Logical Investigations*, three volumes on intersubjectivity, as well as one volume on eidetic variation, in addition to other writings not available in Western Australia. Although the book is not primarily conceived as an exegesis of Husserl's writings, these six volumes of his *Nachlass* formed the backbone of my search for a theorization of language within Husserlian parameters. Two volumes on language deserve special mention, Husserliana XX/1 and XX/2, edited by Ullrich Melle. In addition, there is the *Nachlass* volume on eidetic variation Husserliana XLI, edited by Dirk Fonfara, and the three crucial volumes on intersubjectivity, volumes XIII, XIV, and XV, edited by Iso Kern. I want to applaud the enormous work that has gone into these editions, which, I believe, will gradually generate a much deeper appreciation of Husserl's contribution to philosophy and especially the theorization of language as the backbone of intersubjectivity and language. Two edited volumes on phenomenology have provided useful guidelines for my thinking, *One Hundred Years of Phenomenology*, edited by Dan Zahavi and Frederik Stjernfelt (2002), and *Meaning and Language: Phenomenological Perspectives*, edited by Filip Mattens (2008). I have quoted freely from Husserl and his commentators, partly because much of the *Nachlass* is not yet available to non-German readers, partly to give a flavor of Husserl's style of writing and reasoning. Translations are my own, except where stated otherwise. I acknowledge the influence of a large number of other scholarly works in analytical philosophy of language, linguistics, and semiotics that have contributed to the development of the *imaginability thesis* that informs the present study. Whatever flaws the book may have, they are entirely my own.

I owe a special thanks to the late Maurice Natanson, who generously sparked off my publishing career in the early 1970s. My turn to the social side of intentional acts has its origins in discussions in the 1970s and 1980s with John Frow, who felt strongly that phenomenology needed to engage more seriously with the social and do so beyond the parameters of the writings of Alfred Schütz. I thank him also for his friendship and continuing encouragement over many years. The social dimension that appeared missing in phenomenology has now been rediscovered in Husserl's *Nachlass*, where the elaboration of *sociality* effectively undermines the standard charge of subjectivism and solipsism as methodological flaws of phenomenology. Another special "thank-you" is addressed to the late Lester Embree, founder of the Organization of Phenomenological Organizations (OPO), who bolstered my resolve to practice phenomenology rather than to offer yet another exegesis of Husserl's writings. Intrigued by what Husserl had to say on natural language in the *Nachlass*, I followed Lester's advice to the extent that I sought to balance my desire to reflect Husserl's thinking as much as possible, while at the same time advancing my own ideas.

Among my West Australian colleagues, I want to thank Vijay Mishra for in-depth analyses over peaty single malts, Lubica Ucnik for our many phenomenological conversations, Alec McHoul for strongly defending a radically different position, and Richard Hamilton, whose wit and knowledge of the philosophical landscape I have much appreciated over the years. For their interest in my work, I thank Michael Seats, Kathy Trees, Andrew Turk, Mark Jennings, and Anita Williams. Also, I have always enjoyed listening to the papers offered by our philosophy students. They remain an essential component of the intellectual life of Murdoch University. Last, thanks to our colleagues at the University of Western Australia, whose philosophy seminars have for many years been a source of orientation in the broader arena of philosophical paradigms.

I gratefully acknowledge permission from editors to use materials from previously published work in the present volume. I thank the editors of *Language Sciences* for allowing me to draw on passages from "Implicit Deixis" (2015) in Chapter 5; *The American Journal of Semiotics* for letting me harvest ideas from "Sufficient Semiosis" (2015) for Chapter 6; and the editors of *Philosophy Today, Linguistic and Philosophical Investigations, Review of Contemporary Philosophy*, and *Analysis and Metaphysics* for their permission to use materials from various articles in several chapters. I also gratefully acknowledge approval by the editors of *Phenomenology and the Problem of Meaning in Life and History* for the inclusion of passages from "On the Mode of Being of Language" (2017) in the Conclusion of the book. I gratefully acknowledge the support and guidance by the Bloomsbury editorial staff and especially by Jade Grogan and Joseph Gautham.

Engaging once more with Husserl's texts has also taken me back to my student years at the Universities of Erlangen-Nürnberg and München in the early 1960s, where I studied English literature from Beowulf to Virginia Woolf and the philosophies of Kant, Husserl, Heidegger, and Ingarden. It was there that I benefited greatly from the wisdom of two very close friends, the now-eminent Plato scholar Thomas Szlezák for his philosophical guidance and the Anglist and Germanist Volker Schulz† for introducing me to narratology. The gift of their friendship has been a sustaining influence. Last, and most important, is the thanks I owe to my wife, Dr. Yingchi Chu, who had to live with an often-absent-minded husband composing paragraphs during walks, shopping chores, and meals. Her tolerance, support, love, and reprimands have been a most reliable anchor. It is with much gratitude that I dedicate the book to her.

# Abbreviations

Hua I         Husserl, Edmund. 1950. *Cartesianische Meditationen und Pariser Vorträge*, ed. S. Strasser. The Hague: Martinus Nijhoff.

Hua III/1     Husserl, Edmund. 1977. *Ideen zu einer reinen Phänomenologie und phänomenologischen Philosophie. Erstes Buch: Allgemeine Einführung in die reine Phänomenologie. Erster Halbband. Text der 1.-3. Auflage*, ed. K. Schuhmann. The Hague: Martinus Nijhoff.

Hua IV        Husserl, Edmund. 1991. *Ideen zu einer reinen Phänomenologie und phänomenologischen Philosophie. Zweites Buch. Phänomenologische Untersuchungen zur Konstitution*, ed. M. Biemel. The Hague: Martinus Nijhoff.

Hua VI        Husserl, Edmund. 1976. *Die Krisis der europäischen Wissenschaften und die transzendentale Phänomenologie: Eine Einleitung in die phänomenologische Philosophie*, ed. W. Biemel. The Hague: Martinus Nijhoff.

Hua VII       Husserl, Edmund. 1965. *Erste Philosophie. (1923/24). Erster Teil: Kritische Ideengeschichte*, ed. R. Boehm. The Hague: Martinus Nijhoff.

Hua VIII      Husserl, Edmund. 1965. *Erste Philosophie (1923/24). Zweiter Teil: Theorie der phänomenologischen Reduktion*, ed. R. Boehme. The Hague: Martinus Nijhoff.

Hua IX        Husserl, Edmund. 1968. *Phänomenologische Psychologie. Vorlesungen Sommersemester 1925*, ed. W. Biemel. The Hague: Martinus Nijhoff.

Hua XII       Husserl, Edmund. 1970. *Philosophie der Arithmetik. Mit ergänzenden Texten (1890–1901)*, ed. L. Eley. The Hague: Martinus Nijhoff.

Hua XIII      Husserl, Edmund. 1973. *Zur Phänomenologie der Intersubjektivität. Texte aus dem Nachlass. Erster Teil: 1905–20*, ed. I. Kern. The Hague: Martinus Nijhoff.

Hua XIV       Husserl, Edmund. 1973c. *Zur Phänomenologie der Intersubjektivität. Texte aus dem Nachlass. Zweiter Teil: 1921–8*, ed. I. Kern. The Hague: Martinus Nijhoff.

Hua XV        Husserl, Edmund. 1973d. *Zur Phänomenologie der Intersubjektivität. Texte aus dem Nachlass. Dritter Teil: 1929–35*, ed. I. Kern. The Hague: Martinus Nijhoff.

Hua XVII      Husserl, Edmund. 1974. *Formale und transzendentale Logik. Versuch einer Kritik der logischen Vernunft. Mit ergänzenden Texten*, ed. P. Janssen. The Hague: Martinus Nijhoff.

| | |
|---|---|
| Hua XIX/2 | Husserl, Edmund. 1984. *Logische Untersuchungen. Zweiter Band: Untersuchungen zur Phänomenologie und Theorie der Erkenntnis*, ed. U. Panzer. Dordrecht: Kluwer. |
| Hua XX/1 | Husserl, Edmund. 2002. *Logische Untersuchungen. Ergänzungsband. Erster Teil. Entwürfe zur Umarbeitung der VI. Untersuchung der 'Logischen Untersuchungen'*, ed. U. Melle. Dordrecht: Kluwer. |
| Hua XX/2 | Husserl, Edmund. 2005. *Logische Untersuchungen. Ergänzungsband. Zweiter Teil. Texte für die Neufassung VI. Untersuchung. Zur Phänomenologie des Ausdrucks und der Erkenntnis (1893/94–1921)*, ed. U. Melle. Dordrecht: Springer. |
| Hua XXIV | Husserl, Edmund. 1985. *Einleitung in die Logik und Erkenntnistheorie. Vorlesungen 1906/07*, ed. U. Melle. Dordrecht: Kluwer. |
| Hua XXVI | Husserl, Edmund. 1987. *Vorlesungen über Bedeutungslehre, Sommersemester 1908*, ed. U. Panzer. The Hague: Martinus Nijhoff. |
| Hua XXVII | Husserl, Edmund. 1989. *Aufsätze und Vorträge 1922–1937*, ed. T. Nenon and H. R. Sepp. Dordrecht: Kluwer. |
| Hua XXXII | Husserl, Edmund. 2001. *Natur und Geist. Vorlesungen Sommersemester 1927*, ed. M. Weiler. Dordrecht: Kluwer. |
| Hua XXXIX | Husserl, Edmund. 2008. *Die Lebenswelt: Auslegungen der vorgegebenen Welt und ihre Konstitution*, ed. R. Sowa. Dordrecht: Springer. |
| Hua XLI | Husserl, Edmund. 2012. *Zur Lehre vom Wesen und zur Methode der eidetischen Variation: Texte aus dem Nachlass (1891–1935)*, ed. D. Fonfara. Dordrecht: Springer. |
| CPR | Kant, Immanuel. 1966. *Kritik der reinen Vernunft*. Darmstadt: Wissenschaftliche Buchgesellschaft. |
| CP | Peirce, Charles Sanders. 1974. *Collected Papers of Charles Sanders Peirce 1931–1966*. 8 vols., ed. C. Hartsworth, P. Weiss, and A. W. Burks. Cambridge, MA: Belknap Press. |
| EP | Peirce, Charles Sanders. 1984. *Writings of Charles S. Peirce: A Chronological Edition*, v. 2, 1867–71. Peirce Edition Project. Bloomington: Indiana University Press. |

# Preface

Attempting to write a book that draws substantially on Husserl's writings on language from his *Logical Investigations* (1900/1) to the posthumous *Crisis of European Sciences and Transcendental Phenomenology* (1954, 1970), and especially his *Nachlass*, means to face two obvious options. One is to follow the dominant trend of focusing on Husserl's aim to identify the logical relations embedded in language, discussed in his first big publication and elaborated throughout the remainder of his career. The second option is to attend to those features in his writings that permit a theorization of natural language as open-ended, cultural praxis in its own right. The first avenue has produced impressive results, such as the portrayal of Husserl's "language as calculus" by Martin Kusch and descriptions placing Husserl in the vicinity of Gottlob Frege, as for example by Dagfinn Føllesdal, David W. Smith, and Ronald McIntyre.[1] The majority of publications on Husserl have tended to favor this approach in sharp contrast, for example, to recent treatments of what Martin Heidegger and Merleau-Ponty have had to say about language.[2] In comparison, Husserl's rich and pioneering conception of natural language as *proximate communication* remains an undertheorized topic.

*Husserl's Phenomenology of Natural Language: Intersubjectivity and Communality in the Nachlass* is not designed to rectify this situation by offering a linguistic exegesis of his work. Rather, it attempts to construct a view of language that has its basis in Husserl's remarks about the kind of intentionality that constitutes the expressions of natural language quite apart from their function as logical, "grammatical clothing."[3] To be sure, the bulk of Husserl's descriptions supports the calculus view of Husserl's conception of language, the units of which had to be sifted so that the "logician" can "pick out the components that interest him, the characters of acts, first of all, in which logical presentation, judgment and knowledge are consummated."[4] Although Husserl never gave up on this search for the logic of language, the more remarkable is it that in its shadow there gradually emerged a description of the non-formal features of language as a foil. While Husserl attended to language in this sense only *secondarily*, by the time he wrote *Formal and Transcendental Logic*, he had acknowledged the importance of "vague judgments" and "all the non-formal 'material of cognition'" as key features of natural language.[5] Above all, what makes natural language *natural* comes to the fore most persuasively in the two Husserliana volumes on his revisions of the *Logical Investigations* and, in an ancillary way, in the three *Nachlass* volumes on intersubjectivity.[6] So, the reader will not be surprised to find that they function in the present book as key sources of Husserl's position.

What makes Husserl's approach to natural language unique in my view is what could be called his *expanded linguistic horizon*. Instead of restricting his analysis to the relation of word sounds, syntax, and meaning, Husserl broadens his conception of language to include quasi-perceptual meaning intention, prelinguistic categorial relations, their displacement in merely symbolic *Bedeutung*, and its reversal in nonverbal meaning fulfilment as *Sinn*. This expanded view of language amounts to the creation of a major and neglected paradigm in the theorization of natural language in competition with linguistic, semiotic, semiological, and analytical approaches. A compelling entailment of Husserl's extended meaning chain is that language has to be conceived as a *reciprocal communicative* process rather than a set of sentence-tokens abstracted from the dynamics of utterances. A further consequence of his holistic starting point is that he can eschew the customary separation of semantic from pragmatic concerns, a disjunction that I argue rests on unwarranted and misleading presuppositions.

Beyond Husserl, I want to pursue certain accents, prominent in some of the *Nachlass* volumes, especially on *Anschaulichkeit*, rendered here mostly as vivid imaginability, a foundational feature of both acts of meaning intention and meaning fulfilment. Which led to the formulation of a deceptively simple proposition, the *imaginability thesis*, which can be put like this: "If I can *imagine* what you are talking about, and the manner in which you do, there is meaning. If not, not. And vice versa." In agreement with this formulation and in acknowledgment of the central role of the speech community, natural language can be defined as "a set of social instructions for imagining, and acting in, a world." The methodological profile of the book can be identified as an analysis of our performance of intentional acts without which language could not exist, the adumbrational procedure of repeatedly returning to key components of linguistic expressions from different angles, and the privileging of the speech community as always already present *in* language. A conspicuous feature of the book is the ubiquitous use of quotations, above all from Husserl's two *Nachlass* volumes (Husserliana XX/1 and XX/2) aimed at giving the reader a flavor of Husserl's phrasing and providing access to a substantial collection of passages not yet available in English.

HR

# Notes

1 Martin Kusch, *Language as Calculus and Universal Medium* (Dordrecht, Reidel, 1989); David W. Smith and Ronald McIntyre, *Husserl on Intentionality* (Dordrecht: Reidel, 1982).
2 Cf. Andrew Inkpin, *Disclosing the World: On the Phenomenology of Language* (Cambridge, MA: MIT Press, 2016) on Heidegger, Merleau-Ponty and Wittgenstein; and Dimitris Apostolopoulos, *Merleau-Ponty's Phenomenology of Language* (Roman and Littlefield International, 2019).
3 Edmund Husserl, *Logical Investigations*, trans. J. N. Findlay, 2 vols. (Amherst, NY: Humanity Books, 2000), p. 250.
4 Ibid.
5 Edmund Husserl, *Formal and Transcendental Logic*, trans. D. Cairns (The Hague: Martinus Nijhoff, 1969), p. 71.
6 Hua XX/1, XX/2; Hua XIII, XIV, XV.

1

# Introduction

## Language and Intersubjective Intentionality

*Meaning is a such and such coloured act-character, which* presupposes *an act of* vividly imaginable *presentation (anschaulichen Vorstellens) as necessary foundation.*
(Hua XIX/1, p. 81)[1]

## Methodological Remarks

In this study, language is understood as *a set of social instructions for imagining, and acting in, a world*. This conception of language is derived from Husserl's writings and particularly from his *Nachlass*, where concepts such as *Anschaulichkeit* (vividness, picturability, imaginability), *Anschauung* (intuition), *Ton* (tone, voice), and *Zumutung* (imposition) play important roles and where perception and imagination are treated as equally valid sources of semantic value. In Husserl's treatment of natural language, it is linguistic meaning, not *existence*, that is the focus. Truth, though important for Husserl, cannot be taken as a foundation for the theorization of natural language. This is why throughout the book, the concept of *imaginability* (*Vorstellbarkeit*) will occupy center stage, in two senses, one, as our ability to imagine something in response to the sounds of linguistic expressions and, two, in the sense of language being able to carry and convey *imaginable content*. Neither of the two meanings of imaginability will be used in an optional sense. In the performance of *natural language* both appear at the same time. In the first sense, it will be treated as a form of communal constraint on individual speech performance, and in the second, as a necessary feature of language.[2]

The title of the book *Husserl's Phenomenology of Natural Language: Intersubjectivity and Communality in the Nachlass* is meant to draw the reader's attention to the modifications that Husserl added in his later work, and especially in his *Nachlass*, to what he had to say about language in his *Logical Investigations* (1900/1901), and how we can build on his subsequent insights. In addition, I want to shift the customary emphasis on subjective linguistic, intentional acts toward their *social* dependence relations, a move for which I believe there is significant justification in Husserl's later writings and, again, in the *Nachlass*. The accentuation of the social is not meant as an elaborate confirmation of the fact that language is fundamentally a collective activity.

The observable, social features of language as they are displayed in public discourse have been well canvassed in the philosophy of language, various forms of linguistics, pragmatics, in Peircean semiotics, and Saussurean semiology. Language is clearly a social phenomenon as a visible and audible form of communication. What is not so obvious is that the acts of consciousness that we cannot but perform when we engage in language are likewise fundamentally social, but in diverse and intricate ways. It is the broad aim of the book to demonstrate in what ways the social deep ground of natural language is reflected in our individual intentional, linguistic acts. The method of investigation chosen is a Husserlian form of phenomenology committed to the description and eidetic distillation of the kind of *intentionality* that characterizes linguistic communication.

But why language as *communication* rather than simply *language*? Following Husserl, the restriction of language to an observable objectivity in isolation is the kind of presupposition to be avoided at all cost. The unwarranted assumption here would be that what we can see and hear is all to language that matters. Instead, this study wants to heed Husserl motto "to the things themselves (*zu den Sachen selbst*)," by way of intentional act description.[3] In approaching such a description from a number of adumbrational angles, the study grants predominance to two sets of volumes in the Husserliana edition, Hua XX/1 and Hua XX/2, both dedicated to revisions of *Logical Investigations*, and Hua XIII, XIV, and XV on the phenomenology of intersubjectivity.[4] Together, they form the bedrock on which I will propose my imaginability thesis of natural language. Formulated simply, the thesis states, "If I can *imagine* what you are talking about, including the manner in which you are, there is meaning. If not, not. And vice versa, if you can *imagine* the aboutness of my expressions and its mode of presentation, there is meaning. If not, not."

The skeptical reader may object that our standard, empirical, quantitative, and qualitative research methods are precisely designed for getting us to the things as they are. Husserl answers with an emphatic "No." In the ordinary and scientific way of viewing the world, we are guilty of remaining at the level of the prescientific, *natural attitude* (*natürliche Einstellung*) and the scientific, *naturalistic attitude*, which fail to question our preconceptions of how things are. For Husserl, "the natural attitude is the form in which the total life of humanity is realized in running its natural, practical course."[5] From this stance, we conceive of things as the sum of their properties in contingent relations with all other naturally appearing things in the world around us. The naturalistic attitude can be understood as the natural attitude as far as it appears in the natural sciences. In phenomenology, the sum of the properties of objects is regarded as the unacknowledged result of the sum of intentional acts that we typically and of necessity conduct when we experience things. In doing so, we *constitute* things, not in the sense that we create what is not there but as realizing them in relation to ourselves within community constraints. While the difference between these two attitudes is not immediately obvious in our experience of ordinary objects, his point can be dramatically demonstrated in the viewing of novel artworks where we cannot rely on preconceived, sedimented typifications. Picasso's *Guernica* or puzzle plot films make us aware of the constitutional, interpretive labor that is involved in the process of making objectivities meaningful, that is, what they are for us, an experience, I want to stress, that is always already a communal, intersubjective form of intentionality rather than a merely subjective one. Husserl concedes that this switch in attitude to the phenomenological stance is not easy to make. After all, he says, the phenomenological method demands "thought running counter to deeply ingrained habits."[6] Husserl's critique of the natural attitude demands a *reversal* of our assumed sequence of priorities. Instead of regarding the world as the natural starting point, what we actually do is the obverse. From our act responses *to* the world we draw inferences *about* the world. What appears first, then, is evidence beyond doubt as it appears to us, always given in a certain mode of consciousness. Husserl calls this evidence *apodictic*.[7]

The shift to the *phenomenological gaze* is theorized by Husserl as the *phenomenological reduction*, a technique by which we abandon as much as possible all natural and theoretical preconceptions. However, Husserl's idea of *Voraussetzungslosigkeit* as an absence of presuppositions or the act of bracketing (*einklammern*) should not be confused with acts of eliminationism. "To bracket a belief," Dorion Cairns explains, "is not to destroy it—it is not even to shut one's eyes to it."[8] Read charitably, the Husserlian *epoché* is a methodological constraint in preparation for the description of intentional acts. In the study of language, this amounts to leaving behind all ordinary assumptions about how linguistic expressions work, and especially all theoretical, that is, all linguistic, semiotic, semiological, and philosophical premises with which we happen to be familiar. The very first task, then, is to define the *scope* of our investigation. Here the book adopts Husserl's broad strategy of viewing language as *communication*.[9] As we shall see, this choice has many consequences, one of which is that from the very start we are forced to acknowledge the *social* nature of language, a realization that would be less obvious if we were to restrict our focus, for instance, to the analysis of language as a system of sentences. From a phenomenological perspective such a reductive choice is unwarranted. The answer to a question like "Is there in a sentence a moment of 'act'?"[10] would reveal that sentences are abstractions of utterances from which intentionality has been excised. Only in utterances can intentional acts be individually and socially realized. While the early Husserl still thought that there could be nonsocial, subjective exceptions of language use, as for instance in soliloquy, in his later revisions he rejects any assumption that language could ever be anything but *communicative* through and through.[11] As we shall see, this intersubjective emphasis is put beyond doubt in his *Nachlass* where he draws the encompassing conclusion from his analyses that "experience of the world is from the outset always already *communal* experience," in which language plays a pivotal role. For Husserl, "the home world of humans" is "fundamentally determined by language," transforming as it does the merely sensuous world into an "incomparably larger circle of experience," which "effectively contains experiences of Others that are communicated linguistically." Via linguistic transmission, the Other has a "secondary experience" that cumulatively produces the disposition of a "co-belief" (*Mitglauben*).[12]

Once we have taken the phenomenological turn toward intentional acts, Husserl guides us to noticing that every linguistic utterance begins well before the uttered linguistic expression and terminates well after its utterance. We can call this Husserl's *expanded linguistic horizon* of the verbal meaning chain stretching from nonverbal meaning intention to its verbal displacement, and its reversal in the nonverbal acts of meaning fulfilment as a proximate reconstruction of meaning intention.[13] Were we to attend only to the expressions themselves, their phonemes, morphemes, syntax, and assumed, standard "immanent" meanings, we would have prejudged the very object of inquiry. We would have made language, in T. S. Eliot's words, "a patient etherized upon a table." In contrast, the later Husserl speaks of language as a "linguistic living body [*Sprachleib*]."[14] With this difference in mind, our description of at least *some* of the acts we perforce perform in the production and comprehension of language will generate a very different picture, one that focuses on what makes language a living body nudging us to reflect on the "communicability of what is communicated (*die Mitteilbarkeiten der Mitteilung*)."[15]

How *we mean* by way of language, then, must occupy center stage of our investigation. It is extraordinary, is it not, that an authoritative linguist like David Crystal turns to the question of meaning only on page 186 of *How Language Works*, when nothing he says before would make sense without it.[16] Likewise, Noam Chomsky's entire edifice of syntax is constructed on the assumption that meaning is already in place. Without it, not a single one of his syntactic observations could be comprehended.[17] While this may look like a trivially obvious point, it draws our attention to the centrality of meaning for any theorization of language. For the phenomenologist, the primacy of meaning has also methodological consequences. Once we turn our gaze toward the intentional acts involved in linguistic communication, *all* aspects of language appear to add to the way in which meaning comes about. Readers may object that we are now conflating semantics with *pragmatics*. Indeed, we are, but *deliberately* so. In this respect, the book follows yet another lead offered by Husserl. His focus on language as *communication* stands in stark contrast with the strategy of *minimalist semantics*, which can result in elegantly economic descriptions but changes natural language as the object of inquiry into something it is not in actuality.[18]

Phenomenologists can, however, not stay content with the description of intentional acts in their immediate appearance. That would invite the usual charges of subjectivism and *psychologism*, "methodological individualism" and "solipsism," all of which Husserl rejected by advocating a second methodological constraint, the *eidetic reduction*.[19] Here we vary any individual instantiation of language imaginatively, exploring a range of variants until we are able to abstract an *invariant form*. The question whether the eidetic procedure leads to Husserl's *essences* or merely to concept clarification will have to be postponed to Chapter 3, except to say here that the eidetic procedure allows us to transform individual instantiations of expressions as meaning acts into *metasemantic principles*, allowing for a variety of semantic explications.[20] Husserl's third major reduction, among a range of others, called the *transcendental reduction*, will not be foregrounded in our investigation. The reason for this omission is that the book will offer an alternative path to bridging the apparent gap between subjectivity and intersubjectivity.[21] It will do so by arguing that language is itself a system of eidetic reductions, by which subjective instantiations always reveal their intersubjective ground. Whether it is also a "system of invariants,"[22] in Husserl's sense, will have to be seen. The procedure recommended by Husserl is to attend to actual speech by way of "speech analysis (*Sprachanalyse*)" before proceeding to "thought analysis (*Denkanalyse*)" and from there further to the clarification of the "essential relations (*Wesensbeziehungen*)" between thinking and intuiting (*Anschauen*) and, finally, to the functions of fulfilment (*Erfüllung*) and evidence (*Evidenz*). Husserl hopes that in this way the characteristic features of the "essentially teleological structure of consciousness" will thereby gradually reveal themselves.[23]

## Imaginability (*Vorstellbarkeit*)

From the outset, I want to foreground two mainstays of my argument. One is *imaginability*, now more precisely defined as (1) our ability to *vary perception* under communal guidance and (2) the *capacity* of language to carry what is imagined in displaced fashion for proximate reconstitution in acts of *meaning fulfilment*.[24] The other major emphasis is on the *speech community*, without which language could never have evolved the way it has, nor function the way it does as intersubjective praxis. As will emerge in the ensuing chapters, the two volumes of Husserl's *Nachlass* on language contain materials that, in my view, legitimate arguments in favor of a stronger accent on the central role of imaginability than has previously been acknowledged.[25] A few preliminary remarks on the idea of imaginability may be helpful here. In the *Critique of Judgment*, Kant uses the concept imaginability as our capacity to imagine things (*Vorstellungsvermögen*), but without the second meaning of imaginability as a feature of the object so imagined.[26] More recently, in Ludwig Wittgenstein's *Philosophical Investigations*, imaginability (*Vorstellbarkeit*) serves the purpose of drawing our attention to the question of "the extent to which it ensures that a sentence makes sense." Having rejected imaginability as a contributor to linguistic meaning by relegating it to the incidental role of tunes on the *Vorstellungsklavier* (keyboard of the imagination) earlier in the *Philosophical Investigations*, Wittgenstein now appears to have second thoughts.[27] Likewise, Husserl's early rejection of mental imagery as linguistic meaning is balanced by his later accent on "graded series of fulfilments."[28] Certainly, linguistic *displacement*,[29] that is, language as symbolic proxy for nonverbal grasp, is not thinkable without the precondition of imaginability. It is of course still entirely open what *imagining* consists in when we *imagine* what someone is talking about. However, imaginability is conceived from the outset not as subjective but as part of cultural sociality. From this position, it would seem that Gottlob Frege eliminated *Vorstellung* from linguistic meaning prematurely, on the not entirely cogent assumption that every language user will have too different an "idea" (*Vorstellung*) in response to a linguistic expression. Husserl took the opposite route by granting *Vorstellung* as imaginability (*Vorstellbarkeit*) a pivotal role in his conception of *Wesenserschauung* (seeing essences), the aimed at result of the *eidetic reduction*. The idea that there must be something essential about *Vorstellung* can be traced back to Kant, who writes in a letter to Marcus Herz on February 21, 1772, "I noticed that I still lacked something *essential*, something that in my long metaphysical studies I, as well as others, had failed to pay attention to." In particular, Kant wanted to explore what anchors our ability to relate *Vorstellung* "to the object."[30]

The principle Kant was looking for informs Husserl's eidetic search for a binding generality in which *Vorstellung* is indispensable. After all, the most obvious advantage of language over all other sign systems is *displacement* and, through it, its capacity to communicate about things in absentia. For example, imaginability as the varying of perception is also the basis on which Husserl's concept of *appresentation* does its work. It plays such an important role in the *Cartesian Meditations* not only with respect to the complex constitution of the Other but more generally as a requisite function in the constitution of everyday reality. As Husserl reaffirms from another perspective, not only does imaginability as "reproductive consciousness" belong to every act of perceiving, as a possibility, "every memorial as-if" is a sort of "transforming fiction" and "every experience has as its counterpart a phantasy (a re-presentation) corresponding to it."[31]

## Speech Community

As to the second mainstay of my argument, the prominent role of the speech community, it also takes its cue from Husserl's *Nachlass*, his three volumes on intersubjectivity and specifically from his idea of *linguistic coercion (Zumutung)*. While the role of the speech community is somewhat neglected in Husserl's early writings,[32] we can reconstruct its function by combining what he says about intersubjectivity in *Ideas* and the *Crisis*,[33] and especially his remarks on the community of monads (*Monadengemeinschaft*) and linguistic coercion (*Zumutung*) in the *Nachlass*.[34] This shift is confirmed in Husserl's last writings where he speaks of the "immediate and mediate linguistic community" as a "community of those who can reciprocally express themselves."[35] In particular, Husserl draws our attention to a feature of linguistic expressions that reveals in a quite subtle way the guiding hand of the community in every act of meaning constitution by speakers of a language. He refers to this feature as a "social Ought."[36] Habitual speech (*Sprachüblichkeit*) is viewed as a form of coercion. "For the listener, the sign is affected with the 'ought' of an imposition, in relation to the *Bedeutung*, and the ought is directed at the listener."[37] I will deal with Husserl's idea of language as an imposition (*Zumutung*), under the heading of *Abrichtung* (strict training) and what I have termed the *linguistic linkage compulsion*,[38] a special form of imposition of how "word sound and meaning are associated" by way of a coercion.[39] As I will argue, the association of word sounds with imaginable states of affairs is schematically *typified* and socialized rather than merely *subjective*. The theme of socialized imaginability will also play a role in arguments in favor of intersubjective reciprocity (Chapter 4), the primacy of utterance (Chapter 5), sufficient intentionality as a result of *Abrichtung* (Chapter 6), and degrees of schematization of mental materials (Chapter 7). Whatever the role of imaginability in linguistic meaning will turn out to be, it will be conceived as culturally and socially anchored. In this sense, the imaginability thesis is fundamentally an intersubjective, *social* thesis.

## Meaning as Ideality versus Meaning as Intentional Act

In the *Logical Investigations*, Husserl writes, "meaning is related to varied acts of meaning."[40] The ideality of meaning thus is sharply distinguished from its factuality in linguistic utterance. While Martin Kusch, for example, has based his influential description of Husserl's *semantics* on the former, I will take as my focus the latter, that is, a description of what actually happens when we engage in language. The contrast between the two approaches could hardly be any sharper. Kusch sums up his portrait in the following eight propositions: (1) Semantics is "accessible" and "inexhaustible." Ideal meanings allow for both "ever new metalanguages" and linguistic particulars; (2) "re-interpretation of language *in toto* is possible," permitting different "ways of worldmaking"; (3) Husserl accommodates "model theory" and the concept of "possible worlds" such that "eidetic structures hold in all possible worlds"; (4) "universal grammar" guarantees the intertranslatability among different languages, undermining "linguistic relativism"; (5) "every ego is in principle open to empathetic understanding," including their objectifying acts, "including the *Ding an sich*"; (6) transcendental language is "a true metalanguage," with respect to "ordinary language"; (7) Husserl's "truth is the total perceptual fulfilment of a meaning intention"; and (8) formal systems have formal objects as "content." Accordingly, Husserl's meanings are taken to be "ideal, abstract, non-temporal (and *eo ipso* non-spatial) entities that are independent of being thought of."[41]

Meanings conceived as linguistic, intentional act events are radically different. They are actual, specific, they take time, and are dependent on individual performance under communal control. To be sure, Kusch's stark distillation of a calculus conception of natural language is legitimized by sufficient evidence in Husserl's writings. However, what such an approach cannot accomplish is to do justice to Husserl's many other remarks on natural language, especially in the *Nachlass*, where the epistemic side of natural language appears to be argued as the sum of necessary, intentional acts. In order to fill this research gap, the present study addresses Husserl's expanded linguistic horizon by paying attention to what he has to say about the various acts that make up the meaning chain from meaning intention via its displacement by arbitrary signifiers that, in turn, require a reversal of displacement via acts of meaning fulfilment. The contrast between the two approaches is summed up by Husserl himself in his distinction between *semantic* and *epistemic essence*.[42] While the former, *semantic ideality*, will be reconceived in terms of *semantic sufficiency*, it is the social practice of the latter that is the main focus of this book.

## Husserl in the Landscape of Alternative Approaches

### Semiology and Semiotics

While it is not at all clear whether Ferdinand de Saussure would have accepted the version of the *Cours de linguistique générale* in the form in which it has come down to us, it remains the main source of information about his semiological conception of language.[43]

The book has, however, been strongly challenged recently by Beata Stawarska in *Saussure's Philosophy of Language as Phenomenology: Undoing the Doctrine of the Course in General Linguistics* (2015).[44] From a Husserlian perspective, her critique is apropos, especially with reference to the problematic, structuralist, *radical arbitrariness thesis*.[45] Three key differences set Saussurean semiology apart from a Husserlian approach to language: (1) phenomenology avoids the Saussurean presupposition that nonverbal signification should be judged by linguistic criteria, (2) the claim that the nonverbal domain is always already fully absorbed by language, and (3) that the *signified* could in any way be regarded as arbitrary. Saussure's linguistic idealism is incompatible with Husserl's theorization on the grounds that language "is related correlatively to the world, the universe of objects which is linguistically expressible in its being and its being-such."[46]

That a Husserlian approach should be much more compatible with the semiotics of Charles Sanders Peirce should not be surprising.[47] After all, both Peirce and Husserl are seriously indebted to Kant. Quite apart from Husserl's early paper on formal semiotics (1890),[48] there is fundamental agreement on language as carrying resemblance relations. Also, both Peirce and Husserl contribute to the Aristotelian tradition of *resemblance relations* (*homoiomata*) by catering for the perceptual and imaginable ingredients of language. In the case of Peirce, "every symbol must have, organically attached to it, its Indices of Reactions and its Icons of Qualities."[49] Then, there is Husserl's *Monadengemeinschaft*, the community of monads, which can accommodate Peirce's conception of the speech community as "a sort of loosely compacted person."[50] Where Husserl distinguishes acts of formal intentionality from the non-formal acts of meaning constitution in language, acts of knowing, feeling, and willing, Peirce draws parallel distinctions at the level of the *interpretant*, distinguishing the logical interpretant[51] from the emotional interpretant,[52] the iconic interpretant,[53] and the hypoiconic interpretant.[54] In doing so, Peirce approaches the interpretant from two viewpoints, from what is an appropriate reading of icon, index, and symbol, on the one hand, and, on the other, from the quality of response. The former he calls the "immediate interpretant" and "proper significate" of the sign,[55] the latter the "dynamical interpretant" or "actual effect" determined by the sign. Under the heading of the dynamical interpretant, we find such responses as the "emotional," "energetic,"[56] "imperfect," "indirect," "successive," "logical," "symbolic," and "final" interpretant,[57] all of which can be rephrased in phenomenological terms. Both Peirce and Husserl stipulate logical and imaginable components as necessary ingredients of the linguistic meaning chain, Peirce in the combination of the logical and hypoiconic interpretant, Husserl in the fulfilment of *Bedeutung* by *Sinn*. Unlike Frege and Wittgenstein, Peirce and Husserl emphasize imaginability in combination with *empathetic introjection*.[58] We also find in Peirce, as in Husserl, more than just traces of Kant's schematism, in Peirce's *diagrammatic hypoiconicity* and,[59] as Dieter Lohmar has cogently argued, in Husserl's type and typification.[60] Peirce's diagrammatic hypoiconicity as schematized iconicity is well covered by Husserl's *gradation of Anschaulichkeit*.[61]

## Linguistics

In spite of impressive advances, traditional linguistics has been battling with the complexities of linguistic meaning without reaching any clear consensus. Where there is some agreement is on David Crystal's recommendation to explain the meaning of linguistic expressions by further linguistic expressions. But this procedure can only work if we already know the meaning of the substituting phrase, highlighting a fundamental flaw in the explanation. For if we are not familiar with either the meaning of the expression to be explained or with that of its substitution, meaning cannot occur. According to Crystal, we should now have at least a semantic inkling.[62] Alas, we remain stuck at the level of word sound and syntax. What is missing is *vividly imaginable, quasi-perceptual* meaning fulfilment (*erfüllende Anschauung*).[63] As we shall see, Husserl avoided this verbal merry-go-round by distinguishing between *Bedeutung*, merely verbal sense, and *Sinn* as an elaboration of *Bedeutung*,[64] that is, as more or less rich, nonverbal fulfilment.[65] But even as social semiotic a theorization as Michael Halliday's *functional linguistics* is parsimonious when it comes to the definition of meaning. In *Learning How to Mean* (1975), Halliday discusses the acquisition of meaning as part of "meaningful actions" within a limited "meaning potential." In short, "the child learns language as a system of meanings in functional contexts," which are always "social contexts." As language competency evolves, meaning is distributed across three domains, *ideational* components of *aboutness*, an *interpersonal* component relating to the speech situation, and a *textual component* covering the "operational" side of the presentation of utterances. This "direct dependence of a speech situation on the perceptual environment" gives way to the "lexico-grammatical level of words and structures," by which we have an "abstract" grasp of the linguistic meaning potential. Intergrammaticality replaces perceptual reference.[66] This picture of meaning remains largely intact also in his later works.[67] Yet how precisely we grasp the specificities of the world by verbal means remains unanswered. What is missing is the way the perceptual world enters language as imaginable content.

Among competing branches of linguistics, *cognitive linguistics* is arguably the closest to Husserl's pioneering project, even if its empirical conception of cognition is not easily reconciled with phenomenology since empirical mental schemas have been stripped of their Kantian, transcendental character.[68] To be sure, superficially, the concepts of image-schema,[69] cognitive maps, and mental imagery have a strong affinity with Husserl's *Anschaulichkeit* as a necessary component of meaning fulfilment.[70] Likewise, many other findings in cognitive linguistics are anticipated in principle in his writings. Husserl's accent on *gradation*, for example,[71] is resumed in the cognitive semantics of Leonard Talmy.[72] Ronald Langacker's point that linguistic grammar reflects nonverbal structures of perception (2008) is reminiscent of Husserl's categorial intuition and core forms.[73] Husserlian resemblance relations reappear in Jordan Zlatev's theme of cognitive mimesis,[74] as they do in Gilles Fauconnier's notion of mental mapping.[75] Husserl's embodiment thesis is transformed into a biological conception in *Philosophy in the Flesh: The Embodied Mind and Its Challenge to Western Thought*, resulting in a reduction of Husserl's intersubjective typifications to asocial *neural concepts*.[76] Last, the notion of *conceptual blending* divides empirically transformed *Vorstellung* into mental spaces as "small conceptual packets" by which we form cognitive networks of varying degrees of complexity.[77] What appears undertheorized are olfactory and other non-visual modalities, and a serious engagement with the all-important social dimension of language.

## The Propositional Path

Gottlob Frege's celebrated paper "Sense and Reference" (*Sinn und Bedeutung*, 1892) is broadly regarded as the beginning of modern language philosophy in the analytical style.[78] In spite of the fact that Frege thought that natural languages was "incoherent in the sense that no complete systematic account of the use of the sentences of such a language could be framed,"[79] he must be credited with having launched the most powerful tradition in the theorization of natural language, from Bertrand Russel's reformulations to present-day *hyperintensional semantics*.[80] Nonetheless, the main alternative to analytical language philosophy remains Edmund Husserl's program of intentional act description. In a way, Frege and Husserl epitomize two opposing paradigms for the analysis of language, both of which take their initial cues from Aristotle. Frege does so from Aristotle's remarks on linguistic expressions as *propositions*, useful for decisions on the truth or falsity of statements, and Husserl from Aristotle's more primary emphasis on *homoiomata*, that is, resemblance relations.[81] While the focus on propositions reflects Frege's allegiance to the ideal of mathematical logic and geometry, Husserl's approach, though initially sympathetic to that ideal, increasingly addresses the kind of complexities that distance natural language from formal signification, a difference neatly summed up by the distinction Dieter Lohmar draws between "artificial convention-and-contiguity semantics" and "natural similarity semantics."[82]

## Further Alternatives

Other approaches include *formal theorizations* resting on the presupposition that natural language works in principle like any symbolic sequence, such as $x = y^3$. This amounts to a reduction of language to defined relations among signifiers with neither *aboutness* nor *modality*,[83] while *applied formal approaches* (the tape measure analogy) result in a reduction of verbal communication to quantifiable sign-to-world relations.[84] They take as fact that linguistic expressions function like predefined measuring units, which, however, fail to account for natural kind terms and other expressions that display world-to-language relations.[85] Any approach assuming that natural language operates like any *technical language* (e.g.; welding instructions) is flawed since it caters only for *aboutness* and neglects the essential modalities of *voice*. A weakness of *truth-conditional theories* is that they are parasitic on meaning,[86] and that truth is irretrievable in principle in a vast number of linguistic expressions. Husserl avoids the truth trap by arguing the independence of *meaning* from *existence*.

*Syntactic explanations* cannot get off the ground without semantics and pre-predicative *protosyntax*. Based on the *chess fallacy*,[87] syntactic approaches presuppose and hide *meaning*. Externalist approaches restricted to *observables*, including those of Wittgenstein and Quine, eliminate *Vorstellung*, which is a necessary component in the bulk of language, especially where we speak of absent phenomena. Theories stipulating a *language of thought*, conceived as a formal language of the brain on which natural languages supervene, court infinite regress undermining *meaning* as social event.[88] Arguments in favor of neural concepts look like committing the *genetic fallacy* of confusing the functioning of language with its origins, while failing to address the all-important social dimension of language.[89] A similar criticism can be leveled against other biologically based theorizations of language.[90] The view of language as an infinite chain of signifiers, as proposed by Jacques Derrida, treats language as a *monosemiotic* system.[91] As I shall argue, with Husserl and Peirce, meaning fulfilment is *heterosemiotic*, in that *Sinn* is made vividly imaginable by the substitution of nonverbal semiosis for verbal syntagms, allowing *Sinn* to "coalesce with the object."[92] In contrast with the majority of competing theorizations of natural language, the concept of linguistic meaning that will emerge in the wake of Husserl's *Nachlass* can be abbreviated as the *nonverbal reversal of linguistic displacement under social constraints*, which is very much in the spirit of Husserl's *Nachlass* where the *Anschaulichkeit* (imaginability) of language receives a decisive accent.[93]

## Sketching the Argument

Following the Introduction—Language as Intersubjective Intentionality, Part I of the book looks at Husserl's early theory of language in relation to his later revisions and his conception of natural language as a socially organized, eidetic system. Against this background, I will derive a theorization of language on phenomenological principles from language samples as they typically occur in the lifeworld. Part II will do the main lifting in this task, while Part III will address some of the implications of a Husserlian theorization of language.

### Part I: Two Husserlian Points of Departure

Chapter 2, *Husserl's Philosophy of Language and Its Revisions*, has two aims, to recapitulate some of the main features of Husserl's early language theory and to foreshadow how the ideas of his later writings can assist in bringing his theorization up to date. In doing so, the chapter assembles the main themes that characterize Husserl's expanded linguistic horizon and his conception of language as a form of communication, with an emphasis on what he added in the *Nachlass* volumes.

In Chapter 3, *Language as Eidetic Reduction: The Fuzzy Eidos*, I sum up his blueprint for the method provided in *Experience and Judgment*. The *eidetic reduction* is then tested in different contexts, in formal systems, in the use of natural kind terms, and in relation to cultural objectivities. I raise the question whether our eidetic findings will always amount to a form of linguistic concept clarification. The chapter argues that language is itself an eidetic sign system, though language cannot be reduced to the point where Husserl's accent on *vivid imaginability* is jettisoned, and that the speech community is an *invariant in* language itself.

### Part II: Intersubjective Intentionality *in* Language

Chapter 4, *Introjective Reciprocity—Meaning as Communal, Cognitive Event*, claims that every individual instantiation of language is of necessity always already a *communal*, cognitive event. In arguing this relation, the chapter claims that we can arrive at intersubjectivity from a description of individual acts by showing that all linguistic expressions contain communal instructions and that linguistic comprehension cannot occur without the activation of the social ingredients that are part and parcel of language. A second major theme is the necessity of communally guided *introjective reciprocity* as a condition of meaning, resulting in the linguistic community of monads as a *being-within-one-another* in spite of its separate individualities. Thus, the chapter concludes, language is the main catalyst of the meeting of minds.

Chapter 5, *From Husserl's* Tone *to* Implicit Deixis, takes Husserl's remarks in the *Nachlass* on *tone* as its cue for arguing that marked or *explicit deixis* is no more than the tip of the iceberg of general deixis, the main submerged portion of which is *implicit deixis*, the modal shadow of all signifiers. Since implicit deixis modifies linguistic aboutness, the chapter argues the primacy of utterance as the actual carrier of intentionality. Hence, the very idea of a *sentence meaning* is claimed to be untenable. Sentence types are said to have no more than sentence potential, sentence-tokens only meaning potential, and only utterances are argued to have meaning in natural language.

Chapter 6, *From Meaning Sufficiency to Communal Control*, explores the social constraints that we are bound to infer from our linguistic, intentional acts. With reference to Leibniz's *sufficient reason*, the concept of *meaning identity* is replaced by the notion of *intersubjective sufficiency*, a claim that is supported by Husserl's concession of the "more or less" of meaning fulfilment. Abandoning meaning identity, the chapter elaborates Husserl's remarks on linguistic coercion via the idea of *Abrichtung* as strict language pedagogy and guarantor of communicability. Since whenever linguistic communication occurs it does so as a combination of individual instantiation of linguistic expressions and communal constraints, meaning in language is viewed as an always *indirectly public* event.

Central to the concerns of the book is Chapter 7, *A Phenomenological Redefinition of Linguistic Meaning*, which opens with the claim that the bulk of language is about the world in absentia. If so, the chapter argues, then imaginability must play the central role in the meaning chain from meaning intention to meaning fulfilment. Categorially organized, nonverbal typifications as quanta of experience are shown to be *displaced* by symbolic, linguistic expressions as Husserlian *Bedeutung*, which in turn is replaced by resemblance relations of aboutness, categorial relations, and voice in acts of meaning fulfilment, Husserl's *Sinn*. The chapter concludes with identifying the minimal ingredients of *Sinn* as *directionality*, *quantity*, *quality*, and *degree of schematization* of mental-material content.

## Part III: Implications for the Theorization of Language

Chapter 8, *Why Language Is Not Simply a Symbolic System*, develops a contrast between intentional acts characteristic of language and those that are mandatory in the instantiation of formal signs under the heading of *desedimentation*. Husserlian concepts such as *meaning intention, expression, aboutness, voice, indication, intimation, introjection, word consciousness, empty intentions, categorial relations,* and *meaning fulfilment* are canvassed to demonstrate the radical difference between *desedimented* formal systems and the minimally symbolic system of natural language. Against this background, a number of favorite analytical topics are tested, such as *truth-conditional, compositionality, sorites arguments*, and one of Zeno's paradoxes.

In Chapter 9, *Displacement, Mental Time Travel, and Protosyntax*, Husserl's prelinguistic categorial relations are invoked to provide the likely basis for *linguistic displacement, mental time travel*, and *perceptual* as well as *gestural protosyntax*. The recent literature on mental time travel is charged with failing to distinguish clearly between its spatial and temporal components. Imaginability as spatial variation of perception under communal guidance is then proposed as a precondition of the emergence of symbolic systems. The chapter also takes issue with the claim that syntax is the product of language, suggesting instead that nonverbal protosyntax was probably inherited by language and refined during its further development and so is likely to have assisted in the continued conveyance of the iconicity of the *signified*.

Chapter 10, *Conclusion—The Social Mode of Being of Language*, completes the book with a turn from the epistemic stance of the preceding chapters to an ontological perspective. I argue that natural language cannot be satisfactorily described within a dualist ontology restricted to the categories of ideality and materiality. Because intentional acts have been shown throughout this study to play such a central role in the constitution of language as a compound intersubjective phenomenon, the Conclusion avers that a phenomenological, tripartite ontology is more appropriate in which materiality and ideality are subservient to the separate category of intentionality. Accordingly, and with reference to Roman Ingarden's ontological writings, the mode of being of language is said to be best described as an *ontically heteronomous, intersubjectively intentional, social process.*

# Notes

1 "Das Bedeuten ist ein so und so tingierter Aktcharacter, der einen Akt *anschaulichen Vorstellens* als notwendiges Fundament *voraussetzt.*" (Hua XIX/I, p. 81; my emphasis).
2 In its emphasis on imaginability, the book takes an approach to Husserl's philosophy of language as a theorization of the proximate character of linguistic meaning, an angle that contrasts sharply with the kind of approach taken, for instance, by Martin Kusch in *Language as Calculus and Universal Medium: A Study in Husserl, Heidegger, and Gadamer* (Dordrecht: Kluwer, 1989), without, however, denying the validity of such readings. Likewise, the influential paper "Husserl, Language, and the Ontology of the Act" by Barry Smith in *Speculative Grammar, Universal Grammar, and Philosophical Analysis of Language*, ed. D. Buzzetti and M. Ferriani (Amsterdam: John Benjamins, 1987), pp. 205–27, foregrounds the logical relations Husserl identifies in natural language, leaving the vividly imaginable side of meaning fulfilment undertheorized. Much the same can be said about the otherwise brilliant analyses of Jaakko Hintikka, who, in "The Notion of Intuition in Husserl," *Revue Internationale de Philosophie* 224 (2003), 57–79, places the accent on the immediacy of the givenness of objectivities rather than the role of *Anschauung* and *Vorstellung* in language where objectivities are not given but have to be *imagined*. Nor does

Husserl's *Nachlass* on language play a major role in the comprehensive *Handbook of Phenomenology and Cognitive Science*, ed. S. Gallagher and D. Schmicking (Dordrecht: Springer, 2010).
3   Edmund Husserl, *Ideas: General Introduction to Pure Phenomenology*, trans. W. R. Boyce Gibson (London: George Allen and Unwin, 1969), p. 92.
4   Hua XX/1; XX/2; XIII; XIV; XV. I quote Husserl frequently throughout this study to give a flavor of Husserl's terms and phrasing, to invite the reader to get as close as possible to passages available so far only in the original German, and to ground my extensions of Husserl's theorization of language as firmly as possible in his original thought. Where there are no existing English translations, they are my own.
5   Hua VII, p. 244.
6   Edmund Husserl, *Logical Investigations*, trans. J. N. Finlay (New York: Humanity Books, 2000), p. 255.
7   Hua I, pp. 55f.
8   Dorion Cairns, *The Philosophy of Edmund Husserl*, ed. L. Embree (Dordrecht: Springer, 2013), p. 7.
9   Husserl, *Logical Investigations*, pp. 276f.
10  Jocelyn Benoist, "Non-Objectifying Acts," in *One Hundred Years of Phenomenology: Husserl's* Logical Investigations *Revisited*, ed. D. Zahavi and F. Stjernfelt (Dordrecht: Kluwer, 2002), pp. 41–9 (43).
11  This 'communicative presumption,' Kant Bach and Robert M. Harnish, *Linguistic Communication and Speech Acts* (Cambridge, MA: MIT Press, 1979), p. 61 is foreshadowed in *The Logical Investigations*, pp. 276f. and consistently maintained in the remainder of his writings.
12  Hua XV, pp. 221ff.; 224f.; cf. Heidegger's later Hölderlinian phrasing of language as "the house of being."
13  Husserl's expanded linguistic horizon is announced as early as in the first volume of *Logical Investigations* (1900) where he identifies the goal of "the clarification of the phenomenological essential relations between expression, sense (*Bedeutung*), meaning intention, and meaning fulfilment (*Sinn*)" (Hua XIX/I, p. 19).
14  Edmund Husserl, "The Origin of Geometry," in *The Crisis of European Sciences and Transcendental Phenomenology: An Introduction to Phenomenological Philosophy*, trans. D. Carr (Evanston: Northwestern University Press, 1970), pp. 353–78 (358).
15  Hua XV, p. 218n2.
16  David Crystal, *How Language Works* (London: Penguin, 2008), p. 186.
17  Noam Chomsky, *Syntactic Structures* (The Hague: Mouton, 1957); *Aspects of the Theory of Syntax* (Cambridge, MA: MIT Press, 1965).
18  Cf., e.g., Emma Borg, *Minimal Semantics* (Cambridge: Cambridge University Press, 1984); Herman Cappelen and Ernst Lepore, *Insensitive Semantics: A Defence of Semantic Minimalism and Speech-Act Pluralism* (Oxford: Blackwell, 2005).
19  Dermot Moran and Thomas Szanto, *Phenomenology of Sociality: Discovering the 'We.'* Research in Phenomenology, v. 3 (New York and London: Routledge, 2016), p. 2.
20  Vittorio de Palma, "Die Fakta leiten alle Eidetik: Zu Husserls Begriff des materialen Apriori," *Husserl Studies* 30, 3 (2014), 195–223.
21  See Chapter 4; cf. Teven Galt Crowell, *Husserl, Heidegger, and the Space of Meaning: Paths Toward Transcendental Phenomenology* (Evanston: Northwestern University Press, 2001); Dieter Lohmar, "Zur Vorgeschichte der transzendentalen Reduktion in den *Logischen Untersuchungen*: Die unbekannte 'Reduktion auf den reellen Bestand,'" *Husserl Studies* 28, 1 (2012), 1–24.

22 Edmund Husserl, *Experience and Judgment: Investigations in a Genealogy of Logic*, ed. L. Landgrebe, trans. J. S. Churchill and K. Ameriks (Evanston: Northwestern University Press, 1997), p. 232.
23 Hua XX/2, pp. 22f.
24 In this double sense, imaginability is to be distinguished from the related concepts of imagination and imagining as argued in the literature. Cf., for example, Edward S. Casey, *Imagining: A Phenomenological Study* (Bloomington: Indiana University Press, 2000), esp. pp. 49–86; Jean Starobinsky, "Jalons pour une histoire du concept d'imagination," in *La relation critique* (Paris: Gallimard, 1970), pp. 174–95. For a useful overview of the literature on the imagination, see Casey, "Introduction," *Imagining*, pp. 1–20; or more recently in Edward S. Casey, "Imagination, Fantasy, Hallucination, and Memory," in *Imagination and Its Pathologies*, ed. J. Philips and J. Morley (Cambridge, MA: MIT Press, 2003), pp. 65–87, where he sets the imagination eidetically apart from perception, hallucination, memory, and anticipation via possibility and omni-temporality.
25 Hua XX/1; XX/2.
26 Immanuel Kant, *Critique of Judgment*, trans. J. C. Meredith (Oxford: Oxford University Press, 2007), § 29; cf. also his use of the terms *Vorstellungskraft* and *Einbildungskraft* (power of the imagination).
27 Ludwig Wittgenstein, *Philosophical Investigations*, trans. G. E. M. Anscombe, P. M. S. Hacker, and J. Schulte (Oxford: Blackwell, 2009), §§ 395; 6. Cf. Saul A. Kripke, *Wittgenstein on Rules and Private Language: An Elementary Exposition* (Oxford: Basil Blackwell, 1982), p. 3.
28 Husserl, *Logical Investigations*, pp. 299ff., 250, 291, 295, 668; *bedeutungsverleihende Akte*, pp. 17, 281f., 284, 497, 735.
29 Charles F. Hockett, "The Origin of Speech," *Scientific American* 203 (1960), 88–96; "The Problem of Universals in Language," in *Universals of Language*, ed. J. Greenberg (Cambridge, MA: MIT Press, 1966), pp. 1–29.
30 Arnulf Zweig (ed.), *Kant: Philosophical Correspondence 1759–1799*, trans. A. Zweig (Chicago: University of Chicago Press, 1967), p. 71.
31 Edmund Husserl, *Phantasy, Image Consciousness, and Memory (1898–1925)*, trans. J. B. Brough. Collected Works, ed. R. Bernet (Dordrecht: Springer, 2005), pp. 369, 700f., 707.
32 Except, for instance, in Hua XIV, p. 229.
33 Husserl, *Ideas*, p. 105; *Crisis*, pp. 142ff, 163f., 173, 184, 259.
34 Hua XIII, pp. 469ff.; XIV 47, 53; Hua XX/2, pp. 104f., 170.
35 Husserl, "The Origin of Geometry," pp. 358f.
36 Hua XX/2, p. 313.
37 Ibid., pp. 104f.
38 On '*Abrichtung*' see Wittgenstein, *Philosophical Investigations*, §§ 5, 86, 129, 146, 151f., 441, 630; on the 'linguistic linkage compulsion,' see Horst Ruthrof, "Recycling Locke: Meaning as Indirectly Public," *Philosophy Today* 57, 1 (2013), 3–27, 23.
39 Hua XX/2, p. 170.
40 Husserl, *Logical Investigations*, p. 330; my emphasis.
41 Kusch, *Language as Calculus vs. Language as Universal Medium*, pp. 131–4, 57.
42 Husserl, *Logical Investigations*, p. 745.
43 Ferdinand de Saussure, *Cours de linguistique générale*, ed. C. Bally, A. Séchehaye, A. Riedlinger, and T. de Mauro (Paris: Payot, 2005).
44 Beata Stawarska, *Saussure's Philosophy of Language as Phenomenology: Undoing the Doctrine of the Course in General Linguistics* (Oxford: Oxford University Press, 2015);

cf. also her more recent *Saussure's Linguistics, Structuralism, and Phenomenology* (London: Palgrave Macmillan, 2020), where she qualifies the radical arbitrariness thesis of the linguistic sign, pp. 33–48, and tones down the structuralist overemphasis on *langue* at the expense of *parole*, pp. 117–24.

45 de Saussure, *Cours*, p. 100; a useful summary of the structuralist opposition to Husserl can be found in Maria Golebiewska's "Edmund Husserl's Semantics and the Critical Theses of Late Structuralism," *Eidos: A Journal for Philosophy of Culture*, 3, 1 (2019), 30–50.

46 Edmund Husserl, "The Origin of Geometry," pp. 353–78 (359).

47 Charles Sanders Peirce, *Collected Papers of Charles Sanders Peirce 1931–1966*, 8 vol., ed. C. Hartsworth, P. Weiss, and A. W. Burks (Cambridge, MA: Belknap Press, 1974).

48 Edmund Husserl, "On the Logic of Signs (Semiotik)," in *Early Writings in the Philosophy of Logic and Arithmetic*, trans. D Willard (New York: Springer, 1994 [1890]), pp. 20–51.

49 Peirce, CP 5.119.

50 Ibid., CP 5.421.

51 Ibid., CP 5.467.

52 Ibid., CP 5.475.

53 Ibid., CP 1.158.

54 Peirce, EP 2.273.

55 Peirce, CP 2.294; 5.473.

56 Ibid., CP 4.536; 5.475.

57 Ibid., CP 2.294; 2.303; 5.476; 5.569. The "final" interpretant is conceived by Peirce as a tendency toward which successive interpretants point. "Letter to Lady Welby," March 14, 1909. In Philip P. Wiener (ed.), *Charles S. Peirce: Selected Writings* (New York: Dover, 1966), p. 413.

58 Husserl, *Logical Investigations*, p. 277; Peirce, CP 7.591.

59 Cf. Robert Sokolowski, "Semiotics in Husserl's *Logical Investigations*," in *One Hundred Years of Phenomenology: Husserl's* Logical Investigations *Revisited*, pp. 171–83;

60 Peirce, EP 2.273; Dieter Lohmar, "Husserl's Type and Kant's Schemata: Systematic Reasons for Their Correlation or Identity," in *The New Husserl: A Critical Reader*, ed. D. Welton (Bloomington: Indiana University Press, 2003), pp. 93–124. Support for Husserl's debt to Kant can also be found in B. Elliot, *Phenomenology and Imagination in Husserl and Heidegger* (New York: Routledge, 2005). More recently, Lohmar has defended the role of 'weak phantasy' from a phenomenological perspective, in "The Function of Weak Phantasy in Perception and Thinking," in *The Handbook of Phenomenology and Cognitive Science*, ed. S. Gallagher and D. Schmicking (Dordrecht: Springer, 2010), pp. 159–77. The topic of 'weak phantasy' is taken up by Lajos Horváth, Csaba Szummer, and Attila Szabo in "Weak Phantasy and Visionary Phantasy: The Phenomenological Significance of Altered States of Consciousness," *Phenomenology and the Cognitive Sciences* 17, 1 (2018), 117–29.

61 Husserl, *Logical Investigations*, pp. 735ff.; *Experience and Judgment*, p. 336; Hua XX/2, pp. 2f.

62 Crystal, *How Language Works*, p. 189.

63 Hua XX/2, p. 3.

64 Husserl, *Ideas*, p. 382.

65 Strong support for the presence in Husserl's meaning fulfilment of the nonverbal can be found in Dieter Lohmar, "Language and Non-Linguistic Thinking," in *The Oxford*

*Handbook of Contemporary Phenomenology*, ed. D. Zahavi (Oxford: Oxford University Press, 2012), pp. 377–98.
66 Michael A. K. Halliday, *Learning How to Mean: Explorations in the Development of Language* (London: Arnold, 1975), pp. 15, 9, 17, 141f.
67 Michael A. K. Halliday, *Language as Social Semiotic* (London: Edward Arnold, 1978); *An Introduction to Functional Grammar* (London: Edward Arnold, 1985).
68 George Lakoff, "The Invariance Hypothesis: Is Abstract Reasoning Based on Image-Schemas?" *Cognitive Linguistics* 1 (1990), 39–74; cf. Jordan Zlatev, "Phenomenology and Cognitive Linguistics," in *Handbook of Phenomenology and Cognitive Science*, ed. S. Gallagher and D. Schmicking (Dordrecht: Spinger, 2010), pp. 415–43.
69 Mark Johnson, *The Body in the Mind: The Bodily Basis of Meaning, Imagination, and Reason* (Chicago: University of Chicago Press, 1987); "The Philosophical Significance of Image Schemas," in *From Perception to Meaning: Image Schemas in Cognitive Linguistics*, ed. B. Hampe (Berlin: Mouton de Gruyter, 2005), pp. 15–34; Ronald Finke, *Principles of Mental Imagery* (Cambridge, MA: MIT Press, 1989).
70 Hua XX/2, pp. 2f.; 291.
71 Husserl, *Logical Investigations*, pp. 735f.; Hua XX/1, pp. 129; 240; Hua XX/2, p. 364.
72 Leonard Talmy, *Towards a Cognitive Semantics* (Cambridge, MA: MIT Press, 2000).
73 Edmund Husserl, *Experience and Judgment*, pp. 221f.; Hua XX/2, pp. 409f.; 417; 439; cf. Ronald Langacker, *Cognitive Grammar: A Basic Introduction* (New York: Oxford University Press, 2008).
74 Jordan Zlatev, *Situated Embodiment: Studies in the Emergence of Spatial Meaning* (Stockholm: Gotab Press, 1997); "Embodiment, Language, and Mimesis," in *Body, Language, and Mind*, ed. T. Ziemke, J. Zlatev, and R. Frank (Berlin: Mouton de Gruyter, 2007), pp. 297–338.
75 Gilles Fauconnier, *Mappings in Thought's Language* (Cambridge: Cambridge University Press, 1997).
76 Mark Johnson and George Lakoff, *Philosophy in the Flesh: The Embodied Mind and Its Challenge to Western Thought* (New York: Basic Books, 1999).
77 Gilles Fauconnier and Mark Turner, *The Way We Think: Conceptual Blending and the Mind's Hidden Complexities* (New York: Basic Books, 2002).
78 Gottlob Frege, "On Sense and Reference," in *Translations from the Philosophical Writings of Gottlob Frege*, trans. P. Geach and M. Black (Oxford: Blackwell, 1970), pp. 56–78.
79 Michael Dummett, *Truth and Other Enigmas* (Cambridge, MA: Harvard University Press, 1978), p. 116.
80 Cf. Ernie Lepore and Barry C. Smith (eds.), *The Oxford Handbook of Philosophy of Language* (Oxford: Clarendon Press, 2006); Michael Devitt and Richard Hanley (eds.), *The Blackwell Guide to the Philosophy of Language* (Oxford: Basil Blackwell, 2006); Steven Davis and Brendan S. Gillon (eds.), *Semantics: A Reader* (Oxford: Oxford University Press, 2004); Peter V. Lamarque (ed.), *Concise Encyclopedia of Philosophy of Language* (Oxford: Pergamon, 1997); Marie Duzi, Bjorn Jespersen, and Pavel Materna, *Procedural Semantics for Hyperintensional Logic: Foundations and Applications of Transparent Intensional Logic* (Dordrecht: Springer, 2010).
81 Aristotle, *De Interpretatione*, trans. J. L. Ackrill (Oxford: Oxford University Press, 2002), pp. 1, 16a, 3–8; *Categories*, trans. E. M. Edghill (Adelaide: Adelaide University, 2013), pp. 4b. 8f.
82 Dieter Lohmar, "Language and Non-Linguistic Thinking," in *The Oxford Handbook of Contemporary Phenomenology*, ed. D. Zahavi (Oxford: Oxford University Press, 2015), pp. 377–98, (395).

83 E.g. Scott Soames, *Philosophy of Language* (Princeton: Princeton University Press, 2010), p. 1.
84 E.g., Günther Grewendorf, Fritz Hamm, and Wolfgang Sternefeld, *Sprachliches Wissen: Eine Einführung in moderne Theorien der grammatischen Beschreibung* (Frankfurt: Suhrkamp, 1987).
85 Soames, *Philosophy of Language*, pp. 88ff.
86 E.g., Donald Davidson, "Truth and Meaning," in *Semantics: A Reader*, ed. S. Davis and B. S. Gillon (Oxford: Oxford University Press, 2004), pp. 222–33.
87 Ferdinand de Saussure, *Cours de linguistique générale*, ed. C. Bally, A. Séchehaye, A. Riedlinger, and T. de Mauro (Paris: Payot, 2005), pp. 43, 125, 153; Wittgenstein, *PI* §§ 33, 108, 190, 563.
88 Jerry A. Fodor, *The Language of Thought* (Cambridge, MA: Harvard University Press, 1975); *Lot 2: The Language of Thought Revisited* (Oxford: Oxford University Press, 2008).
89 Johnson and Lakoff, *Philosophy in the Flesh*.
90 Tecumseh Fitch, *The Evolution of Language* (Cambridge: Cambridge University Press, 2010).
91 In spite of his expressed sympathy for Peircean hypoiconicity; see *Of Grammatology*, trans. G. C. Spivak (Baltimore: The Johns Hopkins University Press, 1976), pp. 48ff.
92 Husserl, *Ideas*, p. 398.
93 Hua XX/2, pp. 2f.; 291.

Part I

# Two Husserlian Points of Departure

2

# Husserl's Philosophy of Language and Its Revisions

In light of the quantity and philosophical weight of Husserl's writings that remained unpublished during his lifetime, it is only to be expected that the gradual publication of his *Nachlass* in the *Husserliana* series has already resulted in some serious revisions in the reception of his philosophy. One such revision is the recognition of Husserl's ontological embedding of epistemic subjective acts of consciousness in *intersubjectivity*, an urgent adjustment in light of the frequent charge laid against phenomenology as a *subjectivist* paradigm unable to rid itself of psychologism. Another necessary readjustment concerns Husserl's theorization of natural language. This has been noted by the editor of two volumes on language, Ullrich Melle, as it has been by a number of other phenomenologists.[1] Melle draws our attention to Husserl's remarks in the *Nachlass* as to a significant shift in his analysis resulting in an "essentially different conception" and his aim to eradicate the "half-measures and errors (*Halbheiten und Irrtümer*)" of his *Logical Investigations*.[2] As noted in the Introduction, what makes Husserl's contribution to the theorization of natural language unique is his expanded linguistic horizon. Instead of shrinking his description to the sense-reference relation in the style of Gottlob Frege, Husserl's phenomenological act description aims to capture a much broader set of phenomena, from nonverbal meaning intention and their categorial relations to word sound and *Bedeutung*, that is, verbal directionality, and to *Sinn* as imaginative, proximate reconstitution of meaning intention.

Central to Husserl's linguistic holism is his conception of language as a form of *communication*, an opening move in the *Logical Investigations* that is never abandoned throughout his later writings and elaborated in detail in his *Nachlass*. All the linguistic intricacies introduced after his early observations have to be understood within the parameters of the communicative function of language. One significant consequence of this broad focus is the collapse in Husserl of semantics and pragmatics under a single, comprehensive thematic: the phenomenological description of the intentional acts without which natural language could not exists the way it does. Another consequence is that what matters foremost is what we are communicating *about*, Husserl's *Worüber*,[3] rather than other matters, such as the question of the truth or falsity of sentences. Where the analytical tradition in the philosophy of language has favored Aristotle's path via propositions and the truth value of sentences,[4] Husserl embraced the question of *resemblance*, Aristotle's *pathemata* (affections of the soul) as *homoiomata* (resemblance relations) of *pragmata* (actual things), and their imaginable variations.[5] In this chapter, I want to show that Husserl's early theory of language in the *Logical Investigations* contains important insights that require restoration; how Husserl's recently published revisions assist us in that repair work; and how seminal concepts from his later writings could be used in rendering his ideas competitive once more in the contested arena of the theorization of natural language.

## The *Logical Investigations*

The elegance of Frege's reduction of natural language to its skeleton of sense and reference in *Sinn und Bedeutung* (1892) shall not be disputed.[6] After all, Frege launched the highly successful tradition of analytical inquiry up to current pursuits in hyperintensional semantics[7] and remains the undisputed discourse founder of geometrically grounded, linguistic *externalism*. Yet, Frege's economy of analysis is achieved at a price that Husserl was not prepared to pay. Husserl felt that it was wrong not to address all those features of language that make it a system of *communication*, its foremost communal and so *social* purpose.[8] Crucially, this decision involved of necessity the instantiation of linguistic expressions in the minds of individual speakers, though in a depsychologized form. Thus, Frege's geometrical externalism stands in sharp contrast with Husserl's holistic approach, in which the inclusion of a form of *intersubjective mentalism* is an inexorable, methodological corollary. A second dramatic disparity between the two philosophers is the way each secures the transmission of *resemblance*. In Frege, sense (*Sinn*) is definitionally fixed and reference (*Bedeutung*) is scientifically guaranteed. Sense "determines the semantic value of the expression," that is, "on the assumption that the contribution of extra-linguistic reality is being taken into account," a contribution provided by Frege's *reference*.[9] Thus, sense determines reference. The identity of what is said and what is comprehended is assured, much as it is in formal relations and interpreted calculus.[10] In this respect, Husserl faced a much more complicated situation and, as we shall see, struggled to reconcile his picture of language with his own stipulation of meaning identity.[11] What makes Husserl's early analysis so intricate is that he wants to capture what actually occurs when we employ language as a social activity, even if he rarely refers to the speech community. It is only later that Husserl places the "world of life,"[12] the *Lebenswelt*, "the community of life," and the "linguistic community" at the center of his investigations.[13]

Like Frege, Husserl was tempted on many occasions to identify linguistic meanings with their formal cousins, and yet at crucial points in the *Logical Investigation* he lets go of his ideal of meaning identity to note that "the intentional essence of the act of intuition gets only *more or less perfectly* fitted into the semantic essence of the act of expression."[14] Qualms about a radically abstractive semantics also surface in his qualification that meaning ideality is not so much "normative" as "practical," qualms usually overridden though by a fear of loss of *semantic identity*.[15] When identity is stipulated via "ideal objects" that, for Husserl, "exist genuinely," it is illustrated by "the number 2, the quality of red, the principle of contradiction."[16] Note here how the "fuzzy" ideality of "the quality of red" is embedded in arithmetic and logical expressions, suggesting that Husserl attempted to stabilize his linguistic meaning identity in language by formal notions. This suspicion is strengthened in a long series of formal examples throughout the *Logical Investigations*. Extending meaning identity to our acts of color terms, as for instance in the Introduction to Investigation II, Husserl writes, "when we mean Red *in specie*, a red object appears before us."[17] What remains identical is the imagined species of redness. This is so even if "mental imagery lies outside the essence of an expression" performing no more than a "fulfilling role" of a "provisional character."[18]

Yet elsewhere in the *Logical Investigations*, Husserl deviates quite radically from semantic identity, noting that the "generality of words" belongs "to an endless array of possible intuitions."[19] He clearly saw "a difficulty connected with the otherwise illuminating notion of the unity of identity or recognition." So, Husserl wondered whether we should say "that an emphasis of attention decides the matter? Or ought we not rather grant that *there is not here a fully constituted act of identification*?" Instead, "the nucleus of this act, the connective union of significant intention and corresponding intuition is really present, but it represents no objectifying interpretation (*Auffassung*)."[20] Elsewhere, Husserl has tried to retain meaning identity in perception and the imagination, in the form of "*noematic essential stock*."[21] Such *semantic essence* should, however, not be confused with the *epistemic essence* that characterizes the qualitative, imaginative, nonverbal reconstitution of meaning intention in meaning fulfilment as *Sinn*.[22] We shall see whether or not full meaning identity in the sense of "self-same meaning," as stipulated elsewhere in the *Logical Investigations*, is at all necessary or even possible in natural language.[23] After all, what makes meaning identity unlikely is the transit from acts of meaning intention to those of meaning fulfilment and their distinction from linguistic expressions themselves.

"What marks off an expression" from mere word sounds is the "meaning-intention" in which the expression "undergoes an essential phenomenal modification."[24] This "*act* of meaning" (*Bedeuten*) in turn is differentiated from idealized "meaning" (*Bedeutung*) itself.[25] Husserl's early concept of *Bedeutung* can be taken roughly as Frege's sense (*Sinn*) such that "'meaning' is further used by us as synonymous with 'sense.'"[26] Yet, as we shall see later, *Bedeutung* in a purely logical sense will prove problematic. Where Husserl parts company with Frege is in his setting apart the "act-complexes" of "sense-conferring acts" and "sense-giving acts" from the acts of the "intimation of mental states," both in "speaking and reception." Here Husserl leaves behind any minimalist program by insisting that language as communication cannot be described without a methodological commitment to intentionality. Accordingly, the "*intimating* function" consists in the way "inner experiences" are conveyed from speaker to hearer.[27] Husserl uses the term *intimation* in two different senses: a narrow one as "acts which impart sense" and a wider one as "all acts that a hearer may *introject* into a speaker on the basis of what he says."[28] *Introjection* is yet another cardinal concept at the heart of Husserl's intersubjective agenda, which anticipates his later notion of *appresentation* or *copresenting*, that is, intentional acts that fill out by way of *Vorstellung* what is not immediately given in apperception.[29] However, as a component of intimation, introjection is not to be confused with "indication," Husserl's *Hinweisfunktion*, by which he strictly refers to the resemblance relations between the content of an expression and an object or, in his own words, the relation of an expression "to the object it stands for or that it is to signify."[30] In "*communicative speech*" all expressions "*function as indications.*"[31]

On the side of meaning uptake, "the hearer intuitively takes the speaker to be a person who is expressing this or that" or "perceives him as such."[32] Intuition here likewise requires acts of *appresenting*. It is already clear at this point that in the kind of meta-semantic schema Husserl is constructing, linguistic comprehension could not be argued without a firm commitment to *Vorstellung* and *Vorstellbarkeit*, or *imaginability*, or perhaps "intelligibility" in Sokolowski's sense.[33] Note, however, that Sokolowski's rendering weakens the very feature of *Vorstellung* that Husserl so strongly accentuates in his *Nachlass*: vividly imaginable *Anschauung*.[34] So firmly is the later Husserl committed to *Anschauung* that he finds *intuition* too weak a term to get across the sense of *picturable* saturation characteristic of *Sinn* as meaning fulfilment. At the same time, linguistic communicability requires *intersubjective reciprocity*, a theme to be addressed in detail in Chapter 4. "Mutual understanding," says Husserl, "demands a certain *correlation among the mental acts mutually unfolded in intimation* and in the receipt of such intimation, but *not at all their exact resemblance*."[35] Two crucial concerns are entailed in this quotation, intersubjective *reciprocity* as a necessary condition of language and the *proximate* character of Husserl's *Sinn*, that is, meaning fulfilment.

The principle of the intersubjective reciprocity of mutual intentional acts is resumed in Husserl's distinction between "meaning-conferring acts" and "meaning-fulfilling acts," the former transforming "meaning intentions" into linguistic expressions via *displacement*,[36] the latter as a necessary receptive condition of comprehension as Husserlian *Sinn*.[37] As Wittgenstein is to observe half a century later, in language, "an expectation and its fulfilment make contact," without, however, granting intentionality any significant role in the meaning process.[38] By contrast, Husserl is emphatic in dealing with meaning intention and uptake in reconstructive acts in and by *Vorstellung*, producing as it does an "intimately fused unity" of "meaning-intention" and "meaning fulfilment." Because of his commitment to *Vorstellung*, Husserl resolutely rejects the formulation that an "expression expresses its meaning."[39] Expressions by themselves do nothing. Rather, what is required for meaning to occur is the intentional act of "understanding" that "shines through the expression," lending it "meaning and thereby relation to objects."[40] The question now arises how Husserl's reciprocal intentional acts can be reconciled with a degree of accuracy of meaning transfer that would guarantee efficient communication. Husserl's solution is the introduction of the concepts of "*exclusive directionality*" and the "*steering of attention.*" The function of a word sound, for Husserl, "is to awaken a sense-conferring act" in order "to point to what is intended," an "intuitive fulfilment," and "to guide our interest *exclusively* in this direction." In the same section, Husserl speaks of the steering of attention from "name to the thing named," from expression to "what is expressed." In language, "our interest, our intention, our thought ... *point exclusively* to the thing meant in the sense-giving act."[41] The concept of exclusive directionality, defined by Husserl also more sharply as "determinate direction to objects," thus tightens the relation between speech community, meaning intention, and meaning fulfilment.[42] Linguistic directionality is not merely suggestive but compelling.

Husserl's concept of directionality also points us to linguistic extensionality, in the Leibnizian sense of extension in contrast to intension (formal sense), the former pointing beyond the expression to aboutness, of which Fregean *reference* is a special case. Aboutness, Husserl's "*Worüber*," or[43] its *noematic nucleus*[44] links acts with actuality, as well as with its imaginative variations. Husserl addresses extensionality in two ways. It appears in the *matter* of a meaning act in contrast to its *quality*. It also appears in what an expression says *of* something, by way of "the objective correlate of an expression," defined as "the objective correlate meant by a meaning" in distinction from any actual object.[45] Here, exclusive directionality results in our attention being pointed to something outside the intentional acts that we cannot but reconstruct in the event of meaning, that is, what an expression is about.[46] What Husserl is accentuating here is that "the object never coincides with the meaning."[47] Husserl also distinguishes *aboutness* as the *Worüber* of an expression from its *reference*, defined as the directionality of an expression pointing "to certain objects." As such, it appears in the well-trodden examples of "The victor of Jena," which is about someone who has been victorious somewhere, and about "the vanquished of Waterloo." Each different aboutness *refers* to one and the same person, Napoleon. In Husserl, expressions can have "different meanings but the same object"; vice versa, the same meaning, of "this table," can be used to refer to different objects.[48] Husserl's competitors here are Russell in "On Denoting" (1905), P. F. Strawson on reference as the "referring use" of expressions (1950), and Gareth Evans in his much later analysis in *Varieties of Reference* (1982).[49] The distinction between aboutness, on the one hand, and reference as a special kind of language use, on the other, has the advantage of showing that the former is part of meaning and so semiotically homogeneous as intentional object, while the linking of meaning and objects is *heterosemiotic*. At the same time, Fregean reference has the disadvantage that it can be applied to too broad an array of things beyond specific objectivities, such as thin things or modes of being. It would seem that aboutness does a better job of identifying anything an expression is *about*, no matter how vague, leaving reference to cater for the identification of specifics.[50] Aboutness and reference derive from distinct intentional acts and so should be carefully extricated from one another.

Seminal, too, in *Logical Investigations* is Husserl's discussion of "essentially occasional expressions."[51] The idea was taken up in Adolf Reinach's speech-act phenomenology of 1913 and by Bertrand Russell in his treatment of *egocentric particulars* in *Human Knowledge: Its Scope and Limits* (1948).[52] The former must be regarded as an important precursor of Wittgenstein's "multiplicity of the tools in language,"[53] as well as of the speech-act theories of John Langshaw Austin and John R. Searle. In Husserl the meaning of "essentially subjective and occasional" expressions is relative to "occasion, speaker and situation" and to the presence of "universally operative indication," such as provided by the shifters I, you, we, now, here, and so forth.[54] Using his distinction between "act character" and "ideally unified meaning," Husserl reasons that while the former differs from case to case, the sense of the sentence "should remain identical."[55] In Husserl's own terms, one could agree that its merely indicated meaning does not change, while its intimated meaning introduces a principle of modification, part of linguistic *modality*, in a broad sense, that would undermine any strict notion of identity.

The early Husserl, however, insists that such modifications do not affect the meaning itself but only "the act of meaning."[56] Here, Husserl bridles at the consequences of his own theorizing. In the *Nachlass* Husserl changes his early convictions when he demonstrates the double-layered character of acts of tone and intonation and the significance they have in the process of meaning production and fulfilment.[57]

Yet another fertile insight in the *Logical Investigations* is Husserl's concept of the "haziness" of linguistic expressions, a topic taken up by Bertrand Russel in his paper on "Vagueness" (1923).[58] As Husserl writes, terms "such as 'tree,' 'shrub,' 'animal,' 'plant' etc., are *vague*," their meaning "oriented towards *types*, only partially conceived with clearness and definiteness." Like Frege, he notes that "the *haziness* of such expressions" is not conducive to "definite identifications," because they reflect "phenomenal properties" that "*shade continuously into one another*," producing "*fluid*" relations and "*vague* borders."[59] A serious tension then exists between Husserl's observation that the majority of natural language expressions falls under this kind of description and his reluctance to give up on meaning identity. Only once he places *type* and *typification* at the center of his investigation is he ready to resume the theme of semantic vagueness for a revision of his initial philosophy of language.[60]

## Resemblance

Husserl's writings from *Ideas* onward are a treasure trove for any attempt at reconstructing a phenomenological theory of language in his spirit. Clues for such a reconstruction can be found in Husserl's distinction between materialization and dematerialization, the *nonformal noema, nonessential typifications*, and the subtle distinction between *Sachverhalt* and *Sachlage*. Husserl's definition of formalization as the empty end point on the axis of mental "dematerialization" in contrast to generalization on the axis of despecification provides a useful tool for inquiring whether formal emptiness and fullness should not be replaced by the notion of degree of generalization at the verbal level and by *degrees of schematization* for the nonverbal domain.[61] Degrees of schematization will be useful for showing how Husserl's *Sinn* can be fulfilled by nonverbal *imaginability*, without being hampered by talk of mental images.[62] Likewise expedient is Husserl's argument in favor of two kinds of noemata, the formal noema, which remains congruent with Husserl's demand for meaning identity in the *Logical Investigations*, and a nonformal noema, as in the notion of *nonessential typifications* in *Experience and Judgment*.[63] Such a reading of Husserl's overall endeavor is shored up by the fact that as early as in the *Ideas* the noema is presented as remaining linked to intuition and so cannot be regarded, as it is by Dagfinn Føllesdal, as *empty* as Frege's *Sinn*.[64] In agreement with Robert Sokolowski and Lenore Langsdorf,[65] this amounts to a strong rejection of reading all noemata as formal.[66] Nor does Husserl's description of the internal structure of the noema alter this fundamental distinction.[67]

Only a non-formal notion of Husserl's noema is suitable for characterizing linguistic meaning. But even the non-formal noema still allows for different approaches to natural language. Here, I want to emphasize the merit of Husserl's tightrope act by neither declaring linguistic intentionality fully social, as does Putnam's externalism, nor falling into the trap of *semantic privacy*, referred to sometimes as Locke's psychologism, or Chomsky's *internalism*. Husserl attempted three distinct solutions: (1) to declare meanings a Platonic *ideal species* or some other kind of universal entity; (2) to make them *formal*, that is, syntactic relations governed axiomatically by definitions; and (3) to *socialize* them, without losing sight of the necessity of individual, intentional instantiation. At the beginning of his career, Husserl appears to be committed to the first option, while at times collapsing solutions (1) and (2), especially in his examples in the *Logical Investigations*. Toward the end of his career he appears to have been ready to embrace solution (3) by shifting the *a priori* to the *Lebenswelt*, without, however, being able to revise his language semantics accordingly. It is one of the aims of this study to suggest ways of facilitating some such revision, by taking seriously Husserl's stronger emphasis on *Vorstellung* and *sociality* in his *Nachlass* and later writings.

For such an argument, Husserl himself provides a number of clues. I propose that we can harvest some of them in our attempt to offer a revised portrait of Husserl's philosophy of language. In addition to non-formal noemata, Husserl speaks of *appresentation* in the *Cartesian Meditations*,[68] of profiles or adumbrations and "differences in vitality,"[69] "analogical representation,"[70] retentions and protentions, "the fullness of presentation,"[71] "graded series of fulfilments,"[72] emphasizing richness, liveliness, and vivacity, "*Realitätsgehalt*,"[73] "combinatory forms,"[74] "abstractive percept,"[75] "semblance acts,"[76] habitual "circles of resemblance," "differing resemblances,"[77] and above all the *a priori Lebenswelt* and its *typifications*. This list suggests that we can reconstruct a notion of the linguistic meaning event in terms of some kind of *graded fulfilment* from Husserl's theory of perception, suitable to a phenomenological theorization of natural language. While his *Nachlass* proves particularly well suited to such a revision, Husserl wrote as early as in the *Logical Investigations* that we must "return to the features of the presented object: *The more of these features enter into the analogical representation* and, as regards each separate feature, the greater the similarity with which the presentation represents it in its content, the greater is the fullness of the presentation."[78] Since objects are the sum of nonverbal acts and since it is again nonverbal acts that reconstitute the object in *Sinn*, graded, schematized meaning fulfilment is a promising candidate for the idea that intentional acts in comprehension are likely to make use of imaginative replications as *typified*. Only as *typifications* will they be sharable in the communicative process. As I will argue in Chapter 3, for language to be able to convey typifications rather than subjective particulars, it must be a system not only of generalities but also of *fuzzy eidetic reductions*.[79]

A promising avenue to explore from the *Logical Investigations* to *Experience and Judgment* is Husserl's concept of *profiles*. In perception, material objects are realized in consciousness as a synthesis of visual, tactile, gustatory, and other heterosemiotic adumbrations. This synthesis is neatly summed up by Sokolowski in his definition, "a profile is a moment of a thing-synthesis."[80] Profiles belong to Husserl's theorization of "parts and wholes" where he distinguishes two kinds of parts, "pieces" and "moments." Profiles are instances of the latter, taken up by Roman Ingarden as "existential moments," to be addressed in the Conclusion. Though in the *Logical Investigations* Husserl mentions profiles together with aspects of an object, the concept of profile seems to me to emphasize more the outline of things rather than their adumbrational sides. As such, the notion of profile is reminiscent of Kant's transcendental schema of a dog as "a rule according to which my imagination is able to sketch in a general manner the shape of a certain four-legged animal, without being restricted to any singular and specific shape, given to me by experience or any possible picture that I could represent *in concreto*."[81] Importantly, Kant draws a sharp distinction between *mental schematization* and *mental image* in that images are facilitated by the "*empirical* capacity of our productive imagination," as part of *Vorstellung*, whereas

> the schema of sensible concepts (as figures in space) is a product and as it were a *monogram* of our pure imagination *a priori*, by which and according to which images become possible in the first place. Yet they are to be connected with the concept only by means of the schema, which they indicate, and with which they are not entirely congruent.[82]

Certainly, the doctrine of *profiles* viewed as a form of schematization offers another way of qualifying Husserl's early commitment to semantic identity and formalization. As generalized abstractions, that is, partially desedimented perceptual grasp, profiles can be held in *Vorstellung* as *schemata* bearing reduced and yet still sufficient resemblance relations for recognition of a meaning intention. A similar comparison between Husserl and Kant has been drawn by Dieter Lohmar in "Husserl's Type and Kant's Schemata" according to which the two notions are "functionally almost identical."[83] If we follow Lohmar in roughly equating schematizations with typifications, then degrees of generalization or desedimentation can be argued within Husserl's own parameters. We can furthermore draw on Husserl's concept of "grades of evidence" in the *Cartesian Mediations* where he distinguishes "apodictic" from "adequate" and "certain" evidence.[84] I will argue that we shall have to lower our sights from certitude to meaning approximation, according to which speakers of a language do not doubt that signifiers direct us toward a certain mental disposition consisting in a certain range of mental materials regulated by its concept. This is why Husserl opposes any conception of the meaning process in terms of "static congruence," talking instead of its "stepped construction (*Stufenbau*)" and "fluid type concepts."[85]

At the heart of any reconstruction of a phenomenological theory of language out of Husserl's later works could be placed such concepts as nonessential *typifications*, *Vorstellung*, and *appresentation*. By the time of the posthumous *Experience and Judgment*, Husserl appears to have changed his description of the way we grasp the world by means of "typifications." Now he distinguishes between "essential" typifications as they function in science and "nonessential typifications" characteristic of understanding in the *Lebenswelt*.[86] Both kinds of typification not only display differing levels of generality but, in agreement with distinctions drawn early in *Ideas*, are also marked as "formal" and "material" generalities, respectively.[87] Husserl stipulates that the greater the extension of an expression, the higher the level of generality. Central to our argument will be that "similarity" requires "gradation" such that "the levels of generality are conditioned by the degrees of likeness of the members of the extension." Which opens the way for degrees of resemblance relations within non-formal typifications. Instead of meaning viewed as a formal species, "complete likeness" will be regarded as a limit phenomenon, "the limit of similarity."[88] By contrast, semantic identity will be reserved for "essential" typification in technical sign systems. Only via nonessential typifications can the *"Totalitätstypik"* and *"Habitualität"* of the *Lebenswelt* be rendered linguistic.[89]

In the *Logical Investigations*, Husserl had raised the question, prominently resumed by Wittgenstein, whether the meaning process "necessarily involves" acts of "fancy, or whether, on the other hand, mental imagery lies outside of the essence of an expression, and rather performs a fulfilling role, even if only of a partial, indirect or provisional character."[90] Without rehabilitating the role of mental images, the later Husserl is nevertheless convinced that typified *Vorstellung* is an indispensable component of the meaning process, where it appears in acts of "quasi-perceiving," "quasi-judging," "quasi-wishing," and a myriad of other intentional quasi-acts.[91] His very concept of "appresentation" that plays such an important role in the *Cartesian Meditations* is all about *Vorstellung* and its function in the meaning constitution of everyday reality. Not only does "reproductive consciousness" belong to every act of perceiving, as a possibility,[92] "every memorial as-if" is a sort of "transforming fiction" and "every experience has as its counterpart a phantasy (a re-presentation) corresponding to it."[93] Even in fantasy can "I feel 'real' desire."[94] In natural language, the vast bulk of our linguistic performance cannot but draw on "semblance acts" and "as-if-modification."[95] For Husserl, then, *Vorstellung* in its *productive* form plays a lead role in the *Lebenswelt* as "inactuality modification."

## Language and the *Lebenswelt*

One of the startling omissions in the *Logical Investigations* is a serious engagement with the speech community without which language could never have emerged in human evolution and without which it could not function the way it does now. This absence is corrected in Husserl's massive *Phenomenology of Intersubjectivity* where the *Sprachgemeinschaft* is essential to the *Heimwelt* and an indispensable component in being-with-one-another, for-one-another, and especially *within-one-another*.[96] Toward the end of his career, the speech community is fully integrated into the *Lebenswelt*. Given Husserl's starting point in the description of the acts of consciousness an individual is bound to perform differently in arithmetic, geometry, logic, perception, linguistic meaning, *Vorstellung*, and other ontological domains, how does he finally arrive at the *a priori* of the *Lebenswelt* and does so in such a forceful manner? How does Husserl transform his first-person starting point into the third-person perspective of communal intersubjectivity? How does the *Lebenswelt* arise in Husserl as his overriding ontological commitment? The short answer seems to be that having described acts of consciousness for almost a lifetime, all of which left dangling the Kantian question of the condition of possibility of such individual acts, the *Lebenswelt* began to loom increasingly large as a pressing *inference* as necessary ground. If our subjective acts are indeed such and such, then only a radical intersubjectivity can answer the question of their genesis, an answer postponed for roughly half a century. Husserl's long-sustained first-person epistemology turns into the methodological basis for his third-person perspective on the "acts of communal life (*Akte des Gemeinschaftslebens*),"[97] in the "community of monads" of the *Lebenswelt*,⁹⁸ Husserl's final ontological commitment. What a post-Husserlian phenomenology of natural language then has to consider is how Husserl's introspective being-within-one-another and for-one-another as an "*Ineinander* of the absolute" would have to modify his early theorization of the linguistic meaning process.⁹⁹

In the *Crisis* Husserl juxtaposes the "formula world" sharply to the *Lebenswelt*. In the former, nature is seen through the lens of "numerical magnitudes," its "meaning" lying in "idealities"; whereas in the latter, intuitive grasp, habit (*Gewohnheit*), and familiarity determine our "non-essential typifications." The "formula world" thrives on "prediction to infinity" and confuses its method of measurement with what the world is actually like, forgetting that its tools of predictive inference are in reality derived from "ordinary inductive knowledge": scientific prediction is the forgotten *Vor-meinen* (meaning in advance) that has always characterized the *Lebenswelt*.¹⁰⁰ Although initially, the *Lebenswelt* was a "scientific critical, not a social-philosophical concept,"¹⁰¹ its social implications were unavoidable. In Husserl's own words, the *Lebenswelt* is "the historical communal life" and the validity (*Geltung*) of "its various subjective ways."¹⁰² How does this shift of emphasis affect our theorization of language?

In Husserl's holism of the *Lebenswelt*, language does not simply occupy a clearly demarcated domain. It is not possible to excise it from the *Lebenswelt* as a practice separate from everything else. Without paying attention to language, the lifeworld could not be described at all. Whatever meanings we are able to produce nonverbally can also be covered by language, even if not at the same level of specificity. Language schematizes the various nonverbal modalities to different degrees and does so *heterosemiotically*. Furthermore, we cannot describe the world we live in without the complication of employing language as both *definiens* and *definiendum*. Husserl's view of the *Lebenswelt* as the ultimate *a priori*, the transcendental ground of all human endeavor, which includes science, is always already saturated by natural language. This is not to say, however, that language has fully replaced nonverbal meaning acts. What it does suggest is that language as our main vehicle of predication, having transformed *S as p* into *S is p*, has inherited and incorporated its nonverbal precursors, perception, and *Vorstellung*, in a way concealed by generalization, idealization, and formalization. What Husserl deplores in the *Crisis* as the nonreflective mathematization of the world is what prevented him in *Logical Investigations* from seeing more clearly that natural language semantics in some way contains and so preserves the *Lebenswelt*. What needs fleshing out is how precisely arbitrary linguistic expressions facilitate such conveyance of content.

## Husserl's Revisions in the *Nachlass*

According to Ullrich Melle, editor of Husserl's *Nachlass* volumes on language, two questions inform Husserl's revisions: the relation of what is physical and psychic, real and ideal in linguistic expressions; and the relation of the expression to its foundations, the expressed acts, and its noematic correlates.¹⁰³ Other revisions include the following: Husserl's new analysis of the role of tone and voice,¹⁰⁴ a change of emphasis from intuition to *Anschauung* and *Anschaulichkeit*,[105] an elaboration of empty intention (*Leerintention*) as a merely transitional stage of consciousness (*Durchgangsbewusstsein*),[106] the widening of the gap between formal identity and *proximate* meaning fulfilment,[107] the foregrounding of "epistemic essence" over "semantic essence,"[108] the cognitive equality of *imagined* and *perceptual* forms of meaning intention and meaning fulfilment,[109] the prelinguistic role of categorial relations and the *core forms* of substantivity and adjectivity as expounded further in *Experience and Judgment*,[110] the *social* revision of his earlier view of the subjective nature of *soliloquy*,[111] and the foregrounding of *sociality* as ontological ground and condition of subjective acts, including linguistic intentionality.[112] Accordingly, we can revise and extend Husserl's linguistic act theory in light of his emphasis on the social ground of language in communal life not only as a being-with-one-another (*Miteinandersein*) but crucially a *being-within-one-another* (*Ineinandersein*).[113] "Communicative consciousness"[114] is viewed as integral to a speech community (*Sprachgemeinschaft*)[115] and as such is purposefully inserted into a "shared spiritual world (*gemeingeistliche Welt*)" and the social intellectual life, Husserl's "*soziale Geistigkeit*."[116] Nor did Husserl retreat from such insights in his later work. As late as 1936, in "The Origin of Geometry," Husserl emphasizes the "linguistic community" as the "community of those who can *reciprocally* express themselves."[117]

Whether word sounds become meaningful (*bedeutsam*) by being individually animated or not is the criterion that sets the speaker of a language sharply apart from strangers to the speech community. Only speakers of the language are able to proceed to this point in the chain. When they do so, their acts respond to a sense of *coercion*, Husserl's *Sollenscharakter* (character of the ought).[118] The *Sollenscharakter* of linguistic expressions is endowed, and gradually altered, by the speech community such that its members habitually actualize it according to the communal language drill. With this proviso, once we have animated the word sound, says Husserl, we live in the consciousness of meaning (*Bedeutungsbewusstsein*), typically extended to *Sinn*, its broader interpretive response.[119] When we recognize the word sound via acts of meaning endowment, we are aware of several things at the same time, the aboutness of the linguistic expression, Husserl's *Hinweistendenz*, and its double directionality, back toward an object in the actual world or a merely imaginable object and forward toward the intended object, usually requiring schematizing acts of iconic mental projection for its reconstruction. *Hinweisen* lends the word *Bedeutsamkeit*, which turns into *Bedeutung* via the meaning-endowing act in use, in which the indication terminates.[120] We could say that the community agreed upon *Hinweisfunktion* (indicative function) is instantiated first as directional *Bedeutung* before it can be imaginatively fulfilled in the meaning-endowing act of *Sinn*. As in the *Logical Investigations,* Husserl's revisions repeat the complication of indication by intimation, now by refining the dual notion of intimating as a "speaker's experience" and the "speaker's acts of judging" based on a perceptual experience. "An experience intimated," Husserl holds, "is an experience expressed."[121] As Koukal puts it, "intimation is *the particular way* in which expressions indicate."[122] If so, then Husserl's intimation is coterminous with voice as implicit deixis, an indispensable component, rather than pragmatic extra, of natural language.[123]

A fundamental terminological difference between the Fregean minimalist portrayal of language and Husserl's holistic elaboration is the reversal of *Sinn* and *Bedeutung*.

Whereas in the *Logical Investigations* Husserl was still committed to meaning as synonymous with "sense," both referring to "the identical element in our intention,"[124] in the *Nachlass* Husserl separates *Bedeutung*, understood as merely verbal or logical sense, more clearly from *Sinn* as its vividly imaginable, and so largely *nonverbal*, meaning fulfilment. As Vandervelde puts it succinctly, in Husserl, *Sinn* is "cashed out" *Bedeutung*.[125] However, this *reversal* is not exactly symmetrical for only in formal sign systems is perfect meaning transmission conceivable. Whereas Frege's *Bedeutung* is defined as scientifically secured reference, Husserl's *Sinn* goes well beyond such conception of indication by including acts of intimation. Whereas in Frege, *Bedeutung* is a consequence of *Sinn*, in Husserl, *Sinn* as meaning fulfilment is directionally constrained by the *Bedeutung* of an expression such that meaning identity is assumed to be retained but at the same time expanded by providing a broader, nonverbal, imaginative meaning-context within which a linguistic expression is realized. Husserlian aboutness, then, transcends Fregean reference, a difference that has serious consequences for any comparison between analytical and phenomenological accounts of how language works. According to Husserl, meaning intentions are further complicated, as Melle points out, in that they can be conducted in "authentic and inauthentic" (*eigentlicher und uneigentlicher*) form.[126] Husserl's phrasing should, however, not be construed as an evaluation. All he is saying is that acts of meaning intention can be performed on perceptual reality as they can on something that is merely imagined. In both cases, an "object" is "constituted" as an "identical X" in consciousness, "whether it is real or not."[127]

Last, an intriguing problematic posed in Husserl's revisions is whether or not thought can occur as "speechless (*Sprachloses*), in nonverbal experiences, nonverbal forms of thinking."[128] Donald Davidson, for one and many others, would deny such an option since thinking should be verbal by definition.[129] The revised Husserl leaves the answer open. Yet he concedes that we cannot simply "remove the linguistic expression like clothing and then retain the thought as naked thought on its own beside it." Husserl here addresses a profound problem in the description of natural language central to this study: the relation between words and *Anschauung*, a topic, he writes, that demands "difficult and important analyses."[130] For it is not at all clear whether or not we have "the word as external to the *Anschauung* and in addition the *Anschauung*."[131] Or whether, for the native speaker, the *Anschauung* is always at least minimally coexperienced with the sound of the linguistic expression, according to the imaginability thesis advocated here.

According to Ullrich Melle, Husserl's posthumously published revisions of his early theorization of natural language are not easily reconciled into a coherent picture, perhaps because they amount to too radical a critique of his position advocated in the *Logical Investigations*.[132] If this is the case, our task is perhaps less to invent a cohesion that would violate Husserl's revisions as to explore which specific revisions to accentuate for a coherent phenomenological portrait of language flexibly based on Husserl's overall oeuvre. I have chosen the option that best sustains the *imaginability thesis*, according to which linguistic meaning is a function of being able to *imagine* what is being talked about and the *manner* in which expressions are presented. In this respect, what does provide an overall sense of cohesion in Husserl's theorization of language is his continuing and all-pervasive emphasis on vividly imaginable, *communicative intentionality*.

## Conclusion: From Language as Calculus to Language as Universal Medium

By way of conclusion, I ask how it is possible that two traditions of theorizing, analytical language philosophy and phenomenology, one taking its point of departure from Aristotle's *propositions*, the other from Aristotle's *homoiomata* or resemblance relations, arrive at such divergent descriptions of natural language. And how is it that two philosophers, Frege and Husserl, both from starting points in mathematics, produce such contrasting descriptions of the very same object of inquiry? The answer, I suppose, can be found in their very different motivation and subsequent methodological choices. Frege was primarily interested in a univocal symbolic sign system, his *Begriffsschrift*, which he wanted to illustrate via the use of natural language terms. His starting point was Euclidian geometry by which he collapsed the sense of natural language into formal sense, while his reference is aligned with the kind of reference we find in applied calculus, secured by definitional boundaries and scientific evidence. While Frege grants "colouring" and "force" a minor mention, they do not amount to anything like Husserl's *intimation* or *introjection*, *tone*, or communal *imposition*. This is why the view of Husserl's theorization as "calculus," as proposed by Martin Kusch, in my view leaves his treatment of language as "universal medium" in the shadows.[133] As we shall see, Husserl's holistic starting point and elaborate descriptions of the intentional acts, which we cannot but perform in engaging in language, should be recognized as a serious challenge to the Fregean analytic tradition of language philosophy. For Husserl's results come much closer to the mark of matching what is actually going on when we use language. It is the richness and subtlety of Husserl's analyses, as well as their compelling evidence, that encourage us to continue his work. In this spirit and in light of the emphasis of this study on the social character of our linguistic acts, the following chapter will argue the case of language as a socially generated and monitored system of *fuzzy* eidetic reductions, a system of proximate generalizations, Husserl's *das Ungefähre*.

## Notes

1 Filip Mattens (ed.), *Meaning and Language: Phenomenological Perspectives*. Phaemenologica 187 (Dordrecht: Springer, 2008); Dan Zahavi and Frederic Stjernfelt (eds.), *One Hundred Years of Phenomenology: Husserl's Logical Investigations Revisited* (Dordrecht: Springer, 2002); Hua XX/1, XX/2.
2 Hua XX/2, pp. 16, 23; Ullrich Melle, "Das Rätsel des Ausdrucks: Husserls Zeichen- und Ausdruckslehre in den Manuskripten für die Neufassung der VI. Logischen Untersuchung," in *Meaning and Language*, pp. 3–26 (p. 8).

3 Hua XX/2, pp. 401, 456.
4 E.g., Ernie Lepore and Barry C. Smith (eds.), *The Oxford Handbook of Philosophy of Language* (Oxford: Clarendon Press, 2006); Michael Devitt and Richard Hanley, *The Blackwell Guide to the Philosophy of Language* (Oxford: Blackwell, 2006); Steven Davis and Brendan Gillon (eds.), *Semantics: A Reader* (Oxford: Oxford University Press, 2004); Peter V. Lamarque (ed.), *Concise Encyclopedia of Philosophy of Language* (Oxford: Pergamon, 1997).
5 *De Interpretatione*, pp. 1, 16a, 3–8.
6 Gottlob Frege, "On Sense and Reference," in *Translations from the Philosophical Writings of Gottlob Frege*, trans. P. Geach and M. Black (Oxford: Blackwell, 1970), pp. 56–78.
7 Marie Duzi, Bjorn Jespersen, and Pavel Materna, *Procedural Semantics for Hyperintensional Logic: Foundations and Applications of Transparent Intensional Logic* (Dordrecht: Springer, 2010).
8 Husserl, *Logical Investigations*, trans. J. N. Findlay (New York: Humanity Books, 2000), p. 276; cf. Ernst Tugendhat, "Phänomenologie und Sprachanalyse," in *Hermeneutik und Dialektik*, ed. R. Bubner (Tübingen; J. C. B. Mohr, 1970), pp. 3–33; *Vorlesungen zur Einführung* in die sprachanalytische Philosophie (Frankfurt: Suhrkamp, 1976).
9 Dummett, *Truth and Other Enigmas*, pp. 121f.
10 Cf. Horst Ruthrof, *Semantics and the Body: Meaning from Frege to the Postmodern* (Toronto: University of Toronto Press, 1997), pp. 59–76.
11 Martin Kusch, "Husserl and Heidegger on Meaning," *Synthese* 77 (1988), 99–127; *Language as Calculus and Universal Medium* (Dordrecht: Kluwer, 1989); Donn Welton, *The Origins of Meaning* (The Hague: Martinus Nijhoff, 1983).
12 Edmund Husserl, *The Crisis of European Sciences and Transcendental Phenomenology*, trans. D. Carr (Evanston: Northwestern University Press, 1970), p. 173.
13 Husserl, *Crisis*, p. 138; Hua XV, pp. 366ff; "The Origin of Geometry," in *The Crisis of European Sciences and Transcendental Phenomenology: An Introduction to Phenomenological Philosophy*, trans. D. Carr, 353–78 (Evanston: Northwestern University Press, 1970), pp. 358ff.
14 Husserl, *Logical Investigations*, p. 694.
15 Ibid., p. 331.
16 Ibid., p. 283.
17 Ibid., p. 337.
18 Ibid., p. 283.
19 Ibid., p. 690.
20 Ibid., p. 697; *Addendum*; my emphasis.
21 Edmund Husserl, *Experience and Judgment: Investigations in a Genealogy of Logic*, ed. L. Landgrebe, trans. J. S. Churchill and K. Ameriks (Evanston: Northwestern University Press, 1997), p. 381.
22 Husserl, *Logical Investigations*, p. 745.
23 Ibid., p. 285.
24 Ibid., p. 283.
25 Ibid., pp. 694ff.
26 Ibid., p. 292.
27 Ibid., pp. 277f.
28 Ibid., p. 277.
29 Cf. Kasimir Twardowski, *On the Content and Object of Presentations*, trans. R. Grossmann (The Hague: Martinus Nijhoff, 1977).

30 Husserl, *Logical Investigations*, p. 270.
31 Ibid., p. 277.
32 Ibid.
33 Robert Sokolowski, *Phenomenology of Human Person* (Cambridge: Cambridge University Press, 2008), p. 167.
34 Hua XX/1, pp. 3, 31, 33, 38f., 41, 44, 105, 129, 145f.; XX/2, pp. 2f., 7, 135f., 151, 292, 329.
35 Husserl, *Logical Investigations*, p. 278; my emphasis.
36 Charles F. Hockett, "The Origin of Speech," *Scientific American* 203 (1960), 88–96; "The Problem of Universals in Language," in *Universals of Language*, ed. J. Greenberg (Cambridge, MA: MIT Press, 1966), pp. 1–29.
37 Husserl, *Logical Investigations*, p. 281.
38 Wittgenstein, *Philosophical Investigations*, §445.
39 Husserl, *Logical Investigations*, p. 281.
40 Ibid., p. 302.
41 Ibid., p. 283; my emphasis.
42 Husserl, *Logical Investigations*, p. 290.
43 Hua XX/2, pp. 401, 456.
44 Edmund Husserl, *Ideas: General Introduction to Pure Phenomenology*, trans. W. R. Boyce Gibson (London: George Allen and Unwin, 1969), p. 361.
45 Husserl, *Logical Investigations*, p. 287.
46 Cf. Andrew Woodfield, "Intentionality," in *Concise Encyclopedia of Philosophy of Language*, p. 55.
47 Husserl, *Logical Investigation*, p. 287.
48 Ibid., p. 287.
49 Cf. Barry C. Smith, "Husserl's Theory of Meaning and Reference," in *Mind, Meaning, and Mathematics: Essays on the Philosophy of Husserl and Frege*, ed. L. Haaparanta (Dordrecht: Kluwer, 1994), pp. 163–83; Bertrand Russel, "On Denoting," in *Essays in Analysis*, ed. D. Lackey (New York: George Braziller, 1973), pp. 103–19; P. F. Strawson, "On Referring," *Mind* 59 (1950), 320–44; Gareth Evans, *The Varieties of Reference*, ed. J. McDowell (Oxford: Clarendon Press, 1982).
50 Husserl, *Logical Investigations*, p. 293; I must differ from Husserl's remark, "To use an expression significantly and to refer expressively to an object (to form a presentation of it) are one and the same."
51 Ibid., pp. 313ff.
52 Kevin Mulligan, *Speech Act and Sachverhalt: Reinach and the Foundations of Realist Phenomenology* (The Hague: Martinus Nijhoff, 1987).
53 *Philosophical Investigations*, trans. G.E.M. Anscombe, P.M.S. Hacker, and J. Schulte (Oxford: Blackwell, 2009), §23.
54 Husserl, *Logical Investigations*, pp. 315f.
55 Ibid., p. 329.
56 Ibid., p. 322; cf. Herman Philipse, "The Problem of Occasional Expressions in Edmund Husserl's *Logical Investigations*," *Journal of the British Society of Phenomenology* 13 (1982), 168–85; Peter Simons, "Meaning and Language," in *The Cambridge Companion to Husserl*, ed. B. Smith and D. W. Smith (Cambridge: Cambridge University Press, 1995), pp. 106–37.
57 Hua XX/2, pp. 102ff.; see Chapter Five.
58 Bertrand Russell, "Vagueness," *The Australian Journal of Psychology and Philosophy* 1 (1923), 84–92.

59 Husserl, *Logical Investigations*, pp. 319f.; my emphasis; cf. Kant, on empirical concepts, CPR A727ff/755ff.
60 Hua XX/1, pp. 38, 40; XX/2, p. 139.
61 Husserl, *Ideas*, pp. 72f.
62 Husserl, *Logical Investigations*, pp. 299ff.; Steven M. Kosslyn, William L. Thompson, and Giorgio Ganis, *The Case of Mental Imagery* (Oxford: Oxford University Press, 2006); Zenon Pylyshyn, "Mental Imagery: In Search of a Theory," *Behavioral and Brain Sciences* 25 (2002), 157–82; *Seeing and Visualizing* (Cambridge, MA: MIT Press, 2003); Michael Tye, *The Imagery Debate* (Cambridge, MA: MIT Press, 2000).
63 Husserl, *Experience and Judgment*, p. 334.
64 Dagfinn Føllesdal, "Husserl's Notion of *Noema*," *The Journal of Philosophy* 66 (1969), 680–7; likewise, David W. Smith and Ronald McIntyre, *Husserl and Intentionality* (Dordrecht: Reidel, 1982) and Kusch, *Language as Calculus and Universal Medium*.
65 Sokolowski, *Introduction to Phenomenology* and Lenore Langsdorf, "The Noema as Intentional Entity: A Critique of Føllesdal," *Review of Metaphysics* 37 (1984), 757–84.
66 Dagfinn Føllesdal, "Noema and Meaning in Husserl," *Philosophy and Phenomenological Research* 50 (1990), 263–71; "Husserl on Evidence and Justification," in *Phenomenology: Critical Concepts in Philosophy*, v. 1, ed. D. Moran and L. E. Embree (London: Routledge, 2004); cf. also Smith and McIntyre, *Husserl on Intentionality*.
67 Cf. Rudolf Bernet, "Husserls Begriff des Noema," in *Husserl-Ausgabe und Husserl-Forschung*, ed. S. Ijsselling (Dordrecht: Kluwer, 1990), pp. 61–80; John Drummond and Lester Embree (eds.), *The Phenomenology of the Noema* (Dordrecht: Kluwer, 1992).
68 Hua I, pp. 138ff.
69 Edmund Husserl, *Phantasy, Image Consciousness, and Memory (1898–1925)*, trans. J. B. Brough, *Collected Works*, ed. R. Bernet (Dordrecht: Kluwer, 2005), p. 373.
70 Husserl, *Logical Investigations*, p. 729.
71 Ibid., p. 728.
72 Ibid., p. 735.
73 Ibid.
74 Ibid., p. 475.
75 Ibid., p. 795.
76 Husserl, *Phantasy, Image Consciousness, and Memory*, p. 710.
77 Husserl, *Logical Investigations*, p. 408.
78 Ibid., p. 729.
79 Hua XLI, p. 230; cf. Alfred Schütz, "Type and Eidos in Husserl's Late Philosophy," *Philosophy and Phenomenological Research* 20 (1959), 147–65; as well as Dieter Lohmar, "Husserl's Type and Kant's Schemata: Systematic Reasons for Their Correlation or Identity," in *The New Husserl: A Critical Reader*, ed. D. Welton, 93–124 (Bloomington: Indiana University Press, 2003).
80 Robert Sokolowski, "The Logic of Parts and Wholes in Husserl's *Investigations*," in *Readings on Edmund Husserl's* Logical Investigations, ed. J. N. Mohanty (The Hague: Martinus Nijhoff, 1977), pp. 94–111 (102).
81 Kant, CPR A141/B180.
82 Kant, CPR A141f./B181; cf. Horst Ruthrof, "From Kant's Monogram to Conceptual Blending," *Philosophy Today* 55, 2 (2011), 111–26.
83 Cf. Lohmar, "Husserl's Type and Kant's Schemata," p. 93.
84 Hua I, pp. 55f.

85 Hua XX/2, pp. 3, 439; XLI, p. 230.
86 Husserl, *Experience and Judgment*, p. 334.
87 Ibid., pp. 337f.
88 Ibid., p. 336.
89 Husserl, *Experience and Judgment*, pp. 36, 52.
90 Husserl, *Logical Investigations*, p. 283.
91 Husserl, *Phantasy, Image Consciousness, and Memory*, p. 413.
92 Ibid., p. 369.
93 Ibid., pp. 700f., 707.
94 Ibid., pp. 436, 447f.
95 Ibid., pp. 709f.
96 Hua XV, pp. 224f., 366ff., 471; cf. also "The Origin of Geometry," pp. 358f.
97 Hua IX, p. 246.
98 Hua I, pp. 149ff.
99 Hua XV, p. 366ff.
100 Husserl, *Crisis*, pp. 44ff.
101 Klaus Held, "Husserl's Phenomenology of the Life-World," trans. L. Rodemeyer, in *The New Husserl*, ed. D. Welton (Bloomington: Indiana University Press, 2003), pp. 32–62 (50).
102 Husserl, *Crisis*, p. 152.
103 Melle, "Das Rätsel des Ausdrucks," p. 8.
104 Hua XX/2, pp. 102f.
105 Hua XX/1, pp. 4n3, XX/2, pp. 2f, 7, 135f., 143f., 291f., 298, 329.
106 Hua XX/2, 151, 205.
107 Ibid., p. 139.
108 Husserl, *Logical Investigations*, p. 745.
109 Hua XX/2, pp. 144, 291f., 243.
110 Husserl, *Experience and Judgment*, pp. 210, 221f., 224, 317, 377, 401.
111 Hua XX/2, pp. 49, 465.
112 Hua XIII, XIV, XV.
113 See especially Hua XV, pp. 366–77; my emphasis.
114 Hua XX/2, p. 13.
115 Hua XV, p. 224.
116 Hua XX/2, pp. 75, 23.
117 Husserl, "The Origin of Geometry," pp. 358f.
118 Hua XX/2, pp. 104, 75, 170, 57, 74f.
119 Hua XX/2, p. 126.
120 Cf. Melle, "Das Rätsel des Ausdrucks," p. 18.
121 Koukal, "The Necessity of Communicating Phenomenological Insights and Its Difficulties," p. 261.
122 Ibid., p. 262; my emphasis.
123 A topic to be addressed in Chapter Five.
124 Husserl, *Logical Investigations*, p. 292.
125 Pol Vandervelde, "An Unpleasant but Felicitous Ambiguity: *Sinn* und *Bedeutung* in Husserl's Revisions of the *Logical Investigations*," *Meaning and Language*, pp. 29–48 (31); Hua XX/2, p. 137.
126 Melle, "Das Rätsel des Ausdrucks," p. 14.
127 Husserl, *Ideas*, p. 377.
128 Ibid., p. 20.

129 See Donald Davidson, "Thought and Talk," in *Mind and Language*, ed. S. D. Guttenplan (Oxford: Clarendon Press, 1975), pp. 7–23; "Rational Animals," *Dialectica* 36 (1982), 317–28; "Seeing through Language," *Royal Institute of Philosophy Supplement* 42 (1997), 15–27.
130 Hua XX/2, p. 22.
131 Ibid., p. 145.
132 Melle, "Das Rätsel des Ausdrucks," p. 15.
133 Kusch, *Language as Calculus and Universal Medium*.

3

# Language *as* Eidetic Reduction
## The Fuzzy *Eidos*

"In the world of intuition," writes Husserl, "there is only approximation."[1] Much the same appears to be the case in natural language, in contrast with specialized formal and technical sign systems. And yet, the principle of approximation does not undermine the *systemic* character of natural language. For what is lost in accuracy at the level of approximate meaning reconstruction in language is made up for, I suggest, by the eidetic deep ground of communal meaning agreement. As I want to claim here and try to demonstrate in subsequent chapters, the kinds of acts of consciousness that we are bound to perform when we engage in language seem to indicate that natural language is itself a socially generated and monitored system of *eidetic reductions*. To begin with, a common feature of the eidetic reduction and natural language is the central role played by *generality* in both. There can be little doubt that language draws much of its power and efficiency as a sign system from this characteristic of generality (*Allgemeinheit*). What Husserl says of the single word applies to language in toto. "The generality of the word" means that "one and the same word, through its uniform meaning, encompasses an ideally fixed multiplicity of possible intuitions (*Anschauungen*) in such a way that each of these *Anschauungen* is able to function as basis for an *identically naming verbal act* of cognition."[2] To what extent Husserl's ideal of "identically naming" can be taken as the norm in language will have to be seen. Certainly, Husserl's phrasing allows the inference that any word in a language can be used as the starting point of a *reversal* of an eidetic reduction, that is, whenever we imaginatively fill the general schema provided by the word sound with specific nonverbal states of affairs. Yet in any given speech community, such forms of meaning endowment are not entirely free but appear to be constrained in several ways. One such constraint, I argue in this chapter, is the way the speech community dictates to its members how to reanimate the *eidetically* reduced linguistic structures by means of imaginative, nonverbal acts of meaning fulfilment. If language can indeed be viewed as an eidetic system, the chapter asks what sort of *eidos* we are dealing with.

## Eidos, Similarity, and Imaginability

As indicated earlier, imaginability is employed here in two senses: one, as the human capacity to vary perception under social guidance and, two, as comprising those features of language that permit members of a speech community to render it *anschaulich*, that is, vividly imaginable, to use a crucially important term in Husserl's *Nachlass*. In doing so, I foreground Husserl's distinction between what it is in linguistic expressions that is *unanschaulich* and what makes them *anschaulich*, that is, intuitively empty versus vividly imaginable.[3] With reference to language, Husserl speaks of the "*Lebendigkeit der ganzen Vorstellung*," the liveliness or vividness of the overall intentional projection,[4] and the necessity to always begin with "originary *Anschauungen*."[5] What is *anschaulich* addresses the problematic of the presence of the nonverbal *in* language. In this respect, the eidetic reduction plays an elemental role in the relation between the symbolic side of language and its intuitive, nonverbal side in acts of meaning intention and meaning comprehension. Husserl's *Wesensschau*, the seeing of essences, here fulfils the function of guiding us "from the unthematic to the thematic" and so "increases the clarity of the given essence."[6] According to Dieter Lohmar, Husserl's procedure of essential seeing is an exemplification of *categorial intuition*.[7] Understood as a reduction of particulars to essences, the eidetic reduction has been defined as a process of "free variation" by which the individuating and contingent characteristics of phenomena are bracketed out of consideration and are replaced by "necessity and generality."[8] As Sokolowski explains, in enabling us to grasp "an *eidos* or a form," Husserl's eidetic reduction is best described as "a special kind of intentionality" yielding "identity within manifold appearances." This is not the strict kind of identity we associate with Leibniz's substitution *salve veritate*, his identity of indiscernibles, but rather the "weak kind of identity" we understand as *typicality*.[9]

Here, Husserl draws the decisive distinction between "empty essences as the domain of pure logic (*die leeren Wesen der Domäne der reinen Logik*)" and the "typical essence (*typisches Wesen*)" of what is merely approximate (*Ungefähres*). The former can be exact, the latter is to be conceived as consisting of "*Typen*," that is, "apperceptive generalities." In the first case, we are able to establish full congruence, in the second, we have to retreat to the mere "congruence of similarities (*Deckung von Ähnlichem*)" within a "circle of similarity (*Ähnlichkeitskreis*)" or a "milieu of similarity (*Ähnlichkeitsmilieu*)."[10] On the side of the typical, approximate eidos, Husserl observes a "flow of similarity and sameness," which allows us to perform predicative judgments in the empirical sphere of the "more or less" (*im Ungefähren*). This does not mean, however, that Husserl has given up entirely on his ideal of exact equivalence. While "the empirical sphere is the sphere of fluidity (external, but also inner sensuousness)," at the eidetic level of analysis he still pursues "the possibility of a method of approximation which leads to exact limits." Accordingly, Husserl speaks of a "series of increasing similarity (*Steigerungsreihe in Ähnlichkeit*),"[11] a topic resumed in *Experience and Judgment*, where he draws fine-grain distinctions between grades of similarity, between "partial similarity," "total similarity," and "the magnitude of the divergencies in similarity."[12] In the *Nachlass*, such non-formal concepts are no longer simply viewed as "the meaning of names"[13] but as "fluid type concepts (*fliessende Typenbegriffe*)."[14] This, I suggest, allows for the typical, eidetic fuzziness of natural language concepts, such as "democracy," "culture," "art," or "love." We know roughly what we are talking about and so are able to *imagine* relevant schematizations of such conceptual indications "in a flash."[15] To that extent, Husserl's exclusive directionality holds sway. Yet when it comes to precision of semantic scope, the eidos of "democracy" is replaced by meaning negotiation. At the level of *qualia*, the eidos turns *fuzzy*.

It is sometimes assumed that the eidetic variation indicates a break in Husserl's philosophical trajectory. This is not convincing. Quite the contrary, it could be regarded as a crystallization of his procedure employed from the start.[16] As such, it fulfils several purposes. It allows us to see clearly the difference between empirical perception and its quasi-perceptual intentional counterpart. It functions as concept clarification and as a stepping-stone toward arguments in favor of his stipulation of the transcendental ego. It allows us to distinguish between empirical universality, referring to features shared by empirical objects and eidetic universality, indicating their features as *conditiones sine qua non*. Last, the eidetic procedure can also be shown to be useful in a broad range of research, including the natural sciences.[17] One can argue, then, that Husserl's eidetic reduction is both important philosophically and useful. And if the claim goes through that natural language is a system of eidetic reductions, then the procedure turns out to be a common component of everyday life, even if its performance remains unnoticed. But how precisely does it work?

## The Eidetic Reduction: Husserl's Blueprint

In spite of a large body of literature on the eidetic reduction, there is no better starting point for grasping this nettle than Husserl's own, lucid explication in §87 of *Experience and Judgment*. We can sum up his "method of essential seeing" in twelve easy steps. (1) We take anything that is "empirically given" and free it "from its character of *contingency*" by way of bracketing. This provides us with a *phenomenon* ready to undergo phenomenological manipulation. (2) We now modify the phenomenal experience into "an arbitrary example," which prepares it for a new function in consciousness. (3) The new function is the transformation of the arbitrary example into "a guiding model" requiring a "different attitude." (4) The task of this model is to channel our ray of attention along a line of *variation* in "pure consciousness." (5) Imaginative variation is to be understood as a partial exploration of "an infinitely open multiplicity of variants," driven "by an act of volition," and resulting in the constitution of "free variants." (6) An important step now is the recognition of "a unity" that "runs through the multiplicity." (7) In this unity, "all variants coincide" such that an *invariant* appears as a "necessary general form," a "general *essence*." (8) We can now define "essence" as "that without which an object of a particular kind cannot be thought." (9) Crucially, this phrasing can be replaced by "without which the object cannot be intuitively *imagined* as such."[18] (10) "This general essence is the *eidos*." (11) Eidos is to be understood "in the Platonic sense," minus any "metaphysical interpretation." (12) Lastly and importantly, we do not have to commence this procedure with an empirical particular. "A mere imagining" will also do.[19] Husserl's lucid synopsis can be taken as his last word *on the doctrine of the nature and method of the* eidetic reduction.[20] What his summary also shows is that he does not conceive the eidos as necessarily *formal*.

## The Eidetic Reduction in Different Contexts

In spite of its generally accepted usefulness in phenomenology and in some other disciplines, it is not entirely clear what exactly is happening when we compare how the eidetic reduction affects formal entities in contrast with natural kinds, and especially in comparison with culturally saturated objectivities. Nor is it entirely transparent in Husserl's writings what precisely the difference is between the reduced results of imaginable objects and relations, on the one hand, and, on the other, their associated linguistic concepts. What Husserl has told us about this relation is that the eidos "is prior to all concepts, in the sense of verbal significations (*Wortbedeutungen*), which must be adapted to it as pure concepts."[21] This is consistent also with his treatment of pre-predicative categorial core forms, as we shall see, and supports the view that perceptual and quasi-perceptual concepts are refined in linguistic concepts, both of which, however, are answerable to the ground of their essence, their generalized correlate. The justification for regarding such correlates as grounding lies in their function of governing any of their instances, including all the necessary ingredients of natural language. Crucial for this study is the question whether or not the eidetic reduction will reveal whatever social ingredients are contained in subjective, linguistic acts. If so, then the fundamentally social character of language does not have to be taken as a presupposition, as it is by Alfred Schütz, but can be derived from our analysis of individual linguistic acts. In other words, the *Lebenswelt* would always already be implicated in the results of the eidetic reductions we are trained to perform via language.

In the eidetic reduction, according to Husserl in the *Ideas*, "empirical or individual intuition (*Anschauung*) can be transformed into *essential insight* (ideation)," a transformation that is not itself empirical. While experiential *Anschauung* produces an object as self-given, Husserl's material *a priori*, the eidetic reduction generates an essential generality. This process can be accomplished, says Husserl, for "the highest category or one of its specializations, right down to the fully concrete." Compared with the result of empirical intuition, "the essence (*eidos*) is an object of a new type." And yet, "essential *Anschauung* is still *Anschauung*, just as the eidetic object is still an object."[22] So, Lester Embree asks, "what is essential for something to be an exemplification of an *eidos*?" The answer would be, "what I can vary while it remains being an exemplification of a genus or of a species."[23] This allows for Fred Kersten's assertion that "the seeing of an essence or *eidos* is founded on actual or imagined (feigned) perceiving of *individual exemplifications*," even though "there is no analogue in perceiving for the structure manifest in the seeing of essences." Whereas "the perceived is something real" in space and time, in contrast, "space and time are utterly unimportant for the seeing of essences."[24] For Husserl, however, the analogy remains valid.[25] In the conversion from fact to essence, the constitution of "a pure *eidos*, the factual actuality of the particular cases by means of which we progress in the variation is completely irrelevant. And this must be taken literally."[26] By propelling "the constitutive process as far along the spectrum of generality, toward pure essence, as possible," the imaginative variation "enables us to see the *eidos* or idea free from all contingent differences."[27] In this way, "we evidence an essence" via an "identity synthesis."[28]

Since empirical objects are always viewed from a certain perspective, and we have to make a special effort in actuality to explore their adumbrational character, once we turn it into an *intentional objectivity*, its full quasi-appearance is immediately accessible to the imagination, on condition, that is, that we are already acquainted with its empirical source object. In other words, free imaginative variation liberates us from the constraints of empirical data. "When we perform an eidetic variation," writes Andrea Staiti, "we actively move from an awareness of a certain feature belonging to a given instance, through a generalization of that feature for all instances of a certain class, and finally to the redirection of the look from the infinite variety of possible instances to an object of a new kind: the essence of the class at issue, to which the feature is attributed."[29] Which includes its mode of being, its ontological classification. This is why Husserl insists that the so *in-spected* quasi-perceptual cube is an entity that is radically distinct from its empirical counter-object resting on my writing desk, as well as from the logical objectivity captured by its definition. Each of the three objectivities have a fundamentally different ontological status. The mode of being of the cube on the desk is actual, occupies space, is tangible, and has a certain time span of existence. Which distinguishes it sharply from the formally ideal object of the defined cube, in that it is timeless, does not occupy space, exists purely as a definition, and so must not be confused with its possible representations on a whiteboard or with a three-dimensional prop. Nor must the empirical cube be confused with the quasi-perceptual, phenomenologically reduced cube I am imagining. For the latter is neither a material entity nor an ideal object. It is an intentional objectivity. To allow for this third ontological option, Husserl enlarged traditional dualist ontology of materiality and ideality by insisting on intentionality as an additional and indispensable ontological category, a topic to which the reader will be returned at the end of the book. Suffice it here to stress that a phenomenological, tripartite ontology is imperative if we wish to address such ontically heteronomous entities and processes as culture, science, political institutions, and other ontically compound concepts, such as natural language.

## Formal Objectivities

Our freely varied, imagined cube now undergoes a kind of striptease by which we gradually remove all features that we think are merely *incidental*, that is, we think are not essential to its concept. According to Husserl, we will automatically halt this eliminative process when we realize that we have tampered with an *essential* feature of the cube.[30] As long as we only remove such incidentals as color, weight, reflectivity, or roughness of the cube's surface, their deletion turns out not to destabilize our conceptual grasp of the cube. Yet, as soon as we cut off one of the cube's corners, for example, or dent one side, we immediately know that our imagined cube has now been transformed into a *Gestalt* that is no longer compatible with the notion we have of a cube. According to Husserl, if we continue with the process of elimination of incidental characteristics, we will arrive at a set of features that together constitute the cube as what it is. We have arrived at the cube's eidos, that is, at those features without which the cube is neither definable nor *imaginable* as a cube.

However, whether the same can be said of non-formal phenomena, and especially with respect to language, is a moot point. Husserl, though, is confident that we all see *eide* and routinely employ them in our thinking in general. We do so routinely, says Husserl, once we proceed from our "passively pre-constituted" grasp of things to eidetic reflection. While the "pure essence" of things is ordinarily concealed, in the eidetic reduction the eidos "proves to be that without which an object of a particular kind cannot be thought, i.e. without which the object cannot be intuitively *imagined* as such."[31] Or as Sokolowski puts it, "When we bump up against such impossibilities, we have succeeded in reaching an eidetic intuition."[32] The eidetic reduction, then, "renders the eidos explicit" by laying bare the "laws of necessity which determine the necessary features of an object." In the eidetic reduction "the absolutely identical is thrown into relief," thus providing "the necessary invariable form" that "sets the limit to all variability."[33] An alternative description would be to say that the essence, or eidos, is "an ensemble of predicates belonging to a particular kind of object." They "are not contingent features of an object." Rather, our imagination has afforded us "a glimpse of necessity," which reveals itself "in the impossibility of what we tried to imagine."[34] Nevertheless, unless the sum of predicates facilitates imaginative reconstruction in recollection (*Rückerinnerung*) or in linguistic meaning fulfilment, we would not be able to have an *Anschauung* of the object. Even if one were to argue that such imaginative reconstruction can be no more than an incidental by-product, as does Wittgenstein, a claim, however, that Husserl rejects, the reversal of eidetic reduction by imaginatively fleshing out the eidetic skeleton seems unavoidable in acts of cognition of particulars. Certainly, as argued by Sokolowski, "the move into imagination gives us a deeper insight than does empirical induction" because "eidetic necessities are deeper and stronger than empirical truths."[35]

But what precisely is it that sets this limit to variability? Is it the social rule of the concept itself that we already have of things, even if such a concept is interiorized in a somewhat vague manner by the individual speaker and becomes more sharply delineated in the process of the eidetic reduction? And if eidetic limits are already in our minds, though require sharpening by the eidetic procedure, how did they get there? In other words, what determines the constraints within which such sharpening takes place? It seems unlikely that the eidetic reduction brings to consciousness a precision that is *naturally* already within us, even if we are not normally aware of it. Phenomenology here points us to the limits of Chomskyan *recursivity*, the ability of our innate language faculty to get it right. Isn't it much more likely that eidetic necessities are determined by something outside our minds, such as nature on the one hand and, on the other, the speech community of which we are members? And if so, isn't it pedagogy that has channeled and *naturalized* this determination? But would Husserl allow his eidetic reduction to be characterized as socially guided *concept clarification*?

This, of course, would make the eidetic reduction a fairly straightforward procedure. Husserl rules out such a simplification. After all, for Husserl, the eidos is logically "*prior to all concepts*," while linguistic signs "must be adapted to the *eidos*."[36] This means that Husserl's eidos has to be located at a level of generality and universality that is above (or below) those of any specific concept. Any purified cube concept is only what it is because of an essence that does not permit it to be otherwise. But how would such an eidos differ from the formal definition of a cube? Husserl might say that we should not be surprised that our formal definitions and the results of our eidetic reduction match. After all, the former are intersubjective agreements among mathematicians who have all performed the reduction. But Husserl's claims reach well beyond the formal domain, stipulating as he does the radical universality of an eidetic ground for *all* phenomena. To test this broader contention, we must let go of formal examples and address non-formal phenomena.

## Non-formal Objectivities

When we apply the eidetic reduction to non-formal entities, questions arise that threaten to subvert the neat structure of the eidetic reduction. When we apply the eidetic reduction to triangles, circles, oblongs, hyperboles, cones, rotating geometrical bodies, and so on, we notice that we always end up with their definitions of which their imagined or actual representations are derivative. So, can formal objectivities serve as a model for natural kinds (trees, camels) or human artifacts (chairs, houses, machines)? And what about ontologically heteronomous compounds, such as education, democracy, law courts, works of art, culture, or language? Formal analogies must not dazzle us, especially when we look at language through the lens of the eidos. But first, let us put the eidetic reduction to the test by applying it to natural kinds, such as an empirically perceived rabbit. After transforming the empirical rabbit in front of me into a quasi-perceptual, *intentional* rabbit, liberated from existential constraints, varied freely in my imagination, and stripped of all incidental features, I now perform only those intentional acts with respect to the imagined rabbit that cannot be further reduced without destroying the very concept "rabbit." But what is this essence? Is it, as Husserl laconically says, "what it is"? A peculiarly ordered collection of essential rabbit features? An ensemble of predicates? Here, Husserl draws a decisive distinction in the *Nachlass* between "species eidos (*Gattungswesen*)" and "feature eidos," the deep characteristics of its properties or predicates (*Merkmalswesen*), the sum of the latter constituting the eidetic unity of the former,[37] the rabbit as species versus the rabbit as the sum of essential rabbit characteristics. In the rabbit eidos, the two essences appear to coincide.

Now, we ask whether this rabbit eidos is a linguistically overdetermined concept that acts as a guide for the imagination, or is it the abstractive result of having seen several actual rabbits? Or is it the compelling consequence of training in *typification* and *sedimentation* by the culture to which I belong? If so, then different cultures sharing the same species should produce different rabbit *essences*. However, isn't this a case of the physical world rather than culture calling the shots? As Kant, speaking of a ship moving downstream, observes, "the order in which the perceptions succeed one another in apprehension is in this instance determined, and to this order apprehension is bound to. *Therefore, we must derive the* subjective succession *of apprehension from the* objective succession *of appearances*."[38] This not only deflates the charge of Kant's alleged subjectivism, it can also be used to support Husserl's non-subjectivist conception of the *Sachen selbst*. As Husserl insists, "each being is in a broadest possible sense an '*an sich*' [on its own] and has itself in juxtaposition to the incidental for-me of individual acts."[39] Nor can it be a mere coincidence that in dictionaries as different as those of Chinese and English, natural kind terms have similarly concise entries. It is not primarily the cultural lexicon but the world that makes this similarity possible. At the denotative level cultures tend to respect the physical world of appearances.

Still, the rabbit example, and more obviously so any culturally saturated objectivity, could not be said to produce the same kind of conceptual eidos as the eidetic procedure generates in the formal domain. Both Kant and Husserl provide sound explanations why this is so. "Empirical concepts," according to Husserl, reflect a "typical generality" (*typische Allgemeinheit*) rather than formal universality.[40] For this difference, Kant had already laid a firm and still useful foundation. Empirical concepts, he writes, "cannot be defined at all, but only *made explicit*." And this on two grounds: (1) "the limits of the concept are never assured"; and (2) "the analysis of my concept is always in doubt."[41] Kant also distinguished the empirical concept from both *formal* and *pure* concepts, and the latter two by their reverse genesis. Formal concepts are generated by stipulation, pure concepts by ideation of empirical ones. Husserl echoes this characterization when he writes, "empirical concepts are changed by the continual admission of new attributes." The empirical concept is thus an "open, ever-to-be-corrected concept" as a result of "the continual admission of new attributes."[42] This seems to me to be a crucial concession as to the variable nature of the eidos under changing cultural conditions. As to all typified concepts, Husserl confirms, their "horizon of familiarity (*Bekanntheitshorizont*) . . . is still open and waiting for possible further experience," an observation that triggers the self-reflective question, "Can I vary there as I wish?" The answer has to be "No." As to empirical concepts, our imaginative, eidetic variation can only unfold within the conceptual boundaries set by the speech community. As Husserl remarks about language, "I can always realize the word according to its *Sinn* in an identifying manner, fulfilling and identifying it by means of purely thought examples."[43] Yet whatever I so identify, I do so "*unter Korrektur*."[44] This is how we can build *semantic drift* into the character of empirical concepts, if not also into that of theoretical concepts, as for instance "the eternal recurrence of the same," "*Seinsvergessenheit*," or "differance."

Husserl's eidetic reduction appears to survive the Kantian test when applied to natural kinds. In spite of the relative instability of empirical concepts, natural kinds are certainly less changeable than the concepts of cultural phenomena. But is this so whenever nature dictates our concepts, and does this allow for their grounding in essences? Husserl's answer appears to be that it does not matter where we find what we wish to subject to the eidetic reduction because the domain of eidetic possibilities is independent in its existence from any corresponding reality. According to Husserl, idealization frees us to transform reality into its manageable potential variants. In this way, "idealizing thinking conquers the infinity of the experiential world."[45] In Husserl, then, idealization is a human capacity for producing eidetic abstractions as a habit of mind. Even so, different kinds of objectivities appear to pose different constraints on our eidetic idealizations.

## Cultural Objectivities

Ho do such constraints affect the eidetic reduction performed on culturally saturated objectivities? Can any member from a spatially and temporally distant culture arrive at the same eidos as someone embedded in a specific culture? For example, how would a person unfamiliar with Chinese culture arrive at the eidos of an example of a *cha pan*, a typical part of a traditional tea set? Does knowledge of the object, word sound consciousness (*Wortlautbewusstsein*), and its linguistic concept (*Bedeutungsbewusstsein*) not form an inseparable unity for the speaker of a language? To be sure, in the case of such practical objects, an outsider could still discover their eidos by learning about its essential purpose. But how about the traditional daoist mirror? Would the cultural stranger not be likely to construct the wrong eidos? This would suggest that the more deeply saturated culturally a concept we are dealing with, the more difficult for someone from another culture to perform the appropriate eidetic reduction and the fuzzier the result.

Given the complex relations in the way we come to master culturally saturated concepts, it stands to reason that the further we depart in our exemplification from the formal domain toward the realm of culture at large, the more unlikely is it that formal entities can serve as a model. That much Husserl states clearly himself in *Ideas*. In contrast with the mathematical sciences, "which cannot be appealed to for guidance," the "apprehension of the essence" of non-formal entities has "its own *grades of clearness*."[46] And although "phenomenology must be built up, or can be built up, as a '*geometry*' *of experiences*," Husserl draws a sharp line between *ideal concepts* which "one cannot see" and *descriptive concepts* "drawn directly from simple intuition" and, likewise, between formal essences as correlates of stipulated concepts and "*morphological essences*, as correlates of descriptive concepts."[47] So it should not come as a surprise that performing the eidetic reduction should "in the case of a material essence" be "different from what it is in the case of formal essence."[48] But if so, then we must accommodate the notion of a *fuzzy eidos* in our revision of Husserl's scheme. Which is not to say that in the descriptive domain, essences have to be abandoned, as asserted in popular anti-essentialist arguments. Anti-essentialists tend to miss the important point that in Husserl "every object (*Gegenstand*) *has* its essence," the "object itself *is* not an essence."[49]

Equally important is the fact that we are able after all to distinguish between non-formal objectivities, an ability that cannot be reduced to a mere difference in the kind and number of their predicates. We know what things are *in principle*. Why this is so, Husserl is aiming to explain. What my three-step argument is trying to show is that there appears to be a graded scale, rather than one rule fits all, from formal operations toward the domain of *experiential essences* (*Erlebniswesen*) where the invariant among imaginative variations cannot produce a likewise complete, universally valid result and on to culturally saturated objectivities that make the very notion of universality appear problematic. At least, here universality requires a different kind of abstractive process. To complicate matters, natural language poses additional challenges in that, I will argue, it is an ontically compound, heteronomous phenomenon the aspects of which do not amount to a generally agreed-upon collection of particulars ready to be imaginatively varied for eidetic results. Hence some of the striking explanatory differences among different language paradigms.

Let us once more look at our three categories. In the formal domain, the ideal shape of the cube appears dependent on a comprehensive mathematical or verbal definition. Could the cube shape be maintained *without* that definitional backup? Is it not that very definition that sustains the cube as a formal ideality? So, is it the case that we can imagine the perfect cube only because we have a definition that dictates the quasi-material relations between the essential features of the cube? This would fit the bill of de Warren's eidos as a necessary "ensemble of predicates belonging to a particular kind of object."[50] The ideal cube then *only* exists as a definition and not in terms of its representations, which are incidental. So, in the formal domain the relation between language and nonverbal entity is extremely tight if it is not altogether resolved in favor of purely logical predicates. In the domain of natural kinds, are we certain that our imaginative striptease of incidental characteristics is not similarly dictated by linguistic constraints, as it is most certainly the case in our third category, culturally well-saturated objectivities? Such a dependence relation seems especially likely for all instances of concepts that are fundamentally language dependent, that is, only exist because of their linguistic constellation, such as the institutionalized concept "murder" as against that of "manslaughter." Here it is not nature that calls the shots but the communally circumscribed use of language. We could say then that neither non-formal nor formal *eide* are thinkable outside their respective, community controlled, sign systems, the latter outside their domain of univocal signs, the former outside natural language.

*All* essences, then, appear to be dependent on the *semiotics* in which they are expressed, a dependence relation that even applies to the domain of *natural kinds* where, notwithstanding natural constraints, we are typically trained by a speech community as to how imaginatively vary the aspects of objectivities and recognize the eidetic threshold we must not overstep. But does this square with Husserl's conception? Such training should not be necessary. Should not any passively preconstituted phenomenon yield its essence by itself? Can the sedimentation of essences by training be reconciled with Husserl's eidetic genesis? Attempting answers to such questions goes well beyond the aim of this study. So, I will restrict myself to addressing in subsequent chapters how we can show to what extent linguistic expressions *contain* the speech community in the form of social instructions. Before we are in a position to do so, the crucial question needs airing whether or not the speech community is an eidetic invariant in natural language.[51]

## The Speech Community: An Invariant in Language?

Consider the following four utterances.

(1) "What do you think of the purple carpet?"
(2) "Hello!"
(3) "Democracy is under siege."
(4) "Only if you promise to study will I grant your wish."

Here I only want to draw attention to some of the eidetic principles without which comprehension of such utterances could not occur. In sample (1) the object "purple carpet" has to be imaginatively identified before the question can be answered. We do so at first merely eidetically, guided by Husserl's exclusive directionality, which reveals itself in the fact that we are not in a position to think of a green chair or a white wall as a first response. We have been trained by the speech community to strictly follow the *linguistic linkage compulsion*, a form of social coercion that is built into the fabric of every language. Sample (2) illustrates two essential features of language: aboutness and voice, Husserl's *Worüber* and *Ton*. We grasp the word sounds as a greeting, but more importantly, in our meaning uptake respond to its manner of presentation. Every "hello" is identified as what it is above all by its tone. And it is in its manner of delivery that the community instructions are revealed as friendly, warm, skeptical, challenging, or icy. Such intersubjective nuances have at their eidetic core different communal agreements. The aboutness of the word sound "democracy" in sample (3) illustrates the way we have been drilled to construe the eidos of what constitutes democracy for us. Its eidetic fuzziness allows for speakers from different democracies to construe somewhat different eide. But again, the linguistic linkage compulsion forces us to comprehend the word sound in a flash. Last, sample (4) exemplifies the eidetic principle of Husserl's categorial relations in the "only-if-then" syntax of the utterance as an inescapable, communal, linguistic rule.

Such examples should count as apodictic evidence that the speech community trains us how to typically imagine what language is about, how it is presented, and in what typical order its meanings are to be constructed. In each sample, the eidetic reduction is typically performed as an intersubjective dynamic of intentional acts by both speakers and listeners. While it is always conducted by a subject, in habitual speech this performance tends to be no more than the necessary individual *instantiation* of a community practice. Once we apply the eidetic reduction to the genesis of this practice, the role of the community in the training of our perception, imagination, and linguistic representation appears to be an essential feature rather than a mere pragmatic extra. In other words, Husserl's eidetic reduction would have always already been a social phenomenon as realized in individual performance. Yet, this in no way undermines Husserl's focus on subjective intentionality. Epistemically, it remains the foremost starting point of description. Ontologically viewed, that very starting point turns out to be possible only within the parameters of the lifeworld as all-enveloping social sphere and enabling horizon, the multi-monadic community. On this argument, there would have been no need then for Husserl to stipulate a transcendental ego that would facilitate the transition from individual acts of consciousness toward the appresentation of the alter ego and from there to the *Lebenswelt* as a whole. If the social were already part and parcel of our performance of subjective intentionality, at least in language, there would be no contradiction between subjectivity and intersubjectivity. Subjectivity, then, would always already and of necessity be intersubjective. In Husserl's own words, "to be sure, language is intersubjective from the very outset."[52] In this respect, language as a *fuzzy eidetic system* plays a decisive role in levelling the peaks and troughs of *multisubjective intentionality*.

So, Husserl's egocentric predicament can be resolved by demonstrating how members of a speech community shed their subjective idiosyncrasies to the degree to which they cannot but participate in language as an *eidetic practice*. Leaving the possibility of linguistic deviance aside, as it functions for example in creative, poetic acts, language harmonizes individual use in a number of ways. One is the way native speakers are drilled to apply the rules of the speech community in associating word sounds with schematized quasi-perceptual, iconic slices of world in line with the linguistic linkage compulsion.[53] It is communal agreement at the eidetic level of meaning fulfilment that secures compatibility in this associative process. More specifically, language schematizes the subjective acts of members of a speech community by typifying the constitution of aboutness and voice. Aboutness is anchored in cultural specification of *substantivity* and *adjectivity*, two of Husserl's core categories of human nonverbal grasp of the world. Adjectivity exerts its schematizing effects in *attribution* and *predication*, both serving the specification of aboutness in a generalizing manner and does so differently in different languages.[54] Much the same can be said about the typical ways in which voice is employed in a speech community.

Then there is *displacement*,[55] the transformation of nonverbal meaning intention into linguistic expressions, which not only allows us to speak of absent things, of things past, present, and future, but in doing so also specifies the way in which we schematize imaginable mental scenarios to varying degrees in the process of meaning fulfilment. This too appears to be communally regulated at the *eidetic level* of what counts as an acceptable transformation of meaning intention into verbal expressions. If the boundaries of that eidetic commonality have been transgressed, meaning intentions cannot be reliably retrieved. We can further add different forms of schematization by the way the community monitors the standard linguistic ordering of mental iconic materials required for meaning fulfilment. A useful critical mechanism is, for example, Husserl's double axis of *specification and generalization*, on the one hand, and of *materialization and dematerialization* (formalization), on the other,[56] by which we schematize our linguistic acts via the *subsumption* and *hierarchization* of nonverbal mental materials. Most importantly, however, we must avoid any rigid conception of such schematizations. This would fall foul of Husserl's objection to the "false theory of the static congruence of meaning intention and fulfilling *Anschauung*."[57] In spite of the eidetic fuzziness reiterated in Husserl's *Nachlass*, whichever acts in the overall linguistic meaning process we make our task to describe will reveal the submerged yet inescapable presence of the speech community. All of which strongly suggests that the speech community is very likely an *invariant* in the fuzzy eidos of natural language, a claim that can be further buttressed by Husserl's "eidetic doctrine of sociality."[58] One important aspect then of the "objective spatio-temporal world as *the world about us that is there for us all*"[59] is the speech community as a constant of and *in* language. Thus, the speech community is *contained* in every standard linguistic expression as a coercive, transcendental condition without which language would not be what it is.

## Language *as* Eidetic Reduction

Now we are in a position to return to our initial claim that language itself is a system of eidetic reductions. Dictionaries do not contain meanings but only strings of verbal substitutions. In Husserl's revised picture of language, they offer the reader *Bedeutungen* but not *Sinne*. So, we can agree with Quine that the lexicographer, as representative of the speech community, does not provide us with meanings but rather with instructions for the use of linguistic expressions.[60] Where the phenomenologist must part company with Quine is of course on his behaviorist conception of meaning as use, which disavows intentional acts as necessary components of the meaning process. And yet, we need intentionality in advancing from word sound consciousness and word consciousness to being able to *imagine* what linguistic expressions are about, that is, aboutness, Husserl's *Worüber*.[61] A much neglected act in looking up expressions in dictionaries is the *neutrality modification* that we impose on them in our intonation (aloud or silently).[62] When we comprehend the neutralized aboutness of the near synonyms and strings of predicates in the dictionary, they are not yet imagined according to resemblance and degrees of similarity, that is, in terms of "gradation."[63] Only when they are, can we transform the *Bedeutung* of expressions into *Sinn* as vividly imaginable *Anschauung*. The lexicographer thus assists us in negotiating "material general concepts."[64] Yet this can only ever be a stepping-stone toward meaning as *Sinn*.

For the speaker of a language, a dictionary entry like "breeze" and its substitute "gentle and light wind" appear to function as eidetic, linguistic summaries of our recollections of what it is like to be standing in a breeze. "This" and "that" are deictic signs for eidetic, categorial abstractions of verbal pointing to something close and something more distanced, respectively. Likewise, all adjectives, adverbs, and other verbal forms. Every word reflects Husserl's rule of "the generality that lies in all terms (*Bezeichnungen*)."[65] Which suggests the following observations. Only the trained speakers of a language are in a position to perform the semantic substitution of two expressions provided by the lexicographer, on condition that they have been instructed how to *imagine* the aboutness of both *definiens* and *definiendum*. What Quine does not address is that even at this level, comprehension requires minimal nonverbal grasp as *Vorstellung*. Mere verbal substitution without nonverbal grasp results in meaning failure. Only on this condition can the linguistic linkage compulsion do its work. Minor deviations in the acts of association of word sound and imagined scenario tend to pass without much notice. Major deviations are gradually repaired according to community standards. In his regulatory process, a somewhat fuzzy eidos of linguistic concepts suffices. Thus, the basic directionality of expressions is maintained in verbal pointing, Husserl's indication as *Hinweisfunktion* and *Hinweistendenz*.[66] Also, to serve the displacement of meaning intentions by verbal expressions, language must allow for a very broad spectrum of options from the most abstract to the most concrete representations of the *vouloir dire*, the what we want to say. By its eidetic generality, language affords us *sharable* meaning production and meaning fulfilment, both of which can be further specified by accessing the comprehensive combinatory potential of linguistic expressions.

In this sense, dictionaries are ensembles of verbal clusters of *eidetic summaries*, the complexity of which is a function of the size and purpose of the represented lexicon. Long before we consult dictionaries, we are trained to interiorize and gradually enlarge our lexicon, as well as in the way we are supposed to employ its *eidetic* word clusters at different levels of concreteness and in standard categorial constellations of grammar and syntax. In this process, *recursivity* plays a significant, even if not as radical a role as claimed by Chomsky and his followers.[67] In principle, then, transforming meaning intention into verbal expressions consists in substituting appropriate eidetic summaries for nonverbal meaning intentions. At the same time, we guide the reception of our words by an intimation of the way we would like to be understood.[68] The necessary acts of linguistic comprehension as meaning fulfilment require "saturation,"[69] the filling of the *eidetic schemata* of our lexicon to appropriate degrees of specificity of nonverbal imaginability, Husserl's *Anschaulichkeit*.[70] We could say, then, that natural language is a fuzzy, eidetic system permitting its users to communicate meaning intentions by a process of eidetic reduction and its imaginative *reversal*.

As we enrich empty linguistic expressions with mental material typifications to varying degrees of schematization according to the requirements of speech situations, we *reverse* the activity of the lexicographer. In meaning fulfilment, words in their categorial relations undergo a *volte-face* of the eidetic reduction. Words in their generality then are a transitional phase in the semantic process ranging from nonverbal meaning intention via Husserl's merely verbal *Bedeutung* to nonverbal meaning fulfilment in *Sinn*. Given the complexity of the linguistic meaning process in comparison with formal sign operations, our eidetic grasp must retain a certain degree of fuzziness, an *Ungefähres*.[71] Yet, the picture of the fundamentally eidetic character of language in no way undermines Husserl's position that it is not language that is the guiding principle of meaning but on the contrary, meaning "is the guiding principle of language."[72] One could specify Husserl's communicative thesis by saying that language is primarily a means of transmitting eide, which, to be sharable, must at least have *eidetic sufficiency*. This permits us to recognize the fundamentally *social* nature of language as an eidetic system, which makes possible the transition from Husserl's individual monad to the "monadic plurality as the absolute (*Monadenvielheit als dem Absoluten*)" that guarantees "*Miteinander- und Ineinanderleben*." In pursuing this line of thinking, with a focus on the mode of being of language, I feel encouraged by Husserl's observation that this entire monadic process "is subject to the universal laws of genesis, and above all the essential laws the explication of which is the most pressing task of phenomenology."[73]

So, can language as social process be arrived at via eidetic reduction of its identifiable components? The answer, I suggest, is affirmative, on condition that we are content to accommodate a certain degree of fuzziness in our conception of the linguistic eidos. In fact, it is inevitable if we follow the Husserlian procedure. What Friedrich Uehlein has to say about the starting point of every eidetic reduction equally applies to natural language: "experiential life" must be "the point of departure for eidetic reduction."[74] As a result, we should be able to raise the reality of the empirical specifics of language "to pure possibilities," the eidos of language.[75] At the same time, Husserl's own conception of language and its eidos as argued in the *Logical Investigations* will have to undergo certain modifications as a consequence of our inquiry. In particular, Husserl's conception of linguistic concepts as *pure concepts* cannot survive their later characterization as "fluid types,"[76] embedded always in a sequential increase (*Steigerungsreihe*) of comprehension.[77]

Such linguistic meaning acts can be either based on perception or performed "in parallel phantasy."[78] In either case, to have *Sinn* "is the fundamental characteristic of all consciousness."[79] The difference between the two modes lies in their relation to *essentia* and existence. For Husserl, "every object has *essentia* and existence," while phantasy acts only have *essence*.[80] If so, then the foundational role that Husserl bestows on his notion of *Sinn* as meaningfulness beyond Fregean reference can likewise be taken as an *essential* feature of natural language. At the same time, given Husserl's holistic perspective of language embedded in an all-embracing *Sinn*, it should not be surprising that "one somehow always already has an awareness of what is to be clarified."[81] This is why Husserl can confidently distinguish between experienced and "expected" features. "When we see a dog, we immediately anticipate its additional mode of behaviour: its typical way of eating, playing, running."[82] Everything is experienced as typified, an insight that became the starting point of Alfred Schütz's social phenomenology. Husserl's "sense-giving consciousness," which we must "presuppose," affords us at least a vague intuitive grasp of things before we make precision judgments.[83]

In this respect, language as a socially monitored eidetic system sharpens our nonlinguistic grasp of the world by a process of ideation and idealization. Thus, the "infinity of imperfection" of the perceptual world is healed by language and the gradual idealization of the "properties of things" toward their ideal "identifiability."[84] We could read this as Husserl's amendment to Leibniz's sufficient reason, whose pragmatic solution is replaced here by a fuzzy, eidetic alternative. However, such linguistic repair work cannot be achieved in any formal sense. If "the factual world of experience is experienced as a *typified* world," then is language not likely to have inherited such "passively constituted typifications" as "a stock of typical attributes with an open horizon of anticipation of further such attributes?"[85] Importantly, and in contrast to the eidetic procedure valid for formal signification, Husserl's remark concerning "subjects, whose fluid types cannot be apprehended with exactitude" seems to me to be pertinent to natural language.[86]

As to the formation of eidetic, linguistic concepts, Husserl guides us in forming concepts as "the *meanings of names*"[87] in the *Logical Investigations* to the *Nachlass* where meaning is transitional as *Bedeutung*, grasped by merely verbal or logical concepts, and more or less fulfilled in *Sinn* by the mental material and vividly imaginable reconstruction of meaning intention. Semantic essence now gives way to *epistemic essence*. We always have to start from "originary apprehensions,"[88] which facilitate reconstructive saturation (*Sättigung*).[89] In Husserl's later writings, concepts range from material, "concrete" concepts if they precede "all explication and syntactical linkages" to "purely formal concepts" at a high level of abstraction, as in "likeness, difference, unity, plurality," and so on.[90] Husserl conceives of them as a result of the transformation of *percepts* into conceptual grasp. At this stage, "the possibility of the formation of general objectivities, of 'concepts,' extends as far as there are associative syntheses of likeness."[91] This kind of transformation seems likely to have produced "a presumptive idea, the idea of a universal" out of "empirical induction." Here we see that the role of imaginability (*Vorstellbarkeit*) is decisive in that the concept of a thing requires that we vary imagined things "as pure possibilities." Once we have so acquired a concept it has a "pure ideal being," covering both actual and merely imaginable particulars and enabling "an infinite extension of purely possible particulars, of purely possible conceptual objects." But even as an ideality, Husserl insists, it is "an open, *ever-to-be-corrected concept*" that contains the "rule of empirical belief." On this, according to Husserl, "rests the universality of the operation of the formation of concepts."[92]

As everything else on the semantic side of language, *resemblance* can be conveyed by linguistic expressions only in eidetically reduced form. Here, Husserl's general remarks on resemblance are pertinent. Husserl draws a key distinction between "material" and "formal generalities." Since, as I will claim, the vast bulk of language is about things in absentia, Husserl's "mental material generalities" are a vital contribution, providing as they do aboutness as independent of actuality.[93] As abstract generalities, they add such relations as likeness, difference, unity, plurality, and other *categorial* features. Which is compatible with Husserl's position that both mental material generalities and their categorial differentiation have been inherited, at least in a rudimentary form, from perception and perceptual protosyntax, a topic to be addressed in due course.[94] Resemblance relations are also dealt with by Husserl in terms of *divergence* among similarities. "Different similarities," he writes, "can have different divergencies, and the divergencies are themselves again comparable." Here Husserl anticipates Wittgenstein by providing a theoretical basis for the influential notion of "family resemblance."[95] "Complete likeness," on the one hand, and, on the other, absence of any likeness are Husserl's limit phenomena of *resemblance*.[96] Husserl's contribution to the theorization of language is profound in that he explores the polarities between which language is able to convey resemblance relations. It can only do so eidetically, leaving imaginative specification to the meaning event of *Sinn*.

## Conclusion: *Bedeutung* as Fuzzy Eidos

In *Zur Lehre vom Wesen und zur Methode der eidetischen Variation*, Husserl speaks of the *Wesenswort*, an eidetic word such as "friendship, marriage, family," by which he is not referring to anything individual but the "essence friendship," and so on. At the same time, he concedes that "we do not make all essences clear to ourselves, starting from unclear meanings; not all are the final result in a process of clarification of a fuzzy word meaning," as when we entertain "a vague thought and bring it to clarity."[97] Such remarks are best viewed in the context of his cascading distinctions between "identity, sameness, similarity." The eidetic fuzziness of a word like "democracy" well illustrates Husserl's difficulties in demonstrating that commonality "under incongruence" within a "stream of similarities" can lead to a univocal "abstraction of an essence (*Wesensabstraktion*)."[98] Husserl struggles to convince us that complex expressions such as "friendship" or "human decency" will reveal their deep eidos because "there is evidence that the diminishing distance" between our concepts in the process of clarification of necessity "leads to congruence."[99] This difficulty is alleviated if we weaken the thesis of the essence of language to that of a fuzzy eidos.

What our investigation of linguistic intentionality has revealed is that Husserl's path from formal eidos, where fully defined essence is guaranteed, to essence as sameness among morphological concepts, and to nonessential similarity characteristic of culturally saturated phenomena does not lead us to eidetic certitude when it comes to natural language. The "increasing trajectory (*Steigerungsreihe*)" of "proximate commonalities" that characterize our attempts at clarifying complex linguistic expressions cannot deliver any eidetic univocity beyond "inexact essences."[100] We know *roughly* what we are talking about but continue to negotiate how this rough *Bedeutung* can be cashed out by the qualia of *Sinn*. What remains convincing in Husserl's analysis is that natural language is characterized by "fluid type concepts," "similarities and gradualities," "grades of commonality," and that its "concepts are 'valid,' if they *allow* themselves to be clarified."[101] Clarification, however, can mean no more than a socially agreed-upon form of intersubjective sufficiency.[102] As Husserl concludes toward the end of his *Nachlass* on the eidetic reduction, in apperception as in language there is only the "more or less" (*mehr oder minder*), the "*Ungefähre*." Language, then, should be viewed as a "practice of approximation (*Praxis der Approximation*)."[103] In short, linguistic essence is always a fuzzy eidos.

## Notes

1 Edmund Husserl, *Zur Lehre vom Wesen und zur Methode der eidetischen Variation. Texte aus dem Nachlass (1891–1935)*, ed. Dirk Fonfara, Hua XLI (Dordrecht: Springer, 2012), p. 71.
2 Hua XX/1, p. 33; my emphasis.
3 Hua XX/2, p. 2.
4 Hua XX/1, p. 240.
5 Hua XX/2, p. 3.
6 Andrea Staiti, "The *Ideen* and Neo-Kantianism," in *Husserl's Ideen*, ed. L. Embree and T. Nenon (Dordrecht: Springer, 2013), pp. 71–90 (82).
7 Dieter Lohmar, "Husserl's Concept of Categorial Intuition," in *One Hundred Years of Phenomenology: Husserl's Logical Investigations Revisited*, ed. D. Zahavi and F. Stjernfelt (Dordrecht: Springer, 2002), pp. 125–45.
8 Suzanne Cunningham, *Language and the Phenomenological Reductions of Edmund Husserl* (The Hague: Martinus Nijhoff, 1976), p. 58.
9 Robert Sokolowski, *The Formation of Husserl's Concept of Constitution* (Washington, D.C.: The Catholic University of America Press, 2006), pp. 177f.
10 Hua XLI, pp. 42f., 63f., 71ff., 106f., 109ff., 237, 236.
11 Ibid., pp. 230f., 231, 233.
12 Edmund Husserl, *Experience and Judgment*, trans. James S. Churchill and Karl Ameriks (Evanston: Northwestern University Press, 1997), p. 336.
13 Husserl, *Logical Investigations*, trans. J.N. Findlay, 2 vols. (Amherst, NY: Humanity Books, 2000), p. 430.
14 Hua XLI, p. 230.
15 Ludwig Wittgenstein, *Philosophical Investigations*, trans. G.E.M. Anscombe, P.M.S. Hacker, and J. Schulte (Oxford: Blackwell, 2009), §§139, 191, 318f.
16 Dieter Lohmar, "Die phänomenologische Methode der Wesensschau und ihre Präzisierung als eidetische Variation," *Phänomenologische Forschungen*, ed. T. Breyer, J. Jansen, and I. Römer (Hamburg: Felix Meiner, 2005), pp. 65–91; cf. Staiti, "The *Ideen* and Neo-Kantianism."
17 Friedrich Uehlein, "Eidos and Eidetic Variation in Husserl's Phenomenology," in *Phenomenology, Language and Schizophrenia*, ed. M. Spitzer, F. Uehlein, M. A. Schwartz and C. Mundt (New York: Springer, 1992), pp. 88–102 (88).
18 My emphasis.

19 Husserl, *Experience and Judgment*, pp. 340f.
20 Cf. Hua XLI, *passim*.
21 Hua I, p. 105.
22 Edmund Husserl, *Ideas: General Introduction to Pure Phenomenology*, trans. W. R. Boyce Gibson (London: Allen and Unwin, 1969), pp. 54f.
23 Lester Embree, "Dorion Cairns, Empirical Types, and the Field of Consciousness," in *Husserl's* Ideen, ed. L. Embree and T. Nenon. Contributions to Phenomenology 66 (Dordrecht: Springer, 2013), pp. 225–39 (239).
24 Fred Kersten, "Thoughts on the Translation of Husserl's *Ideen, Erstes Buch*," in *Husserl's* Ideen, ed. Lester Embree and Thoman Nenon (Dordrecht: Springer, 2013), pp. 467–75 (474).
25 Husserl, *Experience and Judgment*, p. 348.
26 Ibid., p. 350.
27 Cunningham, *Language and the Phenomenological Reductions*, p. 59; cf. Husserl, *Experience and Judgment*, p. 411.
28 Sokolowski, *The Formation of Husserl's Concept of Constitution*, pp. 177, 179.
29 Staiti, "The *Ideen* and Neo-Kantianism," p. 82.
30 Hua I, pp. 78ff.
31 Husserl, *Experience and Judgment*, p. 341; my emphasis.
32 Sokolowski, *The Formation of Husserl's Concept of Constitution*, p. 179.
33 Uehlein, "Eidos and Eidetic Variation in Husserl's Phenomenology," pp. 94f.
34 Nicholas de Warren, "Emmanuel Levinas and a Soliloquy of Light and Reason," in *Husserl's* Ideen, ed. L. Embree and T. Nenon (Dordrecht: Springer, 2013), pp. 265–82 (271).
35 Sokolowski, *The Formation of Husserl's Concept of Constitution*, pp. 179ff.
36 Hua I, p. 105.
37 Hua XLI, pp. 104f.
38 CPR A193/B238.
39 Hua I, p. 96.
40 Hua XLI, p. 222.
41 CPR A727f./B755f.
42 Husserl, *Experience and Judgment*, p. 333.
43 Hua XLI, p. 259.
44 Ibid., pp. 233, 371.
45 Edmund Husserl, *The Crisis of European Sciences and Transcendental Phenomenology*, trans. David Carr (Evanston: Northwestern University Press, 1970), p. 346.
46 Husserl, *Ideas*, pp. 194, 201.
47 Ibid., pp. 202, 208.
48 Embree, "Dorion Cairns, Empirical Types, and the Field of Consciousness," p. 234.
49 Jitendra N. Mohanty, *The Philosophy of Edmund Husserl: A Historical Development* (New Haven: Yale University Press, 2008), p. 234; my emphasis.
50 de Warren, "Emmanuel Levinas and a Soliloquy of Light and Reason," p. 271.
51 The answer to this question will be of paramount importance to the argument in favor of linguistic meaning as communal, cognitive event in Chapter 4.
52 "Die Sprache ist ja von vornherein intersubjektiv," Hua XVII, pp. 8b–9a.
53 Ruthrof, "Recycling Locke: Linguistic Meaning as Indirectly Public," p. 23.
54 Husserl, *Experience and Judgment*, pp. 210f.
55 Charles F. Hockett, "The Origin of Speech," *Scientific American* 203 (1960), 88–96; "The Problem of Universals in Language," in *Universals of Language*, ed. J. Greenberg (Cambridge, MA: MIT Press, 1966), pp. 1–29.

56  Husserl, *Ideas*, pp. 71ff.
57  Hua XX/2, p. 3.
58  Hua XLI, pp. 368–73.
59  Husserl, *Ideas*, p. 105.
60  Willard van Orman Quine, *Pursuit of Truth* (Cambridge, MA: Harvard University Press, 1993), pp. 56ff.
61  Hua XX/2, pp. 401, 456.
62  Cf. what Husserl has to say on tone in linguistic expressions, Hua XX/2, pp. 102f., a topic to be addressed in detail in Chapter Five.
63  Husserl, *Experience and Judgment*, p. 336.
64  Ibid., p. 338.
65  Hua XX/2, p. 408.
66  Husserl, *Logical Investigations*, p. 277; Hua XX/2, pp. 152f.
67  Marc D. Hauser, Norm Chomsky, and Tecumseh Fitch, "The Faculty of Language: What Is It, Who Has It, and How Did It Evolve?" *Science* 298, 5598 (2002), 1569–79.
68  Husserl, *Logical Investigations*, pp. 277f.
69  Hua XX/2, p. 136.
70  Hua XX/1, pp. 3, 38; Hua XX/2, pp. 143f.
71  Hua XLI, pp. 71ff., 230.
72  Lothar Eley, "Afterword to Husserl, *Experience and Judgment*: Phenomenology and Philosophy of Language," in Husserl, *Experience and Judgment*, pp. 399–429 (402).
73  Hua XIV, pp. 265–71.
74  Uehlein, "Eidos and Eidetic Variation in Husserl's Phenomenology," p. 100.
75  Husserl, *Experience and Judgment*, p. 354.
76  Ibid., p. 353n2.
77  Hua XLI, p. 231.
78  Ibid., p. 33.
79  Hua III/1, p. 185.
80  Hua XLI, p. 33.
81  Embree, "The Field of Consciousness," p. 232.
82  Husserl, *Experience and Judgment*, p. 331, where Husserl is resuming and elaborating Kant's motif of the outline of a dog in the schematism chapter of the first *Critique*.
83  Husserl, *Ideas*, p. 168.
84  Husserl, *Crisis*, p. 348n.
85  Husserl, *Experience and Judgment*, pp. 330ff.
86  Ibid., 353n2.
87  Edmund Husserl, *Logische Untersuchungen. Zweiter Band. Untersuchungen zur Phänomenologie und Theorie der Erkenntnis*. Ed. U. Panzer (Dordrecht: Kluwer), p. 430.
88  Hua XX/2, p. 3.
89  Hua XX/1, p. 67; Hua XX/2, pp. 136, 205.
90  Husserl, *Experience and Judgment*, p. 338.
91  Ibid., p. 329.
92  Ibid., pp. 329ff.; my emphasis, drawing attention to Husserl's Kantian phrasing in CPR A728/B756.
93  Husserl, *Experience and Judgment*, pp. 337f.
94  See Chapter 9.
95  Wittgenstein, *Philosophical Investigations*, § 67.

96 Cf. the description of limit phenomena as "not arbitrary," "relative determinations," "necessary," and so on. in Anthony Steinbock, *Limit-Phenomena and Phenomenology in Husserl* (London and New York: Rowman and Littlefield, 2017), pp. 4f.
97 Ibid., p. 49.
98 Hua XLI, pp. 223, 237, 243.
99 Ibid., p. 237.
100 Husserl, *Logical Investigations*, p. 450.
101 Hua XLI, pp. 51, 230, 231, 233 ; my emphasis.
102 The topic of Chapter 6.
103 Hua XLI, pp. 71, 234.

Part II

# Intersubjective Intentionality
## *in* Language

# 4

# Introjective Reciprocity

## Meaning as Communal, Cognitive Event

The main aim of this chapter is to dissolve the apparent paradox of language as the sum of individual instantiations of linguistic expressions and at the same time as the product of a *speech community*. I will attempt to resolve this tension by arguing that every expression carries within it a number of social instructions that speakers must follow in producing and comprehending the expressions of a natural language. In this way we can demonstrate that subjective speech intentionality can be reconciled with intersubjectivity as its necessary condition. Husserl contributed to this topic in the three volumes of *Zur Phänomenologie der Intersubjektivität* (On the phenomenology of intersubjectivity),[1] in which the concept of *empathetic apperception* plays a critical role. Just as Husserl specifies perception as *apperception* (*Vergegenwärtigung*), so too does he reduce the concept of empathy to the narrower notion of "empathetic apperception."[2] As discussed, the concept of empathetic introjection (*Einfühlung*) indicates more precisely than "empathy" that we have to present something to ourselves that is not perceptually given. Husserl felt justified in granting empathetic apperception a high degree of apodictic certitude on the grounds that if our reconstructions of the intentional acts of other subjects were consistently wrong, the "communicative community" could not function as "sociality" the way it does.[3] Even in empathetic reconstructions, then, Husserl regards apperception as a form of "objective perception."[4] Reading "objective" charitably, Husserl's empathetic apperception shifts the emphasis from a mere feeling (*pathos*) to an identifiable, intentional act and its eidetic principle. Such acts always include forms of "appresentation,"[5] by which we routinely copresent to ourselves what we feel justified in assuming about the mental disposition of our cosubjects. And we do so via "vivid apperception (*anschauliche Vergegenwärtigung*)."[6]

For Husserl, "the I constitutes itself first in contrast to the You, which is an I for itself and finds itself as an I in contrast to a You, which it posits itself." So, we cannot but posit "the entire ego-life of the other" by way of an analogous process of "empathetic apperception."[7] Husserl's early insights in this field are now receiving increasingly strong support from neurological research, for example, on *mirror neurons*.[8] In language, the fundamental dynamic of reading the minds of others reveals itself in specific ways via a phenomenological description where *indication, intimation,* and *introjection* turn out to be critical components. Husserl's concept of introjection deserves special attention here as a motif that first appears in the *Logical Investigations* and again later in his *Phenomenology of Intersubjectivity*.[9] Accordingly, I want to argue that the communicative function of Husserl's indication can function as effectively as it does only if *intersubjective reciprocity* is a precondition of linguistic meaning conceived as a *communal, cognitive event*. In contrast to the kind of linguistic externalism crystallized in Hilary Putnam's slogan "meanings just ain't in the head," I will argue that without a description of what goes on in the minds of language users under community instructions, we will be able to produce no more than a reductive portrait of language.[10] I begin my argument with a summary description of two communal, linguistic meaning events.

## Meaning Fulfilment as Communal, Cognitive Event

In *Know the Song—Know the Country: The Ngardangarli Story of Culture and History in Ngarluma and Yindjibarndi Country* (2004), the Juluwarly Aboriginal Corporation and Frank Ricavec have put together a moving testimony of the cultural resilience of a people who have survived what must now be regarded as atrociously callous treatment by European settlers of Australia. What is the more remarkable is how vibrant the language of the Ngardangarli people and their mythological connection with the land has remained in spite of the ugly story of colonialization and postcolonialization. In particular, the language of traditional law is still at the heart of the Ngarluma and Yindjibarni clans of Western Australia. Their law ceremonies include the creation myths of the Ngurra-Nyujung Gama (when the world was soft), the Marrga (creation spirits) who are believed to continue to animate mountains, rocks, gullies, and waterholes. The country, birds, animals, and, last, the Ngardangali (all Aboriginal people) are believed to have been created by the Marrga, in that order. This is generally called the *Dreamtime*, but here specifically named Ngurra-Nyujung. The ancient ceremonial ring, the Burdu, where Birdarra, the language of the law, is periodically reenacted, bears the marks of thousands of years of ritual dance steps. The Burdu is visited regularly by tribes from all over the north of Western Australia, and by Aboriginal people from as far away as Uluru, the red center of Australia. When the law is respoken, as it has been for many thousands of years, its word sounds, syntax, and meanings are shared as a communal, sacred inheritance. Who can participate in specific parts of the law ceremonies and how to do so is strictly proscribed and guarded by tribal elders. Thus, the Birdarra tradition has survived and is now beginning to regain its cultural prestige. In this process of rehabilitation, the communal grasp of the language is critical. In conjunction with nonverbal practices, it remains the main communicative vehicle for guaranteeing the continuation of a culture that is profoundly rooted in a mythical conception of the land and landscape. So, individual act intentionality is thus ritually aligned to coincide with a communal, cognitive grasp of the meanings of language. And only to the extent that individuals are able to partake of this communal heritage are they members of the speech community.

Another striking example of linguistic meaning as a communal, cognitive event was provided in a paper presented at the "Symposium" of the Academy of the Humanities of Australia, in November 2014, at the Australian National University in Canberra, where linguist Nick Evans showed a videotaped Aboriginal tribal gathering dedicated to the celebration of traditional songs and ceremonies. According to Evans, this particular gathering is repeated from time to time, each time consolidating the cultural meanings of the song.

Central to one song was a complex word richly suggestive of communal belonging, "Iwaidja *angmarranguldiny*." According to Evans, the word conveys to the community an experience of nostalgia and "a strong feeling of emotion for a place one is associated with, typically as a result of a change in weather conditions." Evans translates the verb "*ang-*" as "pertaining to land, place." In the absence of any precise definition, Evans sums up the meaning of "*angmarranguldiny*" in English as referring to particular meteorological conditions (e.g., lightning, wind) bringing back memories associated with a place from which sensory cues are transmitted, be it the smell of a wind changing as one sits on a beach or the sight of a place burning after being struck by lightning.[11] What the Aboriginal word is *about*, how it is given *voice*, and what role it plays in the culture is thus explained by a sequence of English terms providing adumbrational meaning aspects for the benefit of an English-speaking audience.

There is then an acute discrepancy between what was provided as "meaning" by way of an English paraphrase by which words of one language are substituted for a word that is foreign and mysterious, on the one hand, and, on the other, by the evidence of a communal, cognitive meaning event. In the ceremony, *meaning* "simply" *occurred* and was comprehended within its context by a community, defined appropriately by Husserl as "a personal, many-headed, as it were, and yet integrated subjectivity."[12] The English paraphrase "meaning," as verbal substitution, only served as an approximating bridging device for cultural outsiders. Indispensable as this device is for them, it highlights a problem in its very definition of meaning as verbal replacement.[13] The paper also demonstrated that language as social process reveals that subjective linguistic instantiations are always already embedded in what Husserl calls "a communalized life (*ein vergemeinschaftetes Leben*)."[14] The ceremony clearly fulfilled the function of Husserl's communalization (*Vergemeinschaftung*) as a "within-one-another" and "through-one-another." Husserl appropriately speaks of such meaning events as a "within-one-another of constitution" and its communal thinking and willing as acts of a "through-one-another."[15] The two diametrically opposed notions of meaning are well captured by Husserl's *unanschauliche Bedeutung*, which is always "demanding fulfilment (*erfüllungsbedürftig*)."[16] Meaning in this fulfilled sense always consists in the transformation of the sounds of an expression into a nonverbal, imaginable content, Husserl's *anschaulicher Sinn*. The former is homosemiotic, the latter heterosemiotic, requiring a shift from verbal signs to their nonverbal, mental material contingencies as olfactory, tactile, emotional, visual, and other kinds of quasi-perceptual content.

A description of linguistic meaning in the wake of Husserl's philosophy is well placed to accommodate such a heterosemiotic account by starting with acts of meaning intention, their transformation into linguistic expressions, a merely verbal grasp, his *Bedeutung*, and meaning fulfilment in acts of rendering them *vividly* intelligible, by "*Veranschaulichung*,"[17] where our acts "become imaginable (*Anschaulichwerden*)" as "redeeming fulfilment (*einlösende Erfüllung*)."[18] In this way, Husserl incorporates both definitions of meaning, verbal substitutions, and their nonverbal realizations, in the linguistic meaning process. In the *Nachlass*, Husserl calls the merely verbal meaning event a "transitional experience" made up of "transitional acts of consciousness."[19] Our act of "empty meaning finds its fulfilment in a vividly imaginable (*anschaulichen*) act in the manner of a directional intention."[20] Thus, "the empty consciousness (*Leerbewusstsein*) is superseded by what is imaginable (*anschaulich*)."[21] However, Husserl struggles with the *limit phenomenon* of an "empty consciousness" throughout the *Nachlass*.[22] At one point, Husserl sees this dilemma clearly when he writes, "the *Anschauung* as a whole can never vanish altogether."[23] There could hardly be a stronger affirmation of the nonverbal *in* language, a position that seriously qualifies the standard account of the predominance of *logic* in Husserl.

## Can One Demonstrate Intersubjectivity via Subjective Acts?

It is all very well to describe linguistic meanings as part of the social process in the *natural attitude*, as an obvious empirical fact, but it is not so obvious how to demonstrate this phenomenologically from *within* the acts that I cannot but perform as I engage in language. To be sure, Husserl "tries to provide an accurate description of signs as they occur in conscious experience,"[24] while at the same time assuring us of the ontic embeddedness of all conscious experience in the social world. In interaction with others, our acts tell us that we are external beings *to* one another (*Auseinandersein*) but also *with* one another (*Miteinandersein*) and, at the same time, that in mutual mental engagement we also live "within-one-another (*Ineinandersein*)."[25] Language, I suggest, is the example par excellence with which to validate Husserl's contention. Whether or not phenomenology enables us to demonstrate intersubjectivity via a description of subjective acts is a well-rehearsed problem, the problem of other minds. In the phenomenological tradition, the contributions to this debate by Max Scheler, Ernst Cassirer, and Alfred Schütz are especially pertinent.

In his paper "*Wesen und Formen der Sympathie*" (The Nature and Forms of Sympathy, 1923), Max Scheler discards earlier views of the perception of other minds that rest on specific "analogical inference" and on "empathetic projection of the self into the physical manifestations" of other persons. Instead, he insists that intention-reading of others is only possible on a *holistic* reading of the other, a reading that includes motives, intentions, interests, sympathetic and antipathetic attitudes, and a large number of other corroborating inferences, as well as their adjustment over time. Scheler here follows Cassirer's assertion that "our conviction of the existence of other minds is earlier and deeper than our belief in the existence of Nature."[26] Whatever we experience we do so via "patterns of wholeness." The emphasis here is on a gradual and "holistic reading of persons." The commitment to "patterns of wholeness" as a necessary condition of reading other minds entails the broader presupposition of intersubjective reciprocity as necessary social baseline.[27] Yet not all phenomenologists agree on the validity of Husserl's assertions on "empathetic apperception."[28]

Schütz, for one, rejected the very possibility of deriving "the intersubjectivity of the world from the intentionalities of my own conscious life."[29] And even for Husserl himself, Schütz notes, it was "painfully puzzling" as to how precisely we could bridge this divide, how to arrive at the transcendental we-community (*Wir-Gemeinschaft*) as an "*intentionales Ineinander*" from the immediacy of subjective acts, that "dark corner haunted by the ghosts of solipsism, psychologism, or relativism."[30] Not that Schütz disagrees with Husserl on the reality of intersubjectivity as a sphere in which I-subjects are apprehended as *Nebenmenschen* striving for and largely achieving "mutual understanding." Schütz fully agrees on the "reciprocal understanding between animate subjects belonging to one world." What he questions is that transcendental intersubjectivity can be coherently argued via "empathetic evidence" since it can never yield "originary verification." So, Schütz cannot accept Husserl's derivation of the "transcendental ego at large" from the "personal I" as the "substratum of habits," the "monad" or "ego in its full concreteness."[31] Schütz reverses this relation such that "reciprocal understanding and communication already presupposes a community of knowledge, even a common surrounding world." What makes communication possible is "reciprocal orientation" as necessary precondition of social relationships in our engagement with other living bodies, existential simultaneity, and counter subjects (*Gegensubjekte*). Instead of viewing transcendental intersubjectivity as the result of "constitution," Schütz takes it as a "datum" or *primitivum*, as "the fundamental ontological category of human existence."[32]

Husserl's answer is the apodictic evidence of our intentional acts: "I turn to others in wishes, commands, I address them and impute to them an answer, they fulfil my wishes, they respond to me, we enter into personal, *reciprocal interaction* (*Wechselverkehr*)."[33] To shore up Husserl's position, we could add that *epistemically*, the actual world, Husserl's "*uns allgemeinsame Umwelt* (our generally shared environment)," must be a function of transcendental subjectivity. We can derive it only from our subjective acts.[34] *Ontologically* viewed, the reverse is equally undeniable. Yet, our starting point can only be cognizance of the acts that we cannot but perform in engaging with the constitutive cognition of objectivities. All subsequent acts are inferential. In Husserl's scheme of things, each of us is individually faced with an "open plurality" of alter egos, in which "the Other has sense only with reference to me." This, for Schütz, sets the trap of "solipsism." How this problem evolved is traced by Schütz back to a gradual semantic drift in the meaning of the term "constitution," having changed from its initial use as a clarification of the sense-structure of conscious life and the process of sedimentation, from "explication to creation." Yet "the creation of a universe of monads and the objective world for everyone proves to be impossible within the transcendental intersubjectivity of the meditating philosopher."[35]

Of course, we do not have to accept Schütz's word on this point. An alternative conception can be found in Martin Kusch where the "study of constitution is the study of those acts in and through which objects are self-given."[36] This seems to me to better reflect Husserl's understanding of the relationship between "transcendental subjectivity" and the "intersubjective transcendental community (*Sozialität*)," the former transforming into the latter as "transcendental ground for the intersubjectivity of nature and of the world in general."[37] So, it would be wrong to say that Husserl merely stipulates transcendental intersubjectivity as *sociality*. After all, he argues that we cannot but come to the conclusion from the description of our subjective acts that we all share the same physical world "as common existential ground of work activities and a shared human world as ground of ethical and generally mental achievements."[38] Such observations are afforded communally through "the windows of empathetic apperception." Husserl speaks of the community as a "monad of monads" and an "absolute entanglement of many monads" that stand to one another in "reciprocal relations of influence."[39] Such mutual influencing occurs most effectively in "linguistic communication."[40] The burden of proof then consists in substantiating that each and any individual instantiation of linguistic expression always already and of necessity contains markers of empathetic reciprocity and communal instructions as the hallmark of their fundamentally intersubjective character.

## Sample Expressions and Analysis

Our investigation of subjective meaning endowment thus should bring to light (*phenesti*) the intersubjective ground of linguistic expressions. Consider the following examples.

(1) On a building site: "Slab!"
(2) A tennis racquet advert: "Lift your game beyond ordinary."
(3) A waiter spills a drink over a customer, who mumbles, "Nicely done."
(4) A person entering a dentist's waiting room says, "Hello."
(5) A reckless politician in an election speech: "We will restore funding to the much-neglected universities."
(6) At a party: "Do you think Mrs. Quail was being facetious when she complimented Dorothy on her short dress?"
(7) In a pub, an Australian says to someone, "Don't come the raw prawn."
(8) During a conversation: "You can't be serious."

What are the things I do when I see the printed expression (1) "slab!"? First, I instantiate it according to the instructions provided by the exclamation mark that tell me what sort of tone should inform my reconstructed prosodic contour. When it occurs on the building site, the expression is instantiated by someone in a certain voice. In either case, tonal instantiation is a sine qua non. The utterance is reimagined by the apprentice in a proximate manner. Even in grammar and logic books, linguistic expressions can only mean if they are uttered, even if, typically, in a literal tone. As Filip Mattens explains, in Husserl, the sign "consolidates two heterologous acts of consciousness into the unique phenomenon of language, namely word-perception and meaning-consciousness,"[41] whereby meaning consciousness includes of necessity the *manner* in which a linguistic expression is given.

At the same time, an equally important intentional act in grasping linguistic meanings is the realization of aboutness. Proceeding from word sound consciousness, Husserl's *Wortlautbewusstsein*, to meaning, *Wortbedeutungsbewusstsein*, results in knowing what "slab" is *about*, and what it refers to. Now how does the apprentice on the building site know what to do? Assuming that the slabs are out of sight, perhaps behind a shed, the imperative "slab!" makes special demands on the hearer. Since the slab can't be seen, it must be *imagined*, together with its location. If the apprentice cannot imagine a slab, she cannot know what the expression is about. This is where Husserl's apperception, to make present to oneself what is absent, shows itself as a necessary component of language. It is on this point that Wittgenstein's *Philosophical Investigations* offers only an incomplete picture of meaning as use, a picture that a Husserlian approach is well placed to correct.[42] We require *Vorstellung, presentation*, or *mental projection*, in order to construct aboutness, even if we do so at camera-shutter speed, and in a highly schematic fashion.[43] For Husserl, "word sound and meaning are associated" such that the "empty intention" of the sound of the linguistic expression is "fulfilled" by *Vorstellung*.[44] In more complex linguistic contexts our "understanding" is deepened by an accumulation of "new *Vorstellungen*" providing semantic "saturation."[45] The expression appears to "demand" an apperceptive and *vividly imaginable*, that is, *anschauliche*, reconstruction. What is shared by all our sample expressions are the indispensable intentional acts on the part of listeners (readers) of vivid *apperception* and *appresentation*, both of which are habitually performed within the rules of community pedagogy. The majority of apprentices tend to construct compatible social rules in response to the imperative "slab!"

Putting myself in the shoes of the apprentice, I grasp the command by the tone of the person laying the slabs, suggestive of a purpose. All linguistic expressions carry a sense of *communicative purpose* as part of their *intrinsic* character. When I read the expression, I am guided by the explicit deixis of the exclamation mark. Prosodic contour and exclamation mark fulfill the same function in providing the categorial structure of commands. In addition, the manner in which the expression is presented often can play a decisive role in the modification of propositional content, most conspicuously in its reversal through verbal irony. It follows that tone must be included in the way linguistic expressions "fulfil a communicative purpose,"[46] and do so prior to their indicative role (*Hinweisfunktion*). For it is the tone that tells us two things, that it is a command and that it demands an urgent response. While the "*Hinweisfunktion*" of "slab!" makes clear that "the speaker is *indicating* something (*Der Redende weist auf etwas hin*),"[47] the tone *intimates* something that the apprentice must reconstruct via an act of introjection. The apprentice must *read* the person giving the order in conjunction with the linguistic expression. In order to grasp its communicative function, we must *inhabit* the linguistic sign by activating its manner of presentation as well as "its pointing and meaning functions." This affects not only our phrasing as a sequence of words but also its habitualized prosodic contour and emphasis. In this way we "'breathe life' into the sign."[48] And in doing so we fulfill a linguistic, *social* obligation.

My meaning-fulfilling acts thus require the animation of a sound sequence in tune with a split-second construction of the intimation the expression conveys, that is, perhaps a sense of impatience on the part of the speaker, who is likely to be annoyed by the apprentice's inability to foresee what is needed and act accordingly. What the expression then demands is a greater degree of empathy (*Einfühlung*) on the part of the apprentice, that is, acts of introjection, of which intention-reading is a part. In this context, Husserl calls *Einfühlung* a "higher level of intentionality" (*eine höherstufige Intentionalität*) in his "Theorie der *Einfühlung*," which requires for its existence an "intentional intertwining" (*intentionale Verflechtung*) between ego and alter ego,[49] at least as a minimal form of *being-*

*within-one-another* (*Ineinandersein*).[50] Even as trifling a sample as our "slab!" suggests mental *reciprocity* as a component of language, as it does certain presuppositions, social instructions, "the *pointing-tendency* proceeding from the words themselves,"[51] and "the directions of meaning in language that arise in speaking to another."[52] We are obviously also dealing here, as in all linguistic exchange, with a degree of communal *coercion* as to how to respond, an evocative force, a communicative style, and a certain degree of social significance, all summed up in Husserl's *Sinn* beyond *Bedeutung*.

Sample (2) illustrates the power of "the *seduction of language*" by appealing to my vanity, ambition, or dream of becoming a more competent tennis player.[53] The link between command and what I should do in response is indirect; it remains an unspoken allure, insinuating that my purchase of the advertised racquet will produce the promised result. Seduction in this sense is of course not restricted to the language of commerce, it is a potential feature of all language. The same can be said about the power of language to impart the sense of a certain kind of *advocacy*. In Koukal's formulation, "expressions can be thought of as attempts to *persuade* the hearer to intuit the meaning of an experience in a way so that they will understand it in its essence, whereas an indication merely designates an experience. To this extent, expressions are inherently *rhetorical*." Or more subtly, "expressions can be thought of as a sort of advocate from a given experience, as opposed to merely pointing to the experience."[54] Addressed in speech-act theory as a *performative*, the act of promising is likewise a typical feature of linguistic expressions.[55] The utterance in (5) works with an explicit promise that the politically savvy reader wisely takes with a grain of salt. Aboutness here is an absent state of affairs in a temporal sense, demanding the projection of a possible future scenario, an act requiring my imaginative construction of resemblance relations in contrast with the status quo. As in our first sample, all the criteria listed there can be made relevant to promises of this kind. In samples (3), (4), and (8) voice, or implicit deixis, is foregrounded, even if very differently so in each. In (3) we are dealing with ironic reversal of propositional content, a feature that sharply distinguishes natural language from formal sign systems. In Husserl's *Nachlass*, the vital feature of voice, technically discussed later as implicit deixis and understood as the modal shadow that accompanies every word in any linguistic expression, is dealt with in his discussion of "tone."[56] Nor is irony merely the binary opposite to literality. The very existence of verbal irony alerts us to an infinite variety of possible modifications of aboutness. Importantly, in their habitual or standardized form, such modifications are likewise shared *social* instructions. The voice we construe in (4) differs subtly from an ordinary "hello" in the street, while the likely tones available for (8) range from astonishment to put-downs. Last, sample (6) demonstrates that acts of meaning fulfilment occur irrespective of whether we could in any way reconstruct the actual speech intention of Mrs. Quail. Nor can truth-conditional semantics come to the rescue in such cases.[57] As the example makes clear, meaning is an immediate event, while the imaginative construal of truth conditions is a laborious affair, if not altogether impossible. It would seem then that our constructions of meaningful aboutness always precede, both logically and chronologically, the checking mechanism of truth-conditional semantics. Truth and falsity supervene of necessity on Aristotle's *homoiomata*, resemblance relations.

Without doubt, all our samples (1) to (8) carry a sense of social *coercion*. What Husserl calls an "imposition (*Zumutung*)" is not restricted to direct commands, as in (1) "slab!" or in (7) "Don't come the raw prawn!" Rather, our intentional meaning acts tell us that *Zumutung* is an all-pervasive characteristic of all linguistic expressions.[58] As Husserl writes,

> for the listener, the sign is affected with the "ought" of an imposition, in relation to the *Bedeutung* and the "ought" is addressed to the listener and the "should" of attending to the *Bedeutung*, as an imposition by the speaker, is a component of the entire described context, which is grasped apperceptively as the unit of a psychophysical fact by the listener and perceptually given.[59]

That this general form of *Zumutung* attaching to linguistic expressions is not a subjective trait of utterances but rather a *social* feature of language sanctioned by the speech community comes to the fore in Husserl's idea that habitual speech (*Sprachüblichkeit*) is itself a form of coercion: an "ought" attaches to the word form.[60] Husserl here anticipates the kind of compulsion that was radicalized half a century later by Deleuze and Guattari under the heading of "order words."[61]

## The Ego among Other Egos

Turning our phenomenological gaze from the social instructions embedded in language to the perspective of the relationship of the individual to other individuals in a community, Husserl has provided yet another angle from which to view the social dimension of linguistic intentionality. In this respect, his theory of the eidetic reduction of experiencing oneself (*Sebsterfahrung*) and experiences of the Other (*Fremderfahrung*) is pertinent as a vital part of our intentional, inductive-imaginable projection (*induktiv-anschauliche Vorstellung*) of the world at large.[62] The constitution of our eidetic self is achieved in a continuing process of "eidetic variation of myself." Yet since "even relative completeness of evidence is here impossible," my subjectivity is forever "(an identity) in contradictions."[63]

The eidetic constitution of the Other is quite different. "Others," writes Husserl, "I gather by *Fremderfahrung*." The crucial difference is that the Other is always "an intentional variation of myself in my present and co-present existence (*Dasein*)." After all, "I am not in a position to familiarize myself with his past, the way I can to a certain degree in my own case." Accordingly, all "communal experience" as a "variation of others is always at the same time self-variation and a variation of the whole world." The Other is always "a variant of an 'I.'" As a result, Husserl arrives at an "eidetic doctrine" of the "ego amongst other egos, an eidetic doctrine of sociality (*Sozialität*)."[64] Natural language, as economizing matrix partly constituting and partly superimposed on this imaginable totality, cannot be empty in its production and fulfilment but must carry, in both its expressions and as a totality, the world as imaginable content. However, the totality of the world as imaginable content cannot be present to us at the level of imaginative specificity. It is present to every ego typically in two ways, as detailed, vividly imaginable slices of world and as a radically reduced and all-encompassing eidos. At the same time, this totality is always also a human world in which the perceiving ego is interacting with other egos. Because of its eidetic character, language fulfils the role of facilitator of such interaction. The eidetic, systemic nature of language guarantees that a meeting of minds can occur at all, while its fuzziness renders it flexible enough to accommodate individual difference. As such, we can regard natural language as the great leveler in the arena of sociality, facilitating a meeting of minds via *introjective reciprocity*.

## Intimation, Introjection, and Reciprocity

As we saw, "slab!" carries the social instruction of *imagining* the object before the command can be executed. Such imagining is typically enacted within the constraints of communally agreed-upon categorial relations. Imaginability is likewise vital in granting us a path to the appropriate reconstruction of Husserl's intimation as a part of an utterer's "mental states." What makes reciprocal discourse possible, according to Husserl, is the "correlation among the corresponding physical and mental experiences of communicating persons." However, intimation via language does not amount to a full-scale reconstruction of a speaker's personality by an interlocutor. "To understand an intimation," says Husserl, "consists simply in the fact that the hearer *intuitively* takes the speaker to be a person who is expressing this or that," or "*perceives* him as such." So, "the hearer perceives the intimation in the same sense in which he perceives the intimating person—even though the mental phenomena which make him a person cannot fall, for what they are, in the intuitive grasp of another." By contrast, in the construction of meaning by a speech partner, Husserl's "*gemeinsames Gegenüber*," a relation to an object is established.[65] Yet we must never confuse "what an utterance *intimates* with what it asserts."[66] Via intimation, then, meaning intention receives additional directionality, which guides us in understanding the sort of experience a speaker wishes to convey.

To be able to reconstruct the linguistic component of intimation, we have at our disposal another important concept introduced by Husserl in the *Logical Investigations*, the notion of introjection.[67] Husserl himself was not entirely happy with the term because it could be easily misinterpreted (the "*freilich missdeutbaren Ausdruck Introjektion*").[68] Nonetheless, the concept is critical in that it caters for both mutual and one-sided empathy ("*wechselseitige und einseitige Einfühlung*").[69] What can be said with certainty is that in introjection, "the hearer *perceives* the speaker as manifesting certain inner experiences."[70] As such, introjection is an indispensable, communicative condition of language. Many of Husserl's social concepts, such as the entanglement of interests (*Interessenverflechtung*), horizon of unanimity (*Horizont der Einstimmigkeit*), or communal subjectivity as "many-headed unified subjectivity," all require introjection as a practical set of acts and condition of possibility.[71] Introjection as *Einfühlung* looms large in Husserl's three volumes on *Intersubjectivity* and is crucial for his description of what happens when we engage in language.[72] Nor is Husserl's term a merely subjective concept; it needs to be seen in association with his notion of the *Einfühlungsgemeinschaft*, the community of empathizing persons,[73] a community "produced through empathy."[74] Only in this way can we account for the speed and efficiency of habitual language exchanges, as well as for the fact that intensely personal dialogue relies heavily on reciprocal anticipation.

But even in mundane acts of linguistic comprehension, I find myself in the position of participating in Husserl's being-within-one-another. In attempting to match in my acts of meaning fulfilment of what I see or hear with what I take to be a meaning intention conveyed by an expression, I cannot but participate in a special form of *reciprocity*. In natural language, reciprocity looms large. So much so that it seems a safe assumption that this is how language has evolved. It could not and cannot function *as* language without the performance of not just external reciprocal acts but at the same time without mutual acts of intentionality. Hence, reciprocity can be said to be a core feature of natural language.

Reciprocity has been dealt with, for instance, as early as in Kant's extended style of judgment and his distinction between a vulgar "common sense" (*gemeiner Menschenverstand*) and *sensus communis* as a socialized sensibility of an "internal feeling," which allows us to "take account of the mode of representation of everyone else" as part of the formation of "collective reason."[75] Reciprocity reappears in Charles Sanders Peirce not only as "the natural judgments of the sensible heart" in communicative interaction but also as "a general semiotic principle." Peirce speaks of both a broad mental reciprocity as well as the specific reciprocity that sustains language.[76] As we saw, in *Logical Investigations*, Husserl resumes the theme of reciprocity in the context of the role that "introjection" must play in language, while Alfred Schütz's social philosophy cannot do without the stipulation of his "other orientation" and the "reciprocity of standpoints,"[77] and for Patočka reciprocity is a fundamental presupposition of all discourse.[78] From a Husserlian perspective, reciprocity is part and parcel of his broadly conceived semantics, one in which the linguistic expression itself is meaningful only as a result of reciprocal intentionality. As a consequence of the eidetic character of language, in habitual speech, "intersubjective discrepancies" are leveled into a social "harmony of validity" as an "overarching community consciousness." In complex meaning negotiation, mutual understanding can be reached only by "reciprocal correction."[79]

The intentionality of reciprocity as a necessary social component of communication, verbal and nonverbal, involves awareness and self-awareness. In an important sense, consciousness as awareness is not only vital, it is also, as David Chalmers has argued, the only thing we can be absolutely certain of.[80] Accepting Chalmers's explication of consciousness in the sense of "conscious experience" as a philosophically "hard problem" and yet unavoidable fact, together with Husserl's description of imaginative, intentional acts, we can feel reassured that the methodological commitment to an intersubjective mentalism in the description of language and its precursors is justified.[81] The necessary presence of internalized reciprocity in the performance of language should therefore not be eliminated from any description of language, adding as it does another buttress to its intersubjective, social character in contrast to internalist and externalist accounts. So, it should not come as much of a surprise that one of the most frequently employed terms in Husserl's writings is *Vorstellung*.

It appears more than 3,500 times, significantly outstripping his use of the signifier *Anschauung* (intuition), a ratio that reinforces the contention that in the investigation of natural language, *Vorstellung* (imaginable presentation) takes pride of place over *Wahrnehmung* (perception).

Yet the concept of *Vorstellung* continues to remain something of a mystery to readers in the Anglosphere. One hurdle is that the English term "perception" covers two concepts: one, the straightforward notion of "what we take from our senses," much as the German *Wahrnehmung* (taking for true what we perceive). The other concept covered by "perception" is "what we imagine about something," as in "the perception is that he is a bit unreliable." It is in this second sense that the German concept of "*Vorstellung*" splits off from that of "perception." Nor are its various standard translations entirely satisfactory, such as "presentation," "mental presentation," "mental representation," "idea," or "imagination." *Vorstellung* covers everything and anything we are able to entertain intentionally, anything we are able to *imagine*, be it actual or fictive. As such, the term could be rendered as "perceptual modification" or "mental projection." I have rendered *Vorstellung* most frequently as "mental projection" or left the German term, which entered phenomenology via Kant (1781), Brentano (1874), Twardowski (1894), Husserl (1900/1901), and Meinong (1921). At the same time, it is an indispensable concept in everyday German. Wittgenstein uses the concept consistently throughout his *Philosophical Investigations*, even if he employs it mainly in his ubiquitous invitations to the reader to "imagine," "think of," or "consider" an imaginable scenario, while at the same time still following in the footsteps of Frege by arguing for its elimination from the description of language.[82] In the sharpest possible contrast, phenomenology grants *Vorstellung* center stage, and our investigation of linguistic meaning in terms of intersubjective intentionality could not proceed without it. Let me put this in the strongest possible terms: without seriously addressing the role of *Vorstellung* in the meaning constitution of linguistic expressions, it is impossible to even get close to a comprehensive description of language. As our analysis of samples (1)–(8) showed, the comprehension of aboutness, categorial relations, deixis, animation, intimation, reciprocity, introjection, voice, and, above all, *Sinn*, all rely on acts of *Vorstellung*. Nor can *Vorstellung* be conceived in subjectivist isolation. As suggested in Chapter 3, the intentional acts of the linguistic monad are always overdetermined by the intersubjective intentionality of the monadic community.

## The Linguistic Monad in the *Monadengemeinschaft*

What cannot be addressed in externalist accounts of language is the central paradox of language requiring at the same time individual, intentional acts, and publicly observable instantiations. To make headway on this apparent incongruity it helps to return to Husserl's discussion of speakers of a language as *linguistic monads* functioning not just as a "monadic multitude (*Monadenvielheit*)" but as "*Monadengemeinschaft*," a "communicative human manifold."[83] Husserl's resolution of the paradox hinges on the crucial notion of *Ineinandersein*, being-*within*-one-another, as a key component of human sociality.[84] In *Zur Phänomenologie der Intersubjektivität*, Husserl goes to considerable lengths to argue the case of the seeming contradiction between subjects as separate monadic entities, "*das Auseinandersein der Monaden*," and their simultaneous, total and necessary entanglement in the *Monadengemeinschaft*, "*das Ineinander der Monaden*."⁸⁵ As a consequence of this apparent inconsistency, we have to deal with both individual acts and intersubjective reciprocity. As Husserl was to write much later, in the concept of being-within-one-another, humans, world, and language are "inseparably intertwined" in the "manner of a horizon."⁸⁶

Husserl's argument on monadic intersubjectivity can be summed up somewhat arbitrarily under the following ten points. In doing so, I will attempt to stay as close to the text of the *Nachlass*, drawing freely from the three published volumes on intersubjectivity. (1) Husserl poses the question whether "externality" can "indicate full [intentional] interiority inductively."⁸⁷ In the remainder of the *Nachlass* on intersubjectivity he wrestles with this question, arriving at persuasive results. (2) Subjects understand themselves as "centers of orientation (*Orientierungsmittelpunkte*)" in one and the same spatiotemporal world that, "in its indefinite infinity is the environmental totality of every ego."⁸⁸ As such, every subject can be regarded as a monadic unity of "inner meaning."⁸⁹ To that extent, every subject is clearly separate from the world, including other subjects. (3) Yet, Husserl writes, the monad "has windows" through which it can absorb the external world. "These are the windows of empathetic apperception."⁹⁰ (4) What the monad sees is other egos as "neighboring centers" (*Umgebungspunkte*), whose personalities are in the first instance constructed via bodies.⁹¹ And while in the world of facts there cannot be any identity, corporeality facilitates the communication between the minds of those bodies.⁹² For, according to Husserl's theory of empathetic apperception, the meaning I construe of the alter ego "refers back to my own ego" such that the Other "does not exhaust itself" in being an object but is of necessity conceived as a subject.⁹³

When a person is gradually realized in empathetic apperception, the Other is (5) apprehended as an "analogon," that is, as another bearer of consciousness. For Husserl, this is not a matter of choice. "Every one of us must allocate a mental life to the Other in apperceptive positing (*vergegenwärtigender Setzung*) as an analogon of one's own inner life (*Innenlebens*)."⁹⁴ Having projected itself into the Other "understandingly," the monad finds itself related to others in an intersubjective contingency of consciousnesses.⁹⁵ However, such acts of introjection do not mean that the individual subject experiences the feelings and emotions of the other in an identical fashion.⁹⁶ Rather, such shared acts can only have the status of approximate apperception (*Vergegenwärtigung*), claiming no more than "congruence of resemblance and resemblance," that is, "at best sameness."⁹⁷ Husserl speaks of the "appresentation of the intentional interiority of another" as a supplementary set of intentional acts.⁹⁸ What is so appresented is "a person of a personal life." As to my experience of the Other, "I co-live his life in appresentation," and as I do so, "my intentionality directed at the Other" is able to bridge "the separate subjectivities."⁹⁹ In sum, then, the reciprocal intentional construction of alter egos inevitably produces the "*within-one-another* of the monads."¹⁰⁰ (6) Beyond the intentional realization of other alter egos, each and every subject experiences the one and same common external world "as an index for a determined, regular coordination which, as it were, brings every nomad in relation with every other."[101] By way of strong inference, Husserl argues that since "every process of consciousness is something entirely separate," there could be "no window of common understanding (*Verständigung*) if there did not exist *intersubjective phenomena*."[102] On this basis, Husserl reminds us of the fundamental intersubjectivity of natural science and mathematics: "Every cognition in physics is intersubjective." In short, the external world as well as its methods of investigation are "accessible in principle to any given subject."[103] And "only because minds are there for one another, can everything else exist for them as *commonality*."[104] The external world thus functions as a reliable *tertium comparationis*. Thus, the commonality of experience, as "universale *Welterfahrung*" given by our individual acts via an analogical process,[105] for Husserl counts beyond doubt as apodictic evidence of transcendental intersubjectivity.[106]

As a result of the inevitability of our intentional construals of other monads as subjects and their necessary participation in a shared external world at one and the same time,[107] we cannot deny that the monads not merely "orient themselves according to others" but (7) constitute "an absolute entanglement" as a "monadic multitude."[108] As members of a multitude, the monads, though separate entities, are characterized by their dependence on others (*Unselbständigkeit*) within the "ego-universe (*Ichall*)."[109] This dependence relation generates, and is alleviated by, the "for-one-another (*Füreinander*)" of subjects.[110] Husserl here speaks of an "infinite 'mirroring' (*Spiegelung*)" and an "iteration" as a "potentiality for stages of empathetic apperception."[111] When we thus perform acts of "putting oneself in the position of the Other, we live a quasi-life, as it were, and a quasi-reflection, by which the subjectivity of the Other and the Other himself as subject will become thematic."[112] Thus, Husserl says, "transcendental subjectivity extends itself to intersubjectivity" or, more precisely, transcendental subjectivity "understands itself better" as *intersubjectivity*.[113] (8) An important aspect of the monadic multitude is that it constitutes of necessity a "*communicative* human manifold." As such, "humans are bound together as a unity of a communicatively experiencing subjectivity," a unity created by the all-pervasive "I-You-acts" of communicative relations.[114] This unity expresses itself in the formation of a community of the will, of ethics and sociality.[115] For Husserl, all sociality is based on "the actual connectivity of the communicative community (*Mitteilungsgemeinschaft*)," the community of "addressing and listening."[116] (9) What Husserl terms the "harmony of monads" as a harmony of "souls" is, however, not to be understood as a unity without conflict.[117] As Husserl emphasizes, the Other is "in congruence with me" only to the extent that we form a "conflictual unity (*Widerstreitseinheit*)."[118] The fact that ego and alter ego exist in a unity of conflict appears necessary for the creation of a critical "community spirit," of "conventions and cultural acts," a "cultural life," and "social habituality."[119]

Last, (10), communicability expresses itself most forcefully and effectively through language. In this respect, the intersubjective community appears to us as a speech community, made up by persons who "stand in the unity of a tradition" and "are conscious of the norm of the habitual means of reciprocal communication and mutual influence."[120] The speech community trains and monitors its members in the use of linguistic expressions, both as to public discourse and the kinds of intentional acts without which language would be meaningless. The latter involve mutual introjection and empathetic apperception of intimation and the appresentation that together guarantee meaning, Husserl's *Sinn*, as vividly imaginable. The linguistic, social connection is seen by Husserl as the "basic form of the communicative agreement in principle, the *Urform* of a special congruence between myself and the Other."[121] In the process of comprehending a linguistic expression, the subject "gains an originary experience if he realizes [its meaning] *vividly*, 'as if' he was seeing it."[122] This is what Husserl indicates by the phrase "*anschauliche Vergegenwärtigung*," rendered here as "vividly imaginable apperception," which is a necessary response to word sounds if language is to "participate in the construction of the experiential meaning of the world."[123] Husserl later adds that expressions can be "understood emptily, without transitioning into vividly imaginable quasi-realization, and they can be so understood . . . by virtue of the general, relatively persistent typicality of language."[124] Even if Husserl's notion of empty intentions (*Leervorstellungen*) must remain a moot point, the claim should be uncontroversial that language as an eidetic system functions as a *tertium comparationis* by which we can assert that our "*Umwelt* is now typically one and the same for all." If this is so, language can be invoked as the main vehicle for consolidating Husserl's central arguments in favor of transcendental intersubjectivity. We could say that language levels the peaks and troughs of merely subjective intentionalities into the plane of intersubjective communicability such that "the home world" is "fundamentally determined by language."[125]

## Conclusion: Linguistic Meaning as Introjective *Praxis*

Everything we do with language involves intersubjectivity. Even soliloquy can be shown to be part of accepted practice in reflecting the social constraints set and monitored by the speech community. In the *Nachlass*, Husserl reprimands himself for having treated soliloquy as a primarily subjective performance of intentionality in the *Logical Investigations*. As he now confesses, "a pretty bad blunder I made there (*Da hab ich einen schönen Fehler gemacht*)."[126] Now, he recognizes that no matter how private the use of language may be de facto, any use of linguistic expressions, and conspicuously so habitual speech, is by definition *always already social*.[127] What is less obvious, but central to the argument of this study, is that the social character of language relies heavily on introjective reciprocity, a linguistic ingredient that appears only once we view language through the lens of Husserl's intentional acts of empathetic apperception, understood as introjective appresentation. As a consequence, we are compelled to adopt a method of investigation informed by the principle of intersubjective mentalism.[128]

What has emerged is that meaning fulfilment can ever only be social *Sinn*. This is so even if viewed via externalism, as in Szanto's *collective intentionality*, which "presupposes, but significantly differs from, intersubjective, social, and communal intentionality" as to its "subject, object and content" in that it is "based on mutual interest," in contrast to "asymmetrical social acts."[129] Because linguistic meaning has to be individually instantiated and yet obey social rules as communal, cognitive event, it cannot exist merely as public manifestation. Rather, linguistic meaning must be an indirectly public phenomenon. Linguistic intentionality, then, appears to the phenomenological gaze as a form of intersubjective intentionality grounded in introjective reciprocity. By insisting that "I am aware, through empathy, not only of the acts of others" but also by "co-accomplishing these acts," by way of "co-performance,"[130] Husserl has carefully anchored his portrait of sociality in the absolute of the being-within-one-another of the monadic community such that "every monad has constituted the same world in its 'consciousness.' In an implicit way there is contained all being and transcendentally the universe of monads and everything that constitutes itself in each single one and in the community."[131]

## Notes

1. Hua XIII, XIV, XV.
2. Hua XIII, pp. 234, 188.
3. Hua XV, p. 475.
4. Hua XIII, p. 358.
5. Ibid., p. 224.
6. Ibid., pp. 288ff.; cf. "*quasi*-Auffassungen (quasi-conceptions)," p. 290.
7. Ibid., pp. 247, 249, 234.
8. E.g., Vittorio Gallese, "Embodied Simulation: Mirror Neurons, Neurophysiological Bases of Intersubjectivity, and Some Implications for Psychoanalysis," *Psicoterapia e Scienze Umane* 40, 3 (2006), 543–80; Dieter Lohmar, "Mirror Neurons and the Phenomenology of Intersubjectivity," *Phenomenology and Cognitive Science* 5 (2006), 5–16; Maxine Sheets-Johnstone, "Movement and Mirror Neurons: A Challenging and Choice Conversation," *Phenomenology and the Cognitive Sciences* 11, (2012), 385–401. These and similar papers not only confirm many of Husserl's early insight, but also lend support to the claim that Husserl's type of 'introspection' is philosophically sound.
9. Edmund Husserl, *Logical Investigations,* trans. J.N. Finlay (New York: Humanity Books, 2000), p. 277; Hua XIII, p. 249.
10. Hilary Putnam, "The Meaning of 'Meaning,'" in *Mind, Language, and Reality: Philosophical Papers* (Cambridge: Cambridge University Press, 1975), pp. 215–71 (227).
11. Nicholas Evans, "Anything Can Happen: The Verb Lexicon and Interdisciplinary Fieldwork," in *The Oxford Handbook of Linguistic Fieldwork*, ed. N. Thieberger (Oxford: Oxford University Press, 2012), pp. 183–208. Linda Barwick, Bruce Birch, and Nicholas Evans, "Iwaidja Jurtbirrk Songs: Bringing Language and Music Together," *Australian Aboriginal Studies* 2 (2007), 6–34.
12. Hua XXVII, p. 22.
13. Cf. the definition of "meaning" by the authoritative linguist David Crystal in *How Language Works* (London: Penguin Books, 2008), pp. 186–97.
14. Hua VII, p. 280.
15. Hua XV, p. 371.
16. Hua XX/2, pp. 2, 4.
17. Hua XX/2, p. 144.
18. Ibid., p. 143.
19. Hua XX/1, p. 38; XX/2, p. 205.
20. Hua XX/1, p. 38.

21  Hua XX/2, p. 151.
22  For a discussion of Husserl's *limit-phenomena*, see Anthony Steinbock, *Limit-Phenomena and Phenomenology in Husserl* (London and New York: Rowman and Littlefield, 2017).
23  Hua XX/2, p. 298.
24  Filip Mattens, "Introductory Remarks: New Aspects of Language in Husserl's Thought," in *Meaning and Language: Phenomenological Perspectives*, ed. F. Mattens (Dordrecht: Springer, 2008), pp. ix–xix (iv); cf. also Donn Welton in "Intentionality and Language in Husserl's Phenomenology," *The Review of Metaphysics* 27, 2 (1973), 260–97, on *genetic analysis*.
25  Hua XIV, pp. 268f.
26  Max Scheler, "The Perception of Other Minds," in *Phenomenology: Critical Concepts in Philosophy*, v.2, Phenomenology: Themes and Issues, ed. D. Moran and L. E. Embree (London: and New York: Routledge, 2004), pp. 119–42 (136).
27  Scheler, "Other Minds," p. 139; cf. Matthias Schlossberger, "The Varieties of Togetherness: Scheler on Collective Affective Intentionality," in *The Phenomenological Approach to Social Reality*, ed. A. Salice and H. B. Schmid (Dordrecht: Springer, 2016), pp. 173–95; Søren Overgaard, "The Problem of Other Minds," in *Handbook of Phenomenology and Cognitive Science*, ed. S. Gallagher and D. Schmicking (Dordrecht: Springer, 2010), pp. 254–68. Cf. also Shaun Gallagher and Dan Zahavi, *The Phenomenological Mind* (London: Routledge, 2012).
28  Hua XIV, p. 295.
29  Alfred Schütz, "The Problem of Transcendental Intersubjectivity in Husserl," in *Phenomenology: Critical Concepts*, v.2, Themes and Issues, ed. D. Moran and L. E. Embree (London and New York: Routledge, 2004), pp. 143–78 (147).
30  Schütz, "Transcendental Intersubjectivity," p. 145; cf. Husserl, *Formal and Transcendental Logic*, trans. D. Cairns (The Hague: Martinus Nijhoff, 1969), p. 236; and *The Crisis of European Sciences and Transcendental Phenomenology: An Introduction to Phenomenological Philosophy*, trans. D. Carr, 353-378 (Evanston: Northwestern University Press, 1970), pp. 244ff.
31  Ibid., pp.143ff.
32  Ibid., pp. 151ff.
33  Hua XIV, p. 369.
34  Hua VII, p. 280.
35  Schütz, "Transcendental Intersubjectivity," pp. 145, 166f.
36  Martin Kusch, *Language as Calculus and Universal Medium* (Dordrecht, Reidel, 1989), p. 133.
37  Edmund Husserl, *The Paris Lectures*, trans. P. Koestenbaum (The Hague: Martinus Nijhoff, 1975), p. 35.
38  Hua XIV, pp. 291f.
39  Ibid., pp. 295f.
40  Hua XV, p. 220.
41  Mattens, "Introductory Remarks," pp. xivf.
42  Wittgenstein, *Philosophical Investigations*, trans. G.E.M. Anscombe, P.M.S. Hacker, and J. Schulte (Oxford: Blackwell, 2009), §§ 19ff.
43  Horst Ruthrof, "Shutter-Speed Meaning, Normativity, and Wittgenstein's Abrichtung," *Linguistic and Philosophical Investigations*, 13 (2014b), 33–54, 47.
44  Hua XX/2, pp. 170, 175f.
45  Ibid., p. 205.

46 Ibid., pp. 102f.
47 Hua XX/1, p. 77.
48 Dave R. Koukal, "The Necessity of Communicating Phenomenological Insights and Its Difficulties," in *Meaning and Language: Phenomenological Perspectives*, ed. F. Mattens (Dordrecht: Springer, 2008), pp. 257–79 (261, 274f.).
49 Hua XV, pp. 12f.
50 Ibid., p. 366ff.
51 Mattens, "Introductory Remarks," p. xiv.
52 James Risser, "The Incapacity of Language," *Journal of the British Society of Phenomenology* 40 (2009), pp. 300–311.
53 Cf. Husserl, *Crisis*, p. 362.
54 Koukal, "The Necessity of Communicating Phenomenological Insights," pp. 261, 274.
55 However, in the speech-act theories of John L. Austin and John R. Searle, what we do with "words," such as promising or reprimanding, are not regarded as intrinsic features of language but rather as pragmatic uses of language. Cf. John L. Austin, *How to Do Things with Words* (Oxford: Oxford University Press, 1962); John R. Searle, *Speech Acts: An Essay in the Philosophy of Language* (Cambridge: Cambridge University Press, 1969), pp. 56, 60, 62, 68; cf. especially Austin, *How to Do Things with Words*, p. 103n1, where he asks, "Won't all utterances be performative?"
56 Hua XX/2, 102ff.
57 E.g., Donald Davidson, "Truth and Meaning," in *Semantics: A Reader*, ed. S. Davis and B. S. Gillon (Oxford: Oxford University Press, 2004), pp. 222–33.
58 Hua XX/2, p. 86.
59 Ibid., pp. 104f.
60 Ibid., p. 170.
61 Gilles Deleuze and Felix Guattari, *A Thousand Plateaus: Capitalism and Schizophrenia*, trans. B. Massumi (Minneapolis: Minnesota University Press, 1987), pp. 76f.
62 Hua XLI, pp. 362ff.
63 Ibid., p. 367n1.
64 Ibid., pp. 368–73.
65 Hua IV, p. 196.
66 Husserl, *Logical Investigations*, p. 286; my emphasis.
67 Ibid., p. 277.
68 Hua IV, p. 176.
69 Hua XIV, pp. 133, 135.
70 Husserl, *Logical Investigations*, pp. 277f. The theme of introjection has recently been resumed under the heading of "mindreading" and with reference to neurocomputational arguments and relevance theory by Marco Mazzone in *Cognitive Pragmatics: Mindreading, Inferences, Consciousness* (New York: de Gruyter Mouton, 2018). Cf. also Nini Praetorius, "Intersubjectivity, Cognition, and Language," in *Handbook of Phenomenology and Cognitive Science*, ed. S. Gallagher and D. Schmicking (Dordrecht: Springer, 2010), pp. 301–16.
71 Hua XIV, p. 170 and XXXIX, p. 386; Hua XXXIX, p. 396; Hua XIV, p. 220.
72 Hua XIII, XIV, XV.
73 Hua XV, pp. 461, 461–665.
74 Husserl, *Crisis*, p. 259.
75 Immanuel Kant, *Critique of Judgment*, trans. J. C. Meredith, rev. N. Walker (Oxford: Oxford University Press), §40.

76  CP 6.292; CP 5.313; CP 7.591; CP 5.232; cf. also CP 3.433; CP 5.249.
77  Alfred Schütz, *The Phenomenology of the Social World* (London: Heinemann, 1972), pp. 144ff.
78  Jan Patočka, *Body, Community, Language* (Chicago: Open Court, 1998), p. 55.
79  Husserl, *Crisis*, pp. 163f.
80  David Chalmers, *The Conscious Mind: In Search of a Fundamental Theory* (Oxford: Oxford University Press, 1996), pp. 26ff.
81  Cf. also, for example, Donald Favareau, "Beyond Self and Other: On the Neurosemiotic Emergence of Intersubjectivity," *Sign System Studies* 30, 1 (2002), 57–100.
82  Wittgenstein, *Philosophical Investigations*, § 6.
83  Hua XIV, p. 266; Hua I, p. 158; Hua XIII, p. 378.
84  Hua XV, pp. 366–77.
85  Ibid., pp. 371, 368; cf. Karl Löwith, *Das Individuum in der Rolle des Mitmenschen* (Freiburg and Munich: Karl Alber, 2013).
86  Edmund Husserl, "The Origin of Geometry," in *The Crisis of European Sciences and Transcendental Phenomenology: An Introduction to Phenomenological Philosophy*, trans. D. Carr, 353-378 (Evanston: Northwestern University Press, 1970), p. 359.
87  Hua XIII, p. 483.
88  Ibid., p. 116.
89  Hua XIV, p. 47.
90  Ibid., pp. 295.
91  Hua XIII, pp. 116, 244.
92  Ibid., p. 244.
93  Hua XV, p. 13; XIII, p. 464.
94  Hua XIII, p. 269.
95  Ibid., p. 267.
96  Ibid., pp. 184, 188.
97  Ibid., p. 342.
98  Ibid., p. 225.
99  Hua XV, p. 462; XIV, p. 370.
100 Hua XV, p. 368; my emphasis.
101 Hua XIII, p. 229.
102 Ibid., p. 230; my emphasis.
103 Hua XIII, pp. 214, 217.
104 Ibid., p. 484; my emphasis.
105 Hua XV, p. 220.
106 Hua XIII, p. 235.
107 Hua XIV, p. 103.
108 Ibid., p. 266f.
109 Ibid., p. 374.
110 Hua XIII, p. 483.
111 Hua XV, p. 608.
112 Ibid., p. 427.
113 Ibid., p. 17.
114 Hua XIII, p. 469; XIV, pp. 199, 369.
115 Hua XIV, pp. 169f., 180ff.
116 Hua XV, p. 475.
117 Hua XIV, p. 290.

118 Ibid., p. 143.
119 Hua XIV, p. 161; XIV, pp. 225ff.; XV, p. 461.
120 Hua XIV, p. 229.
121 Hua XV, p. 475.
122 Ibid., p. 223.
123 Ibid., p. 220.
124 Ibid., p. 223.
125 Ibid., p. 225.
126 Hua XX/2, p. 49; this in principle anticipates Wittgenstein's "private language" argument.
127 A point elaborated by Wittgenstein in his *Philosophical Investigations*, §§ 270ff.
128 This is where any post-Husserlian inquiry must part company with Wittgenstein's account.
129 Thomas Szanto, "Husserl on Collective Intentionality," in *The Phenomenological Approach to Social Reality*, ed. A. Salice and H. B. Schmid (New York: Springer International Publishing, 2016), pp. 145–72 (152).
130 Husserl, *Crisis*, p. 259.
131 Hua XV, p. 377.

5

# From Husserl's *Tone* to *Implicit Deixis*

"I speak in a contemptuous tone, in a lively tone, in an icy tone," writes Husserl in the *Nachlass*.[1] This heralds a major revision of what he now has to say about *natural language* in that it introduces a decisive emphasis on the way in which "tone (*Ton*)" affects every single linguistic signifier. Instead of speaking of "essentially subjective and occasional expressions" foregrounding individual nuances as a deviation from "objective expressions," as he did in the *Logical Investigations*,[2] Husserl now treats *tone* as a de-individualized and major feature that affects all of language, the "sentence, statement, interrogative sentence, expression of wish," and so on.[3] So fundamentally is tone reconceived in the *Nachlass* that it now adds a second "layer (*Schicht*)" to every word, seriously qualifying our acts of meaning fulfilment.[4] Thus has Husserl contributed a pioneering insight to the theorization of *deixis* and speech-act theory. However, if anything, this shift has strengthened rather than weakened his early and abiding commitment to his communicative conception of language. At the same time, it further highlights Husserl's refusal to split the meaning process into two separate categories, one to be treated under *semantics*, the other under the label of *pragmatics*. Instead, Husserl continues to subsume all acts from meaning intention via mere *Bedeutung* to meaning fulfilment under one unifying umbrella, *linguistic intentionality*. It is the main aim of this chapter to build on Husserl's remarks on tone under the broader concept of *implicit deixis*,[5] to be defined shortly.

## Meaning and Utterance

The standard distinction between semantics and pragmatics is described, for example, by Zoltan Gendler Szabo as "the distinction between the study of linguistic meaning and the study of context of utterance." As Szabo elaborates, "semantic knowledge is context-independent," even if "semantics does meddle with context to the extent that part of its task is to settle what the truth-conditional content of various expressions is relative to context."[6] Considering deictic expressions, Brendan Gillon adds, "a sentence is alternatively judged as true and judged as untrue with respect to a fixed state of affairs and with respect to different occasions of use."[7] As to Szabo's description, we can't have it both ways. Either meaning is defined in the context-independent sense or it has to be replaced by a comprehensive conception of utterance meaning. The context-independent option fails since, as I will argue in this chapter, sentences by themselves cannot mean at all. Objectivities do not mean on their own. When we read a sentence, speak, or comprehend it, we have already transformed it into an utterance. Furthermore, linguistic expressions require a prosodic contour, even if only a *neutral* or *literal* one. To admit utterances into the purified conception of semantic meaning on the grounds that they are needed for a truth-conditional checking mechanism is dubious for two reasons. First, meaning has to be realized *before* truth conditions can be entertained. Second, meaning does not *require* truth. With regard to Gillon's observation, truth-conditional considerations constitute a specialized, additional language game that can be played on top of meaning, as it were, but cannot claim to be one of its necessary conditions. In imagining what is being talked about and the manner in which this occurs, we depend on the construction of aboutness and voice. Here voice is crucial because it guides our acts as to how to *take* an expression, as for instance a "hello," or a sarcastically modified aboutness. So, if we wish to account for what is actually happening in living speech, it is impossible to avoid addressing voice as linguistic manner of presentation. What Husserl has to say on the role of tone in language encourages us to review voice, prosodic contour, intonation, emphasis, and so on, under the broader principle of implicit deixis, to be understood as the deictic shadow accompanying all parts of linguistic expressions. In this sense, implicit deixis is the modal counterpart of *explicit* or *marked deixis*.

That voice in this broad sense is a fundamental feature of language becomes apparent when we attempt to answer the phenomenological question: how is language *given*? The answer should be obvious; language as speech is typically given as a certain sequence of word sounds, under the umbrella of a specific intonation, and a prosodic contour, even in so-called *literal meaning* contexts. In reading, we supply an imagined sound sequence, a fact that reveals itself when we hesitate because we have noticed that we have misread the tone of a passage. We then reread the relevant expressions with an appropriate silent, or even audible, intonation. In reading, Husserl observes, "the acoustic words sediment themselves over the written ones and *primarily* carry the comprehension."[8] This observation in the *Nachlass* announces nothing less than an important new thesis about linguistic expressions: the *primacy* or, at the very least, the so far neglected *prominence* of voice in natural language. In spite of constituting a major shift in Husserl's description of linguistic intentionality, the accent on tone is entirely in tune with Husserl's opening gesture in the *Logical Investigations*, his enlarged scope of language as a communicative process. If anything, the new deictic emphasis reinforces much of the comprehensive focus of his earlier writings on language.

Yet, if the sounding of expressions is so important, it is a bit surprising, is it not, why linguistic utterance should be excised from semantics in our dominant discourses as belonging to the separate discipline of pragmatics, a strategy that has resulted in semantics being conceived as a static and so unrealistic approach premised on formal presuppositions. One of two main sources here is the Fregean reduction of main characteristics of natural language to a relation between a sense derived from geometry and algebra and a definitionally securable and scientifically conceived reference. The other source is the Saussurean conception of the radically arbitrary linguistic sign trapped within a *homosemiotic* circularity of differential relations. These formal and structuralist presuppositions have covered up the fact that in social reality, where language does its actual work, we do not hear the manner of speaking *after* the sentence. A skeptical interjection, such as "Is that so?" is not first taken up as a mere sentential sequence followed by the pragmatic reconstruction of a certain utterance attitude, or voice. To the listener, both *appear* at the same time and so are co-experienced as an intimate unity of two strata that, writes Husserl, "are expressed in a unified manner."[9]

Why the theoretical separation of semantics and pragmatics should be surprising is because empirically oriented, linguistic externalism would so radically sideline one of the *observables* of natural language, namely the way linguistic expressions are uttered. After all, an ironic tone, sarcasm, an encouraging or deprecatory style of speaking, the tones typical of skepticism, and doubt are all as public as the words themselves to which they are inextricably tied. To untie the two components is of course analytically possible, but when we do so we are changing our object of inquiry. As our sample expressions "Hello" in and "Nicely done!" in Chapter 4 showed, its meaning fulfilment cannot be divorced from its utterance situation without construing an unrealistic meaning event. And yet, both analytic language philosophers and the majority of linguists have reified the unspoken sentence as the central unit of meaning to the point where its decisive modification by voice is banished to another discipline, to pragmatics. As a result, *sentence meaning* has for decades occupied center stage in the theorization of language, with utterance having been granted only a secondary kind of existence. This has produced some remarkable results, as for example the argument by Donald Davidson that the literal meaning of a metaphor such as "My husband is a pig" is strictly its literal meaning, which is false.[10] Such secondary meanings as "a piggish husband" are relegated to notions of "utterance meanings" or other meanings that the metaphor "nudges" us to imagine. An alternative strategy would have been to question the very definition of analytical meaning if it cannot cope with what ordinary language users typically regard as the meaning of the metaphor.

For the phenomenologist, this relation is reversed. A description of our intentional acts in the performance of language tells us that all we come across in daily speech exchanges are utterances. Sentences on their own do not exist as language. Nor are linguistic expressions *given* as formal relations. To *appear*, sentences have to be uttered, aloud or silently, that is, they require a prosodic contour to become meaningful. Even a literally intended linguistic expression has an utterance voice, namely that of literality. The convention of speaking of sentence meanings rests on a distortion of empirical facts. Our primary uptake of language is immediate and holistic. Here, following Husserl's rule of returning *zu den Sachen selbst* discloses a peculiar blindness toward the unified phenomenon of utterance. So, what was the purpose of and promise in reducing language to a self-sufficient system of sentence meanings? The obvious answer is theoretical manageability in analogy with other, especially technical sign systems. Unfortunately, this has been accomplished at the expense of finding out what is actually going on when we use language. Husserl, of course, was well aware of the analytical option of drawing a sharp line between an ideationally abstractive semantics and its pragmatic remainder. He dealt with this divide early in his career under the contrast between semantic and epistemic essence. Whereas "the semantic essence" of our acts produces "meaning in our ideal sense," the content of the "epistemic essence of an objectifying act" has "relevance for its knowing-function."[11] This why, in the *Nachlass*, the epistemic analysis of linguistic communication increasingly attends to the graded and contiguous character of meaning fulfilment.

## The Ubiquity of Tone

In *Logische Untersuchungen* (1900/1), Husserl had distinguished "essentially occasional expressions" from expressions at large and so seemed to allow for precisely the sort of distinction between semantics and pragmatics challenged above. However, reading his *Nachlass* demands a very different assessment of what Husserl had to say in the end about natural language as a system of utterances.[12] At the heart of his reorientation is his discussion of the function of tone in linguistic expressions. "When we speak of tone," Husserl writes, "we mean specific tonal characters, which are grasped in their peculiarity and guide the understanding."[13] In light of this new information, a brief, critical look back at his treatment of *"wesentlich okkasionelle Ausdrücke"* in the *Logical Investigations* may be instructive. I take Aaron Gurwitsch's analysis as my stalking horse in arguing that *all* natural language expressions can be regarded as *essentially occasional* once we take the essential component of voice into consideration. According to Gurwitch, "a theory of such expressions must fulfil two requirements: (1) it must account for their essential ambiguity and (2) it must take the circumstances of their occurrence into account."[14] Gurwitch resolves the first demand by pointing out that meaning is often disambiguated by way of perception or its equivalents in *Vorstellung*. Yet, since "the meaningfulness of essentially occasional expressions," according to Husserl, "does not derive from any specifying act but resides entirely in these expressions themselves as bearers of meaning functions," perception and other mental representations can only be viewed as "meaning-*specifying*" but not as "meaning-*bestowing*." And yet, it is only once the meaning-specifying circumstances of utterance are taken into account that the expressions themselves can be disambiguated. After all, says Gurwitch, "the singular status of the essentially occasional expression derives from the particular *organizational aspect* with which the perceptual world presents itself."[15] In short, the perspective from which something is given, its manner of presentation, or voice as implicit deixis affects aboutness elementally.

We should take issue though with the not so phenomenological assertion that the "meaningfulness" of linguistic expressions resides "entirely in these expressions themselves." Expressions by themselves are meaningless unless they are activated in meaning-endowing acts performed under the auspices of the speech community, a process that can be distilled eidetically into an a posteriori, broadly conceived semantics, in contradistinction to the *a priori* semantics of formal systems. We should take Husserl's intersubjective mentalism of meaning acts seriously by asserting that meanings do not reside *in* signifiers but in the intentional acts of the speakers of a language as a corollary of the pedagogy of language drills. It is only the trained individual-as-social-user of signifiers that has the capacity to produce linguistic meanings. Only as a member of a speech community can I say, on hearing certain sounds, "I interpret them as indications of dispositional phenomena, of *Vorstellungen*, apperceptions, etc., of the person who is uttering those sounds." In this context, Husserl explains that by "indications" he means that we "attribute" emotional phenomena and other mental acts to a speaker, which we assume reveal themselves in the manner of utterance.[16] At the same time, as a consequence of the eidetic character of language, argued in Chapter 3, and the intersubjectivity of communal training can meaning acts, though individually instantiated, be rendered compatible. After all, in habitual speech, which makes up the vast bulk of language use, we cannot but follow the rule of the linguistic linkage compulsion in generating socially guided and tightly circumscribed semantic *appresentations*.[17] Members of a speech community have been drilled to co-perform the rules of how to associate the sounds of linguistic expressions with imaginable nonverbal scenarios.

A second possible objection to Gurwitch is that the special status that the early Husserl grants *essentially occasional expressions* rests on the assumption that linguistic deixis occurs only when it is explicitly marked. Only when it is physically signalled in a sentence are we supposed to be aware of an expression's *enunciative modalities*, to use Foucault's comprehensive term.[18] And yet, the *manner* of presentation of any communicative sign sequence is part and parcel of the communicative process, whether marked or merely implicit, and cannot simply be excised as a redundant residue. When we analytically strip the voice from an utterance, the sign sequence is no longer a form of communication. Husserl's holistic approach to the communicative function of linguistic expressions declares such approaches illegitimately reductive. Without use, language does not exist *as* language. In their normal, social setting, all language expressions carry, for the native speaker, the *manner of their utterance*, and they do so quite apart from whether this presentational component is marked or unmarked. In fact, in the vast bulk of actual speech events, the manner of presentation is unmarked. I take this as justification for granting deictic primacy to the phenomenon of *implicit deixis*, the submerged iceberg of general deixis, the small visible tip of which is marked or explicit deixis. If this is indeed a universal feature of language, then all expressions must be grasped in terms of a double intentionality, Husserl's "dual strata,"[19] on the part of users via acts of constituting aboutness and voice. So, we can say that by investigating the intentionality of tone in the *Nachlass*, Husserl added a crucial correction of his earlier views on essentially occasional language use.

In natural language, Husserl now tells us, aboutness is never alone. It is always accompanied by a certain tone of voice. In addition to a standard "pronunciation," the expression also "always has its 'tone.'" While we are performing acts of constructing aboutness in response to word sounds, we entertain at the same time decisions about the specific manner in which expressions are presented. Such constructions, once more, of necessity involve acts of intimation on the part of the utterer and acts of introjection on the part the speech partner (or reader), together amounting to an intentionality of *intersubjective reciprocity*. As Husserl writes, "I can produce the sound arbitrarily with the intention that the other understands me *thus*, and eventually the other understands me and my intent, since he entertains a *similar intent* in the same circumstances, and so he grasps the sound as a request," or some other intended meaning. In speech exchanges, I assume that the other will respond to my voice, that is, "interpret what I say *in a certain way.*"[20] On my part, "in response to certain sounds, I am inclined to interpret them as indications of dispositional phenomena, mental projections, apperceptions, etc. of the person uttering those sounds."[21] Husserl extends this mechanism of intersubjective exchange to the reading situation where "if necessary, I repeat the word sound silently."[22] Here, Husserl's distinction between "essence" and "existence" is once more critical in that the quality of the sound does not change whether it is actually uttered or merely imagined.[23]

Whenever we come across a definite article that, in standard speech, expresses the positing of an aboutness, the indicated aboutness is never neutrally presented but always already modified by the kind of voice by which speakers "intimate" their speech attitude.[24] Husserl's introduction of the concept of intimation in the *Logical Investigation* can be seen as the seed that grew in the *Nachlass* into the related but more complex concept of tone, now argued as an indispensable intentional component of language as speech. The presence of tone is least noticeable and usually irrelevant in scientific and theoretical expressions, but of paramount importance in everyday language use. Even minimal "explicit naming" (*explizite Nennung*) is always qualified by a certain tone.[25] Since tone effects a crucial *deictic* modification of aboutness in the process of meaning fulfilment, it makes sense to cover it under the broader technical notion of implicit deixis. Defined simply as the unmarked manner of presentation of linguistic expressions, implicit deixis is a ubiquitous feature of all language. Whereas explicit deixis is easily recognized by deictic markers, implicit deixis functions as the *modal shadow* (in a broad sense) that informs every component of an expression, irrespective of whether it also contains marked or explicit deixis. In the *Nachlass* we find the following example of explicit deixis in the form of a shifter: "'Now' (*Jetzt*) is a word that necessarily changes its meaning whenever it is repeated." "Whenever I say 'now,' there is something that is shared. By means of it, I indicate the conscious present of the imagined state of affairs, that is, the possible present, the simultaneity with what is apperceived."[26] By looking at the intentional acts we perform when we use such shifters, Husserl draws our attention to the necessary contribution imaginability makes to secure meaning. However, the absence of explicit deixis should not suggest that linguistic expressions could ever be voiceless. As long as they are unuttered, they are not *linguistic*. Though not as conspicuous, implicit deixis, understood as the general manner of presentation of expressions, could be argued to be even more important in the sense that it is easier to misconstrue and so demands more careful, interpretive labor.

In the *Nachlass*, Husserl cautiously develops his theory of tone only after he has established the aboutness (*das Worüber*) of linguistic expressions. First, the state of affairs of an expression is inspected: "*der Sachverhalt ist angeschaut.*"[27] As to the speaker, "the judgment is primary." The utterer "has what he wants to say," whereas "for the listener the sign comes first." What connects the two acts is our "communicative consciousness, active and passive. Addressing and comprehending."[28] At the same time, Husserl acknowledges the fact that speaking consists of "practical events"; it is a "form of doing." From this double perspective, the focus on mental acts and the character of speech as a "fully concrete expressing" as "unity of word sound consciousness and meaning consciousness," Husserl derives the key insight that we are not dealing here with a second consciousness but an "intimately unified consciousness (*ein innig einiges Bewusstsein*)."[29] This insight has momentous consequences. For example, Husserl notices that witnessing a speech event is a special kind of apperception, for it includes the uptake of voice, requiring as it does the anticipation of a spectrum of different forms of communicative response: doubt, skepsis, disagreement, approval, agreement, and such modalities as certitude.[30] Yet Husserl is not quite ready yet to embrace the concept of tone as a critical tool. Instead, he cautiously distinguishes the "realizing consciousness" as a continuous "flow" from its relatively stable content, "the positing of the contents of imaginability," "imaginable aboutness," or the positing of *Vorstellung* or, in Husserl's term, "*Vorstellungssetzung*," the positing of a merely presentational projection. He also distinguishes between the relative clarity of categorial acts and the more open acts of cognition in response to single terms. Hence, "sign consciousness and cognitive consciousness are not as unified as in predications." Our acts of comprehension then are "clear or dark."[31] For example, "Help!" is read as a sign of an urgent request for assistance. In response, we first form acts of cognition that are "clear" to the extent that help is needed and "dark" as to the precise nature of assistance required. Much the same applies whenever a single word functions "as a closed sentence, even if expressed only incompletely,"[32] as would be the case in single-word utterances such as "Tsunami!" or "Fire!" and many other such expressions.

It is only in "*Beilage IX (Der Ton as Anzeige für die Satzart. Die Einheit von Ton und Wortsubstrat)*," probably written in March/April 1914, according to the editor Ullrich Melle, that Husserl is able to grant the notion of tone his full attention. Husserl can now categorically state that "*the tone is a component of the word, . . . of the sentence, the declarative sentence, the interrogative sentence, the sentence of wishing*, etc."[33] While in written expressions the uptake of tone is often aided by markers, such as question marks and exclamation marks, in the absence of such explicit signs, the reader needs to invent a voice according to context. In other words, in the absence of explicit deixis, the reader of the written text is required to reconstruct a tone that matches as closely as possible the speaker's reconstructed, intended conveyance of values, irony, sarcasm, doubt, approval, disapproval, prioritization, and so on, beyond what is explicitly predicated. Once again, we cannot fail to notice the broader implications of Husserl's initial choice of the scope of his inquiry. Because he has cast his net wide enough to capture all the necessary ingredients of language responsible for its *communicative* efficiency, tone turns out to be an integral part of all linguistic expressions, rather than merely a pragmatic adjunct. Accordingly, tone needs to be reincorporated in a broadly conceived *semantics*.

Yet again, at first Husserl is careful not to open the floodgates threatened by too encompassing a notion, such as *implicit deixis*. He starts by restricting tone to the indication of kinds of sentences. "The tone does not express the 'belief' that is everywhere part of it, but the 'kind of sentence.'" Here, Husserl uses the notion of tone to address the question of "what distinguishes the kinds of sentences (predicative judgment, rejection, affirmation, guessing, etc.)."[34] Viewing tone as a tool with which to identify different sorts of sentences, however, leaves us with the need to identify it also as a vehicle of speech nuances beyond any basic taxonomy. For example, in the construal of the meaning of a sentence like "Can I help you?" we must be able to differentiate speech tones ranging from intimating a genuine offer of help to an aggressive intimation that an approaching person is not welcome. This, then, concerns the second function of tone, such as *degrees of intensity* of request, appeal, sympathy, agreement and disagreement, and other *implicit* deictic nuances. Accordingly, as quoted at the beginning of the chapter, Husserl differentiates speaking "in a contemptuous tone, a lively tone, an icy tone, and this *in addition* to the choice of words."[35] As to the choice of words, Husserl also mentions "colouring" as in "rascal," "liar" ("*Färbungen wie Lump, Lügner*"), inviting comparison with Frege's acknowledgment of the presence of tone (*Färbung*) and force in addition to sense and reference, a complication, however, that was outside the much narrower scope of his analytical description of language.[36] To reiterate the two conclusions Husserl draws from his own observations. One, "when we speak of tone, we mean specific tonal characters that are grasped in their peculiarity and guide understanding"; and two, "the unity of the word has two strata, which are expressed in a unified manner."[37] We were able to identify the two strata as (1) aboutness and (2) voice, which may be (2.1) marked or (2.2) merely *intimated* and so *implicit*.

## Explicit Deixis

In linguistics and analytic philosophy of language, deixis has mainly been investigated in its *explicit* or *marked* appearance.[38] From the first systematic study of deixis by Karl Bühler (1934) to the writings of Charles Fillmore (1975), the semantics of John Lyons (1968, 1995), the structuralist contributions of Roman Jakobson (1971, 1981), and the input by Geoffrey Nunberg (1993), Paul Manning (2001), and Ellen Fricke (2007), attention has primarily been given to deixis in its explicit forms.[39] A second strand of inquiry, Charles Sanders Peirce's theorization of indexical signs, has likewise been influential on the manner in which linguistics and language philosophy have dealt with verbal indexicality.[40] Although this body of research is impressive, it has also contributed to the growing rift between living speech as an intentional, communicative continuum and language as a system of observables. From the holistic perspective of a phenomenological viewing of deixis as made up of intentional acts, which reveal what we typically do when we use language communicatively and what kinds of processes, relations, and objects are involved in linguistic performance, our account of deixis generates a quite different emphasis, one that points us toward a broader avenue of inquiry. First, phenomenology guides us to the acknowledgment of the ubiquity of deixis in language beyond its explicit markers. Second, it invites us to justify in what way *implicit deixis* is as legitimate an object of linguistics as is *explicit deixis*. Since in natural language there is always a speaker, and not only when deixis is marked, implicit deixis should reveal itself as affecting all the signifiers of linguistic expressions as a kind of *modal shadow*.

But because this modal shadow of language is not immediately given, depending as it does on intentional, interpretive labor, it should not come as too much of a surprise that Husserl was an early pioneer in drawing our attention to the function of tone in language. Nor that deixis as a form of grammaticalization of the context of speech events was first recognized by a psychologist, Karl Bühler, some twenty years later. Bühler distinguished between the "symbol field (*Symbolfeld*)" and the "pointing field

(*Zeigfeld*)," the domain of linguistic indication of a presented world and the domain of relations between indication and the speech situation. In so doing, he identified two fundamental features of language, which I sum up under broader concepts of aboutness and voice, respectively.[41] Bühler declared deixis as the "here-now-I-system" that is fixed by the "*origo* of the imaginable here" from "which all other positions are linguistically indicated" and the "*origo* of the now" that determines "all other moments in time."[42] Since then, deixis has been appropriately described by Stephen Levinson as the way in which natural language "encodes or grammaticalizes features of the context of utterance."[43] In a similar vein, Benveniste, Jakobson, Rommeveit, and other linguists have contributed to the discussion of the deictic side of language, before Charles Fillmore moved deixis to the center of linguistic concerns, but still mainly in its *explicit* form.[44]

To his credit, Fillmore not only addresses the basic features of temporal, spatial, personal, discourse, and social deixis but also alerts us to the difficulties we face in trying to identify any boundaries that would separate what belongs to deixis as explicitly stated from inferences that fall outside of what is visibly marked. But first, the basic ingredients of the deictic side of natural language. Linguistic deictic features are distinguished from their non-deictic counterparts by viewing the former to be relative to the speaker, the latter as independent of the speech situation. Temporal deixis is defined by Fillmore as the "position in time of the speech act," allowing us to distinguish between "coding time" and "reference time," the latter "made *explicit* by means of a time specifier phrase." Likewise, "reference place" versus deixis as the "speaker's perspective of his position in three-dimensional space,"[45] person deixis as references to speaker, addressee, and audience, discourse deixis as deictic relations in the linguistic context, and social deixis as the relations among participants in speech events. An expression's "deictic anchorage" requires a social context for identifying "participants in the communication acts." More precisely, social deixis is defined as the study of those aspects of sentences that "reflect or establish or are determined by certain realities of the social situation in which the speech occurs." If such anchorage is missing, the recipient of a written message is unable to perform any perlocutionary acts intended by the sender. Fillmore quips about "unanchored occasion-sentences" by giving the example of a bottle message afloat in the ocean: "Meet me here at noon tomorrow with a stick about this big."[46]

Explicit deixis also includes anaphoric, or intradiscursive, deixis, for securing indexical identity, as for instance in "The Queen waved to the crowd. *She* looked a little tired"; the obverse cataphoric deixis in "She wore a green dress. The Queen always looks immaculately dressed"; as well as exophoric deixis (reference to texts outside of an expression), as in "He hurled his spear through the rock at the top of the island," the "he" referring to the mythological hero of the Polynesian island of Morea. Anaphoric deixis also includes phrases foreshadowing later information and such backwards pointing sentence openings as "This being so, . . ."; "As such, . . ."; "Having said that, . . .—which act as linking devices in arguments but at the same time draw deictic attention to the way speakers attempt to make what they are saying more cogent and persuasive. We can distinguish *deictic centers* as personal, temporal, spatial, discursive, and social deixis from "symbolic deixis" as general spatiotemporal knowledge, as well as from "sympathetic deixis" as a shift from speaker to listener, a constant feature in conversation. In a standard linguistics textbook, deixis is described in terms of the relation of the inside and outside of speech by facilitating identification of referents in relation to context. Deixis forges connections between things and "the social, linguistic, spatial or temporal context of an utterance," including "pronouns, demonstratives and adverbs of space and time." As a result, "the reference of these items varies with each context in which they are used" such that deictics specify "referents by indicating whether they are close to the speaker, or distant from the speaker."[47]

In some recent studies, deixis has been refined to include "meta-deixis" as the self-reflective deictic markers provided by a speaker, "qualitative deixis" in *such* and *so*, and "directional deixis" in *towards* and *from*, while traditional spatial deixis has been rephrased as "spatial schema"[48] and "spatial scope deixis."[49] The displacement of personal deixis resulting in a shift of the speaking position has been distinguished as "ego-centric" versus "alio-centric" deixis by Herbermann, who also includes fictional and realist deixis as contrasting speech modalities.[50] An intriguing case is the phony "we" in the doctor's bedside question "How are we this morning?" The "we" here not only functions as deictic displacement but also colors the entire expression by placing a question mark on the sincerity of the speaker, a case of implicit deixis qualifying the likelihood of a merely literal uptake. In his paper "On Social Deixis," Paul Manning argues, persuasively I think, that it is essential to transcend the boundaries of marked deixis to allow for the exploration of broader social configurations.[51] The worry about the restrictions on deictic interpretation of linguistic expressions imposed by too close an adherence to the description of explicit deixis shows itself also in such concepts as "impure deixis" that, according to John Lyons, combines deictic and nondeictic information. While he classifies *I* and *you* under forms of "pure deixis," *he*, *she*, and *it* under the "referential" umbrella, for cases where we have difficulties in drawing such clear distinctions deixis is to be seen as "impure."[52] From the position of intentional act description it should be clear, however, that there cannot be anything like a purely referential signifier. Every signifier must be at least *colored*, as it were, by a speaker's attitude.

This suspicion is supported in Fillmore's *Santa Cruz Lectures*. What is intriguing in this early work is that almost from the very beginning of Fillmore's inquiry the boundaries of what can be empirically observed about explicit deixis appear fuzzy. When he analyzes the deceptively simple expression "May we come in?" through the lens of deixis, he lists a number of assumptions that we cannot but make in the act of meaning fulfilment. They include that there must be an enclosure, a speaker of English as utterer, a speaker of English as addressee, and a person accompanying the speaker. Furthermore, we must deal with appropriate "utterance conditions." Are we then really dealing with a question here? Or is the expression an indirect speech act functioning as a request? Precisely because, as Fillmore observes, "May we come in?" can be taken as a request, we need to specify the "social conditions" informing the utterance. Alone the modal auxiliary "may" is shown to have at least three different functions: epistemic, pragmatic, and magical, as for instance in "He may not see you," "You may enter," and "May you live in interesting times," respectively. The question "May we come in?" also implies that it is the addressee and not the speaker who occupies the position of authority. All this is perfectly persuasive as long as we take into account that Fillmore is dealing with language use in realist settings.[53] His "May we come in?," however, is meaningful also if there is no enclosure, if the person asking the question is alone, and if no sense of authority is at stake, cases in which we would identify the utterance as ironic, frivolous, or as part of fictional discourse.

We can draw two important insights from Fillmore's analysis, one concerning the object of inquiry, explicit deixis, the other concerning the method of his investigation. The first point is that his analysis does not restrict itself to the explication of the deictic markers "I" and "we" but spreads across other signifiers. For example, the unmarked deixis of "Did John seem angry?" merely conceals the deictically explicit "Did you perceive John as angry?" while in "Have you seen him" and the answer "Yes, I have," according to Fillmore, "the interchanged roles may be implicit, not linked to any specific material in the surface sentence." This suggests that even where there is no explicit deixis, deixis is nevertheless present and in need of scrutiny. This is where implicit deixis reveals its explanatory force. My second observation concerns Fillmore's methodological leaning, which is put on view in such self-reflective phrases as "in picturing the situation," "we might find ourselves imagining," and "with a little imagination, it is possible to conceive." Fillmore's mental projectionist approach appears justified by his skepticism toward "straightforward" utterances of sentences as a norm: "If the question is used in absolutely its most straightforward way—*a rare occurrence*, I would guess . . ."[54] Far from hiding his cognitive allegiance, he firmly commits himself to an iconically mental and projectionist method, which I sum up under the heading of a phenomenological semantics of imaginability.[55] In Fillmore, this accent permits him to project real-world scenarios in order to specify features of natural language that are not explicitly given but entailed or merely implied in linguistic expressions. These features fall into two categories, aboutness and voice. Fillmore's pioneering study, apart from its main focus on explicit deixis, strike me as embracing two principles. (1) A phenomenological imaginability thesis such that the comprehension of linguistic expressions of necessity draws on the mental projection of a possible, realist, or merely imaginable scenario for linguistic expressions, a commitment that must not be confused with a propositionally reduced deep structure. At the same time, in order to keep semantic privacy at bay, such a projectionist approach is in need of *socialization* by way of a phenomenologically grounded intersubjective mentalism in which linguistic *signifieds* are argued to be indirectly public. As I will further elaborate in Chapter 6, the social constraints of natural language can be argued via intersubjective sufficiency and the pedagogy of language drills well captured by Wittgenstein's notion of *Abrichtung,* that is, a rigorous from of training via language drills. (2) Fillmore's other thesis appears to be an unstated legitimization of implicit deixis in the sense that deixis, just as Husserl's tone, tends to extend well beyond the immediate semantic confines of explicit deictic markers.

That implicit deixis as continuous modal shadow is a significant component of language finds indirect support also in remarks by Levinson on the "partially deictic character of most linguistic expressions." According to Levinson, "much of the vocabulary" of natural language may really be "quasi-indexical" such that "many kinds of deictics are easily overlooked," that "many expressions have a wide latitude of interpretation," and that "many expressions require further specification." Levinson also questions formal semantic claims about natural language from the perspective of indexicality that, he argues, raises difficulties for the claim that "*intensions* (senses) of expressions" fix the "corresponding *extensions* (references)" in every "possible world (any set of circumstances)."[56] What such borderline cases demonstrate is that deictic intentionality in meaning fulfilment cannot be contained within any neat boundaries of explicit deixis. Another feature of language related to, but not identical with, marked deixis is *indexicality*, a brief summary of which will pave the way for addressing implicit deixis as a procedural generalization of Husserl's *Ton*.

## Indexicality

Husserl's methodological commitment to the description of intentional acts in the performance of language also guides us to question the widespread alignment in the literature of linguistic deixis and philosophical indexicality. A variety of such alignments can be found in Hurford (2007, p. 223n9); Perry (2006); Nunberg (1993); Levinson (2004); Smith (1989); and Bar-Hillel (1970).[57] For one, the linguist John Lyons objects to any such conflation. I also do so, but for additional reasons. Lyons regards linguistic indexicality as a "particular kind of deixis" that is "relevant to the determination of the propositional meaning of utterances," conceived under a "narrow view of meaning." Importantly, Lyons includes within linguistic deixis the imaginable, salient features of bodily gestures of *pointing* as reflected in "any referring expression." In this sense, deixis is an "integral part of the context of utterance" rather than a feature of propositions.[58] And if deixis is defined as a pointer to the speech situation, then in its *explicit* forms deixis is clearly distinct from indexicals for the simple reason that its standard markers *I*, *she*, *us*, *here*, and *now* are *shifters* (*embrayeurs*). For clarification of this relation, it is helpful to briefly return to one of the original sources of the theorization of indexicality, Peirce's semiotics.

In their Peircean sense, indexical signs are defined as signs displaying an *existential* relation to their *interpretants*. In a phenomenological reading of Peirce, what looms large here are intentional acts of imaginability. In the comprehension of an indexical sign, such as the deciphering of the footprints of a fox in the snow, we are able to constitute meaning, that is, construct the appropriate interpretant, only if we are able to *imagine* what sort of animal must have caused the prints. The causal relation is as crucial here as the necessity of our intentional acts of imagining. Likewise, Peirce's weather-vane is existentially related to the wind that directs it, and the rising smoke in the distant forest is existentially linked to the likelihood of fire. As such, Peircean indexicality, contrary to the shiftiness of marked deixis, is firmly anchored in the specifics of systems of cultural aboutness and imaginability, a contention reinforced by Peirce's primacy of *iconicity* and its tripartition in *hypoiconicity* as image, diagram, and metaphor.[59] The claim can be strengthened also by taking into account the relation of the indexical sign to the other two kinds of signs in Peirce.[60] What tends to be overlooked in the literature is that the relation between icon, index, and symbol is *asymmetrical*. The index stands much closer to the icon than to the symbol in that it can be shown to be *indirectly iconic*. The index is characterized by *indirect resemblance* to be reconstructed by acts of inferential iconic intentionality. Only the symbol can be empty of all content, as in arbitrary linguistic signifiers or, more conspicuously, in formal notation. While there is no resemblance between term and concept in Peirce's conventional symbol, icons are defined by direct resemblance and the diagrammatic *hypoicon* by schematized resemblance, the index requires the mental construction of an iconic similarity relation, such as between the footprint and the paws of the fox, or the tactile iconicity of the resistance of objects to the pressure of the breeze. If it is right to associate the symbol with arbitrariness, the icon with resemblance, and the index with indication, both resemblance and indication require intentional, mental material content in the act of meaning fulfilment. After all, our mental projection of aboutness is firmly directed by our relational acts that link sign and object. Not so in the use of symbolic or arbitrary signs where our mental projections are directed entirely by convention. In the pure case of the symbolic sign in formal systems, convention reveals itself as merely *categorial*. One could say then that in contrast with iconic and symbolic signs, indexicality is characterized by *indirect iconic intentionality*. Likewise, in linguistic contexts. Only under these conditions can certain forms of marked deixis function as indexicality, which, however, disallows their conceptual identity.

## Implicit Deixis

My starting point here is once again Husserl's thesis on the necessity of *Anschaulichkeit* in speech intention and uptake, conceived as *anschauliche Vorstellung*.[61] Which, according to Husserl, includes the indispensable role of tone, that is, *implicit deixis*, conceived as the modification of aboutness by tone or voice as a ubiquitous and all-pervasive feature of natural language. If explicit deixis can be viewed as the visible tip of the iceberg of deixis, implicit deixis could be described as its vast submerged bulk. As such, implicit deixis affects every single signifier of every linguistic expression. It is effective most conspicuously in *spoken* discourse and *cultural* contexts. As we demonstrated earlier, the most mundane of expressions, as for instance the humble "hello," is overdetermined by the unmarked manner of its presentation, its implicit deixis. Or consider, for example, two interculturally complex terms, such as the Chinese word "guanxi" and the post-enlightenment Western signifier "critique." While *guanxi* is associated with human relationships, trust, and well-established and reliable business dealings in the Chinese tradition, the same signifier tends to be read in the West as sharp practice or even as a form of corruption. Both readings are carried by the voice or speech attitude with which the same term is spoken in different cultural contexts. An intriguing case in this respect is the way the signifier "critique" has been absorbed into the Chinese vocabulary where it carries a very different speech attitude if compared to its Western usage. To the Chinese political unconscious, individual critical speech is traditionally viewed with suspicion, quite apart from its ideological status under Communist censorship. To a tradition that since the Confucian *Analects* has celebrated the meta-rule of harmony under obedience informing any well-functioning social order, the voice of individual critique sounds shrill, lacking the wisdom of community sentiment. This is why the notion of *critique* has a very different cultural meaning even in contemporary China if compared to the high regard in which it is held in Western democracies.[62] Implicit deixis is active also negatively in the avoidance of certain topics, phrasing, jokes, and references to religious and other cultural taboos. In the practice of natural language, such lacunae are typically concretized along the lines of culture-sanctioned implicit deixis.

Examples of this kind very much justify Husserl's focus on language as a communicative process, as they do Carol Feldman's observation that most sentences are "underdetermined" in that their meaning cannot be properly explained on "sentence-internal grounds" without taking into account "their existence in some speaker-hearer context."[63] Much the same can be reasonably argued from the perspective of implicit deixis, for if implicit deixis carried by voice has any impact on aboutness, as argued, then all sentences, and not just those with visible deictic markers, require anchoring in context and speech situations for adequate semantic explication. The all-pervasiveness of implicit deixis, then, should be beyond doubt, at least as far as linguistic iconicity is concerned. Yet, does this observation also hold for categorial relations and syncategorematic terms, as claimed earlier? More precisely, is it possible to show that and how our intentional acts in meaning bestowal and meaning fulfilment produce a modification of the aboutness of prepositions like "on," "within," "after," of categorial relations, such as the structure of "predication," or binary relations, such as "smaller" and "larger," and of such function words as "yet," "furthermore," and "if," or "if and only if"? No doubt, in all these cases, the thesis of the radical difference between natural language and formal sign systems looks less persuasive than at the level of substantivity, adjectivity, adverbiality, in short, wherever aboutness draws on the rich iconicity of imaginability.

Nevertheless, just as in the camera's pictorial representation of "on" in photographs or cinematic image chains, it makes a substantial difference from which angle a shot is taken, whether from above looking down on a person sitting on a chair or from below or one side. A different quality of "sitting on" appears to attach to our intentional acts of comprehension in each case. The seeming neutrality of "smaller than" and "larger than" and of "slower than" versus "faster than" in a comparison between a toy yacht and an America's Cup catamaran appears to take on a different quality as a result of the modification of aboutness by the manner of its presentation. Likewise, and perhaps more obviously so, the tone we employ in the use of syncategorematic terms like "furthermore," "if," or "if and only if" could be argued to make a difference in linguistic meaning, if only as a nuance of coloring Frege's and Husserl's *Färbung*. Yet, it is of no small consequence that Husserl was able to find a theoretical category for such nuances in his communicative approach to natural language that Frege had to leave unattended.[64] Last, it might seem that John Langshaw Austin's concept of *illocution* adequately captures what implicit deixis is meant to cover. After all, both illocution and Husserl's tone are argued to be "a component" of linguistic expressions, Austin's *locution*. However, illocution is conceived as speech intention as far as it attaches to a locution irrespective of its manner of presentation, while Husserl's tone as implicit deixis varies according to context and speech situation, as well as a result of the kind of intentional acts of intimation and introjection that characterize the linguistic exchange. Since language is always communicative rather than a mere linguistic fact, implicit deixis is always tied to a relation between persons.

## The Very Idea of an Unuttered Sentence

Try as we may to comprehend a linguistic expression *without* uttering it in some way, aloud or merely in our minds, semantic ascent is doomed to failure. Only once we attend to linguistic expressions in a comprehending manner via utterance, will it acquire a certain prosodic contour and with it a definite meaning. This applies even to the most minimal form of linguistic uptake. Whether such responses produce a literal, ironic, icy, or some other speech modality is irrelevant to the fact that in the empirical reality of initial engagement with language the manner of presentation cannot be eliminated. Christine Tanz, for one, disagrees in her opening observations in *Studies in the Acquisition of Deictic Terms*. "When language is spoken, it occurs in a specific location, at a specific time, is produced by a specific person and is (usually) addressed to some specific person or persons." To this she adds the qualification, "Only *written* language can ever be free of this kind of anchoring in the extra-linguistic situation."[65] If this were indeed the case, readers would be at liberty to impose any intonation they wish to choose on any written expression, no matter what the speech intention of the implied speaker. This surely is not the case. Although we are free to misread the ironic tone of a passage, just as we are able to misconstrue the voice of any spoken utterance, we do so at the price of miscommunication. Leaving the Derridean liberation and negotiable nuances aside, language as *communication* demands that we remain within the community-agreed boundaries of the thrust of the tonal intent of speech. But the proximate character of the reconstruction of speech intention is not the issue here. The fundamental question is whether it is at all possible to comprehend linguistic expressions without the construction of *any* sort of implicit deixis. In short, could voice be eliminated from natural language without changing it into something that is *unnatural*? The answer given here is negative. On their own, expression-tokens do not mean at all; they only have *meaning potential*. Unuttered sentences, then, do not exist *as* language. They are no more than a construable formal fiction. Even as innocent looking an expression as "Ice floats on water" can be shown to be dependent on implicit deixis. Contrary to Bar-Hillel's seemingly persuasive assertion that the expression illustrates a sentence type of which all tokens "refer to the same state of affairs,"[66] though correct, does not tell the whole story.

These considerations lead us inevitably to the question of how best to describe the *mode of being* of the meaning of linguistic expressions and whether sentences can have meaning by themselves. One recent answer is to define "the meaning of a sentence" as "a set of constraints on what normal uses of it assert, or express."[67] This formulation, however, functions better as a definition of meaning potential than meaning. After all, meaning is preferably defined as an intentional event that either occurs or fails to occur. When it does occur, the meaning potential of a sentence-token has been realized in and as a specific utterance event. As argued in Chapter 4, a linguistic expression has been transformed into meaning (Husserl's *Sinn*) via the merely transitional consciousness of *Leerintentionen*, that is mere verbal paraphrase, saturated in acts of meaning fulfilment as the generation of mental material states of affairs and, we can now add here, *viewed from a specific perspective* intimated by implicit deixis. Without such acts, we are unable to *imagine* what is being talked about and at least approximately align our understanding with that of the relevant speech intention.

Nor is the distinction tenable between deictic sentences as "context sensitive" from context insensitive expressions. The notion of context-insensitive expressions is alien to natural language. We could rephrase this by saying that what makes language natural is that there is always at least implicit deixis and therefore the aboutness of a linguistic expression is always already modified, potentially radically, by voice. As far as the question of the mode of being of linguistic meaning is concerned as an always emergent phenomenon, meaning is produced in utterance as an association of arbitrary sound sequences and the projection of an imaginable slice of world, as sanctioned by a speech community, and so cannot be stipulated as a mere technical feature of sentence-tokens devoid of voice. So why has the convention of speaking of sentence meanings become such a dominant discourse? And why is it so hard to free linguistics and the philosophy of language from the illusion of the very possibility of unuttered sentences? It would seem that once more the lure of a techno-logos of natural language has been responsible. In formal signification, voice has no role to play. Indeed, mathematical logic has made impressive advances precisely because the murkiness of such features as implicit deixis has been excised by a process of desedimentation, a topic to be breached in Chapter 8. However, we cannot simply transfer formal expectations to the description of language without changing the object of inquiry into something it is not. Natural language without voice is *unnatural*. As the logician Alfred Tarski has cautioned, in taking a formal route we undermine what makes natural language *natural*.[68]

In his investigations of what makes language natural as "communicative speech," Husserl, well before John L. Austin, distinguished "the verbal act" (Austin's locution) from the "act of address (*Ansprache*)."[69] Part of *Ansprache* is tone, which Husserl regards as always already a "component of the word" or, "more precisely," of the expression as a whole.[70] Indeed, all utterances are in a way performative and, more to the point, without being uttered, locutions would not be locutions (Latin *loqui*, to speak). Furthermore, Husserl asks, "Are sentence tones apprehended via the *deviation* from a normal sentence tone?"[71] Which is precisely what the broad notion of implied deixis is attempting to capture. The greater the social complexity of a linguistic expression, the more forceful is the role that voice plays in the meaning event. And just as the manner in which linguistic expressions are uttered point the recipient in a certain interpretive direction with respect to aboutness, so too is the reconstruction of voice in written language a necessary rather than incidental linguistic feature. In natural language, voice is an indispensable form of *pointing* us in the appropriate direction of meaning fulfilment.

## Conclusion: Sentences Do Not Mean by Themselves

One of the aims of the chapter was to acknowledge Edmund Husserl as one of the pioneers of the theorization of linguistic deixis, as documented in his *Nachlass*. Having taken as our point of departure what Husserl had to say on the role of tone in language, a second aim was to place the notion of tone in the broader context of implicit deixis. As a carrier of implicit deixis, tone was found to be a constant of linguistic expressions. This has resulted in a number of conclusions. Explicit and implicit deixis were clearly distinguished from one another. Implicit deixis was shown to affect every single signifier of a linguistic expression, including syncategorematic terms. As such, implicit deixis was defined as the *modal shadow* of the propositional side of language. This was tested by way of a phenomenological description and eidetic distillation of the intentional acts that we typically perform when we utter and comprehend linguistic expressions. The chapter also drew a firm distinction between deixis and indexicality. Last, it was found that the very idea of unuttered sentences was untenable. Some further implications of these findings are as follows. (1) Sentence types have no more than *sentence potential*. (2) Sentence-tokens have meaning potential, yet they cannot mean without being uttered. (3) Only utterances can have meaning. (4) Utterances have meaning as a consequence of meaning fulfilment via the transformation of word sounds into merely directional *Bedeutung* (possible paraphrase) and *Sinn* (imaginable, mental material scenarios placing *Bedeutung* in a broader context). (5) Acts of intimation and introjection are needed to realize the potential of implicit deixis. (6) In utterance, aboutness is always modified by implicit deixis. (7) Voice modifies aboutness on a scale from acts of minimal qualification to its propositional inversion. (8) Literal meanings are utterance meanings.

The next chapter provides arguments against the idea of meaning identity in any comprehensive sense and for its more realist replacement by the concept of *meaning sufficiency*, which raises the question of what other constraints must be in place to guarantee linguistic communicability. The answer will draw on Husserl's notion of *Zumutung* (imposition; coercion), rephrased as *Abrichtung* and defined as inexorable, communal language drills from the cradle to the grave.

## Notes

1  Hua XX/2, p. 102.
2  Edmund Husserl, *Logical Investigations*, trans. J. N. Findlay (New York: Humanity Books), pp. 313f.
3  Hua XX/2, p. 102.
4  Ibid., p. 103.
5  Horst Ruthrof, "Implicit Deixis," *Language Sciences* 47 (2015), 107–16.
6  Zoltan Gendler Szabo, "The Distinction between Semantics and Pragmatics," in *The Handbook of Philosophy of Language*, ed. E. LePore and B. C. Smith (Oxford: Clarendon Press, 2006), pp. 361–89 (387).
7  Brendan S. Gillon, "Ambiguity, Indeterminacy, Deixis, and Vagueness," in *Semantics: A Reader*, ed. S. Davis and B. S. Gillon (Oxford: Oxford University Press, 2004), pp. 157–87 (183).
8  Hua XX/2, p. 114; my emphasis.
9  Hua XX/2, p. 103.

10  Donald Davidson, "What Metaphors Mean," in *On Metaphor*, ed. S. Sacks (Chicago: The University of Chicago Press, 1981), 29–45.
11  Husserl, *Logical Investigations*, pp. 744f., 590ff., 766.
12  Esp. Hua XX/2.
13  Hua XX/2, p. 102.
14  Aaron Gurwitch, "Outline of a Theory of Essentially Occasional Expressions," in *Readings on Edmund Husserl's Logical Investigations*, ed. N. J. Mohanty (The Hague: Martinus Nijhoff, 1977), pp. 112–27 (117).
15  Gurwitch, "Outline," pp. 118ff.; my emphasis.
16  Hua XX/2, p. 103.
17  Horst Ruthrof, "Recycling Locke: Meaning as Indirectly Public," *Philosophy Today* 57, 1 (2013), 23.
18  Michel Foucault, *The Archaeology of Knowledge*, trans. A. M. S. Smith (London: Tavistock, 1986), pp. 55ff.
19  Hua XX/2, pp. 102f.
20  Ibid., pp. 102, 104; my emphases.
21  Hua XX/2, p. 103.
22  Ibid., p. 106.
23  Cf. Hua XLI, p. 33.
24  Husserl, *Logical Investigations*, pp. 277f.
25  Hua XX/2, p. 456.
26  Hua XX/2, p. 371f.
27  Hua XX/2, p. 2.
28  Ibid., pp. 12f.
29  Ibid., pp. 28, 32.
30  Ibid., pp. 37f.
31  Ibid., pp. 65, 78.
32  Ibid., p. 102.
33  Ibid., pp. 102f.; my emphasis.
34  Ibid., p. 102.
35  Ibid.; my emphasis.
36  Cf. Gottlob Frege, "On Sense and Reference," in *Translations from the Philosophical Writings of Gottlob Frege*, ed. P. Geach and M. Black (Oxford: Basil Blackwell, 1970), pp. 56–78; see also Michael Dummett, *Frege: Philosophy of Language* (London: Duckworth, 1973), pp. 84ff.
37  Hua XX/2, pp. 102f.
38  Aone van Engelenhoven, "Deixis," in *The Cambridge Encyclopedia of the Language Sciences*, ed. P. C. Hogan (Cambridge: Cambridge University Press, 2010), pp. 247–8; Rochus Sowa, "Deiktische Ideationen," in *Meaning and Language: Phenomenological Perspectives*, ed. F. Mattens (Dordrecht: Springer, 2008), pp. 105–23.
39  Karl Bühler, *Sprachtheorie* (Stuttgart: Fischer, 1982 [1934]); *Theory of Language*, trans. T. F. Goodwin (Amsterdam: John Benjamins, 1990); Charles Fillmore, *Santa Cruz Lectures on Deixis* (Bloomington: Indiana University Linguistics Club, 1975); John Lyons, *Introduction to Theoretical Linguistics* (Cambridge: Cambridge University Press, 1968); *Linguistic Semantics: An Introduction* (Cambridge: Cambridge University Press, 1995); Roman Jakobson, *Selected Writings*, v. 2 (The Hague: Mouton, 1971); *Selected Writings*, v. 3 (The Hague: Mouton, 1981); Geoffrey Nunberg, "Indexicality and Deixis," *Linguistics and Philosophy* 16 (1993), 1–43; Paul H. Manning, "On Social

Deixis," *Anthropological Linguistics* 43, 1 (2001), 54–100; and Ellen Fricke, *Origo, Geste und Raum: Lokaldeixis im Deutschen* (Berlin: De Gruyter, 2007).

40  Charles Sanders Peirce, *Collected Papers of Charles Sanders Peirce*, vols. 1–8, ed. C. Hartshorne, P. Weiss, A. W. Burks (Cambridge, MA: Belknap Press, 1984 [CP]); *Writings of Charles S. Peirce: A Chronological Edition*, v. 2, 1867–1871 (Bloomington: Indiana University Press, 1984 [EP]).
41  Bühler, *Theory of Language*, pp. 103ff.
42  Ibid., pp. 149, 107.
43  Stephen C. Levinson, *Pragmatics* (Cambridge: Cambridge University Press, 1983), p. 54.
44  Fillmore, *Santa Cruz Lectures*.
45  Ibid., pp. 239, 271, 235.
46  Ibid., pp. 257, 295, 258.
47  William B. McGregor, *Linguistics: An Introduction* (London: Continuum, 2009), p. 145.
48  Asif Agha, "Schema and Superimposition in Spatial Deixis," *Anthropological Linguistics* 38, 4 (1996), 643–82 (643).
49  Fricke, *Origo, Geste und Raum*, p. 97.
50  Clemens-Peter Herbermann, *Modi Referentiae: Studien zum sprachlichen Bezug zur Wirklichkeit* (Heidelberg: Winter, 1988), pp. 55ff.
51  Manning, "On Social Deixis."
52  J. Lyons, *Linguistic Semantics: An Introduction* (Cambridge: Cambridge University Press), p. 307.
53  Fillmore, *Santa Cruz Lectures*, pp. 223, 230, 224.
54  Ibid., pp. 226, 223, 231; my emphasis.
55  Horst Ruthrof, "Metasemantics and Imaginability," *Language Sciences* 35 (2013), 20–31; cf. Ronald Langacker, *Foundations of Cognitive Grammar*, v. 1: Theoretical Linguistics (Stanford: Stanford University Press, 1999).
56  Stephen C. Levinson, "Deixis," in *Concise Encyclopedia of Philosophy of Language*, ed. P. Lamarque and R. E. Asher (Oxford: Pergamon, 1997), pp. 214–19 (215f.); cf. also Ruth Milikan, "The Myth of the Essential Indexical," *Noûs* 24 (1990): 723–34.
57  James Hurford, *The Origins of Meaning: Language in the Light of Evolution* (Oxford: Oxford University Press, 2007), p. 223n9; John Perry, "Using Indexicals," in *The Blackwell Guide to the Philosophy of Language*, ed. M. Devitt and R. Hanley (Oxford, Blackwell, 2006), pp. 314–34; Geoffrey Nunberg, "Indexicality and Deixis," *Linguistics and Philosophy* 16 (1993), 1–43; Stephen C. Levinson, "Deixis," in *The Handbook of Pragmatics*, ed. L. R. Horn and G. Ward (Oxford: Blackwell, 2004), pp. 97–121; Yehoshua Bar-Hillel, *Aspects of Language: Essays in Philosophy of Language, Linguistic Philosophy, and Methodology of Linguistics* (Amsterdam: North Holland, 1970); and "Indexical Expressions," *Mind* 63 (1954), 359–79; Quentin Smith, "The Multiple Uses of Indexicals," *Synthese* 78 (1989), 167–91.
58  Lyons, *Linguistic Semantics*, pp. 303f.; cf. also Christine Tanz, *Studies in the Acquisition of Deictic Terms* (Cambridge: Cambridge University Press, 1980), p. 1, who regards pointing as 'the prototype of an index.'
59  Peirce, CP 1, 158; EP 2.273.
60  Cf. Arthur Burks, "Icon, Index, and Symbol," *Philosophical and Phenomenological Research* 9 (1949), 673–89.
61  Hua XX/1, pp. 3, 31, 33, 38f., 41, 105, 129, 145f., 231; XX/2, pp. 2f., 8, 22, 105, 135, 135n2, 143, 151, 291f., 329, 336.

62  Yingchi Chu and Horst Ruthrof, "Cultural Obstacles to Political Dialogue in China," *Culture and Dialogue* 2, 2 (2012), 31–50.
63  Carol F. Feldman, "The Interaction of Sentence Characteristics and Mode of Presentation in Recall," *Language and Speech* 14, 1 (1971), 18–25 (23).
64  The deictic modification of syncategorematic terms finds strong support in Ann Sweetser, *From Etymology to Pragmatics: Metaphorical and Cultural Aspects of Semantic Structure* (Cambridge: Cambridge University Press, 1990).
65  Tanz, *Acquisition of Deictic Terms*, p. 1; my emphasis.
66  Bar-Hillel, "Indexical Expressions," 359–79 (359); cf. also his *Aspects of Language: Essays in Philosophy of Language, Linguistic Philosophy, and Methodology of Linguistics* (Amsterdam: North Holland, 1970).
67  Scott Soames, *Philosophy of Language* (Princeton: Princeton University Press, 2010), p. 4.
68  Alfred Tarski, *Logic, Semantics, Metamathematics*, trans. J. H. Woodger (Oxford: Clarendon Press, 1956), p. 267.
69  Hua XX/2, p. 455. Cf. Adolf Reinach's speech-act theory in "Zur Theorie des negativen Urteils," in *Münchener Philosophische Abhandlungen. Festschrift für Theodor Lipps*, ed. A. Pfänder (Leipzig: J. A. Barth, 1911), pp. 196–254 and K. Kevin Mulligan, *Speech Act and Sachverhalt: Reinach and the Foundations of Realist Phenomenology* (Dordrecht: Martin Nijhoff, 1987).
70  Hua XX/2, p. 102.
71  Ibid.; my emphasis.

# 6

# From Meaning Sufficiency to Communal Control

In light of Edmund Husserl's early interests in mathematics, especially calculus, the concept of number, and the philosophical foundations of arithmetic and geometry, it is not surprising that in his initial studies of natural language the notion of *meaning identity* looms large. In contrast, reading Husserl's *Nachlass*, especially the three volumes on intersubjectivity and two volumes on the revisions of *Logical Investigations*, which struggle with the complexities of sociality and natural language, meaning identity appears to be increasingly in conflict with the idea of semantic fuzziness and concessions to linguistic meaning as *approximation*. As a consequence, the overall picture of Husserl's analysis of natural language as a communicative sign system reveals a puzzling tension between merely verbal or logical comprehension (*Bedeutung*) as semantic essence, on the one hand, and, on the other, the epistemic essence of iconic, vividly imaginable (*anschauliche*) meaning fulfilment (*Sinn*). However, it is doubtful that either *Bedeutung* or *Sinn* can be identically determined. In the case of *Bedeutung* in natural language, identity is barred because it can be represented by verbal paraphrases of different length and kind. As to *Sinn*, its core characteristic of vividly imaginable *Anschauung* cannot be identical with either meaning intention or *Bedeutung* since the multimodal, intentional acts activated in meaning fulfilment can vary considerably in terms of degree of *saturation*. What can reasonably be claimed is that sameness of linguistic meaning is possible in the sense of a minimal, merely *numerical identity* shared by all three forms of linguistic intentionality, meaning intention, *Bedeutung*, and *Sinn*. Given this reduced claim, we need an additional concept to cover the remainder of ingredients that render meaning fulfilment both rich and realistic.

The kind of clarification offered by Husserl appears to have been sparked by his growing sympathy with *Anschauung* and *Anschaulichkeit*, conceived as vivid imaginability.[1] This shift from meaning identity to the idea of "a varying amount of intuitive fullness" was already hinted at in the *Logical Investigations*,[2] and later more fully explored as the merely *Ungefähre* and *Ähnliche*, the *more or less* and similarity, in actual meaning exchange.[3] To put this in perspective, the chapter opens with a broad-brush sketch of Husserl's commitment to meaning identity as it appears in his writings from the *Logical Investigations* to *Experience and Judgment*. The subsequent sections address the alternative concept of *semantic latitude* under the umbrella of *intersubjective sufficiency*, Husserl's *meaning approximation*, and linguistic meaning sufficiency in communication. The question of how linguistic communicability can nevertheless be assured will be answered via Husserl's idea of a continuous *coercion* imposed by the speech community on its members. For an appropriate characterization of this all-pervasive language drill I choose Wittgenstein's term *Abrichtung*.

## Husserl's Meaning Identity Revisited

Although Husserl never gave up on the idea of some form of meaning identity as a baseline of linguistic communication, in the *Nachlass* and his later writings the notion of semantic approximation in meaning fulfilment is gaining ground. Husserl must have felt that he had to do justice not only to what makes linguistic communication reliable but also to the semantic latitude demanded by the epistemic character of *Sinn*. Unfortunately, as we saw in the *Logical Investigations*, Husserl tends to back up his accent on meaning identity with formal examples, a strategy that does little to convince the reader that identity can be secured at all in natural language. Husserl initially speaks of the "self-identical meaning" in the correspondence between expressions and concepts.[4] With reference to geometrical objects, writes Husserl, they display "an identity in the strict sense," which in natural language reduces to the identity of the "object meant in the meaning" as an "experienced unity of sign [signifier] and signified." What allows identity to be conveyed by expressions mediating between meaning intention and meaning fulfilment is their "determinate direction to objects." In this way, "the *sense* of the sentence should remain *identical*."[5] But when Husserl insists on "the strict identity of what is meant," he regrettably once more exemplifies his assertion by retreating to a formal notion, "π."[6] Nonetheless, the idea of meaning identity can be defended in a non-formal way via Husserl's concept of exclusive directionality,[7] as in "This vase next to me, not that one over there." But then, meaning identity is reduced to our identical grasp of the mere fact of a "this-here" versus a "that-there" of the aboutness of an expression. The qualitative features of meaning fulfilment must then be left to the intentionality of a *more* or *less*, a merely approximate reconstruction of meaning intention.

For the early Husserl meaning identity is justified also from another angle, viewed as "ideal" or "rigid unities (*starre Einheiten*)."[8] Accordingly, meaning is generated in such a way that it functions as a *class* of universal objects or an *ideal species* under which the various necessary mental acts performed by speakers and hearers are particulars united to guarantee semantic identity.[9] Still in *Ideas*, Husserl's conviction of linguistic ideality is an "essence" conceived as "an ideal conceptual totality of possible particulars to which it can be related through a thought that is both eidetic and universal."[10] "The same holds," he writes, "of the other parts of our statements, even of such as do not have the form of propositions."[11] Thus did he close the all-important gap between language as *universal medium* and *calculus*,[12] between natural language semantics and his "pure morphology of significations (*reine Formenlehre der Bedeutungen*)." Yet again, his commitment to "transcendental phenomenological idealism" in relation to language is more easily demonstrated by recourse to geometrical figures and other formal notions than by such concepts as "responsibility," "caring," or "deceitful." What is intriguing in the later Husserl is his shift of emphasis towards *graded typifications*, a notion that qualifies ideality without however dissolving into private singularities.

Husserl's stipulation of meaning identity as a necessary feature of linguistic meaning has been strongly defended, as for example by Jitendra N. Mohanty in "Husserl's Thesis of the Ideality of Meaning." Mohanty opens his paper with an all or nothing contrast. Either we cater for identity of meaning as a triple requirement for (1) the retention of sameness of meaning in varying contexts, (2) sharability of meanings in communication, and (3) the repeatability of meaning by one and the same speaker in different speech acts and contexts or else we reduce meaning to *semantic privacy*.[13] "Identity, context-independence, intersubjective sharability and communicability" provide "reference to things, events, persons, places, and processes in the world." Meanings, though "incarnated in physical expressions," operate at the level of ideality. As Mohanty reads Husserl, linguistic sameness "needs the concept of ideality." For "only what is irreal can defy individuation by spatio-temporal location and can maintain identity in multiplicity."[14] In his more recent analysis of Husserl's *Vorlesungen über Bedeutungslehre*, Mohanty sums up the different notions of meaning that Husserl draws to our attention.[15] (1) The *meant* objectivity (not always the named object); (2) the meant objectivity precisely in the *manner* in which it is meant; (3) the fact that two categorical sentences may mean different *Sachverhalte*, while they denote the same *Sachlage*; they have different categorial relations, while denoting the same aboutness; and (4) the *phansische* concept of meaning versus the ontological or phenomenological concept of meaning, the former having its origin in the acts, the latter being the intentional object, as act dependent versus as such. "The word-sign may be perceived, remembered, or phantasized, it may be written on a piece of paper or may be heard, or quasi-heard. The empirical perception of words then is given." However, writes Mohanty, "the words are not the object of our 'interest.'"[16] It is consciousness of meaning that is the theme. In Husserl, the "word" functions as a "pointing indication (*deutender Weiser*)" from which "radiates a pointing ray of meaning" terminating in the *Sache*. Husserl here speaks of a fulfilling tendency "analogous to other tendencies, for example, the tendency of the will" by which meaning fulfilment occurs.[17] As early as in his *Lectures on Theory of Meaning* of 1908, Husserl had clarified what distinguishes empirical meaning, which is not an eidos, from essential meaning ideality, an investigation that was to result later in the distinction in *Ideas I* between *Bedeutung*, conceived as logical meaning, and *Sinn* as experiential meaning. Now, ideality, Husserl concedes, "is not an ideality in my original sense (with which I have confused it), that of *eidos*, of the essence as a 'generality.' Now Husserl separates general objects as meanings from objects as species." "I should add," he writes, "contrary to the first edition of the *Logical Investigations*," an "empirical meaning cannot be a pure essence,"[18] a distinction that is of the greatest importance for a phenomenological description of language.

In the *Nachlass*, the kind of meaning identity that *appears* in acts of meaning fulfilment is argued with increasing caution. "A certain (*gewisse*) identity is what is objective, which corresponds to the act of fulfilling or which as it were 'appears' in it."[19] The "*gewisse*" here is ambiguous, reflected likewise in the English "certain," allowing for a fuzzy kind of "identity" to be radicalized below under the concept of *meaning sufficiency*. Husserl now qualifies the formal rigidity of his earlier phrasing when he speaks of an "identifying congruence" that may be accomplished even in the absence of any "explicit intention" directed toward identity.[20] *Bedeutung*, though, remains "identical" in contrast with *Sinn*, where identity is undermined by nonidentical meaning components.[21] *Bedeutung* guarantees the "congruence (*Deckung*)" as the identity of judgments, that is, of what is said.[22] The word in its *Bedeutung* is "congruent with the thing as corresponding to the *Sinn*."[23] Meaning identity is preserved in the *Bedeutung* in the form of an "indicative tendency" (*Hinweistendenz*) toward "the thing meant."[24] In his later published writings, too, Husserl is still firmly committed to "the self-same intentional 'object'" that "separates itself off self-evidently from the shifting and changing 'predicates.'" There "the *central noematic phase*" becomes clearly visible as the "*object*," the "objective unity (*Objekt*)," the "*self-same*," the "determinable subject of its possible predicates—*the pure X in abstraction from all predicates*," which "disconnects itself *from* these predicates, or more accurately from the predicate noemata."[25] Whereas in *Logical Investigations*, identity was declared "wholly indefinable,"[26] in *Experience and Judgment*, Husserl offers a definitive description. "Instead of being determined by the fleeting and variable moment," identity is characterized by an "absolute" and "ideal unity" in modes of "repetition or assimilation." As such, identity "goes through all the individual objects and their multiform moments" as a "unity which is not at all a function of the actuality of the moments; it does not come into being and disappear with them, and, though it is individualized in them, it is not in them as a part." Identity has the character of a universal as a "counterpart" of the "individual."[27] In this way, Husserl distinguishes the thing from its "subjective modes of appearing," which serves as the basis for our acts of constituting the object noematically as "self-identical."[28] Likewise, as a result of categorial alternatives, as in *Formal and Transcendental Logic* where Husserl speaks of the "identity of the thematic object throughout changes in *syntactical* operations." Husserl here neatly separates the numerical identity of a thematized object from its possible categorial formulations. "*In its essence the objective focusing, which is at all times an integral part of the judging itself*, is such that the judging makes these *identifications throughout changes of the judgment-modes* in which 'the same' presents itself as differently formed."[29]

In all this, what distinguishes *Bedeutung* and *Sinn* sharply is that in the latter, meaning intention and comprehending meaning endowment combine exclusive directionality with nonidentical, vividly imaginable "saturation."[30] As to meaning fulfilment in *Sinn*, Husserl allows for "approximation" in the cognitive target.[31] It is "vivid *Vorstellung*" that contributes to epistemic realization in such a way that it "grants what is conceptualized fulfilment in *Anschauung* according to matter and form."[32] But although we "transition from *Vorstellung* to ever new *Vorstellungen*, from confused to distinct ones," we yet "retain meaning identity" in the face of forever "renewed substitution."[33] We will have to see what exactly can be retained when the acts of Husserl's *Bedeutung* are "cashed out" by those of *Sinn*.[34] According to Johannes Balle, the former preserves the "identity of the (referential) object intentions," while the latter adds "contextual variations of the (attributive) property dependent content."[35] Another commentator on the *Nachlass*, Rochus Sowa, suggests that Husserl's meaning identity functions as a basis for two kinds of meaning, the meaning of a thing or its moments in principle and meaning as experiential, specializing grasp.[36] Certainly in the latter, as Dieter Lohmar points out, neither Husserl's "parallelism" of thought and speech nor his "picture-analogical parallelism" can produce identity proper.[37] Two meaning forces then interact in Husserl's theory of natural language, meaning identity secured in *Bedeutung* as exclusive directionality that constrains the intentionality of meaning fulfilment in *Sinn*, on the one hand, and, on the other, vividly imaginable features that *saturate* the constraining frame of the minimal comprehension granted by *Bedeutung*. However, there remains the nagging question how *Bedeutung* can provide even a minimal sense if no nonverbal mental material is at all permitted in its semantic activation, a query the deliberation of which must be postponed for the moment. Suffice it here to conclude that the overall conception of linguistic meaning is not well characterized by the notion of meaning identity. A weaker thesis will have to be entertained.

## From Leibniz to Husserl

Contrary to formal systems where reason is assured and so "can be found by analysis," in systems of contingent relations, writes Leibniz, "a sufficient reason" has to be substituted "for the sequence or connexion of things which are dispersed throughout the universe of created beings, in which the analyzing into particular reasons might go on into endless detail." This is so because of his presupposition that "everything in nature proceeds ad infinitum." Leibniz calls the kind of knowledge we can gain about matters contingent at best "adequate," on condition that we have provided at least "some *satisfactory* or sufficient reason." Leibniz thus distinguishes between two kinds of reasoning, one that yields necessary truth resulting from full definitional control; the other, contingent reasoning, which deals with "truths of fact." While the first kind of reason, "determining reason" (a concept resumed by Kant) or analytical reason is unproblematic in the sense that all we need to do is to follow the rules of calculus, reasoning about the "immense variety of things in nature and the infinite division of bodies" poses a more serious challenge. Here, definitional certitude is replaced by the realization of the fact of the irrevocable *underdetermination* of phenomena, which logically would require infinite analysis. Since humans are incapable of infinite reasoning, Leibniz stipulates that "there must be some satisfactory or *sufficient reason*" that would allow us to "complete" our reasoning when we are satisfied that adequate comprehension has been accomplished. *Sufficient reason* steps in "where a perfect reason is not to be found."[38] Leaving aside his ambiguous genuflection to God as the master calculator and ultimate endpoint of all reasoning, the pivotal point here is that Leibniz has introduced into philosophy a *pragmatic* procedure that is guided less by the laws of logic than by negotiation and consensus, that is, what works in actual human discourse. As such, the Leibnizian concept of sufficient reason suggests a plausible solution to the conceptual strains that have become visible in Husserl's theorization of *linguistic meaning identity*. I suggest that it is more congenial to follow the avenue offered by Leibniz and view language through the lens of *sufficiency*. Which, in light of the previous chapters, would mean to analyze natural language under the heading of intersubjective sufficiency as a necessary condition of linguistic communication.

Such a move appears to find support in *The Crisis of European Sciences and Transcendental Phenomenology*, where Husserl himself resumes the Leibizian gesture by attempting to solve the problem of the sufficiency of contingent reasoning by non-formal *idealization* such that "idealizing thinking conquers the infinity of the experiential world." The so "idealized world, then, is an ideal infinity of things." Just as Leibniz bridges the chasm between formal perfection and the imperfect contingency of the world, Husserl's "infinity of imperfection" of perceptual reality is healed by the gradual idealization of the "properties of things" toward their ideal "identifiability."[39] Toward the end of his career, Husserl had finally found a way of freeing himself from the strict concept of meaning identity argued throughout the *Logical Investigations* and in much of his other published work. However, Husserl's refinement of his thinking in this respect is announced as early as in his *Nachlass* where we find indications that the notion of meaning identity was giving way to a conception of linguistic meaning more conducive to what makes language *natural*.

## Husserl's "More or Less"

In his introduction to *Meaning and Language: Phenomenological Perspectives*, Filip Mattens reiterates Husserl's semantic identity thesis to the effect that "the concrete linguistic expression of our thoughts can only be secondary to what remains identical over against a multiplicity of acts."[40] Yet whether the idea of meaning identity in natural language still holds as firmly in his later publications and the *Nachlass* as Mattens suggests is a moot point. After all, Husserl here added a number of qualifications to his earlier account in the *Logical Investigations* that allow for a more *proximate* conception of linguistic meaning as *Sinn*. Meaning is now beginning to look *sufficiently similar* rather than identical. Certainly, all of Husserl's versions of identity must be carefully reviewed in light of his remarks on "modes of similarity" that divide into "total" or "pure similarity" and "partial similarity." While identity is uniform, Husserl's modes of similarity exhibit "gradation."[41] Which of the two, then, identity or similarity, should hold sway in the conception of linguistic meaning? As I will argue, identity in any strict sense is not demonstrable either in Husserl's transitional *Bedeutung*, understood as symbolic, logical, or verbal substitution, or less so in *Sinn*, taken as meaning fulfilment that places word meanings in imaginable contexts. As to *Sinn*, because "the subject plays the key role of inhabiting the sign" and animates "both its pointing and meaning functions,"[42] meaning identity in any strict sense is not plausible, except in its reduced numerical form: the "this-here" rather than the "that-there." As to *Bedeutung*, whatever our intentional acts entertain as verbal alternative varies according to the kind and size of the internalized *lexicon*. *Sinn* as meaning fulfilment is unlikely ever to be identical, relying as it must on acts of recollection, imaginable aboutness, the interpretation of voice, and the degree of communal coercion. There is much material in the *Nachlass* in support of the idea that linguistic meaning events are more appropriately described in terms of graded similarity and approximation than via semantic essence and identity. If so, and in order to remain within the Husserlian project of language as communication, we will have to answer the question of how, without the security of meaning identity, linguistic communicability can be guaranteed. I will return to this problematic in the last section of this chapter under the heading of communal coercion as *Abrichtung*. So, what is Husserl's alternative route to the description of linguistic meaning intentionality that we can glean from the *Nachlass*?

Husserl now speaks of "habitual speech (*Sprachüblichkeit*)" that draws our attention to the communal ground and all-important social dimension of language.[43] This feature tends to be undermined in phenomenological parlance, where individual acts, one the one hand, and, on the other, linguistic expressions take center stage and so threaten a certain degree of reification of the object of inquiry. Epistemically, our description of the linguistic meaning acts is of course the primary phenomenological target. But when we ask the question of the condition of its possibility, then, as Husserl has made clear, we arrive of necessity at the ontological basis of the speech community of *Miteinandersein, Ineinandersein*, and *Füreinandersein* as the ground of language.[44] Against this fundamental background we find observations that indicate that the Husserl of the *Nachlass* is qualifying his commitment to strict meaning identity. Certainly, we can no longer say that "the meaning lies in the definition."[45] After all, we cannot understand either the defined word or its verbal substitution *without* at least minimal acts of nonverbal intentionality. Even the most minimal requirement of directionality is not thinkable without acts of imaginability. As if to confirm this observation, Husserl firmly places imaginable aboutness *before* its categorial representation: "the mental presentation of the lion (*die Löwenvorstellung*) in this connection with the word is itself the *Bedeutung*."[46] In short, without the *Vorstellung* of a lion, in whatever schematized form, there is neither *Bedeutung* nor *Sinn*. We would have neither directionality nor meaning saturation (*Sättigung*).

Husserl clarifies the difference between *Bedeutung* and *Sinn* as follows. As a "transitional experience," he writes, the "act of empty meaning by way of a directional intention finds its fulfilment in the picturing (*veranschaulichenden*) act." What is "merely thought" in the "symbolic act" is "made intuitively present" in the "*Anschauung*." Husserl now allows for a certain slippage between the *Bedeutung* as symbolic displacement or "empty meaning intention and its *more or less* corresponding intuition (*Anschauung*)."[47] *Bedeutung* and meaning fulfilment (*Sinn*) are now not only "temporally stretched apart," they can no longer be viewed as exhibiting congruence, as *in-Deckung-Sein*. Husserl's method of act description results in a "stretching" of the links in the meaning chain at the end of which full semantic congruence is unlikely. What remains objective in the meaning process is no more than "a certain (*gewisse*) identity," which "as it were 'appears'" in *Sinn*.[48] One of the main reasons Husserl provides for these distinctions between *Bedeutung* and *Sinn* is that the latter more than the former involves memory. While *Bedeutung* can be "*identical*," meaning fulfilment, which is bound to draw on recollection, cannot[49] (XX/2, 41ff.). Though meaning intention, *Bedeutung*, and meaning fulfilment are still about the *same objectivity*, instead of identity we now have the *more or less* of intersubjective sufficiency.

Another concept in support of this reading of Husserl is "adequation,"[50] by which he characterizes the meaning chain from meaning intention and expression to mere

*Bedeutung* (*signikativ*; symbolic, logical, or merely verbal) and "*Erfülltsein*." If meaning intention agrees with the *Anschauung* in fulfilment, Husserl says that the object as it appears therein is given the character "*des Erkannten*," of what has been recognized. As such, "signification and intuition" are forged into an "*Erfüllungseinheit*," a unity of fulfilment displaying a peculiar correlate "toward what it is 'directed.'"[51] But even in such a case, writes Husserl, "identifying congruence" may have been achieved by the interpreter of the expression.[52] Meaning identity, congruence, and correlate are of course not the same things. Also, meaning fulfilment does not rule out the possibility of "inadequate *Anschauung*,"[53] allowing for communicative failure. So, Husserl's "unity of congruence" (*Deckungseinheit*) can be accommodated charitably under the idea of sufficiency in the sense that in meaning fulfilment, "the intentional essence of the act of *Anschauung*" appears to "conform, *more or less perfectly*," to "the meaning essence of the expressing act."[54] Meaning fulfilment understood as "intuitive saturation (*intuitive Sättigung*),"[55] or "*Anschauungssinn*"[56] then, always already involves a shift, not the least because linguistic expressions and imaginative saturation belong to two different semiotic domains, the nonverbal *within* the verbal as mental material content. There is reasonable evidence, then, in Husserl's *Nachlass* and later writings that natural language typically functions within the constraints of intersubjective sufficiency, the hallmark of the social as *negotiation*.

## Intersubjective Sufficiency

In contrast to the assumption of meaning identity between meaning intention, *Bedeutung*, and *Sinn*, in living discourse we typically observe *intersubjective sufficiency*, with its emphasis on what satisfies communication at least minimally within flexible boundaries, admitting a certain degree of semantic latitude. Barring formal expectations, we notice that meaning events do occur and do so within pragmatic parameters. The constraints under which natural language utterances operate are much looser than formal ones, warranting a less preemptive but by no means less rigorous approach in analysis. The concept of intersubjective sufficiency assists, for example, in accounting for Locke's principle of "agreement in the signification of common words, within some tolerable *latitude*."[57] It also shores up the claim that an a posteriori procedure, such as a phenomenological description of our acts of comprehending utterances, proves an appropriate path for checking the monitoring mechanisms that are in place in a language. The explanatory contribution that an approach via intersubjective sufficiency can make is to tell us when linguistic comprehension has occurred; when clarification is needed; when a conversation should be continued as promising, or terminated as fruitless; when a certain tone of voice, topic, and vocabulary are warranted; and when silence is the preferable option.

So how does this constraint do its job at the various levels of speech? At the *phonological* level, the limits of pronunciation vary not only among idiolects, as to region, social, class, and gender, but also historically. Even within each idiolect at any specific time there is no such thing as an ideal pronunciation or sentence intonation. No formal notion of identity of sound sequences adequately reflects empirical linguistic performance. Rather, a certain *bandwidth* of sounds allows comprehension, outside of which what is said tends to be unrecognizable, that is, if speech participants cannot perform the *linguistic linkage compulsion*, the way native speakers are trained to link sounds and meanings. The bandwidth analogy makes the point that empirically we are dealing with an extended range of possible pronunciations rather than with any kind of identity. Which, however, is not to say that Husserl's notion of the informal ideality of the word as guarantor of sameness among an empirical *multiplicity* should be discarded. For it allows us to retain an umbrella notion covering instances of *approximate* sameness. At the level of the lexicon, sufficient intersubjectivity operates as a regulating mechanism, roughly governing the semantic scope of words in their manifold available categorial combinations within a network of permissible differential relations. In meaning fulfilment, intersubjective sufficiency also regulates the kinds, quantity, and degree of schematization of nonverbal, mental materials that are appropriate in specific speech situations. Intersubjective sufficiency curtails pragmatic scope, conceptual overlap, and pragmatic meaning satisfaction. Other such sufficient controls include *syntactic constraints*, and what counts as sufficiently grammatical versus elliptic and outright ungrammatical performance. The notion of sufficiency highlights the fact that actual utterance exchange in natural language tolerates all kinds of ungrammaticality before communication breaks down. The sufficiency rule also allows us to identify limits to *recursivity* in idiomatic utterances and constraints on *embedding*, that is, pragmatic boundaries how many subclauses we are able to process without losing touch with the basic sentence structure. Much the same can be observed about *predicability*, or what can be predicated about phenomena in various discursive domains. Tigers cannot be said to enjoy litigation, except in poetic discourse where linguistic rule-breaking is appropriate. At the broader level of linguistic communication, intersubjective sufficiency can be regarded as a social principle that regulates such things as meaning negotiation, clarification, objections, and Gricean presuppositions, implicatures, and maxims, and includes the appropriateness of communicative styles and the limitations imposed by the indispensable *reciprocity* of standpoints. As such, the concept of sufficiency sums up the social boundaries within which habitual discourse takes place at camera-shutter speed.

However, having let go of the formally inspired concept of meaning identity leaves us with the task of explaining what makes linguistic communicability function at all and does so efficiently. The answer is to be sought in yet another communal phenomenon of language, tentatively theorized in Husserl's notes under such terms as *Zumutung* (imposition) and *Sollenstendenz* (tendency of the "ought"). I shall sum up Husserl's concepts under the heading of Wittgenstein's notion of *Abrichtung*, understood here as the strictest form of language training and language drills.[58]

## Husserl's Coercion as *Abrichtung*

Long before Wittgenstein introduced the term *Abrichtung* for the coercion involved in language acquisition to analytical philosophy, Deleuze and Guattari characterized language as a system of "order words,"[59] and Jean-Jacques Lecercle wrote of the "violence of language,"⁶⁰ Husserl had already thematized the compulsion tendency inherent in linguistic expressions. In his *Nachlass*, he speaks of the word as an "imposition (*Zumutung*)," of the "ought" of habitual speech (*sprachüblich*), of a certain "coercion," and the "*Sollenstendenz* (the tendency of an 'ought')," and the "generally prescribed manner" by which linguistic communication is controlled.⁶¹ At first blush, it would seem then that Husserl's *Zumutung* and Wittgenstein's *Abrichtung* are very much coextensive terms. What makes Wittgenstein's choice of the German term *Abrichtung* appealing are its connotations of the strictest possible alignment of intentional acts in the minds of the members of a speech community. Yet ironically, his externalist analysis prevents him from exploring this side of the concept. So, from a phenomenological perspective, Wittgenstein's concept of *Abrichtung* needs to be redefined. What is of key importance for us here is that *Abrichtung* cannot merely refer to the observables of vocabulary, pronunciation, intonation, and word order in written and spoken discourse, in short to observable language games, but must likewise include the kind of linguistic intentionality speakers of a language are bound to perform as part of meaning as *use*. Which amounts to nothing less than a radical revision of Wittgenstein's *linguistic externalism*, a topic dealt with elsewhere.⁶²

In the wake of Deleuze and Guattari's conception of language as a form of oppression, Lecercle pursues the idea of language as a powerful potential for violence, as material violence in its use of voice, as a source of pain, in facilitating aggression in the confrontation of addresser and addressee, in its capacity of insinuation and threat, and as a linguistic form of the enforcement even of "truth."⁶³ Rather than adding to these arguments, the task here is to ask what it is *in* language that lends plausibility to such interpretations. What we experience as language, writes Filip Mattens in the Introduction to his collection *Meaning and Language*, is "the unnoted merging of signs and signification in the form of meaningful expressions" as a "unity of physical sign-appearances and meaning-intentions."⁶⁴ As mentioned, neurolinguists are now in agreement with Husserl that the assumed simultaneity of word sound consciousness and word meaning consciousness is an illusion. The linguistic meaning event takes time.⁶⁵ Phenomenological analysis has demonstrated this fact via "introspection" defined as "inner perception" or "the perception of intentional experience."⁶⁶ But why should the minimal time lag between word sound consciousness and meaning fulfilment play a role in linguistic coercion? As our analysis of sample expressions in Chapter 4 showed, their production and comprehension are anchored in social coercion as an elementary constraint that affects all acts of the meaning chain from meaning intention to meaning fulfilment. Whenever we read a newspaper or view its electronic version on a screen we undergo a kind of refresher drill of what sort of mental states of affairs to evoke on the cue of sign appearances. As early as the *Logical Investigations*, had Husserl been able to ascertain that the meaning process must be a temporal sequence, typically resulting in a "gradual increase in fullness" from *Bedeutung* to *Sinn*.⁶⁷ But how is this possible at camera-shutter speed? How is it that on the word sound of "democracy" members of a speech community conjure up *in a flash* an abbreviated notion that acts as umbrella covering sufficient details that make up the concept? Husserl and Wittgenstein, in spite of some fundamental differences, share the answer that we have been *drilled* that way. Our performance is circumscribed by a social *ought* realized as an imposition on our speech conduct. Even though different speakers will opt for a different selection of mental materials as to size and content, the roughly shared understanding of the term "democracy" does not appear to be endangered, which supports the idea of meaning events satisfying the principle of intersubjective sufficiency as a result of *Abrichtung*.

The concept of Husserl's imposition (*Zumutung*) invites us to address briefly a tendency in phenomenological accounts to foreground language itself as a kind of agent. In the volume by Mattens of responses to Husserl's *Nachlass* on language, Dave Koukal asks, "Why is there no meaning-intention in 'abcaderaf'?"[68] In light of the origin of Husserl's *Sollenstendenz* (tendency of an "ought"), the answer should be: because we have not been "drilled" (*abgerichtet*) to endow the expression with a meaning. It is entirely possible that "abcaderaf" could acquire a *Bedeutung* as well as a *Sinn* should the speech community decide to provide the sound of this combination of letters with instructions for a verbal sense and an associated imaginable state of affairs. In other words, the distinction between what counts as a vehicle for meaning intention and meaning fulfilment is not a matter of language itself but rather a matter of what the speech community deems to belong to the language system. So far, however, that particular sequence of letters has not been bequeathed a social, discursive, and communicative purpose. Less, at least in habitual speech, can we speak of the subjectivity of meaning endowment. As Koukal points out, "with an indication there is no subjective intention that *bestows* meaning."[69] In habitual speech, individual meaning instantiation is rule following via communal *Abrichtung*, the drill function of language pedagogy. Nor should we say, as does Rudolf Bernet, that to bestow a meaning "is the result of a voluntary decision." While such voluntary decisions do occur, they are no more than a minute portion of the bulk of language use.[70] And while we can agree with Mattens in his observation that "a phenomenologist needs to know 'what the word wants from him" (*was das Wort von ihm will*),[71] to know such a thing is not primarily so much a personal demand as a social condition of meaning. It is not that language wants something from us, but rather that we need to know how to satisfy the expectations of the speech community reflected in language. I make this perhaps pedantic point to shift our phenomenological analysis away from the relation between language and an individual speaker and toward its social dimension as its foundation. Indeed, Mattens does acknowledge this social emphasis when he writes that "a concept cannot be passively assimilated—it is only through *practice* that a word acquires its true tone."[72]

But what exactly is being *drilled* into each speaker of a language? The answer that we can develop out of Husserl's schematization of the meaning process looks as simple as it is fundamental: our capacity to link the sounds of expressions with communally agreed-upon *Vorstellungen* schematized according to need. Two claims made early in the book coincide here: (1) the imaginability thesis: if I can imagine what you are talking about, and in the manner that you do, there is meaning. If not, not; and (2) linguistic expressions carry social coercion as *Abrichtung*, of which the linguistic linkage compulsion is a critical component.[73] Speakers of a language combine word sound and meaning under the gun of *Abrichtung*, as it were, and the resulting linguistic linkage compulsion. That is to say, at the split-second event of comprehending an expression,

Reinach's "punctual act of meaning,"[74] lasting about 250 ms for short expressions,[75] speakers are not able to replace their habitual meaning-acts by any alternative, private ones. At the moment of immediate grasp, we simply cannot *imagine* a red chair in response to the expression "green table." Such is the social force of the linguistic linkage compulsion that makes us associate word sounds and imaginable scenarios.[76] If this is so, then meanings cannot be either public in Putnam's sense or merely private, as in Locke,[77] but must be *indirectly public*.[78]

## *Abrichtung*, Word Sound Consciousness, and Semantic Ascent

We can imagine the written form of a word, yet it only becomes a word in the full sense if we imagine it as a word sound. Unpronounced terms like "brief-case" and "brief case" are not linguistic signs. It is only their different word sounds that makes them so. Vandervelde's notion of instantiation as "hearability" is a crucial component of natural language, a fact that tends to be forgotten in a world of screen literacy.[79] Following Husserl's schema from word sound to meaning fulfilment, we are trained (*abgerichtet*) to have word sound consciousness (*Wortlautbewusstsein*) within a socially acceptable range as an act of recognition in a system of differential sound relations. As Husserl writes, "we have word sound consciousness in connection with empty or full meaning consciousness,"[80] whereby "*Wortlautbewusstsein*" is no more than a merely "transitional consciousness" (*Durchgangsbewusstsein*).[81] The next stage can be seen as *insufficient Abrichtung* when the word sound is experienced with a merely vague semantic directionality, as in words that are more or less similar in meaning to other word sounds. *Sufficient Abrichtung* would be the stage where the child masters both near synonymy with other word sounds as well as meaning fulfilment via imaginable scenarios, the recognition of "this is what is being talked about."[82] In this context, it is instructive to look at cases where the transition to Husserl's merely symbolic grasp and, further on to imaginable meaning fulfilment, fails. Two exemplary cases are available to us in the literature.

One is that of the American deaf-mute Helen Keller who, after years of unsuccessful tutoring by Anne Sullivan, was one day able to make the leap from word sound consciousness to meaning fulfilment as decisive intentional act. Sullivan records that she was holding Helen's hand under a water spout, pumping water over her hand, while continuously repeating the word sound "water." Suddenly, Helen, who was reading Sullivan's utterances by touching her tutor's throat, realized in a flash of cognition how language functioned as communication. Contrary to standard explanations, a phenomenological reading of this situation will focus on the intentional acts that had to occur in this situation, as a combination of the sensation of water, the action of her tutor, and the word sounds she had recognized so far as mere sounds. It is the totality of the perceptual, embodied, recollected, and social acts as a combination of verbal and nonverbal intentionality that solved the riddle of linguistic meaning for Helen.[83]

A similarly intriguing case is that of Donna Williams who, in her book *Nobody Nowhere: The Extraordinary Autobiography of an Autistic* (1992), recalls the moment when, again after many years of mere word sound consciousness, she suddenly realized what language was all about. Until she was almost four years old, Donna grasped and used language only at the level of word sound and syntax, repeating the utterances of others verbatim. Though she was regularly punished for her flawed linguistic performance, semantic ascent proved out of reach. The turning point occurred when from glances and whispers of adults and other children in the living room she suddenly realized that they were talking about her, apparently confirming that Donna was still wetting herself. The acute sense of embarrassment Donna felt at that moment apparently catapulted her into the cognition of the purpose of language, the linking of verbal sounds and nonverbal phenomena. As in the case of Helen Keller, the onset of meaning consciousness coincided with embodied recognition of word sounds as having aboutness. Together with aboutness, in Donna's case, is the recognition of voice transforming mere aboutness into shame, which testifies to the thesis that in natural language aboutness is never alone. In fact, it is her reading of communal, implicit deixis that triggered cognition.[84] In both cases, personal handicap had delayed the ontogenetic nexus of word sound consciousness and word meaning consciousness until communal coercion finally achieved its social purpose and integrated both Helen and Donna fully into the speech community.

## Linguistic Meaning as Indirectly Public

Beyond the significance for their personal lives and our understanding of the process of language acquisition, the cases of Helen Keller and Donna Williams also draw our attention to the unpopular fact that language is neither private nor purely public. As our phenomenological act description reveals, language partakes at the same time of individual and social intentionality. The concept of linguistic meaning as *indirectly public* addresses the seeming contradiction inherent in the simultaneity of individual instantiation of linguistic expressions and public discourse.[85] The paradox that is threatening here is the apparent irreconcilability of an inevitable *mentalism* involved in the description of the intentional acts that speakers have to perform, one the one hand, and, on the other, an *externalism* that would restrict itself to the characterization of language as a system of observable phenomena. This incongruity is also sometimes referred to as Locke's paradox, as an inability to reconcile semantic privacy with discourse at large. The idea of linguistic meanings as *indirectly public* intentionality is meant to overcome this impasse. What our phenomenological approach has shown is that linguistic meanings are indirectly public in the sense that the acts that we must perform in the displacement of meaning intentions into symbolic signifiers and their retransformation into *Sinn* cannot be accomplished by mere external manipulation. And yet this very process cannot be called private either since it only functions within a system of rules imposed on speakers and monitored by the speech community. Two things are needed to facilitate a resolution: one is to show that language is itself an eidetic system within which subjective meaning intentions can be systemically absorbed and, two, that *Abrichtung* works as social constraint on individual meaning instantiations.[86] Members of a speech community can thus be described as individuals who have been drilled to *sufficient uniformity* in responding to word sounds in their categorial constellation by acts of standardized meaning fulfilment. In habitual speech, at least, individual meaning constitution as a connection of word sounds and their semantic activation via appropriate intentional acts is thus typically corralled by *Abrichtung* into a communal performance.

## Conclusion: Language as Communicative Sufficiency

Having replaced Husserl's mathematically inspired idea of meaning identity by the weaker thesis of intersubjective sufficiency, the chapter addressed the question whether it is possible to account for the fact of linguistic communicability in a less rigid manner. The trigger for investigating a more flexible notion of meaning as socially negotiable was the puzzling tension between Husserl's merely verbal or logical *Bedeutung* and his vividly imaginable *Sinn*, a tension that renders meaning identity implausible as a global explanation. Instead, the chapter argued intersubjective sufficiency as a more appropriate principle underlying communication via natural language, with a nod to Leibniz's concept of sufficient reason. This move was buttressed by the observation of a shift in Husserl's *Nachlass* from the demand of identical meaning acts toward the "more or less" of meaning approximation. The remainder of the chapter dealt with Husserl's pioneering recognition of the *coercive* ingredients in linguistic expressions, a theme that was explored in terms of a revised form of Wittgenstein's *Abrichtung*, as a strict version of language pedagogy. The speech community, the chapter concluded, uses *Abrichtung* to ensure communicability by instilling its linguistic standards in its members and monitor every aspect of their meaning instantiations from the cradle to the grave. These standards were shown to cover the way in which speakers of a language typically employ the phonetic, syntactic, and semantic features of language, and foremost the manner in which they associate words sounds with imaginable scenarios, a point presented under the concept of the *linguistic linkage compulsion*.

Gathering up the principles argued so far, the following chapter addresses the way the mental material content of *Sinn* is formed in the performance of meaning fulfilment. The aimed at result is a redefinition of linguistic meaning from a Husserlian, phenomenological standpoint.

## Notes

1. Hua XX/1, pp. 3, 4n3, 31, 38f., 41, 44, 105, 231f.; XX/2, pp. 2f., 7, 143, 151, 191, 298.
2. Edmund Husserl, *Logical Investigations*, trans. J. N. Findlay (New York: Humanity Books, 2000), p. 745.
3. Hua XLI, pp. 71ff., 109ff.; XX/1, p. 38.
4. Husserl, *Logical Investigations*, p. 227.
5. Ibid., pp. 282f., 285, 290; my emphasis on *sense*.
6. Ibid., p. 329.
7. Ibid., p. 282.
8. Ibid., p. 149.

9   Ibid., p. 284; e.g., "quadratic remainder."
10  Husserl, *Ideas: General Introduction to Pure Phenomenology*, trans. W.R. Boyce Gibson (London: George Allen and Unwin, 1969), p. 73.
11  Husserl, *Logical Investigations*, p. 286.
12  Cf. Martin Kusch, *Language as Calculus and Universal Medium* (Dordrecht: Kluwer, 1989).
13  Jitendra N. Mohanty, "Husserl's Thesis of the Ideality of Meaning," in *Readings on Husserl's Logical Investigations* (The Hague: Martinus Nijhoff, 1977), pp. 76-82.
14  Ibid., pp. 76ff.; cf. Dorion Cairns, "The Ideality of Verbal Expressions," *Philosophy and Phenomenological Research* 1 (1941), 453-62.
15  Jitendra N. Mohanty, "On Husserl's 'Lectures on Theory of Meaning (1908),'" in *The Philosophy of Edmund Husserl* (New Haven: Yale University Press, 2008), pp. 224-41 (227f.).
16  Ibid., pp. 225f., 227f.
17  Hua XXVI, p. 24.
18  Hua XXVI, p. 217n1.
19  Hua XX/1, pp. 40f.
20  Ibid., p. 43.
21  Hua XX/2, pp. 41ff.
22  Ibid., p. 43.
23  Ibid., p. 146.
24  Ibid., p. 153.
25  Husserl, *Ideas*, pp. 365f.
26  Husserl, *Logical Investigations*, p. 343.
27  Edmund Husserl, *Experience and Judgment: Investigations in a Genealogy of Logic*, trans J. S. Churchill and K. Ameriks (Evanston: Northwestern University Press, 1997), pp. 324f., 327.
28  Ibid., p. 375.
29  Edmund Husserl, *Formal and Transcendental Logic*, trans. Dorion Cairns (The Hague: Martinus Nijhoff, 1969), p. 113.
30  Hua XX/2, p. 136.
31  Ibid., p. 139.
32  Ibid., p. 292.
33  Ibid., pp. 340, 345, 356.
34  Ibid., p. 137.
35  Johannes D. Balle, "Husserl's typisierende Apperzeption und die Phänomenologie der dynamischen Intentionalität," in *Meaning and Language: Phenomenological Perspectives*, ed. F. Mattens (Dordrecht: Springer, 2008), pp. 89-104 (89).
36  Rochus Sowa, "Deiktische Ideationen: Ueber die mit den Wörtern 'dies' und 'so' vollziehbaren okkasionellen Bezugnahmen auf ideale Gegenständlichkeiten," in *Meaning and Language*, pp. 105-23 (108); cf. Hua XIX/1, p. 114.
37  Dieter Lohmar, "Denken ohne Sprache?" in *Meaning and Language*, pp. 169-94 (173); cf. Hua XIX/1, p. 18; Hua XIX/2, pp. 658f.
38  Gottfried Wilhelm Leibniz, *Leibniz: The Monadology and Other Philosophical Writings*, trans. L. Latta (Oxford: Oxford University Press, 1968 [1714]), pp. 62, 235ff., 414.
39  Husserl, *Crisis*, pp. 346, 347, 348n1.
40  Mattens (ed.), *Meaning and Language*, p. xvii.
41  Husserl, *Experience and Judgment*, p. 193.

42  Dave R. Koukal, "The Necessity of Communicating: Phenomenological Insights—And Its Difficulties," in *Meaning and Language*, pp. 257–79, 274f. However, as I argue throughout, linguistic instantiation by subjects is never merely subjective but always intersubjectively overdetermined.
43  Hua XX/1, p. 83.
44  Hua XIII, XIV, XV, *passim*.
45  Hua XX/1, p. 231.
46  Ibid., pp. 231f.
47  Ibid, p. 38.
48  Ibid., pp. 40f.
49  Hua XX/2, pp. 41ff.
50  Hua XLI, pp. 37f.; cf. Lohmar, "Denken ohne Sprache?" p. 173.
51  Hua XX/1, pp. 40f.
52  Ibid., p. 43.
53  Hua XX/2, p. 2; also, as inadequate "ideation," Hua LXI, pp. 37f.
54  Hua XX/1, pp. 44, 38; my emphasis.
55  Ibid., p. 67.
56  Husserl, *Ideas*, p. 370.
57  John Locke, *An Essay Concerning Human Understanding*, ed. J. W. Yolton (London: Dent, 1993), p. 288.
58  For a delineation of '*Abrichtung*' see Ludwig Wittgenstein, *Philosophical Investigations*, trans. G. E. M. Anscombe, P. M. S. Hacker, and J. Schulte (Oxford: Blackwell, 2009), §§ 5, 86, 129, 146, 151f., 189, 320.
59  On "order words," see Gilles Deleuze and Felix Guattari, *A Thousand Plateaus: Capitalism and Schizophrenia*, trans. B. Massumi (Minneapolis: Minnesota University Press, 1987), pp. 76ff.
60  Jean-Jacques Lecercle, *The Violence of Language* (London and New York: Routledge, 1990), esp. pp. 224ff.
61  Hua XX/2, pp. 57, 74f., 75, 104, 170.
62  Horst Ruthrof, "Shutter-Speed Meaning, Normativity, and Wittgenstein's *Abrichtung*," *Linguistic and Philosophical Investigations* 13 (2014), 33–54.
63  Lecercle, *The Violence of Language*, pp. 224ff.
64  Mattens, "Introduction," in *Meaning and Language*, p. xiif.
65  Friedemann Pulvermüller, Yuri Shtyrov, and Olaf Hauk, "Understanding in an Instant: Neurophysiological Evidence for Mechanistic Language Circuits in the Brain," *Brain and Language* 110, 2 (2009), 81–94 (81).
66  Husserl, *Logical Investigations*, p. 412.
67  Ibid., p. 726.
68  Koukal, "The Necessity of Communicating: Phenomenological Insights—And Its Difficulties," pp. 257–79 (265n2); cf. also Roman Ingarden's foregrounding of language compared to the role of the speech community in his otherwise pathbreaking investigations on literature.
69  Ibid., p. 274.
70  Ibid., p. 274n3.
71  Filip Mattens, "Introducing Terms: Philosophical Vocabulary, Neologisms and the Temporal Aspects of Meaning," in *Meaning and Language*, pp. 281–326, 323.
72  Ibid.; my emphasis.
73  Horst Ruthrof, "Recycling Locke: Meaning as Indirectly Public," *Philosophy Today* 57, 1 (2013), 3–27 (23); "Shutter-Speed Meaning, Normativity, and Wittgenstein's *Abrichtung*," *Linguistic and Philosophical Investigations* 13 (2014), 33–54.

74 Adolf Reinach, "Zur Theorie des negativen Urteils," in *Sämtliche Werke*, v. 1, ed. K. Schumann and B. Smith (Munich: Philosophia, 1989), 95–140 (103); cf. Kevin Mulligan, *Speech Act and Sachverhalt: Reinach and the Foundations of Realist Phenomenology* (Dordrecht: Martin Nijhoff, 1987).
75 Pulvermüller, Shtyrov, and Hauk, "Understanding in an Instant," p. 81.
76 Ruthrof, "Recycling Locke: Linguistic Meaning as Indirectly Public," p. 23.
77 Hilary Putnam, "The Meaning of 'Meaning'," in *Mind, Language, and Reality: Philosophical Papers*, v. 2 (Cambridge: Cambridge University Press, 1997), pp. 215–71; Locke, *An Essay Concerning Human Understanding*.
78 Ruthrof, "Recycling Locke: Linguistic Meaning as Indirectly Public," pp. 3–27.
79 Vandervelde, "An Unpleasant but Felicitous Ambiguity," in *Meaning and Language*, pp. 27–48 (39).
80 Hua XX/2, p. 177.
81 Ibid., p. 207.
82 Cf. Lev S. Vygotsky, *The Collected Works of L.S. Vygotsky*, v. 1, *Problems of General Psychology*, ed. R. W. Rieber and A. S. Carton (New York and London: Plenum Press, 1987); this is when the "imagined" apple becomes more relevant than the actual one; p. 63; cf. Chapter 10.
83 Horst Ruthrof, *The Body in Language* (London: Cassell, 2000), pp. 61–6.
84 Ibid., pp. 80f.
85 Ruthrof, "Recycling Locke: Linguistic Meaning as Indirectly Public," pp. 3–27.
86 For arguments in favor of language as a fuzzy eidetic system, see Chapter 3.

# 7

# A Phenomenological Redefinition of Linguistic Meaning

Language is the world in absentia. This is a conclusion we are forced to draw when we analyze our intentional acts performed in the engagement with a wide range of linguistic expressions. They show that the bulk of speech events is not about what is immediately before us but what is spatially and often also temporally distant. "Imagine an angler on a riverbank"; "Did you enjoy the party last night?" "How is your sister in the UK?" "What a surprising election result"; "Bring me four blue slabs from the shed behind the house"; "A cold front has been predicted for tomorrow"; and so on. What such examples demonstrate is that the "modality of intentionality"[1] addressing what is before us comprises only a minute portion of the totality of intentional acts we are bound to conduct in the utterance and comprehension of linguistic expressions. Which demands a reversal of standard forms of exemplification: the application of language to perceptual particularities turns out to be no more than a special case of general language practice. *Apophantic*, that is, declarative sentences about perceptual states of affairs, cannot be claimed to be the privileged starting point for the theorization of language. Externalist theories tend to play down this qualification, whereas phenomenological accounts are well placed to explore the inevitable, intentional role that imaginability (*Vorstellbarkeit*) plays in the bulk of language.[2] Less obviously, but no less crucially, are acts of imaginability indispensable in bestowing meaning on observation expressions. Without being *imaginable*, even in the process of perception, Husserl's *Worüber* (aboutness) simply does not occur.[3]

In light of the centrality of *imaginable aboutness*, this chapter addresses the key question how precisely, in a phenomenological account, language conveys world, present or absent. Because this chapter concludes the first two parts of the book, a very brief recapitulation may assist in preparing the reader for a summary redefinition of linguistic meaning. We recall that Husserl had rejected the option that *linguistic aboutness* can be realized by way of mental images.[4] In their place, Husserl adopted Kant's idea that "it is schemata, not images of objects, which underlie our pure sensible concepts."[5] However, having retreated from images to schematization, Husserl's later emphasis on vivid imaginability (*Anschaulichkeit*) creates a tension with his early meaning grasp "without illustrative intuition."[6] In the *Nachlass*, this option rightly reduces to a mere boundary: now "pure *Anschauung* and pure empty intention" are viewed by Husserl as "limit cases" of cognition such that "the empty consciousness

(*Leerbewusstsein*) is superseded by what is imaginable (*anschaulich*)."[7] In contrast with *Leerintention* (mere *Bedeutung*), what exactly is meant by "*anschauliche Vorstellung*?"[8] And how does *Vorstellung* function *in* language?

Husserl thought that meaning acts differ from other intentional acts, functioning as they do at a more abstract level. Acts of perceiving, judging, and wishing all involve meaning-endowing acts; so, meaning endowment is the broader concept specified by those other acts. What is it that distinguishes them? When I perceive I intend a quasi-sensuous something, when I judge I intend a predicatively organized state of affairs, and when I wish I intend as desirable a state of affairs that does not exist. In what way is the general notion of meaning endowment different? It subsumes all those other acts, embedding them in salient contexts. As to linguistic meanings, Husserl offers us the complex, theoretical scenario of a substantially enlarged chain of relations containing such things as meaning intention, expressions, word sound consciousness, word consciousness, word meaning consciousness, verbal or logical *Bedeutung* as empty intention, and its transformation into vividly imaginable *Sinn* as meaning saturation. As to *Bedeutung*, "I grasp the words and live in meaning consciousness (*ich erfasse die Worte und lebe in dem Bedeutungsbewusstsein*)."[9] While Husserl's *Bedeutung* is reminiscent of Frege's sense as pure thought determining reference, Husserl's *Sinn* takes cognizance of the role of imaginability via a *polythetic* description of intentional acts from meaning intention to *meaning fulfilment*, which presupposes "meaning-conferring acts" making up "the innermost core of intimation."[10] As our analyses of samples of expressions in Chapter 4 showed, meaning fulfilment is possible if, and only if, we are able to entertain such acts in the form of *imaginable* states of affairs in response to word sounds and their categorial syntagms. We do so within the parameters of the speech community, which suggests the validity of some sort of socially guided *semantics of imaginability*. We concluded from the evidence that every single linguistic expression entails, in the strictest possible sense, a *social dimension*. All of which commits us methodologically to the notion of *intersubjective intentionality* within the broader boundaries of an *intermonadic mentalism*, inviting the following hypothesis.

Meaning is a communal, cognitive, indirectly public event generated in the process of meaning fulfilment as an effect of individual instantiations of language by members of a speech community. Meaning fulfilment consists in the transformation of linguistic expressions into lexical and categorial aboutness, modified by voice, as the consequence of an association of arbitrary signifiers with *motivated signifieds*, the latter made up of intentional, mental materials regulated by concepts, under the control of the speech community, in terms of *directionality, quantity, quality, and degree of schematization*. The remainder of the chapter addresses the major components we require in trying to render this hypothesis plausible.

## Typifications: The Quanta of Experience and Basis of Concepts

By stipulating his epoché, especially with regard to the necessary bracketing of theoretical presuppositions, Husserl was able to avoid a number of ontological commitments: the collapse of linguistic meaning into definitional sense as pure thought and the elimination of intentionality,[11] the presuppositions of the primacy of syntax, a brain-language organ, a specialized language faculty with a *universal grammar* as its initial state, an innateness thesis,[12] the language of thought hypothesis threatening infinite computational regress,[13] all of which undermine the *Anschaulichkeit* of *Sinn* with respect to olfactory, thermal, gustatory, gravitational, and emotional features. Yet, if quasi-nonverbal content is observed in our act description as constitutional as a necessary component of the act of meaning intention as well as central to our acts of meaning fulfilment, we must answer the question of how imaginable content combines with linguistic expressions in a Husserlian account?

Husserl's answer is via *typification*, a principle that was turned to seminal use in Alfred Schütz's sociology. With equal justification, typification can be employed in a phenomenological account of natural language. So, what is typification and what role can the concept play in the study of language? First, some broad-brush distinctions. Typification is best described in contrast with *generalization*, on the one hand, and, on the other, with *idealization*. While typification is a largely nonconscious process whereby higher animals and humans economize experience by reducing percepts to their most prominent features, generalization is primarily a conscious process of abstraction by which we can distill a skeletal configuration from a multitude of common and similar features of objects such that we arrive at a set of universal aspects. By far the largest number of generalized material objects are thus recognizable by way of *empirical concepts*. In contrast, idealization is characterized by the absence of spatiotemporal orientation, even though it never quite gives up its determinate mental material content. Idealization is best understood as a process of abstraction toward a concept that subsumes aspects of members of a series such that, for example, Kant's series of succession, simultaneity, and duration together form the ideality of time in human cognition. Contrary to typifications as economizing recipes for storing experience and empirical generalization as hierarchical subsumption, idealization belongs to a more abstract plane of reasoning. In Husserl, idealization is typically illustrated by examples drawn from the formal domain, foremost from geometry, which unfortunately represents only exact essences, rather than general ideality. Perhaps the latter can be described as a stipulated meaning without which empirical concepts are not thinkable as a subsumed multiplicity. In order to account for the systemic *vagueness* at the heart of linguistic expressions, most likely inherited from the phenomenal regress of mental materials of percepts, an explication via Husserl's typification suggests itself as the most congenial path.

According to Husserl, the *type* as typification appears to be the result of a passive synthesis, by which we transform percepts into raw concepts. Raw concepts need to be distinguished from linguistically refined concepts, only the former of which appear to be shared with higher animals as recipes for survival. As Johannes Balle notes, Husserl's typifications should be viewed as a way of dealing with *Objekt-Vorstellungen* (object realizations) as part of his genetic theory of concepts.[14] As such, the type would be a *pre-predicative* component of cognition whereby our typifying apperception renders an object imaginable, that is, *anschaulich*, but does so in an abbreviated, *schematized* form.[15] Viewed from the vantage point of typified experience, Husserl's strong accent on *Anschauung*, as I have argued, deserves a more prominent role in the meaning process than has been granted so far.[16] At the same time, a theory of linguistic meaning that foregrounds imaginability in this way will have to come to grips with how language *schematizes* Husserlian typified experience in a *graded manner*.[17] Typifications can now be viewed as a storehouse of mental material content available for recall at different levels of abstraction and varying degrees of schematization. And if, as argued, it is the speech community that monitors the way linguistic sounds and meanings are combined via the linguistic linkage compulsion, then we have a mechanism for the community-sanctioned way we reconstruct meaning intentions in acts of meaning fulfilment, Husserl's *Sinn*.

Typifications schematized to varying degrees according to discursive needs, then, look like serious candidates for transforming arbitrary linguistic signifiers into motivated signifieds conveying imaginable content. The idea of degrees of schematization would also allow for the graded specification of the generality that stamps all expressions. As already emphasized, in Husserl, expressions are through and through general. Likewise, proper names.[18] Schematized types, then, are well suited to meet the demand of linguistic generality. However, unlike the linguistic concept, the type does not yet have a "strict generality."[19] A more precise regulation of the concept is better conceived as a social rule acting as a frame for typified content. Certainly, Husserl's pre-predicative type invites valuable insights into the dynamics of the overall phenomenon (*Gesamtphänomen*), allowing as it does for both fine-grain changes at the level of property dependent content (as for instance perceptual differences with respect to the same object) in Husserl's "typifying apperception" and the simultaneous rigidity of the directionality of the object intention. The type, then, structures my expectations of a spatial-temporal object and facilitates its cognition as something determined, without the additional precision imposed by linguistic conceptuality. As such, the type can be regarded as a *Vorform*, a preform, of concepts.[20] Importantly, the pre-predicative and dynamic experiential type displays strong *resemblance relations*. And because every perception leads to the evolution of an object type, according to which similar objects are perceived, Husserl's type can be said to mediate communally aligned similarities. So, we can say that the type is characterized by relations of likeness and functions of associations.[21] However, unlike linguistic concepts, it is likely that the way the type mediates preconceptual grasp occurs by aligning characteristics of objects in an *open* manner, Husserl's *Erfahrungsoffenheit*. And because Husserl's intentional, perceptual contents do not presuppose concepts in any strong sense after 1920, we can say with Balle that *the type is on the way toward the concept*.[22] What we should add to Balle's reading of Husserl is the imperative qualification that the sedimentation of such quasi-perceptual contents always occurs under *social* guidance. Instead of saying as that "individual typifications" are not yet "intersubjective,"[23] the typifying human conducts intentional acts under social control from the very beginning. Methodologically viewed, we should be wary of turning typifying acts into an ontological commitment to individualistic type formation. Instead, it makes sense to say that vague mental iconic contents can be sedimented as experiential recipes only by becoming intersubjectively regulated, first nonverbally and later by linguistic concepts. Nevertheless, as Balle rightly highlights, experiential openness (*Erfahrungsoffenheit*) remains an essential feature of the phenomenology of the type, a feature that goes well with the idea of its flexibility.[24] If we can show that typifications are employed by speakers of a language in the activation of expressions as linguistic schemata, then the flexibility of the type has proved itself to be crucial for its role in the linguistic concept; it must be malleable to suit different discursive contexts.

Long before George Lakoff, Mark Johnson, Guy Fauconnier, and Mark Turner championed the ideas of neural concepts, mental spaces, mapping and schemas, as well as their role in *conceptual blending* as components of the linguistic meaning process,[25] Alfred Schütz had introduced Husserl's typification not only as a general concept for his elaboration of the social lifeworld but also as a specific feature of language. It is with Husserl and Schütz then that our investigation should begin, while at the same time acknowledging the inspiration they both drew from Kant's schematism.[26] Typification does its work as a central concept in Schütz's social phenomenology, a development of Husserl's "regional ontology" of the "*systematische Ontologie sozialer Gegebenheiten*," "intentional sociology," and "collective intentionality."[27] As such, typification occupies a special niche in Schütz's conception of sign systems in which individual signs, in agreement with Husserl, have the double function of referring back to "an act of choice on the part of a rational being," its expressive function and its indicating function of pointing to objectivities.[28] At the same time, sign systems are viewed by Schütz as simultaneously *expressive* and *interpretive* schemes of our experience that always operate within a "meaning-context," a concept he subdivides into six aspects: (1) the "for me" context; (2) the coordinating scheme of the sign: its use as *signum* and *signatum*; (3) as "expressive action"; (4) as "communicative act"; (5) a higher-order "perlocutionary" context; and (6) the historicity of the here and now and *manner* of a communicative act.[29] Schütz's summary is pertinent to the claim of the primacy of utterance. At the same time, Schütz shores up the distinction, to be addressed in Chapter 8, between language and formal sign systems.[30]

In contrast with the Husserl of the *Logical Investigations*, the Schützian meaning-context does not require meaning identity, but only "approximation." After all, our "knowledge of another person's perspective is always necessarily limited." Vice versa, "the person who expresses himself in signs is never quite sure of how he is being understood."[31] Meanings are related to one another as *typified*. At the same time, as Schütz and Luckmann argue, "type-constitution, as well as type-structure, is in principle conceivable *without language*." This is so because "the structure of language presupposes typification but not vice versa," an assertion bolstered by the observation that "typifying schemata can also be positively demonstrated in children who do not yet talk." This leads the authors to the general definition of language as a "system of typifying schemata of experience," employing "idealizations and anonymizations of immediate subjective experience," facilitating eidetic grasp. Such typifications of experience are detached from subjectivity and so are "socially objectified."[32] As a result, "by far the largest province of life-worldly typifications is linguistically objectivated" and "the subjective stock of knowledge of the individual" is always already "socialized in this society and language."[33] Here, the authors rehearse Husserl's notions of language as one of the "objectivities of a higher order," as unifying "social acts" as a means of consolidating a unified "supra-personal consciousness (*Einheit des überpersonalen*

*Bewusstseins)*" and as an "overarching communal consciousness (*übergreifendes Gemeinschaftsbewusstsein*)."[34]

In the *Nachlass*, the typical is not a highest possible abstraction to full dematerialization, which would be empty, but rather a package of generalizations from a series of phenomena sharing a generalized, common aboutness.[35] Accordingly, the word sound "democracy" produces typified *Vorstellungen*, schematized to appropriate degrees. But how is it possible that the word sound of "democracy" in a *flash* conjures up in the mind of a member of an English-speaking community an abbreviated notion that acts as umbrella covering many of those details? The simple answer is that we have been drilled that way, the result of *Abrichtung* and the linguistic linkage compulsion. Nor is the same collection of aspects assembled in each act of comprehension. Different speakers will activate different selections, without endangering the roughly shared understanding of the term. Which, once more, suggests the looser principles of the fuzzy eidos and *sufficient intersubjectivity*, a conception that satisfies Husserl's meaning endowment as a "special form of cognition" via "fluid type concepts (*fliessende Typenbegriffe*)."[36] We must not forget, however, to whatever degree we schematize typified mental material content and whatever its fluidity, the main task of typifications is the conveyance of resemblance relations.

## Resemblance

Throughout his career, Husserl's investigations of language were concerned with the question of how language communicates resemblance relations. Relegating identical transfer of resemblance to the formal domain, Husserl's position in his *Nachlass* is persuasive in that linguistic resemblance is viewed in terms of *approximation* and degrees of similarity, that is, Aristotle's *homoiomata*. We have seen how in *displacement* conceived as the symbolic transformation of perceptual reality and its imaginative variants into conventional linguistic signifiers direct, iconic resemblance is jettisoned. We have also seen how this loss is compensated for in meaning fulfilment, Husserl's *Sinn*, where the *symbolicity* of verbal signs is retransformed into imaginable, quasi-perceptual scenarios. The *reversal* of linguistic displacement manifests itself as a replacement of verbal intentionality by nonverbal, mental material intentionality. In this transformation, language, according to Husserl, should be no more than a "faithful" (*treuer*) conveyor of imaginable situations. And while it is the case that such "faithfulness" is part of normativity and so cannot be taken as a logical necessity,[37] what is pertinent is not the logically cogent but intentional, iconic relationship between the *Vorstellungen* of speech partners and how language can serve as a channel for the communication of resemblance. As Husserl remarks, "in its *Sinn*, the word is congruent with the thing as *equivalent* to its *Sinn*" (*das Wort in seinem Sinn deckt sich mit der Sache als Sinn entsprechende*).[38] Again, it is important to recall that Husserl does not privilege perception over imaginability, because "essence can be given without existence" (*Essenz kann ohne Existenz gegeben sein*),[39] and essence is all that matters in resemblance relations. But what sort of similarity is meant here? Husserl speaks of "equivalence" rather than identity as in "pure *Bedeutung*."[40] It would seem that

Husserl's idea of a "picture-analogical parallelism"[41] would best fit the meaning bill, as long as this metaphor is taken to comprise the entire spectrum of nonverbal modalities from olfactory and gustatory to gravitational and emotional communicability. How, we must ask, does language carry this parallelism across from meaning intention to meaning fulfilment? So far, as a result of our phenomenological description of the acts that we cannot but perform in engaging with language, we have specified three linguistic features that are suitable for the task and present in every linguistic expression: what it is *about*, how it is *organized*, and how it is *presented*. Three different kinds of intentional acts must be performed then to secure the linguistic conveyance of resemblance relations: acts of *aboutness*, *categorial relations*, and *voice*.

## Aboutness

Aboutness as Husserl's *Worüber*, that is, "what is posited as aboutness,"[42] can be described as a schematized, mental iconic projection of a portion of the actual or an imagined world. As such, aboutness is neither material nor ideal but rather an intentional objectivity posited under community rules. We can distinguish at least five different kinds of acts under the heading of linguistic aboutness: (1) perceptual intentionality, as in "Here is the control tower, right in front of us"; (2) realistically imaginable intentionality, as in "I need a blue slab from the shed"; (3) realist constructive intentionality, as for example from instructions in a plan, "cover with 200 g/m² woven glass, five staggered layers diminishing from 600x600[mm] to 200x200[mm]"; (4) recollective intentionality, as in "The statues on Easter Island were quite an experience, weren't they?"; and (5) pure intentionality, as in fiction, "How do you imagine Kafka's beetle in his *Metamorphosis*?"

In addition to differentiating various kinds of intentionality, our act descriptions also force us to come to terms with linguistic resemblance as aboutness by acknowledging the deep-seated, *heterosemiotic* nature of language. In the process of meaning endowment, verbal schemata can be shown to be animated by intentional acts that draw on heteronomous nonverbal sign systems, each of which with its own semiotic homogeneity. One and the same objectivity can be realized in terms of visual, tactile, olfactory, and other forms of signification. Useful observations in this respect can be found in what Dorion Cairns has to say about empirical types. He points us to the "homogeneity" we cannot but construe from the "tactile manners of givenness found in the noemata of all tactile perceivings of various things." Yet no matter how a thing is given, its form appears to us "as the one identical shape." When a nonverbal phenomenon is "intersensually" constituted, our *common sense* reconciles the different semiotic sign systems such that we experience a unified phenomenon. Cairns speaks of "prephantomic worlds," a "visual world, a tactile, an auditory, etc. posited alongside each other, not unrelated." So, the structure of the "tone-world" differs radically from the "visual world." To make these worlds commensurate, we perform "inter-sensuous syntheses," thereby reducing "the schematic world" in such a way that "I have bracketed the intersensuous organism-phantom along with others."[43] In this context, we should also address the genetic question of the origins of intersensuous acts. It would seem that the heterosemiotic character of language can be traced to the discrepancies between sound waves (aural readings), pressure (tactile, gravitational readings), molecules (gustatory, olfactory readings), thermal energy (noticing changes in temperature), and photons (visual readings), all of which are absorbed and reconciled in the fuzzy, eidetic generality of language. Thus, the intersensuous syntheses inherited by language as typified content appear to us as *coherent aboutness*. Which suggests once more that language can be regarded as an economizing matrix superimposed over prelinguistic grasp, a topic to be resumed in Chapter 9.

## Categorial Relations

What of resemblance then at the level of categorial relations? Here, Husserl tells us that different languages use different categorial constellations of "logical equivalence" to achieve the adequacy of their expressions in relation to *Anschauung*.[44] As precursors of linguistic syntax such constellations carry resemblance relations as a reflection of how things relate to one another in "situations of affairs (*Sachlagen*)" and "states of affairs (*Sachverhalt*)." As Husserl writes in the *Nachlass*, "In the linguistic expression we do not just have a situation of affairs (*Sachlage*) but a determined categorial formulation, and the state of affairs (*Sachverhalt*) presented in this formulation is meant and exactly in this formulation."[45] To clarify, "a>b = b<a" represent the same *Sachlage* (a is the larger of the two entities), but they display a different *Sachverhalt* (how they relate to one another as viewed from each position). A popular joke nicely exploits this distinction. To the optimist, the glass is half full; from the perspective of the pessimist it is half empty; while to the engineer the glass is twice as big as it needs to be. One and the same *Sachlage* produces three different *Sachverhalte* when viewed from three, different perspectives. More to the point here, both *Sachlage* and *Sachverhalt* have to be *imagined* as a necessary condition of their verbal and formal representations of *resemblance*.

When they are so imagined, *Sachlage* and *Sachverhalt* reveal Husserl's pre-predicative core forms of substantivity and adjectivity, of which nouns and adjectives are linguistic consequences. Aboutness likewise emerges from adverbiality and such categorial relations as *proto-predication*, "when-then" and "if-then" patterns, relations of contrast, negation, and other proto-syntactic combinations. Suffice it here to highlight the remark by Dorion Cairns that "the far more important type of conceptualization is, of course, that which is founded on a syntactical act." As our responses to abbreviated utterances like "Taxi" for "The taxi is here" or "Stop, I need a taxi" illustrate, "such conceptualizations may, in addition to being general—as are all conceptualizations—be incomplete, in that they may not be founded in all the partial theses of the syntactical substratum."[46] The point is that categorial relations in language, inherited most likely from nonverbal precursors, as well as resulting from linguistic refinement, can be regarded as nonlexical vehicles of resemblance as similarity in patterns of relations. In Chapter 9, I will have occasion to return speculatively to the way syntax reflects perceptual, proto-syntactic relations. Suffice it here to mention also that Husserl's elaboration of categorial relations has an antecedent in Peirce's concept of *hypoiconicity* as a transformation of general *iconicity* into schematized, diagrammatical representation.[47] For Peirce, all reasoning is diagrammatic, that is, containing mappable resemblance relations. A third way in which resemblance appears in linguistic expressions is via voice, the manner in which linguistic expressions are presented.

## Voice

As discussed in detail in Chapter 5, intentional acts of voice or implicit deixis are an indispensable, and much underrated, component of the linguistic meaning process. As argued, aboutness never appears except as always already modified by voice. But how can one say that voice, Husserl's "tone (*Ton*),"[48] likewise conveys resemblance? In sum, our acts of reconstructing the appropriate tone of expressions are approximations to the tone in which the expression was conceived in meaning intention. Such reconstructions, at camera-shutter speed in habitual speech, are always in the first instance resemblance relations of utterance intentions. In meaning fulfilment as Husserlian *Sinn*, the reconstituted tone is vital for an adequate comprehension of a speaker's illocutionary purpose. As illustrated by our sample in Chapter 4, "Nicely done," the customer is letting the waiter know by her tone that she is displeased with his clumsiness. Two things warrant separation in this case. First there is the speech intention, John Langshaw Austin's illocution, of disapproval expressed by the verbal irony of the use of "nicely" and, second, there is the sarcastic tone in which the irony is delivered, which introduces vital tonal gradations. The discrepancy between verbal aboutness and perceived situation is sufficient to indicate the ironic use of language but insufficient in conveying the *degree* of annoyance. This is where tone fulfils a critical *semantic* (rather than merely pragmatic) function.

John Searle's indirect speech-act theory is useful here, except that irony cannot be restricted to a mere reversal of propositional content.[49] The implicit deixis of irony delivers a multi-rayed openness of possible contraries, such as an imputation of negligence, disrespect, incompetence, lack of attention, and so on. The sarcastic component of implicit deixis here suggests displeasure, exasperation, irritation, and so on, on the part of the customer. This indicates that we cannot limit language to the polarity of a neutral or literal intonation and its ironic counterpart. Instead of a binary set of contraries, irony opens the spectrum to an indefinite number of possible tonal modifications of aboutness. Without the reconstruction of resemblance relations between speech attitude as part of meaning intention and the intentionality of *Sinn*, linguistic communication would founder in a very large number of cases. If our acts of semantic uptake fail to take account of Husserl's "contemptuous tone," "lively tone," or "icy tone," for example, appropriate and adequate meaning fulfilment will fail even if lexical aboutness and categorial relations have been sufficiently realized.[50]

In terms of resemblance relations, voice should be regarded then as an integral part of the meaning process rather than a mere pragmatic attachment. After all, the manner of presentation is the primary feature we recognize in conversation. To be sure, voice is a secondary construction in reading, but therefore no less important. What is carried across by voice from meaning intention to meaning fulfilment are socially agreed-upon instructions for how to take a series of words as to their aboutness and categorial constellation. In successful linguistic communication, the resemblance between meaning intention and meaning fulfilment therefore is decisively determined by appropriate acts of reconstructing the phenomena of voice. As such, voice as implicit deixis identifies the manner of speaking and comprehending linguistic expressions by which the members of a speech community are able to modify meanings to fine-grain nuances. That the elimination of voice from semantics has been dictated by formal presuppositions about natural language should be sufficient reason for considering its reincorporation in a more encompassing theorization of linguistic meaning.

## Aspects of Linguistic Meaning

According to Vandervelde, Husserl's four parameters of linguistic meaning can be summed up as follows: (1) meaning as performance of an act (*meinen*); (2) what is meant, "which is publicly available and borrowable"; (3) meaning (*Bedeutung*) as "the expressible meaning, which can be cashed out in a *Sinn*"; and (4) "the *Sinn* as the implicit sense, which can be explicitly formulated and expressed in a *Bedeutung*."[51] In light of our discussion so far, we are compelled to add a fifth parameter to Vandervelde's summary, a meta-parameter that must be regarded as a condition without which (1)–(4) would not be possible. (5) We must add the speech community, which does not merely function as the necessary external frame within which language has evolved and continues as its social horizon but at the same time reveals itself as a set of *implicit communal instructions* in language. These instructions appear to the phenomenological gaze as rules for pronunciation and prosodic contours, as well as a control mechanism of imaginability, that is, instructions for the sort of intentional, mental material clusters of contingencies we are meant to entertain in standard responses to the sounds of linguistic expressions.

In the kind of dynamic, communally guided, mental scenario semantics that is emerging from our phenomenological inquiry, the continuum of the *displaced* world reappears in the categorial combination of typifications as the quanta of linguistic content. As is the case in Husserlian apperception, where every content is permanently transformed, typified linguistic content is likewise continuously overwritten and modified. As argued above, language has absorbed not only the dynamic dialectic of sensuous experience of individual objects and experiential openness (*Erfahrungsoffenheit*)[52] but also its multiplication in imaginability. In light of recent neurological findings, the *Vorstellungswelt* is bound to be a radical multiplier of the *Wahrnehmungswelt*, a relationship that is likely to reveal itself as yet another inheritance in language from its nonverbal precursors.[53] How then is language able to cope with experiential openness and the much larger open horizon of human imaginability that it has absorbed from apperception and nonverbal communication? The linguistic expression, viewed as a sequence of arbitrary signifiers, typically points the member of a speech community toward the path of standard meaning fulfilment. But on its own, this indicative function, Husserl's *Hinweisfunktion*, cannot meet the demand of the necessary combination of *content*, typified *Vorstellung*, and the boundaries of semantic scope. The motivated signified, as the linguistic equivalent of Husserl's *Sinn*, needs to be recognized as consisting of two components: mental material *content* and *conceptual* regulation; the former conveying the richness of linguistic communication, the latter its social instructions. The literature on the "concept" tends to conflate these two radically different notions.[54] Yet, without the former, language would be empty; without the latter it would be blind. The double character of the motivated signified as a unity of intentional materiality and communally regulated conceptual regulation help in avoiding two theoretical traps. One is the gradual demise of the signified at the expense of the signifier in structuralist linguistics and its postmodern successors, with the undesirable consequence of the arbitrary signifier now having to carry *semantic load*. The other trap is the forgetting whence the regulatory concept draws its content. Instead, the motivated signified homogenizes quasi-perceptual content grounded in imaginability and conceptual delimiting regulation as its social dimension.

Against this background, the motivated signified, Husserl's *Sinn*, can be shown to be constituted by the following four intentional acts: (1) *directionality*, subsuming *categorial relations*; (2) the *quantity* of aboutness; (3) the *quality* of aboutness and voice; and (4) the *degree of schematization* to which mental materiality needs to be abstracted in meaning fulfilment according to the requirements of the speech situation.

## Directionality

In his early theorization of linguistic expressions, Husserl defined the function of a "word-presentation" above all as "to guide our interest *exclusively*" in a determinate "*direction*," to "the thing meant in the sense-giving act."[55] Husserl's exclusive directionality refers to the "this-there," not those other things but to "the individual as this-determined." Later, in the *Nachlass*, Husserl speaks of "the act of the determinately directed indication" (*Hinweisung*) as the "direct intention" and primary, "indicated *Bedeutung*."[56] The exclusive directionality of the expression determines our "direction of gaze (*Blickrichtung*)"[57] such that our *Vorstellung* is entirely focused on an intentional object or categorial relation at the expense of all other possible objectivities and states of affairs. Husserl's conviction in this respect has been vindicated in the sense that verbal, exclusive directionality appears to be the only way one can successfully assert a certain version of linguistic *meaning identification*.

However, as a consequence of directionality, meaning identity can only ever be *numerical identity*, a this-here, not a that-there. This is so because all our other acts that make up meaning fulfilment, the quantity of mental materials, their quality, and the degree to which they are schematized in each case of vivid comprehension can neither be predetermined nor reconstructed with equal rigor. Apart from the conveyability in language of intentional exclusive directionality, specified by categorial relations, all other acts that constitute meaning events as *Sinn* can only ever be approximations of original meaning intentions. Each case of meaning fulfilment as *anschauliche* realization of a meaning intention appears to consist in a combination of identifying and illustrating acts. So, linguistic meaning can never amount to full *qualitative identity*.

## Quantity

Every act of meaning fulfilment can also be described in terms of the quantity of mental materials that are needed for comprehension. Quantity in this sense can be regarded as a necessary adumbrational aspect of the meaning event. In communicative situations the *how much* or *how many details* are required is subject to negotiation. This is especially an issue when we need to distinguish substantivities with a strong likeness and unfamiliar kinds of aboutness. Another domain where the quantity of imaginable materials is crucial is the relative vagueness of concepts. The "how many" question in response to the word sounds of "population" (people) , "a heap of rice" (grains), "baldness" (hairs), and so on, can be answered by saying that members of a speech community handle the vagueness of concepts pragmatically by imagining at camera-shutter speed the schemata of a typical population, a typical heap of rice, a typical bald head within a broad spectrum of options. If specification is required by the speech situation, additional indicative information can be added either verbally or by gesture or pictorial representation. The rough schematization of quantity involved here illustrates a key difference between natural language discourse and its formalization. A telling exemplification of this contrast is provided in the *sorites* puzzles where linguistic vagueness is presented as posing an obstacle to clarity in acts of comprehension.[58] Here, I want to point out only that the vagueness involved in the mass terms of natural language is no barrier to the intentionality of meaning fulfilment for the not so simple reason that linguistic grasp occurs only if we are able to project appropriate, intentional, mental material states of affairs in response to the relevant word sounds. Which, once more, points us to the imaginability thesis of linguistic meaning.

## Quality

The notion of "quality" refers to the *kinds* of mental materials that form part of the act of meaning fulfilment. What sort of green we are to imagine or what sort of softness, roughness, and so on, we are to associate with the objectivity aimed for in the utterance. The vagueness of "slow" or "fast" is not typically resolved by quantification, although this is of course possible, but rather by *imagining* the appropriate nonverbal context. In addition, the manner of presentation, in short voice, should be regarded as a vital quality component of language indicating what sort of value stance should be adopted in the act of meaning fulfilment. For example, the quality of schematization in the "occasional" or *deictic* sense is argued for in Rochus Sowa's "Deictic Ideations." Sowa addresses the "adverbially general" of a mode of action or procedure via our "such-consciousness (*so-Bewusstsein*)." Accordingly, statements like "I have never seen such a beetle before" or "This is the way you should do this" contain *deictic ideation* particles the nominal intention of which does not primarily aim at specificity but rather at a "type." The so constituted type opens up in a "space of variation (*Variationsspielraum*)" via deictic ideation, while at the same time it always also indicates the "limits of variability" such that species comprehension and the specific coincide.[59] Sowa's analysis invites the specification of deictic ideation by *graded schematization* according to speech situation and raises the question who or what fixes the space of variation of the content of concepts and its limits. By now the not so surprising answer is "the speech community via pedagogy from the cradle to the grave by techniques of *Abrichtung*." A broader implication of Sowa's investigation is the nagging question whether or not *all* of natural language is fundamentally occasional and so deictic,[60] a question reminiscent of John Langshaw Austin's self-critical remark that perhaps all utterances are "performative."[61]

The aspect of the quality of the mental material content of acts of meaning fulfilment also demonstrates the radical difference between Husserl's *Bedeutung* as minimal directional guidance and *Sinn* as reconstruction of nonverbal components of meaning intention. Whereas the former provides directionality to what is being talked about, permitting mere numerical identification of a *this-here* rather than a *that-there*, distinctions of the quality of mental-material intentionality belong firmly to the domain of acts of meaning fulfilment. It is here that the kind of red or the sort of roughness aimed at in meaning intention is to be approximately reconstructed.

## Degree of Schematization

Neither empty consciousness nor full intentionality are relevant to habitual and interpretive linguistic meaning fulfilment. As we saw, "pure *Anschauung* and pure empty intention" are viewed by Husserl as mere "limit cases" of cognition.[62] Which seriously weakens the charge levelled by Derrida that Husserl's enterprise is a paradigm of visual *plenitude*.[63] Instead, we have a broad spectrum of meaning endowment between minimal comprehension and richly imaginable meaning realizations. While directionality is secured in appropriate meaning constitution in response to linguistic expressions, neither the quantity nor quality of the mental materials that make meaning vividly imaginable (*anschaulich*) can be fully predetermined by the speaker. They are constituted by the hearer (reader) according to need. This is where the notion of degree of schematization plays its explanatory role. It allows us to distinguish between lower and higher degrees of meaning *saturation*. Unfulfilled intentions, says Husserl in the *Nachlass*, are gradually saturated (*gesättigt*).[64] With reference to meaning intention and its response, Husserl tells us that "in meaning fulfilment what is intended 'satisfies' itself, 'saturates' itself." It is the "same" intention but in the mode of "saturation (*Sättigung*)."[65] Meaning fulfilment, then, looks like a stepped or graded construction (*Stufenbau*), with "gradations of clarity" as well as "gradation of fullness" in a "series of enhancements of fulfilment," resulting in different "degrees of completeness."[66] In line with Husserl's emphasis on the centrality in meaning of vivid imaginability, that is, *Anschaulichkeit*, he speaks of the "gradations of *vividness* of the entire *Vorstellung* (*Graduationen der Lebendigkeit der ganzen Vorstellung*)."[67]

What does such schematized *Vorstellung* consist in that renders it suitable to making arbitrary signifiers as merely symbolic expressions vividly imaginable in the form of motivated signifieds? The answer cannot possible be "verbal paraphrase." More words merely re-pose the question. Verbal substitution simply offers an infinite regress. We would never know what an expression is *about*, nor how it is meant to be conceived. Following in Husserl's footsteps is to view meaning fulfilment as the at least partial filling of empty linguistic schemata by nonverbal, quasi-perceptual states of affairs.

This invites the analysis of speech in terms of the degree to which typified experience is schematized in language. From the perspective of the heterosemiotic nature of language, it is worth noting that each separate sign system absorbed in language creates different kinds of generalities by the way olfactory, thermal, auditory, haptic, tactile, and emotional, sensuous syntheses are differentially schematized in meaning fulfilment according to communicative requirements.[68] High-level, cultural abstractions, such as the ontically compound concepts of "culture," "democracy," or "educational institutions," can be schematized to differing degrees without ever losing *Anschaulichkeit*.

Thus, the concept of degree of schematization encourages the retention of similarity relations in meaning fulfilment without having to throw out the baby of resemblance with the bathwater of detailed mental images.[69] Differentiated schematization allows for the specification of Melle's meaning acts forming a higher level sort of act by which objects and *Sachverhalte* are conceptualized.[70] Graded schematization is likewise compatible with Balle's view of Husserl's "final demonstrative *Bezugnahme*" according to which "the individual as this-determined as it were, is embedded for Husserl in a complex dynamic system of *typifying gradations*, starting from a 'something at all' and terminating in a 'this individual.'"[71] As such, "fulfilling *Anschauung*" is always a dynamic, intentional process that cannot be pegged at one and the same level of abstraction. In this context, we can build on Husserl's idea of the "*gradation* of fullness and series of enhancement of fulfilment."[72] In support of the graded differentiation among motivated signifieds as acts of meaning fulfilment, degrees of schematization can be said to be an indispensable aspect of linguistic meaning.

## Conclusion: Meaning as Schematized Imaginability

In light of these observations, the revised chain of necessary acts in the constitution of language as communication consists of the following. On the side of the utterer, we have nonverbal meaning intention and *vouloir dire* and the displacement of nonverbal mental materials by a symbolic expression. On the side of the listener (reader), there are word sound consciousness; word consciousness and *Bedeutung*, as minimal directional and so not entirely empty grasp; and the reversal of displacement by nonverbal meaning fulfilment in *Sinn* as schematized, vividly imaginable *Anschauung*. All of these intentional acts are socially overdetermined by the speech community. In line with our opening hypothesis, we can now formulate the following redefinition of meaning in natural language.

Linguistic meaning is a communal, cognitive, indirectly public event generated in the process of meaning fulfilment as an effect of individual instantiations of linguistic expressions by members of a speech community. Meaning fulfilment consists in the transformation of linguistic expressions into lexical and categorial aboutness, modified by voice, as the result of an association of arbitrary signifiers with motivated signifieds, the latter made up of intentional, mental materials regulated by concepts as linguistically specified typifications, under the control of the speech community, in terms of exclusive directionality, quantity, quality, and degree of schematization.

Part III of the book deals with some implications of the portrait of language developed so far, first for analytical approaches and, second, for speculations on language evolution. In the next chapter, I ask how the symbolicity of formal signification compares with that of natural language, viewed from the perspective of the kind of intentionality involved in each.

## Notes

1. Jocelyn Benoist, "Non-Objectifying Acts," in *On Hundred Years of Phenomenology: Husserl's Logical Investigations Revisited*, ed. D. Zahavi and F. Stjernfelt (Dordrecht: Kluwer, 2002), pp. 41–9 (43).
2. Cf., e.g., P. Kung, "Imagining as a Guide to Possibility," *Philosophy and Phenomenological Research* 81 (2010), 620–63; see also his paper "You Really Do Imagine It: Against Error Theories of Imagination," *Noûs* 50, 1 (2016), 90–120.
3. Hua XX/2, p. 456; cf. Kant where imagination cannot be divorced from experience, including perceptual experience: CPR A118; A78/B103; B152; A140/B179.
4. Edmund Husserl, *Logical Investigations,* trans. J.N. Finlay (New York: Humanity Books, 2000), pp. 299ff.
5. Kant, *CPR* A140/B180.
6. Husserl, *Logical Investigations*, pp. 303f.; my emphasis.
7. Hua XX/1, p. 129; XX/2, p. 151.
8. Hua XX/2, p. 291.
9. Hua XX/2, p. 126.
10. Husserl, *Logical Investigations*, p. 281.
11. Gottlob Frege, "On Sense and Reference," in *Translations from the Philosophical Writings of Gottlob Frege*, trans. P. Geach and M. Black (Oxford: Blackwell, 1970), pp. 56–78.
12. Noam Chomsky, *Syntactic Structures* (The Hague: Mouton, 1957); *Aspects of the Theory of Syntax* (Cambridge, MA: MIT Press, 1965); *Language and Mind* (New York: Hartcourt, Brace, 1972); *Cartesian Linguistics* (Cambridge: Cambridge University Press, 2009).
13. Jerry A. Fodor, *The Language of Thought* (Cambridge, MA: Harvard University Press, 1975); *Concepts: Where Cognitive Science Went Wrong* (Oxford: Clarendon Press, 1998); *Lot 2: The Language of Thought Revisited* (Oxford: Oxford University Press, 2008).
14. Johannes D. Balle, "Husserl's typisierende Apperzeption und die Phänomenologie der dynamischen Intentionalität," in *Meaning and Language: Phenomenological Perspectives*, ed. F. Mattens, 89-104 (Dordrecht: Springer, 2008), p. 92.
15. Hua XX/1, pp. 3, 231f.; XX/2, pp. 137, 143f., 151, 291f.
16. Hua XX/1, pp. 31, 33, 38f., 41, 44, 105, 129, 145f, 231; XX/2, p. 298; see also *Anschaulichsein*, XX/2, p. 143 and *Vorstellung* conceived as *Anschauung*, XX/2, p. 454.
17. Husserl, *Logical Investigations*, p. 735; Hua I, pp. 55f.; *Ideas: General Introduction to Pure Phenomenology,* trans. W.R. Boyce Gibson (London: George Allen and Unwin, 1969), p. 194; XLI, p. 233.
18. Ullrich Melle, "Das Rätsel des Ausdrucks: Husserls Zeichen- und Ausdruckslehre in den Manuskripten für die Neufassung der VI. Logischen Untersuchung," *Meaning and Language*, p. 10.

19  Balle, "Husserl's typisierende Apperzeption," p. 92.
20  Ibid., pp. 90, 92f.
21  Ibid., pp. 92f., 95.
22  Ibid., p. 102.
23  Ibid., p. 95.
24  Ibid., pp. 92f., 99, 103.
25  Mark Johnson, *The Body in the Mind: The Bodily Basis of Meaning, Imagination and Reason* (Chicago: University of Chicago Press, 1987); Gilles Fauconnier, *Mappings in Thought's Language* (Cambridge: Cambridge University Press, 1997); Mark Turner, *Reading Minds: The Study of English in the Age of Cognitive Science* (Princeton: Princeton University Press, 1991); Mark Johnson and George Lakoff, *Philosophy in the Flesh: The Embodied Mind and Its Challenge to Western Thought* (New York: Basic Books, 1999); Gilles Fauconnier and Mark Turner, *The Way We Think: Conceptual Blending and the Mind's Hidden Complexities* (New York: Basic Books, 2002).
26  Dieter Lohmar, "Husserl's Type and Kant's Schemata: Systematic Reasons for Their Correlation or Identity," in *The New Husserl: A Critical Reader*, ed. D. Welton (Bloomington: Indiana University Press, 2003), pp. 93–124; apart from their different genesis, Kant's schemata and Husserl's type are aligned by Lohmar in terms of their functions.
27  Hua XII, pp. 102f.; Hua XXXIX, p. 389; Hua XIV, pp. 196ff.
28  Alfred Schütz, *The Phenomenology of the Social World* (London: Heinemann, 1972), p. 119.
29  Ibid., pp. 131f.; my emphasis.
30  Ibid., pp. 133f.
31  Ibid., p. 129.
32  Alfred Schütz and Thomas Luckmann, *The Structures of the Life-World*, trans. R. M. Zaner and H. T. Engelhardt (Evanston: Northwestern University Press, 1973), pp. 233f.
33  Ibid., pp. 234f.
34  Hua XIII, p. 101; XXVII, p. 22; XIV, p. 199; VI, p. 166.
35  Hua XX/2, p. 129.
36  Hua XX/2, p. 279; XLI, p. 230.
37  Dieter Lohmar, "Denken ohne Sprache?" *Meaning and Language,* 169–94, p. 173.
38  Hua XX/2, p. 146; my emphasis on "equivalent," which does not mean "identical."
39  Hua XLI, p. 33.
40  Hua XIX/2, p. 625.
41  Lohmar, "Denken ohne Sprache?" p. 173; Hua XIX/2, pp. 658f.
42  Hua XX/2, p. 456.
43  Lester Embree, "Dorion Cairns, Empirical Types, and the Field of Consciousness," in *Husserl's Ideen*, ed. L. Embree and T. Nenon, 225–39. Contributions to Phenomenology 66 (Dordrecht: Springer, 2013), pp. 148ff.
44  Edmund Husserl, *Experience and Judgment: Investigations in a Genealogy of Logic*, trans. J.S. Churchill and K. Ameriks (London: Routledge and Kegan Paul, 1997), pp. 211, 209f., 222ff.; cf. also Edmund Husserl, *Formal and Transcendental Logic*, trans. D. Cairns (The Hague: Martinus Nijhoff, 1969), pp. 294ff., 301ff.
45  Hua XX/2, p. 11.
46  Embree, "Dorion Cairns, Empirical Types, and the Field of Consciousness," p. 265.
47  Peirce, EP 2. 273.
48  Hua XX/2, pp. 102ff., 112, 131f.

49  John R. Searle, "A Classification of Illocutionary Acts," *Language and Society* 5 (1976), 1–23.
50  Hua XX/2, p. 103.
51  Pol Vandervelde, "An Unpleasant but Felicitous Ambiguity," *Meaning and Language*, 27–48, p. 36.
52  Balle, "Husserl's typisierende Apperzeption," p. 98f.
53  See Chapter Nine.
54  George Lakoff, "What Is a Conceptual System?" in *The Nature and Ontogenesis of Meaning*, ed. W. F. Overton and D. S. Palermo (Hilldale, NJ: Lawrence Erlbaum, 1994), pp. 41–90; Johnson and Lakoff, *Philosophy in the Flesh*; Fodor, *Concepts*; Ray Jackendoff, "Possible Stages in the Evolution of the Language Capacity," *Trends in Cognitive Sciences*, 3, 7 (1999), 272–9; Eric Margolis and Steven Laurence (eds.), *Concepts; Core Readings* (Cambridge, MA: MIT Press, 1999); and much of analytical philosophy of language.
55  Husserl, *Logical Investigations*, pp. 282f.; my emphasis.
56  Hua XX/1, pp. 25f.
57  Hua XX/2, p. 112.
58  See Chapter 8.
59  Sowa, "Deiktische Ideationen," in *Meaning and Language*, pp. 105–23 (110ff.).
60  Husserl, *Logical Investigations*, pp. 313ff.; Hua XX/2, pp. 102ff.
61  John L. Austin, *How to Do Things with Words* (Oxford: Oxford University Press, 1962), p. 103n1.
62  Hua XX/1, p. 129.
63  Cf. Jacques Derrida, *Of Grammatology*, trans. G. C. Spivak (Baltimore: The Johns Hopkins University Press, 1976), p. 215; *Speech and Phenomena: And Other Essays on Husserl's Theory of Signs*, trans. D. B. Allison and N. Garver (Evanston: Northwestern University Press, 1973); the futile search for presence and plenitude is parodied by Derrida in the now famous cadence, "Rising toward the sun of presence, it is the way of Icarus," p. 104.
64  Hua XX/2, p. 364.
65  Ibid., p. 136.
66  Ibid., p. 439; Hua XX/1, pp. 240, 129f.
67  XX/1, p. 240.
68  Horst Ruthrof, "Sufficient Semiosis," *The American Journal of Semiotics* 31, 1 (2015), 117–46.
69  Steven Gans, "Schematism and Embodiment," *Journal of the British Society of Phenomenology* 13 (1982), 237–45.
70  Melle, "Das Rätsel des Ausdrucks," p. 10.
71  Balle, "Husserls typisierende Apperzeption," p. 98; my emphasis.
72  Hua XX/1, p. 129; my emphasis.

Part III

# Implications for the Theorization of Language

8

# Why Language Is Not Simply a "Symbolic" System

If we take Martin Kusch's description of Husserl's theorization of language as calculus as our guide,[1] the emphasis on semantic essence would suggest that natural language is closely related to starkly symbolic signification, such as technical and formal sign systems. If, however, our focus is the "more or less" character of natural language and the "fluid types" that make up linguistic meaning, that is, its epistemic essence, then natural language looks very different from its formal derivatives. The sharp difference that will emerge between the minimal symbolicity of language and its optimization in formal signs could very well point back to its origins, hundreds of thousands of years of gradual evolution compared to the very recent emergence of purely deductive bodies of formal signs. We can be reasonably confident that natural language as we now know it grew out of the iconic and indexical features of its nonverbal, communicative precursors, gradually shedding iconicity at the level of verbal signifiers while retaining resemblance relations at the level of the motivated signified.[2] In this respect, the signifiers of formal systems, such as calculus, can be regarded as radically reduced relations of the signs of natural language. Husserl refers to as formal placeholders as "convenient replacements."[3] Because of the very different genesis of formal sign systems, Husserl remarks that "mathematics, emptied of meaning, could generally propagate itself, constantly being added to logically."[4] In agreement with Husserl, I suggest that the thesis that language is to be viewed as a *symbolic system* in any strong sense, as it is for example by Jacques Lacan (1985), is not tenable, even if *displacement* via its arbitrary signifiers is one of its core components.[5] True, "we require a symbolic vehicle for meaning which is independent of the original cognition in order to represent the meant state of affairs (such as an event) in consciousness."[6] But as argued so far, in language, the loss of iconicity in the arbitrary character of the linguistic *signifier* is compensated for by its dependence on a motivated signified. So, the presence of symbols alone will be argued to be an insufficient criterion for the characterization of language as a symbolic system. At the very least, it cannot be the whole story.

## Desedimentation: From Linguistic to Formal Signs

In support of my reasoning, I draw especially on the work of Burt Hopkins who has identified formalization as the result of acts of "desedimentation."[7] In his paper

"On the origin of the 'language' of formal mathematics," Hopkins gathers the various reductions needed to achieve significatory emptiness by stripping away the sedimented ingredients of language, as, for example, by desedimenting the more specific concept "magnitude" of such and such a size, toward the concept "magnitude in general."[8] In order to better understand the relation between linguistic and formal intentionality, I ask what precisely it is that we have to abandon in language in order to arrive at mere placeholders $(x, y)$ in their categorial relations $(x^2 = y^3)$, which leaves us with their merely syntactic, mutual dependency. Intriguingly, Husserl was reluctant to grant formal entities the term "concept" since they do no longer hold any mental material together (*con-capere*). All they do is making themselves available for indicating categorial contingency minus "core stuff."[9] It does not come as a surprise then that, as Hopkins writes, Husserl identifies "symbolic calculus" as "a concept-less calculational technique."[10] "As to their meaning," Husserl confirms, "symbolic expressions are empty, unfulfilled (*Das symbolische Aussagen ist nach seiner Bedeutung leer, unerfüllt*)."[11] On the way to formalization, the most obvious ingredient that is *desedimented* is aboutness. Yet, aboutness appears to be still present in *applied calculus*.

## *Applied Calculus*

When we design forms of calculus for measurements, we proceed by desedimenting *Anschauung* somewhere halfway to generic magnitudes as strictly defined units, such as mm, nanometers, degrees Celsius, wavelengths, units in Röntgen radiology, and so on. Each such collection of magnitudes is rendered coherent within a closed schema of quantification. In applying such forms of calculus to phenomenal reality, we reverse the procedure of linguistic displacement. Instead of adapting the *expression* to *Anschauung*, we reduce the complexity of perceptual acts to those demanded by the units of a measuring system. It is deceptive to think that when we measure the circumference of a tree trunk with a mm tape that we are performing intuitive perceptual acts. So, are our linguistic terms not very much like the measuring units of our tape? And do we not predicate something about reality much the same way as when we say, "This tree has red fruit"? The difference is revealed as soon as we compare the kinds of intentional acts required for each procedure. We realize that the difference lies in the manner of using two distinct forms of semiosis and in the way the terms of each are secured in each semiotic system. The units of measurement do not yield to perceptual reality, as do the concepts of "fast" and "tall" in natural language. Our very acts of measuring differ from our acts of linguistic description. Quantification diverges sharply from decisions on verdicts of "murder" and "manslaughter." In the first case, we make *Anschauung* pliable to the calculus; in the second case, we negotiate which of the concepts is more appropriate to the *Lebenswelt*. Which highlights an important distinction between empirical, natural language concepts and their desedimented formal counterparts. While the limits of the former are never assured, and their analysis is never complete,[12] the conceptual boundaries of the latter are *always already assured*, and their *analysis is always completed by way of definition*. This is so because the concepts of applied calculus are stipulated, whereas linguistic concepts are *typifications* of cultural experience. That is why we call the former artificial and *a priori* and the latter *a posteriori*, or *natural*.

Since the concepts of calculus guarantee the objective transmission of sense, Husserl's linguistic meaning fulfilment as *Sinn* is inapplicable. Another way of accounting for the difference is to admit formal concepts on the understanding say that the numerical aboutness of applied calculus is an inevitable result of the *desedimentation* of *Anschauung* to generic magnitudes. Furthermore, while the *Bedeutung* of a signifier of calculus is intersubjectively agreed upon by definition it is objectively secured rather than negotiated under the rule of sufficiency. But perhaps the most striking difference between linguistic intentionality and that of applied calculus is the fact that language would not be language without the presence of voice, while in applied calculus it has no function at all. The alleged analogy between applied calculus and natural language is therefore untenable. In the following sections, we look at how Leerintention, aboutness, voice, categorial relations, and imaginability are realized in language and in formal sign systems.

## *Leerintentionen* (Empty Intentions)

Just as the term "*Intuition*" is progressively replaced in Husserl's writings by "*Anschauung*," so too is "*Leervorstellung*" gradually substituted for "*Signifikation*."[13] Both moves indicate Husserl's warming to the idea of imaginability (*Vorstellbarkeit*) on the epistemic side of language. The emptiness indicated by the term *Leervorstellung* may trap us into assuming that formal sign systems would be ideal candidates for this puzzling concept, an option supported in Husserl's remarks that we can have "objective (gegenständliche)" as well as "objectless" acts, in which case they are *Leerintentionen*[14] and that "an emptily imagining consciousness . . . now takes over the function of meaning."[15] We could also misread Husserl's observation that "in the mere symbolic comprehension of the word a meaning is performed (the word means something for us), but nothing is *recognized*." Yet such a reading is quickly rectified by his insistence that what is "merely thought" in the "symbolic act" is "made intuitively present" in the "*Anschauung*."[16] Certainly, the vast majority of Husserl's descriptions of empty intentionality disallow any formal interpretation of his Leerintention. When "I read 'General White,'" Husserl writes, "I have no vivid image nor a mere word sound." Though I "know that it is an actual person, I perform no predication."[17] Leerintention in this form then is a case of linguistic generality rather than a formal phenomenon. Its assumed emptiness remains an unrealizable limit-phenomenon.[18]

This conception finds support also in Husserl's emphasis on Leerintention as providing a merely "*directional intention (abzielende Intention)*" as an act of ephemeral, "transitional experience."[19] Nor can *gradual* clarification be a characteristic of formalization. Only in language can the "empty horizon (*Leerhorizont*)" function as a "a tendency aiming at clarity."[20] Even its minimal "*Hinweistendenz*" disqualifies it as a formal act. As Husserl specifies, the Leerintention "would be fulfilled when I consult a dictionary or a language expert."[21] Yet, the decisive mark of Husserl's empty intentionality is the pervasive linkage between word consciousness and "vividly imaginable—redeeming fulfilment."[22] As empty "act tendencies," Leerintention warrants an "identifying synthesis with intuitive acts."[23] When this demand is met, meaning fulfilment will eventually have "replaced" the empty acts of our *Leerbewusstsein*.[24] The "*Leerintention* transforms into an *Anschauung*,"[25] which renders it a "meaningful sign,"[26] where Husserl's "*Anschaulichsein*," "*Veranschaulichung*," and "*Anschauung* in the concept" dominate.[27] There is then a fundamental difference between Leerintention and our performance of the formal sign. In natural language there is always a fleeting moment of a yet not quite fulfilled act of comprehension, the merely directional act of the *Leervorstellung* as limit-phenomenon. In formal operations, no such directionality is given.

## Aboutness

Perhaps the most obvious disparity between language and its formal derivatives is the presence of aboutness in the former and its absence in the latter. In language, our comprehending acts constituting meaning fulfilment always contain aboutness as a selection from Husserl's "entanglement in contingencies,"[28] desedimented in the formal sign. In semiotic terms, the *heterosemiotic* nature of language can be transformed into the *homosemiotic* character of algorithms by a process of shedding olfactory, gustatory, tactile, visual, emotive, and higher-level typifications. Whereas in language, the symbolic signifier functions as a "vehicle of our mental projection (*Vorstellung*)," the mere placeholders of formal sign systems bar any such acts. But more importantly, *Vorstellung* in and by language is also the condition for three distinct forms of comprehension: the cognition of an object "in its individuality," its mediate recognition, and reimagining as the same object, cognition in its entangled contiguity, and as merely directional indication without full cognition.[29] In the formal domain, symbols serve only to guarantee the univocity of categorial relations.

Another way of looking at the relation of aboutness in the linguistic and formal domains is to return to Husserl's distinction between *substantitivity* and *adjectivity*. In language, the "aboutness of objects can be determined by way of substantivity (*Gegenstände-worüber können substantivisch bestimmt werden*)."[30] In this respect, substantivity diverges from adjectivity that is mediately dependent on the object and so is subsumed under its concept. In Husserl's words, "every concept that determines an aboutness falls under substantivity," whereas adjectivity characterizes the "concept of a dependent moment." That is, substantivity captures objects "directly." Adjectivity, on the other hand, subsumes concepts that "capture moments and abstracta" and in so doing determines an aboutness "indirectly and predicatively." In language, objectivities are named and only then mediately qualified by subordinated predication.[31] One could continue Husserl's dependence relations by adding that adverbial qualifications are dependent on adjectivity and verbality, with similar relations pertaining to participles and other linguistic features. Neither the *core forms* discussed by Husserl nor their possible extensions can be removed from language without destroying the very concept of *natural language*. In formal signs, they have to be radically desedimented.

In the aboutness of perception, what is meant "is given,"[32] writes Husserl; in language it is displaced by arbitrary signifiers. This is why in linguistic communication meaning has to be reconstructed via "perception" and "parallel fantasies," which form the "foundation (*Grundlage*) of language."³³ This is why Husserl calls them "elementary intentions" (*Elementarintentionen*). They assemble the typifications out of which we forge linguistic meaning intentions. Meaning intentions conveyed by natural language, in turn, are "*erfüllungsbedürftig* (demanding fulfilment)."³⁴ No such saturation is present in formal signification. To advance from perception to linguistic expressions, Husserl says we require "an appropriate direction of gaze (*Blickrichtung*)."³⁵ The right *Blickrichtung* functions as a bridge for crossing from the things we wish to indicate to finding expressions appropriate for the kind of statement we intend to make about them, whereas the reverse process occurs in the restoration of a quasi-perceptual meaning intention in meaning fulfilment. In contrast, when we perform such formal sign sequences as "$x^2 = y^3$" our acts of meaning intention and *Blickrichtung* entirely lack quasi-perceptual iconicity. The complexities of symbolic calculus lie immanently and entirely intensionally within the domain of the formal. The distinction drawn in the *Nachlass* between "sensuous and categorial acts" (*von sinnlichen und kategorialen Akten*) and "sensuous and categorial objects" (*sinnlichen und kategorialen Gegenständen*) likewise highlights the opposition between natural language and its artificial derivatives.³⁶ In formal systems there is no projection of *sinnliche* objects; there are only categorial relations.

Mindful of the intricate relation between perception and language, Husserl defines linguistic expressions as "the apperceived in its categorial formation (*das Wahrgenommene in seiner kategorialen Formung*)."³⁷ As such, linguistic signifiers are typically "bearers of intentional indications."³⁸ The apperceived quasi-perceptual content in its specific categorial sequence and manner of utterance is the *displaced form* that functions as the vehicle for an intended statement in need of restoration. This is the way members of a speech community live in the meaning consciousness of their mother tongue, providing as it does an all-encompassing, cultural and existential *Umwelt*. When we perform symbolic algorithms, our acts are fully predetermined by the rules of a formal sign system, where meaning consciousness reduces to categorial relations among fully defined terms within an axiomatically stipulated framework. An obvious source of difference between the univocal senses of formal systems and linguistic expressions is polysemy. As Husserl writes, "one word sound—a number of meanings," which means that "a number of meaning intentions (*Bedeutungsintentionen*) attach to the word sound," a complication that has been purposefully *eradicated* from calculus as well as its applied varieties. However, adds Husserl, "only the word sound can have more than one meaning," that is, can function as the foundation for "more than one word, even if they sound the same."³⁹ Therefore, "instead of the mere word sound," we must take the "actual and full word which always has the same character of meaning as the ground of the naming relation."⁴⁰ According to Husserl, "the mere word sound and any habitual tendency [associated with it] is yet not the situation of affairs (*Sachlage*); rather the word in its *Sinn* coincides with the thing as corresponding to the *Sinn*."⁴¹ In sharp distinction from the word that we must read through the word sound, "the appearing word sounds" have no more than "the character of something secondary and additional."⁴² The word as a meaning ideality is here strictly separated by Husserl from its empirical sound event. Accordingly, it is the word, "by its uniform meaning" that "encompasses an ideally limited multiplicity of possible *Anschauungen* such that every one of these intuitions can function as the basis of an identically naming, [and] verbal act of cognition."[43] In its entanglement of social contingencies demanding as much as facilitating a multiplicity of *Anschauungen*, the word is "objective" also as a "cultural object (*Kulturobjekt*)."[44] No such secondary character attaches to the terms of strictly symbolic signs.

Another vital difference between formal and linguistic signs is marked by Husserl by the term "indication" (*Hinweisung*), the intended and reconstructed act of "determined directional pointing" (*bestimmt gerichtete Hinweisung*). Meanings in this sense are "indicating and indicated," to be realized in meaning fulfilment by "supplementing imaginability (*ergänzende Vorstellung*)."[45] Although in this sense, "the word indicates,"[46] Husserl extends the concept of indication to include what he calls the "indicative function" (*Hinweisfunktion*), the task of which it is to establish a connection between an expression and the "indicated thing," such as "dispositional phenomena."[47] A less rigid linkage is provided by the "indicative tendency (*Hinweistendenz*)."[48] Husserl provides an example. "With respect to an entirely unknown word, the indicative tendency would be fulfilled if I were to check the dictionary or asked someone well-versed in the language."[49] In habitual speech, there is always a "tendency," Husserl writes, "a certain intentional feature," a pointing "through-the-word-towards-the-thing."[50] Even if Husserl does not regard tendencies strictly as "acts,"[51] his *Hinweistendenz* is an example of a more comprehensive idea, according to which "every association is a connectedness via a tendency. In each we have the empty tending towards and the fulfilment: unity of congruence, unity of the 'belonging together', in a very broad sense."[52] At the same time, the *Hinweistendenz* is also a "*Hinausweisung*" beyond words and their categorial relation to a world, real or fictional. Thus, *Hinausweisen* "emanates from the word, but is nothing by itself, it is a certain founded mode of act (*Aktweise*)."[53] *Hinausweisen* is a mere "tendency" toward acts of nonverbal projection.[54] At the end of the meaning chain, our acts of word consciousness, statement consciousness, and imaginable, nonverbal scenarios (*Anschauungen*) are combined in one unity in the "mode of saturation (*Modus der Sättigung*)"[55] as one of the cardinal acts that has been desedimented on the way from natural language to formal signification.

## Voice

Aboutness, we contended, is never alone. In language as communication we are always also dealing with *voice*, a feature that, like aboutness, is conspicuously absent in formal sign systems. A sardonic intonation of a mathematical formula leaves its sense unaffected. Even though the signifiers of both language and their formal derivatives are "arbitrary (*willkürlich*),"[56] voice has a semantic purchase only in language. Since the main function of voice in language is the modification of aboutness and since there is no aboutness in formal signs, there is also nothing to be modified by whatever prosodic contour we may wish to impose. Only linguistic expressions, therefore, need to be uttered in a certain way for meaning to occur; formal signs can be mechanically transmitted without loss of sense. In the machinic transmission of natural language, context typically guides our acts of imagining an appropriate sound contour. In his *Nachlass*, Husserl addresses what we assume about speakers on the grounds of the tone with which they deliver a sentence. "I interpret certain sounds as associated with certain experiences of the other as sounds in which those experiences are 'discharged' (*sich entladen*)."[57] No such associations can occur in systems of pure deduction. All the mental material ingredients required for introjection have been eliminated by desedimentation. Moreover, we need to distinguish between the sounds of a standard prosodic contour that I give an expression and the special tone by which I modify what I am saying. This is why Husserl speaks of the "pronunciation that always has its 'tone' (*Aussprache, die immer ihren 'Ton' hat*),"[58] the former serving the identification of different sentence types, the latter the modification of aboutness via implicit deixis. Both varieties of tone are irrelevant in formal signification. Formal signs lack "tonal characters (*tonale Charaktere*)" that are "grasped in their peculiarity and guide understanding."[59] There is no meaning modification when we speak a mathematical equation in a "contemptuous tone, a lively tone, in an icy tone."[60] Our intentional acts in the performance of formal sign operations are a-tonal. So, it makes no sense in formal sign contexts to speak of the production of tone with the intention that the other "understands me in *this* way" and so comprehends my intimated "purpose."[61] Nor is it possible in formal systems to speak of a "deviation from a normal tone of a sentence (*Satzton*)."[62] When I reread a formal algorithm, I merely assure myself that I have grasped the relevant categorial relations. In our natural language acts, the process of meaning constitution "goes through the word sound" as "only a means" as a *Hinausweisung*, pointing beyond itself toward the "ultimate meaning (*Zielmeinen*)."[63] This is probably why Husserl accepts the general principle that "Generally, I 'translate' what is written ... into spoken language," where it is the acoustic words that "primarily carry comprehension."[64] In formal signification, utterances collapse into sentence types. In natural language, any such reduction would mean the loss of both *Bedeutung* and *Sinn*.

## Categorial Relations

Different languages, writes Husserl, use different categorial constellations of "logical equivalence" to achieve the *adequacy* of their expressions to intuitive experience.[65] This suggests that basic acts of categorial relations are in place *prior* to the specific, syntactic choices typically made by speakers of natural languages. Bilingual speakers become aware of this situation when they have chosen a sentence opening that is appropriate in one language, but not in the other language in which they are conversing at a given moment. While prelinguistic categorial relations allow for diverging syntax patterns, at the more specific level of a particular language only socially sanctioned, idiomatic syntagms satisfy the minimal requirement of intersubjective sufficiency. Contrary to the convictions sustaining catastrophe theories of language evolution,[66] the primordiality of categorial relations in the emergence of language should be uncontroversial.[67] In the phenomenological camp, its founding role in the meaning process is supported by Dieter Lohmar who views categorial intuition as the guiding measure in the genesis of expressions. Accordingly, "the categorial intuition is an independent and primary givenness with respect to the adequate linguistic expression."[68] It also had to be in place for language to emerge as displacement in language evolution.[69] When we choose words according to community rules, we retain resemblance relations both at the level of the motivated signified and that of categorial relations, but jettison iconicity at the merely symbolic signifier. In the categorial relations among formal signs, intuitive content has been radically desedimented.

So, language and algorithmic systems demand different acts of consciousness when it comes to Husserl's distinction between "situation of affairs" (*Sachlage*) and "state of affairs" (*Sachverhalt*). Comparing the verbal sequences "John is taller than Jane" and "Jane is smaller than John" and their formal counterpart "a>b" and "b<a", we note that the different categorial relations make us construe different perspectives of the same *Sachlage*, while demanding the projection of a different state of affairs, a different *Sachverhalt*. Although we look at John first as the taller person compared to Jane and then at Jane as the smaller of the two, the *Sachlage* of who is taller and who is smaller does not change. The opposite is the case regarding the state of affairs, the way the two persons *relate* to one another. In the first case the relation is one of tallness, in the second one of smallness. A dramatic difference, then between linguistic and formal signs is that in the first case we have an *Anschauung*, whereas in symbolic calculus all that needs to be imagined is the categorial relation (quantity; degree) itself. In language, then, we are always dealing at the same time with pure categorical relation and its *intuitive*, that is, *imaginable* fulfilment. Not so in formal sign relations, where there is nothing to imagine beyond the signifiers. With reference to the concept of "communicative *Sachlage* (*kommunikative Sachlage*),"[70] Husserl introduces the following example. "The tracks of wild animals indicating wild animals. More precisely, the grasped existence of the tracks indicates the existence of wild animals."[71] The acts I have to perform here are the projection of an imaginable scenario and a strong inference, which I draw on the grounds of my projection, Peirce's *indexical* variety of signs.[72] When such acts are part of verbal communication, we imagine indirectly iconic resemblance. We are forced to conclude, then, that in language, categorial relations require imaginability to function as syntax. Furthermore, at the end of the meaning-making process, our acts of meaning fulfilment involve of necessity *postverbal* categorial relations as imaginable scenarios. The same holds for Husserl's merely "imagined communication (*Phantasiekommunikation*)."[73] We could add here that is typical in language for meaning fulfilment not necessarily to terminate at the end of verbal exchanges. More often than not, we engage in extended, merely imagined communication, a form of intentionality that would be odd if it occurred in response to formal signs.

## Vividly Imaginable Adequation versus Axiomatics

Both the acts we must perform in doing symbolic calculus and natural language are subject to a certain degree of "coercion."[74] Note, however, an important difference, brushed aside by Wittgenstein, between how such coercion is accomplished in each case by the speech community via *Abrichtung*. In the formal realm, Husserl's *Zumutung* is fully covered by the rules of the sign system,[75] whereas in language the hearer (reader) has to reconstruct it interpretively by appropriately responding to implicit deixis. Husserl employs the term "*Richtigkeit* (correctness)" to indicate the possibility of a high degree of adequation between expression and intuitively given cognition.[76]

*Approximation* of initial meaning intentions must suffice to satisfy Husserl's standard of *Richtigkeit*. A certain degree of incongruence is only to be expected, given that meaning fulfilment in natural language is characterized by intersubjective sufficiency. While the word itself is an "intersubjectively constituted objectivity,"[77] the same kind of objectivity cannot be presumed at the end of the comprehension process. In formal languages, intersubjective meaning fulfilment is replaced by the transmission of objective sense. In the *Nachlass*, Husserl refers to the acts we perform in formal operations as "thinking" that excludes "all intersubjectivity."[78] Which, however, is not to deny that formal sign systems too have their genesis in intersubjective agreements.

Other factors that distance language as a merely marginally symbolic form of communication from its fully symbolic derivatives is *semantic sufficiency*, to which Husserl refers in terms of the "more or less" of meaning approximation and the "more or less perfectly" conveyed meaning according to "threshold variations (*Schwellenunterschiede*),"[79] as well as by acknowledging the gradual "approximation towards the aim of cognition (*Annäherung an das Erkenntnisziel*)."[80] Husserl here anticipates the recent emphasis on *semantic gradation* in the work of Leonard Talmy (2000) as well as laying the foundation for what I have referred to as *degrees of schematization* in Chapter 7.[81] A further complication is Husserl's accent on the role of "guessing (*Einstellung des Vermutens*)" in language[82] and the relevance of "recollection" in meaning constitution, which he somewhat ironically calls the "firm belief in the past (*den patenten Glauben an das Vergangene*)."[83] Husserl acknowledges the presence in acts of comprehension of a "*more or less* corresponding intuition (*Anschauung*)"[84] and writes that in meaning fulfilment, "the intentional essence of the act of *Anschauung*" appears to "conform, *more or less perfectly*," to "the meaning essence of the expressing act."[85] He also concedes that we are dealing with "a reproductive, modified picture intentionality (*eine reproductive modifizierte Bildanschauung*)," with "fluid transitions" (*fliessende Übergänge*) among concepts as an essential feature of language.[86] Fluidity of semantic scope must be fully desedimented in calculus.

With reference to language, Husserl asks the question, "How can we describe the unity between the mental projection (*Vorstellung*) stimulated by the word, the imagined meaning (*Bedeutungsvorstellung*), and the vividly imaginable presentation (*anschauliche Vorstellung*) in which the indicated thing eventually appears?"[87] Part of the answer is that the imagined object is only a stand-in (*Repräsentant*) for the one that was intended.[88] More importantly, linguistic intentionality reveals the "essentially teleological structure of consciousness,"[89] which, in communication, involves an "infinite regress" of mutual interpretive acts,[90] though this does not amount to "an *actual* regressus."[91] Husserl lists a range of acts that are responsible for this regress of meaning. Only in language can "*Leerbewusstsein*" be replaced by *Anschauung* and "evolving mental projections (*erwachsende Vorstellungen*)."[92] Only in language can "*Leerakte*" und "*Vollakte*" be "substituted for one another (*füreinander eintreten*)."[93] In accommodating "emotional phenomena (*Gemütsphänomene*)" and "vivid mental projections (*lebhafte Vorstellungen*),"[94] language draws on typified knowledge rather than on axiomatic foundations, a kind of knowledge that is *anschaulich*, rendered here as "vividly imaginable."[95] Meaning regress is unavoidable to the extent that the hearer "has a partially determined and step-by-step self-limiting and determining meaning consciousness until he eventually has the whole," a unified totality.[96] And even then, linguistic meaning can always be deepened by "generating new mental projections step by step."[97] In this process intervene our horizon of recollection and its "chains of past experiences" as "an open multiplicity"[98] supplementing our acts of meaning fulfilment.[99] In language, Husserl's "communicative consciousness" not only takes account of the public and mental acts of speech partners (*Mitunterredner*) but also of our own "corporeality" as well as other bodies.[100] Here, Husserl projects his ambitious research frame as an "immense horizon of a phenomenology of corporeality" as well as one that embraces "individual and *social* mentality (*Geistigkeit*)."[101] Symbolicity, then, plays a very different and comparably minor role in language if compared with that in its derivative, desedimented, formal cousins. In the second part of this chapter I single out some of analytical favorites, such as *truth-conditional semantics*, *compositionality*, and *sorites arguments*, concluding with one of Zeno's parodies on the geometric conception of time and language.

## Essence versus Existence: Truth-Conditional Semantics

Given the preoccupation with propositions in analytical approaches, it is not surprising that *truth* has remained a central concern in language philosophy, whereas in Husserl the narrow focus on truth tied to existence is supplanted by his broader concern with essence. The tight nexus between truth and linguistic meaning, as argued after Frege by Moritz Schlick via the *verification principle*, has long given way to the weaker thesis of truth-conditional semantics. Schlick had advocated the straightforward thesis that to provide a sentence with meaning was to "transform it into a proposition," on condition that the sentence was *apophantic*, that is, referred to actual reality. This required a description of what makes a sentence into a true proposition and stipulated that only true sentences can have meaning.[102] Meaning here is guaranteed by establishing the *existence and replication of aboutness*. On the less stringent thesis of truth-conditional semantics, meaning can be secured by answering the question of what sort of conditions a sentence would have to satisfy to be true. Existence must now be *construable* rather than verifiable. In this respect, arguably the most influential truth-conditional semantics is argued by Donald Davidson in "Truth and Meaning."[103]

First, we note that in Davidson's title "truth" precedes "meaning," a deliberate inversion of the empirical facts. Second, as a procedure that asks what conditions would have to prevail to guarantee the truth of sentences for the purpose of securing their meaning, truth-conditional semantics rests on a number of assumptions. Such that acts of truth and meaning are related; that only acts producing true sentences have meaning; and that the constitution of meaning is dependent on existence. What can be conceded is that truth-conditional semantics operates as a truth-checking mechanism for meaning within a restricted range of utterances, namely declarative assertions. But if our checking procedure cannot be undertaken without having secured meaning as a precondition, then truth-conditional semantics rests on a *petitio principii*.[104] Let us see how Davidson's theory stacks up against our concept of meaning as the result of the constitution of cognitive equivalence via vivid imaginability. For Davidson, the lexicon of a natural language and its categorial rules form a finite, formal grammar that permits the construal of a parallel semantics in a formal metalanguage M, in which lexical semantics, together with its rules for semantic combinations, controls the way in which sentences are deemed meaningful.

At the heart of his approach is Alfred Tarski's "Convention-T" in its well-worn formula "'snow is white' is true, iff snow is white."[105] Davidson adopts this formula, in violation of Tarski's explicit warning against using the Convention-T for an analysis of natural language on the grounds that it would rob language of what makes it "natural."[106] As our description of necessary acts in the meaning chain from meaning intention to meaning fulfilment has shown, what makes language *natural* cannot be separated from intersubjective intentionality, which is lacking in the formal character of Tarski's truth convention. Convention-T cannot account for our acts of *imagining* what others are talking about and the manner in which they do so. From this perspective, truth-conditional semantics of Davidson's variety as well as that of others face a number of difficulties.[107]

One is that the aboutness of a sentence is dependent on voice, as argued. But voice is absent from the truth-conditional machinery, even though it is one of the central ingredients of language as social discourse and demands an elaborate speech act investigation to be formalized. Then there is the difficulty of retrieving truth in complex verbal exchanges. More often than not, truth proves irretrievable, which makes it necessary to elaborate the truth-conditional procedure to include an imaginable scenario of what would be required for truth to be a condition of the meaning of a sentence. Idiomatic expressions further make the approach via the formal structure of sentence-tokens a laborious, if not an inadequate, procedure. It is also doubtful whether Davidson's principles of radical interpretation and charity can be corralled within the confines of his own truth-conditional mechanism.[108] Nor can such necessary components of the meaning process as Husserl's intimation and introjection be glibly associated with any notion of truth.[109] Truth-acts belong to an entirely different category of intentionality, a topic well beyond the present study. So, we should welcome Davidson's own doubts about his procedure. As he himself concedes, he may have taken a far too "optimistic and programmatic view of the possibilities for a formal characterization of a truth predicate for a natural language,"[110] a sentiment that finds additional support in his posthumous *Truth and Predication*, where Davidson resumes his use of Tarski's Convention-T to natural language within a broader horizon. As he had already indicated in his Dewey lectures, he declares that after all "the conceptual underpinning of interpretation is a theory of truth; truth thus rests in the end on belief and, even more ultimately, on *the affective attitudes*."[111] Davidson's phrase of "affective attitudes" perhaps indicates a phenomenological turn to our acts of imaginability as ground of meaning. As such, his final position is also reminiscent of the relation between Aristotle's *pathemata* and *homoiomata*, how Kant's *Anschauungen* rest on "*Affektionen*,"[112]and Wittgenstein's reluctant admission of the "*Affektion der Seele*."[113] It would seem, then, that Davidson's affective attitudes cannot quite escape Kant's idea of "receptivity" as our "capacity of being *affected* in a certain manner with *Vorstellungen*."[114] All of which suggests that the mechanism of truth-conditional semantics cannot but supervene on imaginability. If so, it follows that linguistic meaning is more fundamental to language than truth. The decisive reason why Husserl avoided the path to meaning for natural language via truth is that it restricts us to the criterion of *existence*, which would entail leaving unaddressed the vast portion of language dealing with fictional entities.[115] And this is why Husserl's entire theorization of natural language is more broadly anchored in the *essentia* of aboutness and their eidetic specification by tone as the proper ground for semantic value.[116]

## Compositionality

Another favorite of analytical language philosophy is compositionality, also known as Frege's law, of which numerous, compatible definitions are cited in the literature.[117] "A language is compositional," it is said, "if the meaning of each of its complex expressions (for example, 'black dog') is determined entirely by the meanings of its parts ('black,' 'dog') and its syntax."[118] According to Francis Pelletier, "the principle of semantic compositionality is the principle that the meaning of an expression is a function of, and only of, the meanings of its parts, together with the method by which those parts are combined."[119] Graeme Hirst places the accent on the whole of an expression as a systematic function of its components (1987),[120] while John Haugeland foregrounds the composition of compound expressions (1987).[121] For Michael Devitt and Richard Hanley, "compositionality" means that "the meaning of a sentence is determined by the meanings of the words that constitute it and by the way those words are put together, by the syntactic structure of the sentence."[122] In short, according to compositionality, "the meaning of a compound expression is a function of the meanings of its parts."[123]

A detailed defense of compositionality is provided by Josh Dever's in *The Oxford Handbook of Philosophy of Language* (2006).[124] In his definition, a compositional language is a language in which "each of its complex expressions is derived from the meanings of its simple expressions." He places two theoretical limitations on compositionality, (1) "semantic closure," which stipulates that "only semantic information can go into the determination of the semantic value of a complex expression"; and (2) "semantic locality," demanding that "only information derived from the parts of complex expressions can go into the determination of the semantic value of that expression." In this way, Dever has immunized the concept of compositionality against contamination by verbal as well as nonverbal contexts outside the expression in question. Compositionality is "a tool for limiting what can be relevant to determining the meaning of a complex expression."[125] Since we have already rejected the very idea of unuttered sentences, Dever's dual restriction makes compositionality applicable only to a narrowly conceived notion of natural language. Once again, the theorization of natural language is held to the standards of artificial sign systems.

From a Husserlian position, a major shortcoming of such standard conceptions of compositionality is the conviction of the *semantic immanence* of linguistic expressions, a presupposition carried from formal sign systems across to the very different domain of natural language. Accordingly, Dever feels justified in saying that "compositionality marks the convergence of three components of a semantic theory: the assignment of meaning to the parts, the assignment of meaning to the complexes, and the parthood relation between parts and complexes."[126] However, as idiomatic expressions, metaphors, indirect speech acts, Chinese homophone phrase substitutions, and other forms of circumlocution show,[127] the assumption of meaning as fully contained within the components of compound linguistic expressions does not square with the realities of actual discourse. Dever's own examples highlight the cracks in any hermetic conception of compositionality. Comparing the expressions "Who bought that book?" and "Who the hell bought that book? he declares that "the two are roughly synonymous." The hell they are. For Dever, the difference is no more than their "rhetorical impact," leaving intact "the core semantic value of each" as "a request for information about the identity of the book buyer."[128] This is where things go badly wrong. The phrase "the hell" is an important instruction to the listener (reader) to negate the "Who" altogether in favor of a meaning fulfilment paraphrasable along the lines "What a lousy book!" Which is at least as plausible a meaning construction as the one taken for granted by Dever. An emphasis on "the hell" suggests meanings such as "How could anyone buy such a book?" or even "No one would seriously buy this sort of book!" In short, compositionality needs to be argued in terms of utterances as a necessary condition of linguistic meaning.

A modest account of compositionality is advocated by Francis Jeffry Pelletier, who defends it on the grounds that it provides a way to demonstrating truth, validity, and inference; that semantics must be compositional because our cognitive states are compositional; that language without compositionality would be unlearnable; that compositionality bridges the explanatory gap between language as finite resource and of generating an infinite number of possible sentences; and that without it, we could not make sense of novel sentences. Acknowledging a broad phalanx of criticisms of "compositionality," he concludes that compositionality via functionality "is false."[129] Pelletier's position can be accommodated in the present account on condition that the concept of compositionality is broadened, as proposed. What still needs consolidating is the claim that in sharp contrast with formal assumptions, compositionally in natural language runs into a number of unacknowledged constraints. I will argue this claim in five steps: in terms of the failure of semantic immanence in natural language expressions, the complexity of idiomatic expressions and metaphor, the example of the intriguing case of Chinese homophone phrase substitution, the principle that sentences can have meaning only as utterances, and the indispensable role of imaginability.

On the claim that semantic immanence fails, consider the following examples: "Beats me." "Pass." "Am I Jesus?" "No idea." "You have got me there." "I haven't got a clue." "Sorry, can't help you." "I haven't the faintest." "Beyond my ken." Very roughly, they all mean "I don't know." But how do the individual parts of these expressions contribute to this coarse-grained overall meaning? All of them require acts that point outside the semantic scope of the meanings of the individual components. In this sense, standard compositionality is *insufficient*. As Pelletier concludes, compositionality fails because it cannot deal with the discourse dependence of language.[130] If so, then at least

Frege's law has given a good reason for reuniting semantics and pragmatics.[131] What is missing in immanent accounts of compositionality are

> all kinds of fact, all kinds of information . . . context . . . inferences . . . world knowledge to evaluate an expression, where these facts, etc. are not part of the meanings of the parts of the expression (and they are furthermore not dictated by the "method of combination" used to construct the expression).[132]

In short, the immanent conception of compositionality in natural language is not tenable, a contention consolidated by *idiomatic expressions and metaphor*. For example, the meaning of "Are you pulling my leg?" cannot be retrieved from the parts of this ubiquitous expression. Likewise, the meaning of "She gave me the rough end of the pineapple." And yet, meaning in both cases should be transparent here according to the principle that "it is because the constituents of sentences make repeatable contributions to the meanings of sentences that it is possible to understand a sentence that one has never heard before provided that it is built from familiar words in familiar ways."[133] None of the specifics of "end" or "pineapple" are relevant to the meaning intention of the utterance. What is crucial is the overall idea that can be generalized by the listener with the help of imaginability. While the expression "It would choke a brown dog" is easily reconstructed as "This is inedible," it is not so easy to successfully apply the rule of compositionality to the idiom "Don't come the raw prawn."

A fascinating case in the context of compositionality is *Chinese homophone phrase substitution*.[134] Called *zhengzhi yinyu* in Chinese, this form of complex circumlocution or *hidden language* is a time-honored linguistic tradition by which a speaker can plead innocence in uttering an innocuous expression that has a merely implied, usually offensive, second-order meaning. This device has seen a recent, dramatic revival on the Internet, especially as a form of political criticism. The trope works by the replacement of one character by a homophone or near homophone but very different character with an entirely different meaning. Cases of hidden language are recognized by the reader of a text in which a character, or sets of characters, makes no immediate sense. Its pronunciation then leads the reader to the recognition of a homophone, or near homophone, merely implied character sequence that carries the intended, sensitive meaning. Examples of *zhengzhi yinyu* are *héxiè* (river crab) for the Party slogan *héxié* (harmony), now commonly understood as "censorship," or the character sequence "the Chinese people have begun to tremble," which phonetically almost mirrors the very different characters of the famous slogan of 1949 by Mao Zedong "The Chinese people have risen!" As a form of circumlocution, *zhengzhi yinyu* differs from verbal irony by its contextual incoherence and absence of standard phrase meaning. It differs from metaphor by its lack of directionality at the semantic level and sole reliance on phonetic guidance. However, the trope seriously undermines the customary separation of semantics from pragmatics in that it demonstrates beyond doubt that without utterance meaning fails.

Nor, as the Chinese language demonstrates, is *syntactic order* as reliable a necessary component of compositionality as claimed, for example, by Partee et al., who write,

"The meaning of a compound expression is a function of the meanings of its parts *and* of the *syntactic rule* by which they are combined,"[135] a sentiment echoed in a range of contributions to the debate on compositionality.[136] And even scrambled English more often than not allows meaning construction to occur.

Last, a brief look at the role of imaginability with respect to the analytical concept of compositionality if applied to the idiomatic expression "Where is John? He's driving the big white porcelain truck." If we were to restrict ourselves to the dictionary senses of the expression we would end up with the literal meaning of "steering a large and heavy vehicle made of porcelain." To meet Wittgenstein's demand for clarification of the function of imaginability in the process of comprehending a sentence,[137] without imaginative acts we would remain stuck at the level of senseless literality. The compositionality of our sample is in urgent need of imaginative meaning exploration. We take a step back, as it were, and vary several phantasy scenarios that might fit the expression, a situation in which a person is interacting with something big, made of porcelain, and performing motions reminiscent of holding and moving a sizable steering wheel. When the expression is used as part of the typical language games people engage in at a party, in response for instance to the question "Where is John?" the summary meaning of the metaphor is easily constituted. Our example also well illustrates the distinction that Husserl draws between Leerintention as merely logical or merely verbal grasp, his *Bedeutung*, and vividly imaginable meaning fulfilment, as *anschaulichen Sinn*.[138] The mere word meanings of "driving," "big," "porcelain," and "truck" are demonstrably an intermediate, merely *directional* stage, Husserl's transitional consciousness (*Durchgangsbewusstsein*).[139] Rebuffed by this unsatisfactory meaning, we employ imaginative variations of possible situations for which the expression could make sense. Peirce would say, we perform a series of *abductions*, on the principle of "the surprising fact C is observed; but if A were true, C would be a matter of course. Hence, there is reason to suspect that A is true."[140] In our case "A" would be something like "John is sick, shakily embracing the toilet." When we are finally on the right track by imagining a likely, appropriate situation, the circumlocution has become *anschaulich* in Husserl's sense; one could say it has become *pictorially imaginable*. The complex process of meaning constitution here testifies to the merely directional role that the symbolic signifiers play in natural language. In this sense, we could agree to the weakened thesis that compositionality "provides a strategy for dealing with the complexities of language" and so can be accepted "at least as a heuristic device."[141]

## Sorites Arguments, Recursion, and Predicability

A typical sorites puzzle consists of a series of seemingly harmless assertions followed by an unacceptable solution. For example, "Would we call a person 2m in height 'tall?' 'Yes.' 'A person measuring 190cm?' 'Yes.' '189cm.' 'Yes,' and so on. 'Therefore' a person measuring 1m is tall." Why is it that ordinary language users are not puzzled by *sorites arguments*, while logicians find them so captivating? Two features seem to be prominent here. One is that they highlight the *vagueness* of terms in natural language. And because language terms are typically *underdetermined*,[142] members of a speech community have been trained to cope with vagueness and ambiguity according to the principle of intersubjective sufficiency, as argued above. The second point highlighted by sorites puzzles is that they appear to pinpoint a misalignment between logical procedures and natural language, demonstrated most accurately by accounts where mathematical logic occupies center stage of the discussion.[143] As Sainsbury and Williamson show, "little-by-little" arguments are based on a series of premises, "the gradualness" of which makes each step in the argument "appear true."[144] At the end of their formal representation, Sainsbury and Williamson return to discussing natural language via Russell's observations about the vagueness of linguistic meaning and by drawing our attention to the "epistemic view" to be taken.[145] Phenomenology offers an alternative explanatory path toward solving the problem of vagueness identified in the sorites arguments via vivid imaginability. We typically *imagine* relevant scenarios in response to linguistic expressions by placing linguistic expressions in appropriate nonverbal contexts in the process of meaning fulfilment constituting Husserl's *Sinn* as realistic, "*anschauliche Vorstellung*."[146]

Another formal principle that has played a role in linguistics and analytical accounts is *recursion*, championed as a major ingredient of language by Noam Chomsky and others.[147] While working smoothly in formal systems, it tends to run up against what is idiomatically unaccepted phrasing in natural language. This is an important *social* constraint on Chomsky's language faculty, even if it still allows for a very large number of possible expressions to be phrased in a recursive manner. The reason that idiomaticity is crucial in regulating the production of sentence tokens as utterances is that Chomsky's I-language, our internalized language competence, here must respect the E-language, the external language monitored by the speech community. Recursion in language is restricted by idiomaticity and so dependent on standard use. This is why recursivity has been argued by Stephen Levinson to be more appropriately dealt with in pragmatics.[148] Which, according to our arguments so far, is a kind of theoretical escapism. Instead, we should embrace the limitations of recursion within a conception of a natural language semantics that is designed to acknowledge its social rules of constraint.

Similar restrictions pertain to *predicability*, or what can be predicated about something linguistically. In natural language, the formal expectation of predicability faces two barriers: linguistic convention and nature. We simply don't speak of "vengeful apples," and nature tells us not to refer to "flying elephants" except, once more, in poetic speech. Predicability plays an important role in reminding us of the fact that the perceptual world, shared to a very large extent and to a high degree of accuracy by diverse cultures, is a stubborn backdrop to language rather than a merely linguistic variant. The more closely languages deal with the perceptual world at a corporeal level, the smaller the conceptual differences. Vice versa, the more culturally saturated, the greater the differences at the level of the motivated signifieds. Furthermore, predicability changes over time, observing shifts in the community yardsticks of acceptable speech. When it comes to the representation of intersubjectively shared reality, predicability demonstrates that the intentional acts that we are guided to perform are restrained not by an idealized semantics or a language faculty but by the perceptual world, linguistic idiomaticity, and the social standards of the speech community. Together, they contribute to what makes language *natural*.

## Zeno: The Desedimentation of Achilles

A topic that has often exercised the minds of philosophers, including analytical proponents, is Zeno's *paradoxa*.[149] One of four surviving paradoxes of Zeno of Elea is *Achilles and the Tortoise*, in which Achilles agrees to a footrace with the tortoise, offering it a substantial head start. Zeno shows that Achilles can never win the race because each time Achilles gets to the point where the tortoise was when he started, the tortoise will have moved on beyond that point, and so on *ad infinitum*. The general principle invoked by Zeno is that in order to cover a certain distance, we have to first traverse half of it, then half of the rest, and yet again travel half of the remainder, and so on, which involves us in an infinite regress. Beyond the use of the paradox as a clever narrative, the paradox, like the other three, is making a serious philosophical point. Zeno is performing a *reductio ad absurdum* of the Pythagorean claim that the world consists of geometrically spatial extensions. His critical analysis is accomplished by the spatialization if time. As a result, movement is reduced to punctuality as *discontinuity*. The Pythagorean position of infinite divisibility of space and time is thus shown to lead to a failure of accounting for motion. Zeno advanced his critique of motion in defense of the thesis advocated by Parmenides of the changeless homogeneity of reality.

For some 2,000 years, philosophers have amused their disciples with this paradox. Taking a phenomenological approach, we ask what intentional acts Zeno had to entertain that allowed him to deviate so dramatically from the way a race is normally conceived and narrated. Normally, we would imagine Achilles just pipping the tortoise to the post, given his speed and the fact that he has granted the tortoise a fair head start. What alterations to the natural language version is Zeno guiding us to make? We are made to reimagine the event in geometrical terms by attending exclusively to the spatial relations between the competitors. By endlessly subdividing the distances by which Achilles is getting closer to the tortoise, our geometrical acts of imagining space produce infinitesimally small distances as a timeless process. Our acts of consciousness have transformed the race into purely spatial phenomena, which are thinkable, but distort perceptual reality. By eliminating the crucial component of time, we have violated the very concept of the "foot race." In doing so, we have performed an illegitimate eidetic reduction. Zeno has guided us to collapse the two dimensions of time of succession and duration into simultaneity, producing a timeless geometry. As soon as we reintroduce the full dimension of time into the narrative, Achilles leaps across the tortoise at a certain point of the total distance, winning the race. Zeno's paradox is intriguing well beyond its historical contribution and function in philosophical pedagogy. It could very well be read as a prophetic critique of *minimal* semantics.[150] *Achilles and the Tortoise* prefigures the paradox of post-Fregean philosophy of language. It would seem that the more substantially we hand our investigations over to formalization, the less likely is it that they will be able to capture the complexities of the human mind reflected in language.

## Conclusion: *Anschaulichkeit* Compensates for Arbitrariness

For language to function, we need to fill the merely symbolic and so semantically empty signifiers with typified knowledge to facilitate meaning saturation. Formal signs diverge sharply from this requirement; they are materially empty. In interpreted symbolic systems, typified perceptual materiality is required for quantifying saturation. Which, however, does not justify calling language "an interpreted formal sign system."[151] Applied calculus does not *name* perceptual reality but rather functions as a system of stipulated measuring units superimposed on an already named reality for the purpose of quantification. In contrast, meaning fulfilment in natural language provides Husserl's linguistic "*Sättigung*" as "objectifying imaginative projection in the mode of thematic execution."[152] This is why in the *Nachlass*, Husserl distances the generality of natural language concepts from that of formal emptiness more clearly than he did in the *Logical Investigations*. As he now writes, "the word 'lion' is not a generality like a triangle."[153] Nor is it a merely verbal generality, which would do no more than Husserl's "lion" does already. What sort of generality then is that which is neither formal (*gegenstandslos*) nor a merely verbal abstraction? The answer, once more, is to be sought in Husserl's concept of *anschaulich*, translated here as *vividly imaginable*. The sensuous (*sinnliche*) meaning fulfilment of "lion" is *imaginably* objective (*gegenständlich*).[154]

To call natural language a *symbolic sign system*, then, veils the important differences that dissociates language from its formally symbolic derivatives. The degree of dissimilarity between language and formal signs has been demonstrated by drawing attention to their drastically different forms of "fulfilment (*Erfüllung*)." A mathematical equation is fulfilled when the calculation is completed with always the identical result that, in Husserl's words, must remain "unsaturated."[155] In language, the "modus of saturation"[156] involves intimation, introjection, graded comprehension, intersubjective sufficiency, and the apperceptive "empathy" (*Einfühlung*) into "the psychic life of the other (das *fremde psychische Leben*)."[157] Attempts at fudging this radical otherness of language can produce seductively elegant constructions, but only distance us from understanding the profound way in which language facilitates human interaction as being-within-one-another, Husserl's sociality as *Ineinandersein*.

The following chapter speculatively traces imaginability to its possible prelinguistic origins, in competition with some of the recent literature on language evolution.

## Notes

1 Martin Kusch, *Language as Calculus and Universal Medium* (Dordrecht: Kluwer, 1989), p. 131; cf. also David W. Smith and Ronald McIntyre, *Husserl and Intentionality* (Dordrecht: Reidel, 1982), as well as the stance taken by Dagfin

Føllesdal in "Husserl's Notion of Noema," *The Journal of Philosophy* 66 (1969), 680–7; and "Noema and Meaning in Husserl," *Philosophy and Phenomenological Research* 50 (1990), 263–71.
2. Horst Ruthrof, *The Body in Language* (London: Cassell, 2000), pp. 85ff.
3. Hua XII, p. 351.
4. Edmund Husserl, "The Origin of Geometry," in *The Crisis of European Sciences and Transcendental Phenomenology: An Introduction to Phenomenological Philosophy*, trans. D. Carr, 353–78 (Evanston: Northwestern University Press, 1970), p. 368.
5. Jacques Lacan, "Sign, Symbol, Imaginary," in *On Signs*, ed. M. Blonsky (Oxford: Blackwell, 1985), pp. 203–9; Charles F. Hockett, "The Origin of Speech," *Scientific American* 203 (1960), 88–96; and "The Problem of Universals in Language," in *Universals of Language*, ed. J. Greenberg (Cambridge, MA: MIT Press, 1966), pp. 1–29.
6. Dieter Lohmar, "Denken ohne Sprache?" in *Meaning and Language*, ed. F. Mattens (Dordrecht: Springer, 2008), pp. 169–94 (178).
7. Burt Hopkins, "On the Origin of the 'Language' of Formal Mathematics," in *Meaning and Language*, 149–69; pp. 161ff.; cf. also *The Origin of the Logic of Symbolic Mathematics: Edmund Husserl and Jacob Klein* (Bloomington: Indiana University Press, 2011); and "Husserl and Jacob Klein," *The European Legacy* 21, 5–6 (2016), 535–55.
8. Hopkins, "On the Origin of Formal Mathematics," pp. 161ff.
9. Edmund Husserl, *Formal and Transcendental Logic,* trans. D. Cairns (The Hague: Martinus Nijhoff, 1969), p. 312.
10. Ibid., p. 150.
11. Hua XX/2, p. 296.
12. Kant, CPR A728f/B756.
13. Hua XX/1, p. 4n3.
14. Hua XX/2, p. 325.
15. Hua XX/2, p. 151.
16. Hua XX/1, p. 38; my emphasis.
17. Hua XX/2, p. 329.
18. Hua XX/1, p. 129.
19. Ibid., p. 38; my emphasis.
20. Hua XX/2, p. 157n1.
21. Ibid., p. 187.
22. Hua XX/2, p. 143; my emphasis.
23. Ibid., p. 145. check.
24. Ibid., p. 151; my emphasis.
25. Ibid., p. 3.
26. Cf. Editor's note \*, Hua XX/1, p. 39.
27. Peirce, CP 8.314; 1.158; Hua XX/2, pp. 143f.; 329.
28. Hua XX/2, pp. 396f.
29. Ibid.
30. Ibid., p. 400.
31. Ibid., pp. 400f.
32. Ibid., p. 142.
33. Ibid., p. 95.
34. Ibid., p. 4.
35. Ibid., p. 112.
36. Hua XX/1, p. 7.

37 Hua XX/2, p. 5.
38 Ullrich Melle, "Das Rätsel des Ausdrucks: Husserls Zeichen- und Ausdruckslehre in den Manuskripten für die Neufassung der VI. Logischen Untersuchung," in *Meaning and Language*, 3–26, p. 5.
39 Hua XX/2, pp. 131f.
40 Hua XX/1, p. 31.
41 Hua XX/2, p. 146.
42 Ibid., p. 105.
43 Hua XX/1, p. 33.
44 Hua XX/2, p. 75.
45 Hua XX/1, pp. 25f.
46 Hua XX/2, p. 73.
47 Hua XX/1, 77; XX/2, p. 291.
48 Hua XX/2, pp. 151, 187.
49 Ibid., p. 187.
50 Ibid., p. 154.
51 Ibid., p. 223.
52 Ibid., p. 157.
53 Ibid., pp. 101, 135n2.
54 Ibid., p. 135n2.
55 Ibid., p. 136.
56 Ibid., p. 316.
57 Hua XX/2, p. 103.
58 Ibid., p. 102.
59 Ibid.
60 Ibid.
61 Ibid., p. 104.
62 Ibid., p. 102.
63 Ibid., p. 106.
64 Ibid., p. 114.
65 Edmund Husserl, *Experience and Judgment: Investigations in a Genealogy of Logic*, trans. J. S. Churchill and K. Ameriks (Evanston: Northwestern University Press, 1997), pp. 210f.
66 Marc Hauser, Noam Chomsky, and Tecumseh Fitch, "The Faculty of Language: What Is It, Who Has It, and How Did It Evolve?" *Science* 298 (2002), 1569–79; or the early Derek Bickerton, *Roots of Language* (Ann Arbor, MI: Karoma, 1981); "The Supremacy of Syntax," *Behavioral and Brain Sciences* 10 (1987), 658–9; *Language and Species* (Chicago: University of Chicago Press, 1990); Tecumseh Fitch, *The Evolution of Language* (Cambridge: Cambridge University Press, 2010).
67 Ray Jackendoff, "Possible Stages in the Evolution of the Language Capacity," *Trends in Cognitive Sciences* 3, 7 (1999), 272–9; Robin Burling, *The Talking Ape: How Language Evolved* (Oxford: Oxford University Press, 2005).
68 Lohmar, "Denken ohne Sprache?" p. 173.
69 See Chapter 9.
70 Hua XX/2, p. 50.
71 Ibid., p. 51.
72 Peirce, CP 8.335.
73 Hua XX/2, p. 50.
74 Ibid., p. 57.

75 Ibid., p. 104.
76 Lohmar, "Denken ohne Sprache?" p. 173.
77 Hua XX/2, p. 75.
78 Ibid., p. 22.
79 Ibid., p. 339.
80 Ibid., p. 139.
81 Leonard Talmy, *Towards a Cognitive Semantics* (Cambridge, MA: MIT Press, 2000).
82 Hua XX/2, p. 432.
83 Ibid., p. 109.
84 Hua XX/1, p. 38; my emphasis.
85 Ibid., my emphasis.
86 Hua XX/2, pp. 8, 349f.
87 Ibid., p. 291.
88 Ibid.
89 Ibid., p. 23.
90 Ibid., p. 36.
91 Ibid., p. 76; my emphasis.
92 Ibid., pp. 151, 353.
93 Ibid., p. 4.
94 Ibid., p. 103, 104n1.
95 Hua XIX/2, pp. 658f.
96 Hua XX/2, p. 12.
97 Ibid., p. 176.
98 Ibid., pp. 394, 356, 263n7.
99 Ibid., p. 356.
100 Ibid., p. 26.
101 Ibid.
102 Moritz Schlick, "Meaning and Verification," *Philosophical Review* 45 (1936), 339–68 (339ff.).
103 Donald Davidson, "Truth and Meaning," in *Semantics: A Reader*, ed. S. Davis and B. S. Gillon (Oxford: Oxford University Press, 2004), pp. 222–33 (226).
104 Mark Richard, *When Truth Gives Out* (Oxford: Oxford University Press, 2008).
105 Alfred Tarski, *Logic, Semantics, Metamathematics*, trans. J. H. Woodger (Oxford: Clarendon Press, 1956 [1936]), pp. 153ff.
106 Ibid., p. 267.
107 The "mono-propositionalism" of truth-conditional theories has been challenged, for example, by the notions of "pluri-propositionalism" and "referential truth-conditions" by Kepa Korta and John Perry in *Critical Pragmatics: An Inquiry into Reference and Communication* (Cambridge: Cambridge University Press, 2011).
108 Horst Ruthrof, "Sufficient Semiosis," *The American Journal of Semiotics* 31, 1 (2015), 117–46.
109 Edmund Husserl, *Logical Investigations*, trans. J.N. Findlay (New York, Humanity Books, 2000), p. 277.
110 Davidson, "Truth and Meaning," p. 232.
111 Donald Davidson, *Truth and Predication* (Cambridge MA: Harvard University Press, 2005), p. 75; my emphasis.
112 Kant, CPR A68/B93.

113 Ludwig Wittgenstein, *Philosophical Investigations*, trans. G.E.M. Anscombe, P.M.S. Hacker, and J. Schulte (Oxford: Blackwell, 2009),,, § 676.
114 Kant, CPR A494/B522; my emphasis.
115 Cf. John R. Searle, "The Logical Status of Fictional Discourse," *New Literary History* 6 (1975), 319–32; which demonstrates the laborious and hardly convincing arguments needed to make truth relevant for fictions.
116 Hua XLI, p. 33.
117 Richard Grandy, "Understanding and Compositionality," *Philosophical Perspectives* 4 (1990), 557–72.
118 Mark Richard, "Compositionality," in *The Shorter Routledge Encyclopedia of Philosophy*, ed. E. Craig (London: Routledge, 2005), p. 133.
119 Francis Jeffry Pelletier, "The Principle of Semantic Compositionality," in *Semantics: A Reader*, ed. S. Davis and B. S. Gillon (Oxford: Oxford University Press, 1994), pp. 133–56 (133).
120 Graeme Hirst, *Semantic Interpretation and the Resolution of Ambiguity* (Cambridge: Cambridge University Press, 1987).
121 John Haugland, *Artificial Intelligence: The Very Idea* (Cambridge, MA: MIT Press, 1987).
122 Michael Devitt and Richard Hanley (eds.), *The Blackwell Guide to the Philosophy of Language* (Oxford: Blackwell, 2006), p. 3.
123 Theo M. V. Janssen, "Compositionality of Meaning," in *Concise Encyclopedia of Philosophy of Language*, ed. P. Lamarque and R. E. Asher (Oxford: Pergamon, 1997), pp. 102–7 (102); cf. also his "Compositionality," in *Handbook of Logic and Language*, ed. J. van Bentham and A. ter Meulen, 417–73. For other relevant accounts, see Zoltan Gendler Szabo, "Compositionality as Supervenience," *Linguistics and Philosophy* 23, 5 (2000), 475–505; Markus Werning, "Compositionality, Context, Categories, and the Indeterminacy of Tradition," *Erkenntnis* 60 (2004), 145–78; Jaroslav Peregrin, "Is Compositionality an Empirical Matter?" *Journal of Logic, Language, and Information* 10 (2003), 115–36; Richard Heck, "Is Compositionality a Trivial Matter?" *Frontiers of Philosophy in China* 8 (2013), 140–55; Wilfrid Hodges, "Formal Features of Compositionality," *Journal of Logic, Language, and Information* 10 (2001), 7–28; Josh Dever, "Compositionality," in *The Oxford Handbook of Philosophy of Language*, ed. E. Lepore and B. C. Smith (Oxford: Clarendon Press, 2006), pp. 633–66 and his "Compositionality as Methodology," *Linguistics and Philosophy* 22 (1999), 311–26; Ali Kazmi and Francis Jeffry Pelletier, "Is Compositionality Formally Vacuous?" *Linguistics and Philosophy* 21 (1998), 629–33; Hans Kamp and Barbara Partee, "Prototype Theory and Compositionality," *Cognition* 57 (1995), 129–91; Barbara Partee, "Compositionality," in *Variety of Formal Semantics*, ed. F. Landman and F. Veltman (Dordrecht: Foris, 1984), pp. 281–312.
124 Dever, "Compositionality," pp. 633–66.
125 Ibid., pp. 633f.
126 Ibid., p. 644.
127 Yingchi Chu and Horst Ruthrof, "The Social Semiotic of Homophone Phrase Substitution in Chinese Netizen Discourse," *Social Semiotics* 27, 5 (2017), 640–55.
128 Dever, "Compositionality," p. 648.
129 Pelletier, "Semantic Compositionality," p. 142.
130 Ibid., p. 134.
131 Theo M. V. Janssen, "Frege, Contextuality, and Compositionality," *Journal of Logic, Language, and Information* 10 (2001), 115–36; Francis Jeffry Pelletier, "Did Frege

Believe Frege's Principle?" *Journal of Logic, Language, and Information* 10 (2001), 87–114.
132  Pelletier, "Semantic Compositionality," p. 149.
133  Martin Davies, "Foundational Issues in the Philosophy of Language," in *The Blackwell Guide to the Philosophy of Language,* ed. M. Devitt and R. Hanley (Oxford: Blackwell, 2006), pp. 19–40 (27).
134  Chu and Ruthrof, "Homophone Phrase Substitution."
135  Barbara H. Partee, Alice ter Meulen, and Robert E. Wall, *Mathematical Methods in Linguistics* (Dordrecht: Kluwer, 1990), p. 318; my emphasis.
136  Haugeland, *Artificial Intelligence*; Richard, "Compositionality"; Michael Devitt and Richard Hanley (eds.), *The Blackwell Guide to the Philosophy of Language* (Oxford: Basil Blackwell, 2006).
137  Wittgenstein, *Philosophical Investigations,* § 395.
138  Hua XX/2, p. 143.
139  Ibid., p. 151.
140  Charles Sanders Peirce, *Collected Papers of Charles Sanders Peirce 1931–1966,* 8 vols., ed. C. Hartsworth, P. Weiss, and A. W. Burks (Cambridge, MA: Belknap Press), CP 5.189.
141  Janssen, "Compositionality of Meaning," p. 106.
142  Kant CPR A727ff./B755ff.
143  Mark Sainsbury and Timothy Williams, "Sorites," in *A Companion to the Philosophy of Language,* ed. B. Hale and C. Wright (Oxford: Blackwell, 1999), pp. 458–84.
144  Ibid., p. 462.
145  Sainsbury and Williams, p. 479; cf. Russell, "Vagueness," *The Australian Journal of Psychology and Philosophy* 1 (1923), 84–92.
146  Hua XX/2, p. 292.
147  Marc Hauser, Noam Chomsky, and Tecumseh Fitch, "The Language Faculty: What Is It, Who Has It, and How Did It Evolve?" *Science* 298 (2002), 1569–79.
148  Stephen C. Levinson, "Recursion in Pragmatics," *Language* 89 (2013), 149–62.
149  Wesley C. Salmon, *Zeno's Paradoxes,* 2nd ed. (Indianapolis: Hackett Publishing, 2001).
150  E.g., Emma Borg, *Minimal Semantics* (Oxford: Clarendon Press, 2004).
151  Günther Grewendorf, Fritz Hamm, and Wolfgang Sternefeld, *Sprachliches Wissen: Eine Einführung in Moderne Theorien der Grammatischen Beschreibung* (Frankfurt: Suhrkamp, 1987), p. 377.
152  Hua XX/2, p. 205.
153  Ibid., p. 117.
154  Ibid., p. 325.
155  Ibid., p. 296.
156  Ibid., p. 136.
157  Ibid., p. 68.

# 9

# Displacement, Mental Time Travel, and Protosyntax

The ideas presented in this chapter once again take a foundational theme in Husserl's writings as their point of departure, his treatment of categorial relations, and the core-forms of *substantivity* and *adjectivity*. Since these concepts have already been discussed in earlier chapters, they will remain in the background, merely providing the basis for my arguments. From this perspective, I want to review three related, topical themes: *displacement, mental time travel*, and *protosyntax*. Introduced into linguistics by Charles Hockett in 1960,[1] the concept of *displacement* highlights a significant feature of language, one that marks a radical shift in the evolution of human semiosis. *Linguistic displacement* occurs when we transform *perceptual* and *quasi-perceptual* acts of meaning intention into verbal expressions. However, contrary to structuralist belief, linguistic displacement could not have happened all at one stroke. We can only speculate that it must have gradually emerged out after the ability of nonverbal, perceptual displacement had already become a socially sharable capacity that had proved itself as a useful survival strategy. As such, displacement can be stipulated as *imaginability*, that is, the ability to vary any given apperception into an alternative, merely *imaginable* but relevant *scenario*. Once this communal capacity was established, the emergence of symbolic signs was likely one of the benefits of human evolution. Although veiled by the mists of hominid prehistory, it seems reasonable to assume that displacement must have dramatically advanced communication by gradually replacing nonverbal signification relying on *iconicity* (direct resemblance relations) and *indexicality* (indirect, existential resemblance) by verbal, *symbolic signification*. In this regard, displacement is crucial to the transformation of pre-predicative substantivity and adjectivity into naming and basic predication, as well as of prelinguistic categorial relations into verbal syntax.[2] Via displacement, categorial acts of perception could gradually "come to expression" in language as grounded in the categorial, prelinguistic structures of hominid, *communal intentionality*.[3]

On somewhat less shaky ground, I also want to present a critical view of the recent theorization, foremost in the psychological literature, of mental time travel. Again, my accent will be on imaginability (*Vorstellbarkeit*), defined in the previous chapters as the human ability to *vary perception under social guidance* and the *capacity of language to convey resemblance relations*. Imaginability will be argued as the necessary condition of both the spatial and temporal aspects of mental time travel, two very different kinds of acts that seem to me to be conflated in current accounts. My third topic will be protosyntax, viewed as a likely forerunner of verbal syntax, in opposition to the popular view that syntax is a result of the emergence of language. Instead, in line with Husserl's pre-predicative, categorial forms, and with a nod to Wittgenstein, I am going to contend that modern syntax is more likely a refinement of ordering principles inherited by language from its nonverbal precursors in its evolutionary trajectory from prelinguistic perceptual being and iconic, gestural communication to verbal utterance. Taking a strongly *gradualist stance* on the likely emergence of language, I will discard the structuralist assumption that "language must have been born in a single stroke," when "a passage was effected from the stage where nothing made sense to another where everything did," because "objects couldn't just start to signify progressively."[4] In a similar structuralist vein, Eric Gans proposed the birth of language out of the communal experience of death.[5] Such *catastrophe theories* also include the claim by the early Derek Bickerton that language could not possibly have evolved out of a protolanguage, since there could not have been any intermediate forms. Instead, he insists that syntax suddenly emerged as an organizational mutation in the human brain.[6] Likewise shaky now looks any syntax-driven description of language.[7] However, in some recent literature, a more gradualist conception of language evolution has now taken hold.[8]

## Displacement and Imaginability

### Dual Displacement

We have on several occasions mentioned Charles F. Hockett's notion of *displacement*, a concept proposed in 1960 in an initial list of thirteen essential traits of language, a little later (1966) enlarged to sixteen. It is now appropriate to have a closer look at his comprehensive catalog. In the order proposed by Hockett, language is made up of such indispensable features as (1) the *sounds* of linguistic expressions; (2) their broadcast transmission and directional processing; (3) *transitoriness* of word sounds (a feature that is not falsified by written language or by signed languages, the former because it requires at least a "silent" intonation, the latter because they always piggyback on existing languages); (4) *interchangeability* of messages regardless of facts or truth; (5) *total feedback*, since speakers are able to monitor their own speech; (6) *specialization*, in that language is primarily representational and communicative and yet lends itself also to mumbling to oneself; (7) *semanticity*, the fact that word sounds are tied to meanings; (8) *arbitrariness*, the fact that linguistic signifiers are merely conventional in contrast to their always motivated signifieds; (9) *discreteness*, that in language small meaning units are combined by syntactic and grammatical rules categorically rather than continuously; (10) *displacement*, that word sounds replace the things talked about and that what is being talked about does not have to exist; (11) *productivity*, which appears in the potential infinity of expressions out of finite means (Humboldt's law), the ongoing evolution of sentence patterning, the emergence of new idiomatic expressions, and semantic drift as a result of the changing relations between word sounds and signifieds; (12) *traditional transmission*, that language acquisition always occurs in social settings, both phylogeny and ontogeny of language are culture dependent, and language and culture cannot be disentangled; (13) *duality of patterning*, that meaningful messages are always made up of smaller, nonsemantic units, such as phonemes; (14) *prevarication*, that is, the capacity of language of facilitating deceptive, false, and meaningless statements; (15) *reflexiveness*, or metalinguistic use, whenever we employ language to talk about language; and (16) *learnability*, the fact that all languages can be learned.[9]

As to displacement, Hockett's insight is as crucial as it has been neglected. Though recently resumed, especially in the literature on mental time travel, even in as well-researched a volume as the 921-page analytical *Semantics: A Reader* (2004), displacement fails to receive a mention. In linguistics, the situation is somewhat different, even if not altogether satisfactory. Although Derek Bickerton, for one, regards displacement as the most important "single source" of the emergence of "cooperation, language, and distinctly human cognition,"[10] he views it as a consequence of language, declaring its "absence" as a "defining feature of the pre-human minds."[11] This, I think, is too narrow a conception of displacement of what I believe to be a much more fundamental human skill. Bickerton, I suggest, has put the cart before the horse. For first we need the ability to vary perception, that is, *displace it* by imaginable alternatives. Only once such a faculty has evolved, can it be inherited by and refined through language. Only in this order does it seem possible to conceive of a progression from naming accompanied by pointing at immediately perceivable things to naming in the absence of identified objectivities. Nor can verbal displacement be a mere substitution at the level of sound gestures. Rather, displacement should be viewed as resulting from special acts, as it is by Husserl when he writes that it must involve a "signifying consciousness" (*signitives Bewusstsein*).[12] What appears to be so displaced by language are perceived items or their merely *imagined* substitutes, instantiated by individuals within communal constraints. At the same time, as Ullrich Melle shows, the functions of displacement go well beyond replacing perceived and imagined phenomena by including the *externalization* of the interiority of experience, the intentionality of the expression in and via its meaning, its *immaterial materiality*, and its expressive and communicative functions.[13]

So, it is timely to revisit Hockett's discovery from a phenomenological perspective. In keeping with our basic strategy, I want to investigate the mandatory acts of consciousness that we perform when we *displace* items in the world or in our imagination with linguistic expressions. As it turns out, such a description will reveal displacement to be a much more complex process than Hockett's opening gesture would suggest. First, we need to look at the transformational process involved in moving from an empirical, bound percept to the choice of a word or an expression. The bound percept, a typified, sedimented combination of multimodal perceptual acts, must be grasped as an *intentional object* before we can exchange it for a verbal analogy. Only once we have formed a meaning intention as a "pointing beyond" (*Hinausweisung*) are we in a position to transpose it into an equivalent verbal expression via an act of word consciousness.[14] This applies as much to physical objects as it does to relations and states of affairs. In language as communication, a series of typical "acts of social reciprocity (*Akte der sozialen Wechselbeziehung*)" has to be carried out.[15] In this sense, displacement is never an individual achievement by a speaker of a language but a social phenomenon, Husserl's "communal achievement (*eine Gemeinschaftsleistung*)."[16]

As such, displacement fulfils yet another function. It facilitates the liberation of language from its representational and narrowly communicative immediacy by making its meaning intention an *option*. For it does not matter whether "nice topspin backhand" is uttered while watching a tennis match or used metaphorically to applaud a sharp retort at the dinner table. Here, displacement combines with Hockett's interchangeability, the capacity of language to convey messages regardless of existence, as well as with prevarication, its eminent suitability for deception. At the same time, language as the displacement of nonverbal, perceptual, and imaginative configurations illustrates Husserl's observation that "the appearing word sounds have the character of something secondary."[17] Put more radically, "the level of linguistic expressions is a superficial phenomenon."[18] Language always points beyond itself. It is always also a *Hinausweisung*. Whereas in perception, "what is meant is also given,"[19] in language, what is displaced is placed at a "higher level (*Oberschicht*) of a peculiarly founded consciousness." This higher-level act calls for nonverbal meaning fulfilment, an "approximation to the aim of cognition."[20] By introducing this higher level, "language extends experience, becomes its substitute, as it were, suspends it, but it can do this only insofar experience has a pre-verbal structure."[21] In this sense, linguistic expressions point not only beyond themselves in a forward direction but also backward to their founding meaning intention. Which suggests that language requires a form of *dual displacement*, once from world to word and then, in meaning fulfilment, from word to an imaginatively reconstituted world. In Husserl's chain of the linguistic meaning acts, dual displacement reveals itself as a replacement of acts of quasi-perceptual meaning intention by the transitional consciousness of merely verbal *Leerintentionen*, followed by acts of saturation that transform mere *Bedeutung* into vividly imaginable meaning fulfilment or *Sinn*.

In what sense, then, can *imaginability* as *the organism's ability to vary perception under social guidance* be held responsible for the very possibility of displacement in its phenomenologically revised version? We must not understand displacement as the moment when we leave the perceptual and imaginable world behind. We merely suspend it during an ever so brief phase of *Leerintention*, Husserl's "empty intention," or merely *directional* word sound consciousness. As the analysis of our linguistic acts demonstrates and as the Husserl of the *Nachlass* repeatedly highlights, word sound consciousness as sign consciousness is only a "transitional consciousness (*Durchgangsbewusstsein*)."[22] The word sound merely stimulates "interest" and functions as a "hold for understanding."[23] For meaning to occur, word sounds must "terminate" in "vividly imaginable conception (*Anschauung*),"[24] by which the communicated object is "perceptually given or imaginatively presented (*den Gegenstand selbst gibt oder bildlich gibt*)," that is, either "presented" or "represented (*präsentiert oder repräsentiert*)."[25] In what way, then, can we argue the dependence of displacement on imaginability? I want to say that a long evolution of nonverbal displacement must have preceded the emergence of language for the simple reason that replacing what is before us by something that is not has to become a social, mental, human habit before the more complex advance can be accomplished to applying it to *symbolic substitution*. First, I suggest, hominids must have developed the ability to *vary* perception itself *homosemiotically*, such as imagining a crouching leopard behind foliage, before that ability could be utilized in verbal communication, which is always *heterosemiotic*. It is plausible then, is it not, that *nonverbal displacement* as deliberate perceptual modification was a necessary cause of or stimulus for the emergence of increasingly *symbolic communication*, culminating in verbal displacement.

Thus, imaginability could be viewed as an extension of *exteroception*, or sensory perception, by the evolution of *proprioception*, that is, internal perception. According to the role of the most salient object in perception, being able to perform the act of imagining a leopard before being jumped by one must have been a major advance in the development of hominid communities. After all, in terms of survival, the imagined leopard must have become a top priority according to "the most-primed-wins principle."[26] The same principle operates in language, where perceptual cognition is first displaced by word sounds and then replaced by meaning fulfilment. Nor is such replacement uniform. According to need, we reconcretize the displaced state of affairs "incompletely" or "completely,"[27] as roughly schematized or imagined in a highly realistic fashion. Not surprisingly, this picture of dual displacement is not congenial to a number of competing theories.

## The Argument from Biology

An intriguing case is the Darwinian idea of language having emerged out of bird song in the form of a musical protolanguage. The *musilanguage* thesis has been strongly defended by Fitch (2010), Brown (2000), Hauser, Fitch, and Chomsky (2000), Mithen (2005, 2012), and Slater (2012).[28] Accordingly, instead of viewing perception and gestural forms of communication as the main precursors of language, proponents of musilanguage emphasize the syntactic and symbolic similarities between song and speech. From the angle of displacement, the musilanguage proposal looks plausible in as much as it provides strong grounding for intonation and voice, as well as the symbolic character of terms and their categorial relations. Its main weakness lies in its relatively weak capacity to explain the vast spectrum of linguistic aboutness. Nonetheless, the possibility that music is likely to have played some role in language evolution cannot be denied.

An approach to the emergence of language that is more difficult to reconcile with the fact of dual displacement comprise mono-causal, biological explanations, as presented for example by Tecumseh Fitch in *The Evolution of Language* (2010).[29] What is missing here is the social dimension of language. We must be able to explain how members of a speech community transform meaning intentions into suitable linguistic expressions, and how they have learned what quasi-perceptual acts to perform in meaning fulfilment. In particular, what is not addressed is the linguistic linkage compulsion, the social coercion involved in training speakers of a language how to associate the sounds of linguistic expressions with communally sanctioned mental material projections. As argued, without *Abrichtung*, that is, communally agreed upon language pedagogy, reinforced from birth to old age, linguistic communication would not work, nor could language have emerged in the first place. The lack of the social dimension of the approach taken by Fitch has been forcefully criticized, for instance, by Nick Enfield.[30] The flaw of the undertheorization of the social dimension of language is likewise a characteristic of the work of the Lakoff School, which otherwise has contributed significantly to our understanding, for instance, of the role of metaphor in abstract reasoning as "cross-domain mapping"[31] and of "conceptual inference" as "sensorimotor inference."[32] From the angle of meaning fulfilment involving imaginability, Husserl's *Anschaulichkeit* in a broad sense, the emphasis on *neural concepts* is a retreat to a much narrower horizon of inquiry, in particular with respect to the all-important involvement of language in *sociality*.

## Cognitive Linguistics and Displacement

A cognitive-linguistic reconciliation of individual mental performance and its social constraints can be found in Ronald Langacker's *Cognitive Grammar: A Basic Introduction* (2008) where the accent is on the social control of language by conventions, with grammar being regarded as their individual mastery. As such, language is explored by Langacker as a sociopsychological phenomenon by which our mental life is linguistically organized and the grammar of which reflects nonverbal ways of conceiving the world.[33] Another contribution of cognitive linguistics is Leonard Talmy's *Towards a Cognitive Semantics* (2000) in which the notion of "gradation" of meaning has proved particularly useful,[34] a thought that looms large in Husserl's thinking from the *Logical Investigations* to the *Nachlass* and his later work.[35] Other approaches that can be harnessed to throw additional light on displacement as problematizing the relation between apperception, *Vorstellung*, and language can be found in the discussion of "cross-modal nature of image schemas" (Popova 2005), the concept of "mimetic schemas" (Zlatev 2007), Fauconnier's "mental spaces" (1997), and the theorization of "conceptual blending" (Fauconnier and Turner 2002).[36] I have already drawn attention to the strongly visual bias in much of this research in that it could do with a redirection toward meaning fulfilment via olfactory, gustatory, thermal, gravitational, and emotional quasi-acts, in short, via non-dominant modalities. On the difficult problem of how displacement affects the transition from prelinguistic categorial relations to their syntactic formations in language, a major contribution has been made by Anne Sweetser in her book *From Etymology to Pragmatics: Metaphorical and Cultural Aspects of Semantic Structure* (1990), especially by her arguments demonstrating fundamental differences between the role of function words in natural language and their formal foils.[37] Above all, her claim that the syntagms of natural language can be traced to relations in human perception is congenial to the kind of phenomenological project pursued here. In this respect, too, Husserl's theorization of *categorial intuition* must count as pathbreaking.[38]

## Displacement, Mimesis, and Imaginability

One of the core concerns in this study is the question of how resemblance can survive beyond linguistic displacement, as it is in Greenfield and Savage-Rumbaugh's "Imitation, Grammatical Development, and the Invention of Protogrammar,"[39] and in Zlatev, Persson, and Gärdenfors (2005) who propose that "bodily mimesis" as a "semiotic capacity" beyond animal abilities is likely to have been the "missing link" in the emergence of language. This is asserted to have occurred in three stages, imitation, intersubjectivity, and gesture, culminating in the co-evolvement of representational, mimetic schemes and communicative intentionality.[40] Four phases of mimesis are identified by the authors, *protomimesis* (proto-mimetic mirroring, as in facial expressions); dyadic mimesis (attention sharing, imperative pointing); triadic mimesis (declarative pointing); and *postmimesis* (signed language, conventional signs). However, what is ignored in these accounts is the transition from apperceptive iconicity to imaginative, quasi-perceptual iconicity and hypoiconicity by means of which we can signify objects, relations, and processes in absentia, but nevertheless *mimetically*, as a necessary stage prior to linguistic displacement. For imaginability, conceived as the socially constrained, mental variation of realist situations, must have played a decisive role in the emergence of language, not only in its inheritance of aboutness and voice but also in the way the world and hominid social behavior appeared as *ordered* rather than random.[41] Therefore, the stipulation of a preverbal protosyntax, subsumed under Husserl's pre-predicative categorial relations,[42] well before the emergence of language, would make sense as a reflection of this sense of order. If so, then a rapidly increasing capacity of imaginability must have been a precondition for being able to mentally vary aboutness, voice, and proto-syntactic sequencing. Nor, I suggest, should language be viewed as "postmimetic." After all, the motivated signified continues to function as the vehicle of resemblance relations. This is where much linguistic theorizing has been bedazzled by the radical structuralist arbitrariness thesis of the linguistic sign.

But what is the advantage of multiplying the *Wahrnehmungswelt* before us by a potentially infinite series of imaginable worlds or *Vorstellungswelten*? The explosion of human intentionality involved here cannot be overestimated in terms of the communal advancement of the human mind. Nor, as art history demonstrates, has imaginability diminished in human evolution to this day. That *Vorstellung* is pertinent to language is persuasively observed by Len Vygotsky: "The child prefers the real apple to the imaginary one," yet "it is the *imagined* apple that will play the crucial role in linguistic meaning."[43] Without imaginability, no language. Indeed, imaginability must have reached a certain degree of complexity well before the emergence of language, an assumption that plays a significant role in a favorite topic in recent publications in psychology, mental time travel. My main critical target in the next section will be the assertion in the literature that mental time travel is the linchpin in the emergence of language out of nonverbal forms of communication. While it is likely that it has played a significant role, I want to unpack specifically the hasty assumption that the spatial and temporal acts of mental time travel could have emerged simultaneously.

## Mental Time Travel

In a seminal paper, Thomas Suddendorf and Michael Corballis coined the phrase *mental time travel* to characterize the human mental faculty of forward and backward projection in time (1997), a topic that they have since revisited in several further publications.[44]

Their research relies in part on the distinction investigated by Endel Tulvin between *semantic* and *episodic memory*, the former referring to memory routines required for daily practices, the latter to the human habit of remembering personal involvement in past events, as a feature of *autonoetic* or self-knowing consciousness.[45] Suddendorf and Corballis thematize our ability to project ourselves mentally into the future, accentuating the advantages such projections must have meant for human evolution and the emergence of language. They regard mental time travel as "the most flexible" form of our memory systems and the one that has "most recently evolved."[46] Mental journeys into our personal past are argued to be structurally comparable with mental projections into the future, with similar attention to particular agents and events such that there is a significant difference between merely imagining the fact of possible future occurrences and the mental creation of detailed prospective scenarios. So, the authors propose that mental time travel "provides increased behavioural flexibility to act in the present to increase future survival chances." Thus, "the crux of mental time travel lies in its role in enhancing biological fitness in the future," with episodic retrieval of the past serving as a model for imagining what may occur later. Suddendorf and Corballis acknowledge the "causal asymmetry" that exists between knowing the past in a way we cannot know the future, though they insist that both kinds of projection rely on many of the same cognitive resources and especially on the structural features of episodic memory.[47] In support of this thesis, Suddendorf and Corballis invoke the metaphors of stage, playwright, actors, set, director, executive producer, and broadcaster to characterize what is required in order to perform elaborate human, *mental staging*. By way of conclusion, the authors suggest that in the "cognitive arms race" humans have outstripped anything we know about other species, and that the ability to employ projections of future states of affairs may very well have led to intention-reading (theory of mind) and verbal communication.[48] In more recent papers, Corballis allows for the possibility that mental time travel may have "ancient origins" well beyond the emergence of language, without, however, pursuing the distinction between its spatial and temporal components.[49]

And yet, the assumption of the simultaneous emergence of spatial and temporal displacement in the form of mental time travel appears to be fundamentally flawed in the absence of arguments supporting their co-occurrence. Since temporal displacement of perception by mental excursions into the past and future is much more complicated than the spatial variation of perception, the latter is likely to have occurred first. As Tulving has persuasively argued, *chronesthesia*, as the subjective awareness of time, must have emerged as a separate precondition of mental time travel.[50] So it is much more likely that imaginability as spatial displacement was the critical turning point that must have evolved into a communal habit of mind over a very long period of time before "projection," nonverbal symbolic systems,[51] and finally *verbal displacement* could occur.

## Protosyntax and Categorial Relations

Up to very recent research,[52] Derek Bickerton's thesis that syntax could not have emerged without the development of a substantial vocabulary permitting sophisticated forms of sequencing had been widely accepted.[53] Similar arguments had been proposed by Chomsky and have recently been reiterated.[54] In accordance with my thesis of a *radical gradualism* in the evolution of language,[55] I advocate a long-term view of linguistic development. After all, almost anything we have so far assumed about human evolution is being routinely backdated. Building once more on Husserl, I want to take issue with the orthodox assumption that syntax is a consequence of language. Instead of running with a deus ex machina solution of a recent mutation in *homo erectus* or *homo sapiens*, I suggest that language has inherited categorial principles from its preverbal antecedents in human prehistory, in prelinguistic perception, gestural communication, and especially pointing.

This is a path of thinking we can take with reference to Husserl in *Experience and Judgment*, even if he does not invoke the notion of protosyntax. As Lothar Eley writes in the "Afterword," Husserl's "predicative judgment refers back to pre-predicative experience."[56] Intriguingly, Husserl does not favor the lexicon as the primary beneficiary of prelinguistic sign systems but "the mode of categorical synthesis, which confers signification on the linguistic expression." Resuming his use of the notions of "syntactical" and "categorial" from *Ideas* and *Formal and Transcendental Logic*, Husserl grants logical priority to pre-predicative experience over linguistically informed experience. Syntactic constellations, for Husserl, are options used differently in different languages for ordering "receptivity," which "lies at the basis of predication"[57] the logical form of which consists in two "core-forms," the "core-form of *substantivity*" and the core-form of "*adjectivity.*" Substantitivity, writes Husserl, "should not be confused with the subject-form. It designates 'being-for-itself,' the independence of an object" in contrast to "*adjectivity*, which is the form of 'in something,' of the dependence of the object-determination."[58] Husserl here is not so much interested in linguistic differences but rather in principles underlying all languages.

Accordingly, instead of saying that linguistic syntax is a result of language, we can claim with Husserl that, in their specific ways of sequencing words, languages realize the proto-syntactic or categorial potential of substantivity and adjectivity. What categorial structure permits us to do is to "form new syntactical judgments" about the same objects, which "may be monothetically grasped and reactivated."[59] Like such objects themselves, according to Jitendra Mohanty, the categorial act is "founded on a simple perception—as it must be in the long run" and so, "categorical consciousness is built upon intuition, and is itself intuitive."[60] Husserl's idea of sedimented, prelinguistic categorial relations has been revived recently from the perspective of other disciplines, as for instance by the linguist James Hurford, who speaks of a "pre-syntactic capacity to organize longer sequences of sounds and gestures," contrasting this "proto-syntactic capacity" with a "pre-semantics" of basic concepts, propositions, and "mental calculations of complex concepts." Hurford also allows for the absence of proper names, illocution markers, hypotaxis (subordination of clauses), syntactic classes (nouns, verbs, adjectives), and function words during the early stages of language evolution.[61] What is missing in this account, however, is the dimension of imaginability, that is, our competence in varying perception imaginatively and express merely imagined states of affairs in words. As argued, without imaginability, the bulk of linguistic utterances would lack aboutness, a feature prominently shared by two major precursors of language: communally guided perception and nonverbal communication. Two main candidates, then, appear to offer themselves as likely forerunners of linguistic syntax, imaginatively variable perception, and gestural communication. In this sense, we could speak of a *perceptual protosyntax* as well as a *gestural protosyntax*.[62] Together, I submit, perceptual protosyntax and gestural protosyntax may very well have provided a critical component to the emergence of language: *embryonic syntax*. As we now know it, syntax would thus be the result of linguistic refinement.

## Perceptual Protosyntax

Arguably, the intentional acts by which we intuitively experience the world display demonstrable structures that precede language.[63] Yet like language, perceptual protosyntax and its rudimentary communication should be viewed as social sign systems reflecting the communal interpretation of ineluctable, concrete contingencies. In terms of the relation between language and perceptual reality, then, "the structure of the world is not at all a product of logic and language but rather the indispensable precondition of their applicability."[64] So we cannot but assume a high degree of constancy in both the perceived world and in human perceptual physiognomy. According to the hypothesis of "*sequential isomorphism*," perceptual strings "invariably mirror the external sequence of events in the real world," suggesting a certain "serial order in perception."[65] Observations of this proto-syntactic character of perception are confirmed by examples of multistable perception, as for instance in Wittgenstein's duck/rabbit representation or Rubin's vase. Two sets of constraint appear to be operating here, those imposed by the object world to be perceived and those dictated by the human senses. As to the object world, "object contexts facilitate feature or line detection, and scene contexts facilitate object detection."[66] As Husserl phrased the syntax of the perceptual world, "I am not free, I cannot produce appearances at will [nor] freely vary, but only vary them according to the way the appearance . . . prescribes."[67] Which is reminiscent of Kant's realism in what he says about seeing a ship going downstream. "We must derive the *subjective* succession of apprehension from the *objective* succession of appearances."[68]

To a very large extent, nature dictates how we can cognize a lizard scuttling up the bark of a tree. Our perception does not invent the lizard but rather responds to its movements. The process of perception unfolds as a sequence beginning with an unconscious proximal stimulus, followed by the selection of a conscious distal stimulus and conscious sensory uptake, and on to unconscious neural transduction and finally conscious interpretation. At the time, according to the anthropic thesis, our manner of seeing the world is part of the world such that our visual capacities are in tune with the movement of the lizard. It would seem that language has inherited this pro-syntactic sequencing in such a way that the categorial structures of language are configurations *commensurable* with the world in motion. Extending these insights to include imaginability, Dieter Lohmar declares that even daydreaming must respect "the identity, causality and temporal order of events and so can be regarded as a thinking response to reality."[69] Further complications are added by the perceiver's disposition and cultural preferences. "Higher level nodes must become activated during perception in order to transmit enough priming for connected nodes to reach commitment threshold and, indirectly, to become activated under the most-primed-wins principle."[70]

Husserl's idea of what is thematic in our attention provides an early explanation for this observation, as well as an answer to the question "why we sometimes perceive units that come later in an input sequence more quickly than units that come sooner." Indeed, Husserl's elaboration of theme and horizon is pertinent to the query of "why do higher level units often take precedence in perceptual processing?"[71] Because they have become *thematic*, that is, more centrally salient within the horizon of our needs. In evolutionary terms, the fact that the whole is more important than the detail may very well have to do with what favors survival. Even false perceptual constructions reinforce this idea, as illustrated by the example described by Schütz of the rope being taken for a snake. Although such illusions are "perceptions not represented in sensation,"[72] they tend to dominate our intentional acts until counter evidence persuades us otherwise. Very much in the spirit of Husserl's adumbrational aspect theory, his theorization of outer and inner horizon, and the concept of "appresentation" is the idea of the double structure of *aspects* of objects and objects in toto. Thus, Michael Braund asserts the hypothesis that "perceptual processing involves both aspectual content and intrinsic content."[73] Likewise, Ernst Cassirer's conception of the prelinguistic structure of perception, according to which, "perceptual phenomena possess structural features" that "are experienced as related to one another in a rule-governed fashion." Taking a very broad, encompassing view, perceptual experience, says Cassirer, "provides a basis out of which each of the forms, language, myth, and science, develops." From this he concludes the primacy of perception such that "there must then be pre-linguistic perceptual experiences."[74] And if perceptual sequencing has left categorial traces in linguistic syntax, it is just as likely that nonverbal communication of perception has left its proto-syntactic imprint on the emergent phenomenon of language.

## Gestural Protosyntax

To indicate the polarities between which the debate on the relationship between language and gestures has unfolded in the recent literature, two positions are exemplary. The work of Michael Corballis marks the pole of strong support for the claim of gesture as a forerunner of language, in opposition to David McNeill who regards gesture as always already linguistic. While Corballis argues for a temporal sequence such that language emerged out of gestural communication,[75] McNeill rejects gestures as likely precursors,[76] arguing the obverse relation such that "gesture has the potential to take on the traits of a linguistic system."[77] The thesis of gesture *as* language is also presented by McNeill et al. who propose the twin-system theory of the joint emergence of gesture and speech, whereby gesture and words express "the same idea unit, at the same time." With reference to McNeill (1992), the authors speak of "spontaneous, speech-synchronized gestures" that "should be counted as part of language" on the grounds that because gesture and linguistic content can be "coactive in time and jointly convey what is newsworthy in context."[78]

However, the collapse of gesture into speech is unsatisfactory. Gesticulation does not require speech, as the primate research of Michael Tomasello and others demonstrates. If so, proto-syntactic, preverbal gesture looks like a much older form of communication than language.[79] We could even speak of a *grammar of gestures*. Accordingly, gestural iconicity could reasonably be regarded as a basis for language, a position also congenial to the research conducted by Adam Kendon.[80] And although the parallels we are inclined to draw between the ontogeny and phylogeny of language must remain tentative, the three stages in child language acquisition from gesture without verbal utterance to gesture plus words and the decline of gestures during the stage of syntactic consolidation seem to be mirroring the transition from gestural communication to language.[81] In addition, Marion Tellier's observation of gesture assisting thinking by means of "imagistic mental representation" bolsters the idea of a close connection between perception, gestural communication, and imaginability.[82]

As a conspicuous sort of gesture, *pointing* deserves special attention. It undergoes linguistic displacement in its transformation into deictic features of language. As discussed in Chapter 5, verbal pointing is active in language in two forms, as explicit deixis, in "here," "there," "now," "then," "we," and as implicit deixis, the unmarked, yet all-pervasive presence of *utterance attitude*, or voice, beyond the narrower concept of *illocution*.[83] As the literature on the relationship between language and gestures testifies, pointing has remained alive in human communication in the guise of gestures as separate, auxiliary features accompanying speech.[84] On the plausible assumption that nonverbal pointing had reached a high level of complexity prior to the advent of language, it must have played a vital role in the evolution of natural languages. In addition, there is also growing neural evidence in support of the idea of gestures, such as pointing, being intimately intertwined with verbal communication.[85] Pointing may even mark the moment of the emergence of elaborate syntactic sequences out of perceptual and gestural protosyntax, a view that finds robust support in the sharp division of the use of pointing between primates and humans, as argued by Michael Tomasello.[86]

Tomasello draws our attention to the vital difference between "imperative" and "declarative" pointing. While he has documented that "chimpanzees gesture to one another regularly" and are aware of the "gaze direction" and "line of sight" of other apes, there is no evidence of "one ape pointing *for* another." Husserl's crucial criterion of *Füreinandersein* in his conception of sociality, then, would be absent or only minimally developed in other primates. As Tomasello insists, "no apes point declaratively ever." What is missing in the pointing gestures of apes is the all-important "joint attentional frame." While human infants soon achieve a degree of "sharing of interest and attention," as well as a capacity for "helping and sharing," such attitudes appear to be absent in primates. They "do not have the motives to share experience with others or to help them by informing," nor do they "know what is informationally new for others, and so what is worthy of their communicative efforts." What is of paramount importance is grasping the intention behind the communicative act. In short, apes lack shared "intentionality." On the other hand, as the ontogenesis of language acquisition in human children demonstrates, reciprocal intentionality is already present in "the humble act of pointing." This is why Tomasello concludes his paper on the proposal that the pointing gesture is a promising start for the study of the emergence of language. The proto-syntactic structure of pointing can be argued to be always a form of collaboration. As such, pointing is eminently suited to the transformation of its nonverbal structure into the syntax of verbalized communication.

Arguments in favor of nonverbal protosyntax having fed categorial structures into the emergence of language have recently been strengthened by a number of papers employing the strategy of *reverse engineering*,[87] a kind of bashful Kantian transcendental retrieval of conditions without which linguistic expressions could not have evolved. The papers proceed by stripping a language of its complexities to its minimal features of communicability. What these approaches have in common is a commitment, shared in the present account, to a strong gradualist theory of the evolution of language.

## Conclusion: Language as Heir of Nonverbal, Categorial Relations

In *Formal and Transcendental Logic*, Husserl reminds us that "we are continually busy incorporating categorial formations of every sort into predications" simply "because we *combine judgments themselves conjunctively* (or disjunctively, or in some other manner)." In describing categorial relations, Husserl insists on their "*universality*" as "modes of combinative forming of categorial objectivities."[88] Together with the core-forms of substantivity as the condition of "determinability" of objects and that of adjectivity as "determination" on the side of predication, elaborated in *Experience and Judgment* categorial forms are identified by Husserl as the necessary preconditional skeleton of human thinking.[89] As such, they also provide the necessary basis not only for the syntax of natural language but equally for the chapter's arguments concerning displacement, perceptual and gestural protosyntax, and the critique of the literature on mental time travel by means of imaginability, understood as communally guided variation of perception. Without imaginability as an emerging faculty of substituting *Vorstellung* for perceptual reality under social guidance, the transition from nonverbal, iconic, and indexical communication to increasing symbolization and the birth of language is difficult to explain. In this process, categorial relations as *proto-syntax* appear to have been a constant, from nonverbal semiosis to the gradual evolution of language. In this sense, language can be regarded as the form of communication in which the potential of intuitive categorial acts has been most richly developed.

The Conclusion will unite the central epistemic arguments of the book under the umbrella of a tripartite phenomenological ontology in answer to the question of how best to describe the mode of being of language.

## Notes

1 Charles F. Hockett, "The Origin of Speech," *Scientific American* 203 (1960), 88–96; "The Problem of Universals in Language," in *Universals of Languagei* ed. J. H. Green (Cambridge, MA: MIT Press, 1966), pp. 1–29.
  See his catalog of linguistic features in the following.
2 Edmund Husserl, *Formal and Transcendental Logic,* trans. D. Cairns (The Hague: Martinus Nijhoff, 1969), pp. 294ff., 301ff., 310; *Experience and Judgment,* trans. J. S. Churchill and K. Ameriks (Evanston: Northwestern University Press, 1997), pp. 210, 221f., 224, 401; Hua XVII, pp. 310f., 330.
3 Hua XX/2, pp. 409f.; cf. Hua XVII, pp. 219f.
4 Lévi-Strauss in Julia Kristeva, *Language the Unknown: An Introduction into Linguistics,* trans. A. M. Menke (London: Harvester, 1989), p. 46.
5 See Eric L. Gans, *The Origin of Language* (Berkeley: California University Press, 1981), who proposes the "transcendental hypothesis," according to which mimetic gestures led to conflict, resulting in murder. The repetition of communal death rituals is then seen as the birth of the signifier-signified relation.
6 Derek Bickerton, *Language and Species* (Chicago: University of Chicago Press, 1990); cf. also "The Supremacy of Syntax," *Behavioral and Brain Sciences* 10 (1987), 658–9.
7 Noam Chomsky, *Syntactic Structures* (The Hague: Mouton, 1957); *Aspects of the Theory of Syntax* (Cambridge, MA: MIT Press, 1965); *Language and Mind* (New York: Hartcourt, Brace, 1972); *The Logical Structure of Linguistic Form* (New York: Plenum, 1975); *Reflections on Language* (New York: Pantheon, 1975). However, see Vivian J. Cook, *Chomsky's Universal Grammar* (Oxford: Basil Blackwell, 1988).
8 Ray Jackendoff, "Possible Stages in the Evolution of the Language Capacity," *Trends in Cognitive Science* 3 (1999), 272–9; Sverker Johannson, *Origins of Language— Constraints on Hypotheses* (Amsterdam: Benjamins, 2005); James R. Hurford, "The Language Mosaic and Its Evolution," in *Language Evolution,* ed. M. H. Christiansen and S. Kirby (Oxford: Oxford University Press, 2003), pp. 38–57; *The Origin of Meaning* (Oxford: Oxford University Press, 2007); Franklin Chang, Gary S. Dell, and Kathryn Bock, "Becoming Syntactic," *Psychological Review* 113, 2 (2006), 234–72; Anna R. Kinsella, *Language Evolution and Syntactic Theory* (Cambridge: Cambridge University Press, 2009); Daniel L. Everett, "Grammar Came Later: Triality of Patterning and the Gradual Evolution of Language," *The Journal of Neurolinguistics* 43 (2016), 133–65; Horst Ruthrof, "Speculations on the Origins of Language," *Linguistic and Philosophical Investigations* 15 (2016), 90–107.
9 Hockett, "The Origin of Speech," *pp.* 88–96; "The Problems of Universals in Language," in *Universals of Language,* ed. J. H. Green (Cambridge, MA: MIT Press, 1966), pp. 1–29.
10 Derek Bickerton, "Two Neglected Factors in Language Evolution," in *The Evolution of Language: Proceedings of the 7th International Conference (EVOLANG7),* ed. A. D. M. Smith, K. Smith, and R. F. I. Cancho (Barcelona, March 12–15, 2008), pp. 26–33 (31).
11 Derek Bickerton, "How Proto-Language Became Language," in *The Evolutionary Emergence of Language: Social Function and the Origins of Symbolic Form,* ed. C. Knight, J. R. Hurford, and M. Studdert-Kennedy (Cambridge: Cambridge University Press, 2000), pp. 264–84 (217).
12 Hua XX/2, p. 73.

13  Ullrich Melle, "Das Rätsel des Ausdrucks," in *Meaning and Language*, ed. F. Mattens (Dordrecht: Springer, 2008), pp. 3–26 (3f.).
14  Hua XX/2, p. 101, 135n2.
15  Hua I, p. 159; Hua XIII, pp. 98ff.; Hua XIV, pp. 166ff.
16  Hua XXXIX, pp. 385ff.
17  Hua XX/2, p. 105.
18  Dieter Lohmar, "Denken ohne Sprache?" in *Meaning and Language*, pp. 169–94 (177).
19  Hua XX/2, p. 142.
20  Ibid., pp. 134, 139.
21  Vittorio de Palma, "Die Syntax der Erfahrung," in *Meaning and Language*, pp. 127–48 (144f.).
22  Hua XX/2, pp. 105f., 134f., 205; XX/1, p. 38.
23  Hua XX/2, p. 289.
24  Ibid., p. 151.
25  Ibid., p. 292.
26  Donald G. MacKay, "Perceptual Sequencing and Higher-Level Activation," in *The Organization of Perception and Action: A Theory of Language and Other Cognitive Skills*, ed. D. G. McKay (Berlin: Springer, 1987), pp. 62–89 (69).
27  Hua XX/2, p. 336.
28  Tecumseh Fitch, *The Evolution of Language* (Cambridge: Cambridge University Press, 2010); Steven Brown, "The 'Musilanguage' Model of Music Evolution," in *The Origins of Music*, ed. N. L. Wallin, B. Merker, and S. Brown (Cambridge, MA: MIT Press, 2000), pp. 271–300; Marc Hauser, Noam Chomsky and Tecumseh Fitch, "The Faculty of Language: What Is It? Who Has It? And How Did It Evolve?" *Science* 298, 5598 (2002), 1569–79; Steven Mithen, *The Singing Neanderthals: The Origins of Music, Language, Mind, and Body* (London: Weidenfeld and Nicholson, 2005); "Musicality and Language," in *The Oxford Handbook of Language Evolution*, ed. M. M. Tallerman and K. R. K. Gibson (Oxford: Oxford University Press, 2012), pp. 296–8; and Peter Slater, "Bird Song and Language," in *The Oxford Handbook of Language Evolution*, pp. 96–101.
29  Fitch, *The Evolution of Language* (Cambridge: Cambridge University Press, 2010).
30  Nick J. Enfield, "Language Evolution without Social Context?" *Science* 24, 329, 5999 (2010), 1600–601.
31  George Lakoff, "What Is a Conceptual System?" in *The Nature and Ontogenesis of Meaning*, ed. W. F. Overton and D. S. Palermo (Hilldale, NJ: Lawrence Erlbaum, 1994), pp. 41–90 (43).
32  Mark Johnson and George Lakoff, *Philosophy in the Flesh: The Embodied Mind and Its Challenge to Western Thought* (New York: Basic Books, 1999), pp. 20.
33  Ronald Langacker, *Cognitive Grammar: A Basic Introduction* (Oxford: Oxford University Press, 2008).
34  Leonard Talmy, *Towards a Cognitive Semantics* (Cambridge, MA: MIT Press, 2000).
35  Husserl, *Logical Investigations*, pp. 735f.; Hua XX/1, pp. 129; 240; XX/2, pp. 137f.; *Experience and Judgment*, p. 336.
36  Yanna Popova, "Image Schemas and Verbal Synesthesia," in *From Perception to Meaning: Image Schemas in Cognitive Linguistics*, ed. B. Hampe (Berlin: Mouton de Gruyter, 2005), pp. 421–42; Jordan Zlatev, "Embodiment, Language, and Mimesis," in *Body, Language, and Mind*, v. 1, ed. T. Ziemke, J. Zlatev, and R. Frank (Berlin: de Gruyter, 2007), pp. 297–338; Gilles Fauconnier's, *Mapping in Thought's Language* (Cambridge: Cambridge University Press, 1997); Gilles Fauconnier and Mark Turner,

*The Way We Think: Conceptual Blending and the Mind's Hidden Complexities* (New York: Basic Books, 2002); cf. my comments on the book in "From Kant's Monogram to Conceptual Blending," *Philosophy Today* 55, 2 (2011), 111–26.

37  Ann Sweetser, *From Etymology to Pragmatics: Metaphorical and Cultural Aspects of Semantic Structure* (Cambridge: Cambridge University Press, 1990).
38  Husserl, *Formal and Transcendental Logic*, pp. 294ff.; cf. Dieter Lohmar, "Husserl's Concept of Categorial Intuition," in *One Hundred Years of Phenomenology*, ed. D. Zahavi and F. Stjernfelt (Dordrecht: Kluwer, 2002), pp. 125–45.
39  Patricia M. Greenfield and Sue E. Savage-Rumbaugh, "Imitation, Grammatical Development, and the Invention of Protogrammar," in *Biological and Behavioral Determinants of Language Development*, ed. N. A. Krasnegor, D. M. Rumbaugh, M. Studdert-Kennedy, and R. Schiefelbusch (Hillsdale, NJ: Erlbaum, 1991), pp. 235–58.
40  Jordan Zlatev, Tomas Persson, and Peter Gärdenfors, "Bodily Mimesis as the Missing Link," *Lund University Cognitive Studies*, 121 (2005), 1–43.
41  Cf. Michael Corballis, "The Evolution of Language: Sharing Our Mental Lives," *Journal of Neurolinguistics* 30 (2016), 1–13; Michael Tomasello, *The Cultural Origins of Human Cognition* (Cambridge, MA: Harvard University Press, 1999); *A Natural History of Human Thinking* (Cambridge, MA: Harvard University Press, 2014); Vittorio de Palma, "Die Syntax der Erfahrung"; Barbara Tversky, Jeffrey M. Zacks and Bridgette Martin Hart, "The Structure of Experience," in *Understanding Events: From Perception to Action*, ed. T. F. Shipley and J. M. Zacks (New York and Oxford: Oxford University Press, 2008), pp. 436–64; Ernst Cassirer, *The Philosophy of Symbolic Forms*, v. 3, The Phenomenology of Knowledge, trans. R. Manheim (New Haven: Yale University Press, 1957).
42  Husserl, *Formal and Transcendental Logic*, pp. 294ff.
43  Lev S. Vygotsky, *The Collected Works of L.S. Vygotsky*, v. 1, *Problems of General Psychology*, ed. R. W. Rieber and A. S. Carton (New York and London: Plenum Press, 1987), p. 63.
44  Thomas Suddendorf and Michael Corballis, "Mental Time Travel and the Evolution of the Human Mind," *Genetic Social and General Psychology Monographs* 123 (1997), 133–67; "The Evolution of Foresight: What Is Mental Time Travel and Is It Unique to Humans?" *Behavioural and Brain Sciences* 30, 3 (2007), 299–313.
45  Endel Tulving, "Episodic and Semantic Memory," in *Organization of Memory*, ed. E. Tulving and W. Donaldson (New York: Academic Press, 1972), pp. 381–402; "Episodic Memory and Autopoiesis: Uniquely Human?" in *The Missing Link in Cognition*, ed. H. S. Terrace and J. Metcalfe (Oxford: Oxford University Press, 2005), pp. 4–56.
46  Suddendorf and Corballis, "The Evolution of Foresight," pp. 2f.
47  Ibid., pp. 6f.
48  Ibid., pp. 25f.
49  Michael Corballis, "Wandering Tales: Evolutionary Origins of Mental Time Travel and Language," in *Frontiers in Psychology* 4, 485 (2013a), 49. DOI: 10.3389/fpsyg.2013.00485 Corpus ID: 6588425; "Mental Time Travel: A Case for Evolutionary Continuity," *Trends in Cognitive Science* 17 (2013b), 5–6; cf. also Tulving, "Episodic Memory and Autopoiesis," pp. 6, 47; Kourken Michaelian, *Mental Time Travel: Episodic Memory and Our Knowledge of the Personal Past* (Cambridge, MA: MIT Press, 2016) and Thomas Zentall, "Mental Time Travel in Animals: A Challenging Question," *Behavioral Processes* 72 (2006), 173–83.
50  Endel Tulving, "Chronesthesia: Awareness of Subjective Time," in *Principles of Frontal Lobe Functions*, ed., D. T. Stuss and R. C. Knight (New York: Oxford University Press, 2002), pp. 311–25.

51 Peter Gärdenfors and Mathias Osvath, "Prospection as a Cognitive Precursor to Symbolic Communication," in *Evolution of Language: Biolinguistic Approaches*, ed. R. Larson (Cambridge: Cambridge University Press, 2010), pp. 103–14.
52 Ray Jackendoff and Eva Wittenberg, "Linear Grammar as a Possible Stepping-Stone in the Evolution of Language," *Psychonomic Bulletin Review* 20 (2017), 219–24; Corballis, "The Evolution of Language"; Everett, "Grammar Came Later: Triality of Patterning and the Gradual Evolution of Language," pp. 133–65; Sverker Johansson, "Working Backwards from Modern Language to Proto-Grammar" (Jönköping: School of Education and Communication University, 2016).
53 Derek Bickerton, *Language and Human Behaviour* (Seattle: University of Washington, 1995).
54 Hauser, Chomsky and Fitch, "The Faculty of Language: What Is It? Who Has It? And How Did It Evolve?"
55 Ruthrof, "Speculations on the Origins of Language."
56 Lothar Ely, "Afterword to Husserl, Experience and Judgment: Phenomenology and Philosophy of Language," in *Experience and Judgment*, pp. 399–429 (400).
57 Husserl, *Experience and Judgment*, pp. 228f.
58 Ibid., pp. 210f.; my emphasis.
59 Dorion Cairns, *The Philosophy of Edmund Husserl*, ed. L. Embree (Dordrecht: Springer, 2013), pp. 234, 237.
60 Jitendra N. Mohanty, "On Husserl's Lectures on Theory of Meaning (1908)," in *The Philosophy of Edmund Husserl* (New Haven: Yale University Press, 2008), pp. 224–41 (232).
61 Hurford, "The Language Mosaic"; cf. also Hurford, *The Origin of Meaning*.
62 Adam Kendon, "Kinesic Components of Multimodal Utterances," in *Berkeley Linguistics Society Proceedings* (Berkeley: Linguistics Society, 2009); *Gesture: Visible Action as Utterance* (Cambridge: Cambridge University Press, 2004); Michael Corballis, *From Hand to Mouth: The Origins of Language* (Princeton: Princeton University Press, 2002).
63 Cf. Hua XXXII, p. 101.
64 De Palma, "Die Syntax der Erfahrung," p. 142.
65 MacKay, "Perceptual Sequencing," p. 84; cf. also Michael Land and Benjamin W. Tatler, *Looking and Acting' Vision and Eye Movement in Natural Behaviour* (Oxford: Oxford University Press, 2009); John Foster, *The Nature of Perception* (Oxford: Oxford University Press, 2003).
66 MacKay, "Perceptual Sequencing," p. 64.
67 Hua XX/2, p. 66.
68 Kant, CPR A193/B238.
69 Lohmar, "Denken ohne Sprache?" p. 189.
70 MacKay, "Perceptual Sequencing," pp. 75ff.
71 Ibid., pp. 67, 76.
72 Ibid., p. 65.
73 Michael Braund, "The Structures of Perception: An Ecological Perspective," *Kritike* 2, 2 (2008), pp. 123–44 (189); cf. also John Dilworth, "The Twofold Orientational Structure of Perception," *Philosophical Psychology* 18, 2 (2005), 187–203.
74 Ernst Cassirer, "The Concept of Group and the Theory of Perception," *Philosophy and Phenomenological Research* 5, 1 (1944), pp. 1–36 (26f., 28).
75 Michael Corballis, "The Gestural Origins of Language," *WIREs Cognitive Science* 1 (2010), 2–7; as well as in *From Hand to Mouth*.

76  David McNeill, *How Language Began: Gesture and Speech in Human Communication* (Cambridge: Cambridge University Press, 2012); *Gesture and Thought* (Chicago: University of Chicago Press, 2005); *Hand and Mind: What Gestures Reveal About Thought* (Chicago: University of Chicago Press, 1992).
77  David McNeill (ed.), *Language and Gesture* (Cambridge: Cambridge University Press, 2000), p. 4.
78  David McNeill, Bennett Bertenthal, Jonathan Cole, and Shaun Gallagher, "Gesture-First – But No Gesture," *Behavioral and Brain Sciences* 28 (2005), 138-9; 138f.
79  Benjamin W. Tatler, Mary M. Hayhoe, Michael F. Land, and Dana H. Ballard, "Eye Guidance in Natural Vision: Reinterpreting Salience," *Journal of Vision* 11, 5 (2011), 1-23; Palma, "Die Syntax der Erfahrung"; Dilworth, "The Twofold Orientational Structure of Perception"; Sotaro Kita, *Pointing: Where Language, Culture, and Cognition Meet*; cf. review by David Leavens in *Cognitive Systems Research* 5 (2004), 157-65; Rachel Mayberry, "Gesture Reflects Language Development: Evidence for Bilingual Children," *Current Directions in Psychological Science* 9, 6 (2000), 192-6.
80  Adam Kendon, "The Study of Gesture," in *Gesture: Visible Action as Utterance*.
81  Marion Tellier, "The Development of Gesture," in *Language Development Over a Lifespan*, ed. K. de Bot (London: Routledge, 2009), pp. 191-216; 11f.
82  Ibid, p. 8; cf. also Vyvian Evans, *The Structure of Time: Language, Meaning, and Temporal Cognition* (Amsterdam: John Benjamins, 2003); *How Words Mean: Lexical Concepts, Cognitive Models, and Meaning Construction* (Oxford: Oxford University Press, 2009).
83  Horst Ruthrof, "Implicit Deixis," *Language Sciences* 47 (2015), 107-16.
84  Sotaro Kita, "How Representational Gestures Help Speaking," in *Language and Gesture*, ed. D. McNeill (Cambridge: Cambridge University Press, 2000), pp. 162-85.
85  Roel M. Willems and Peter Hagoort, "Neural Evidence for the Interplay Between Language, Gesture, and Action: A Review," *Brain and Language* 101, 3, 1 (2007), 4-6.
86  Michael Tomasello, "Why Don't Apes Point?" in *Roots of Human Sociality: Culture, Cognition, and Interaction*, ed. N. Enfield and S. C. Levinson (Oxford and New York: Berg, 2006), pp. 506-24. Cf. also
Michael Tomasello, and H. Moll, "Why Don't Apes Understand False Beliefs?" in *Navigating the Social World: What Infants, Children, and Other Species Can Teach Us*, ed. M. R. Banaji and S. A. Gelman. Oxford Series in Social Cognition and Social Neuroscience (Oxford: Oxford University Press, 2013), pp. 81-7.
87  Daniel L. Everett, "Grammar Came Later"; Sverker Johansson, "Working Backwards from Modern Language to Proto-Grammar," Jönköping: School of Education and Communication University, 2016; Ray Jackendoff and Eva Wittenberg, "Linear Grammar as a Possible Stepping-Stone in the Evolution of Language," pp. 219-24.
88  Husserl, *Formal and Transcendental Logic*, p. 301.
89  Husserl, *Experience and Judgment*, pp. 222, 224.

## 10

# Conclusion

## The Social Mode of Being of Language

From an *externalist* angle, the claim of the social nature of language looks uncontroversial. Language as public discourse renders the social character of language self-evident. What has been shown to be missing in this perspective is the intersubjective intentionality that is at the heart of language. From the *internalist* angle, as exemplified by the Chomskyan tradition, language is said to have "no objective existence apart from its mental representation."[1] Language as internalized *competence* becomes public only as individual *performance*. Much the same lack of attention to the social dimension of language can be observed in the writings of cognitive linguistics. Nor is any analytical, *immanent* theorization up to the task if it strips language of voice by the reduction of utterance events to idealized sentences types. A very different portrait of language has emerged from our phenomenological description, one at the center of which are the kinds of intentional acts that speakers of a language cannot but perform when they engage in linguistic communication. Instead of arguing the social character of language with reference to *observables*, the book attempted to show that the intersubjective nature of language reveals itself most clearly via a description of the interpretive labor involved in the analysis of individual linguistic expressions. From our retrospective position in the Conclusion, we can now turn from the epistemic standpoint of the preceding chapters to an ontological overview and address the broad question of the *mode of being* of language. Unfortunately, traditional ontologies restricted to the two categories of ideality and materiality cannot accommodate the kind of description presented in the previous chapters. In order to account for the role of intersubjective intentionality *in* language, we have to replace traditional, dualist ontologies by a phenomenological ontology that grants intentionality full membership. It does so by encompassing three ontological domains: *ideality*, *materiality*, and *intentionality*. Moreover, the ontological description of language to be offered demands that intentionality be granted a subsumptive role. By way of concluding the book, I will suggest that in language, ideality and materiality supervene on intersubjective intentionality such that the mode of being of language appears as an *ontically heteronomous, social process*.

# Tripartite Ontology

Traditional ontologies are dualist constructs, dividing the cosmos into the two domains of ideality and materiality. A pertinent example of a dualist ontology is Quine's "On What There Is" in *From a Logical Point of View*. As Quine quips, "A curious thing about the ontological problem is its simplicity." We can compress it into the question "What is there?" and provide the even shorter answer "Everything," even if "there remains room for disagreement over cases."[2] This, however, is not very helpful to an understanding of the mode of existence of natural language. That it is *there* is not in doubt. Its existence is ubiquitous. What is in doubt is the manner of its being there, its *Seinsweise*. As to the question of the ontological status of language, the dualist answer fails to resolve this puzzle because it remains committed to a binary ontology of ideality and materiality, represented in Quine by sets and particles, respectively, yet leaving unaddressed the essential work done by socially guided intentional acts in language as cultural practice. And since our description of language has shown intentional acts to be a necessary condition of the very existence of language, we must turn to ontologies that transcend this methodological dualism.[3] Such ontologies we find in Husserl, Heidegger, Merleau-Ponty, Jitendra Mohanty, and, in their most elaborate form, in the writings of Roman Ingarden.[4]

To account for the ontological status of complex phenomena, such as works of art,[5] education, justice, language, and culture, phenomenologists have added a third dimension to traditional ontology: intentionality. While ideal entities are independent of time and space and material entities are bound to both space and time, intentional entities and processes have neither ideal nor material existence. Rather, they exist *as* the sum of intentional acts. Ontological descriptions able to accommodate intentionality are most convincing when they are applied to ontically compound phenomena that partake of all three ontic domains, ideality, materiality, and intentionality. This is why it is one of Husserl's major philosophical accomplishments to have provided meticulous elaborations of the role of intentional, epistemic acts in the constitution of multi-ontic entities. His analyses of aspects of natural language are a case in point. They show that without intentionality in what we want to say, in deciding on appropriate verbal displacements via material expressions, in performing the ideality of categorial relations, and in the reconstruction of meaning intention via the reversal of symbolic displacement by acts of vividly imaginable meaning fulfilment, language could not exist *as* our dominant system of communication. Which becomes apparent when we attempt to answer the innocuous-looking question of what we *know* when we "know a language."[6]

## Husserl

In the *Logical Investigations*, the kind of ontology of natural language we can infer from Husserl's epistemic analyses addresses as essential components of natural language such things as meaning intention, linguistic expression as an articulate sound complex, ideal meaning units as directional, and imaginable scenarios in meaning fulfilment or *Sinn* as an intentional elaboration of *Bedeutung*. In his *Nachlass* and later writings, Husserl felt compelled to accentuate the intentionality of *intersubjective reciprocity* as a methodological consequence of having conceived of natural language early on in terms of its *communicative* function. From the very beginning this methodological commitment led Husserl to view language through a wide-angle lens permitting him to purvey linguistic intentionality broadly, encompassing both aboutness and tone, in contrast with theories that deal with language under the two separate headings of semantics and pragmatics. While intuitive meaning fulfilment is restricted in his early account to a largely provisional role, in the revisions of his initial position, Husserl gradually places a stronger accent on the work of imaginability in the acts of meaning fulfilment, replacing the notion of intuition by the stronger concepts of *Anschauung* and *Anschaulichkeit*, translated here as *vivid imaginability*. I have tried to justify their rendering as *Vorstellbarkeit* because of the filter of intentionality through which things become *anschaulich* in linguistic comprehension.

Initially, Husserl was reluctant to let go of an austere conception of meaning and its retention in linguistic exchanges via meaning identity. Yet, already in the *Logical Investigations*, the notions of intimation and introjection had complicated any assumption of a slick transfer of meaning intention via linguistic expressions. Husserl's observation of the necessity of intersubjective reciprocity as being-within-one-another further confounded any straightforward alignment of meaning intention with meaning fulfilment. For it is precisely the admission of reciprocal *appresentation* that produces a problematic tension with the exactitude stipulated by Husserl's geometrical, semantic congruence. Instead, the mode of being of language is increasingly argued as characterized by grades of *similitude* in *proximate* meaning events, resulting in the curtailment of exclusive directionality of *Bedeutung* to mere numerical identification. Perhaps the most important contribution to an ontology of natural language by Husserl is his radical expansion of the linguistic meaning chain from Frege's sparse sense-reference relation to a comprehensive act description addressing meaning intention, symbolic displacement, merely verbal and logical *Bedeutung*, word consciousness, and the reversal of displacement in meaning fulfilment as *Sinn* and his embedding of language in the lifeworld of the linguistic *Monadengemeinschaft*. In the absence of a fully developed ontology of language in Husserl, we are encouraged to round out his portrait by drawing on the work of some other phenomenologists.

## Heidegger

As mentioned in the Introduction, the main reason for excluding Heidegger's writings from the methodological commitment to a post-Husserlian act description was that what is concealed but disclosable is not strictly part of what *appears*. Husserl's disapproval of Heidegger's reappraisal of the *phenomenon* early in *Being and Time* as *concealment* was an expression of his disappointment that his most prominent disciple would so radically turn away from phenomenology in the strict sense toward the philosophy of Being as a kind of anthropology. In Husserl's view, phenomenology is to describe and eidetically distil acts that we cannot but perform in constituting an "objectivity," whereas Heidegger's philosophy of Being elaborates acts of *disclosure* of *Sein*. And yet,

Heidegger's contribution to an ontological perspective on language is both original and profound. What Heidegger's *Fundamentalontologie* unveils, in contrast with the ontological positions of Husserl, Merleau-Ponty, and Ingarden, is that language itself bars being described as an objectivity vis-à-vis others, on the grounds that language is the very foundation of how humans exist. For Heidegger, because *"language speaks,"* our reflection "demands that we enter into the speaking of language in order to take up our stay with language." Only "within *its* speaking, not within our own," will language "call to us from there and grant us its nature."[7] Language now assumes an *agency* beyond the communicative function of expressions and the stewardship of the speech community. Foremost in this important shift is Heidegger's accent on the function of language in the constitution of human reality. It is language that creates the way we see the world. "Only once the word has been found for the thing, is the thing a thing." The objectivities of the world cannot be anything for us unless they have been transformed into language. The thing only exists once it is named. For Heidegger, "it is the word that grants the thing Being." This leads him to his post-Husserlian dictum, "*Das Wesen der Sprache: die Sprache des Wesens,*" the essence of language is the language of essence. Furthermore, "*Das Wesen der Sprache ist die Sage als die Zeige,*" the essence of language is saying as showing. Language then is the key to disclosure, yet "language cannot be captured by way of expression."[8] Rather, we have to enter language in such a way that we see that "in naming, the things named are called into their thinging." And by "thinging, they unfold world." Only in their capacity of "thinging" can things be things. As such, by "thinging, they gesture—gestate—world." In this way, language "calls out to the things, commending them to the world out of which they appear." Extending Husserl's concept of aboutness, Heidegger posits that language "names not only things. It simultaneous names world" such that "things bear world" and "world grants things." World and things then do not simply "subsist alongside one another"; rather, "they penetrate each other."[9] Because we have language in this sense, humans are *weltreich*, rich in world, as against animals, which are poor of world (*weltarm*), and inanimate nature, which is worldless (*weltlos*). However, different uses of language achieve different degrees of richness of world. While "everyday language is a forgotten and therefore used-up poem, from which there hardly resounds a call any longer,"[10] it is *poetically thoughtful speech* where the event of language amounts to Heidegger's *Ereignis*, defined as "the relation of all relations,"[11] that can lift us from the level of mere *Seiendes* to the level of *Sein*. Thus, language defies being described as an objectivity among the things of the world. Unlike objectivities, language is the way human are in their capacity to comprehend anything. We are defined by language. We are language, through and through. In contrast to Heidegger's *Fundamentalontologie* of Being, Merleau-Ponty's contribution to phenomenological ontology takes a Husserl inspired, *corporeal turn*.

## Merleau-Ponty

A well-canvassed aspect of Merleau-Ponty's ontology is his resumption of Husserl's distinction between body as a biological and physical objectivity (*Körper*), and body as our epistemic base and center of orientation (*Leib*).[12] In this second sense, my "living body" is my "*leibliche Ichlichkeit*."[13] In Merleau-Ponty's phenomenology, we can reconstruct an ontology of language with the corporeality of the I as its foundation. Human corporeality is also the basis for his critique of the Saussurean *signified* as always *motivated* and of his rejection of the pure conventionality of formal sign systems as inappropriate analogues for the description of language. Here too, Merleau-Ponty follows in the footsteps of Husserl by conceiving the linguistic meaning chain as a "surpassing of the signifying by the signified" via vivid imaginability.[14] Starting from the intentionality of the lived body, language is viewed as absorbing the "world of silence" as an instrument for "singing the world."[15] At the same time, "the spoken word is a gesture" indicating the meaning of the "world."[16] Nor is the spoken perceptual world the only world. Language empowers us to create infinite "possible worlds," as intentional "variants" of actuality. As in Husserl, perception and imagination are equally valid sources of semantic value. A shift beyond Husserl is Merleau-Ponty's insistence on the body as exclusive source of phenomenological description. So, "it is the body and it alone" that "brings us to the things themselves."[17] It is the "motility" of the body that constitutes "the primary sphere in which initially the meaning of all significations in the domain of represented space is engendered."[18] At the same time, the distinction between *corporeal* meaning as primary and *linguistic* meaning as the "immanent meaning of language"[19] is reconciled by the thesis that the meanings of words are accomplished via a "deduction from *gestural meaning* which is immanent in speech." This is so, because language has absorbed perceptual being. Yet speech, for Merleau-Ponty, is not something that we simply encounter and use. Speaking is always a "taking up a position in the world of meanings," in social contexts,[20] which allows for the vital role of the speech community.

In light of this summary, it comes as a bit of a surprise that, as I have remarked elsewhere,[21] in the end, Merleau-Ponty appears to lose faith in the rock bottom of his embodied ontology. Language falls victim to a deeper level of organization, "the *Logos* of the perceived world."[22] Instead of staying committed to a corporeal conception, "the being of language" is returned to a "logic in contingency," as an "incarnate *logic*."[23] Husserl's methodological restriction to what *appears* is in the end abandoned in favor of a yearning for a metaphysical deep ground, "an essence beneath us, a common nervure of the signifying and the signified."[24] Instead of the primacy of human corporeality, there is after all something else, something deeper than is phenomenologically retrievable, a universal logos.

## Derrida

I include Jacques Derrida in this synopsis of phenomenological approaches to ontology even if this may strike the reader as odd. After all, Derrida has been celebrated as a destroyer of all metaphysical schemes. Indeed, Derrida has a good deal to say (write) about language, most of which looks like a consistent attempt to de-ontologize what appears to *present* itself to us as and via language. And yet, there is a quasi-ontological consistency in his writings that provides an entry for asking what *Seinsweise* of language emerges from its *deconstruction*, as demonstration of "the heterogeneity of the text."[25] In answering this question Derrida's methodological debts to Husserl and

Heidegger can be taken for granted, which declares him a phenomenologist of sorts. Yet the deep anchor of his philosophical convictions holds on much older ground: Kant and Nietzsche. Specifically, Derrida's entire tool kit of *infrastructures* from *differance* to the supplement and *undecidability* looks like a sustained and radical elaboration of two decisive moments in Kant's first *Critique*, his remarks on the empirical concept that "the limits of the concept are never assured" and that "the completeness of the analysis of my concept is always in doubt."[26] As to Nietzsche, it would seem that Derrida's accent on *metaphoricity* is a resumption of Nietzsche's famed characterization of language as consisting of nothing but "metaphors, metonyms, and anthropomorphisms," and so, what we take as truths are "illusions of which we have forgotten that they are worn-out metaphors that have lost their sensuous force."[27]

Thus, "in a meta-phorical culture, man can do no more than guess or interpret."[28] And since truth is illusory, interpretations should not be measured by its yardstick but by other criteria, such as novelty, ingenuity, marginality, that is, by critical interventions as deconstruction. Originally, Derrida's translation of Heidegger's *Destruktion*, or critical dismantling, deconstruction "acquires its value from its inscription in a chain of possible substitutions."[29] As such, it invites us to inhabit any text with an attitude of reading against the grain, looking for displacements and dislocations and so it can be regarded as the meta-term for Derrida's infrastructures, a collection of interpretive tools expounding the critique of the assumed stability of the linguistic concept. Thus, undecidability is viewed as the condition of decidability;[30] differance as the condition of spatial and temporal difference;[31] *pharmakon* as the condition of opposing meanings; the *arche-trace* as the principle of the disruption of the sign, *aporia*, the blind spots of metaphysics; *chora*, the possibility of textual shift; *parergon*, the essential and at the same time nonessential character of ornamentation; *play* as disrupting presence;[32] *supplementarity*, the principle of the impossibility of identity by adding "only to replace" as an intervention in the process of repetition;[33] *dissemination*, the dissolution of meaning by its proliferation; *iterability*, as ideality, since nothing else can be repeated;[34] and the metaphoricity of language as making impossible the early Husserl's "exclusive directionality" by disseminating meaning fulfilment.[35] Intriguing here is the answer to the question by which methodology Derrida has arrived at his infrastructural conditions. It is intriguing, because all of them can be stipulated only by a Kantian transcendental procedure.[36] Applying this method to the meta-device deconstruction itself, would it be possible then to claim that Derrida's infrastructures permit the reconstruction of a quasi-ontology of language that would be attuned to his broad *critique* of the metaphysics of *presence* in Western philosophy, the misleading and blinding "sun of presence"?[37] If so, it would seem that Derrida's theorization of language is part of his critique of appearances as unknowable beyond Kant's unknowable *Dinge an sich*.[38] If this is not too far off the mark, what would emerge from Derrida's writing would be a *Seinsweise* of language as a system of proliferating, fleeting appearances defying all ontologies, including Heidegger's *Fundamentalontologie* by which we are able to fathom Being itself. Returning to safer ground, in the following I want to address the way the phenomenological ontology of language can be approached through the lens of Roman Ingarden.

## Ingarden

The most detailed exploration of phenomenological ontology in Husserl's wake has been achieved by his student and colleague, the Polish philosopher Roman Ingarden, whose writings especially on literature and art have been highly influential, foremost in reception theory.[39] Sadly, his contributions to general ontology were neglected for a long time. More recently, however, a series of critical analyses have revived interest in his work.[40] In many ways, Ingarden can be regarded as one of Husserl's closest followers, with the exception of the rejection of his teacher's transcendental turn. But despite this difference, as far as the ontological status of language is concerned, Ingarden shares Husserl's core commitments. Like Husserl, Ingarden insists on the "intersubjective identity of sentences" in "different conscious subjects."[41] Ideality is embraced also in the sense that "every language system is as it were an ideally formed, abstractly conceived 'system'" in a "peculiarly potential state."[42] Like many other ontically heteronomous entities, natural language for Ingarden appears as neither mind-independent nor merely subjective but rather as an *intersubjectively intentional objectivity*. And so, as in Husserl, the ontological status of language can be adequately assessed only by way of a description of the intentional acts involved in its constitution and their eidetic distillation.

In ontology, Ingarden's most convincing contributions are in the domain of aesthetics, his analyses of literary works, music, painting, and architecture,[43] while his most ambitious work can be found in his four volumes on *The Controversy about the Existence of the World* (*Der Streit um die Existenz der Welt*).[44] What makes his ontological approach attractive is that it is well suited to addressing ontically compound entities, that is, entities that defy analysis from the dualist perspective of ideality and materiality. The strength of Ingarden's ontology rests on its capacity to embrace intentionality as an ontological domain in its own right, characterized by its lack of causal relationships and spatiotemporal extension.[45] In the four volumes of *Der Streit*, Ingarden divides ontology into three branches: (1) *formal ontology* addressing the *Seinsweise* of properties, relations, and states of affairs; (2) *existential ontology*, which deals with real, ideal, and purely intentional modes of being; and (3) *material ontology* focusing on temporality and causality. As Ingarden demonstrates, the directional acts of consciousness that Husserl sums up under intentionality call for an ontology that can handle its special existential, graded dependency relations. A core contention of his ontology is that we must attend not only to different kinds of entities but also their "mode of existence" made up of identifiable "existential moments,"[46] a specification of Husserl's concept of dependent *moments*. These existential features, Ingarden announces, "form the first attempt to go beyond the vague phrases in which one ordinarily speaks of modes of being (*Seinsweisen*) and to replace them with rigorous concepts."[47] His four fundamental *Seinsweisen* are *absolute being*, as in the stipulation of an absolute authority; *formal being* pertaining to the extra-temporal existence of formal ideality; the *material*, temporal being of real objects; and *purely intentional* being. Entities in which intentionality is a necessary component include such ontically compound examples as universities, states, societies, works of art, imagined communities, and culture. Ingarden asks in what *Seinsweise* an entity exists and whether a single mode of being is sufficient for its identification. No thing can be given, he contends, without clarification of its special mode of existence. In what *Seinsweise*, we should ask then, does language exist?

Unfortunately, Ingarden did not produce an ontology of natural language itself, but he listed "language" among "ontically heteronomous (*seinsheteronomer*)" objectivities,[48] and as such a prime candidate for an intentional, phenomenological investigation. What little he has to say about language in general very much corresponds to Husserl's description, as for instance concerning the minimally necessary components of semantic relations as made up of linguistic expression (materiality), meaning (ideality), and a corresponding intentional entity (intentionality).[49] In spite of the richness of Ingarden's ontological analyses, what is granted little attention is the *communal* aspect of ontically heteronomous objectivities. In contrast, as this study has maintained, language is through and through *social* by virtue of the intersubjective intentionality that informs all our acts that we cannot but perform in producing and comprehending linguistic expressions. The book's many references to Husserl's *Nachlass* on intersubjectivity testify to the ontological centrality of the social.[50] By way of a description and eidetic reduction of acts of consciousness, which we perforce perform in the use of language, the all-pervasive presence of the social has been shown to appear in multiple and ontically heteronomous ways. With this proviso, Ingarden's summary thesis of language as an example of *ontic heteronomy*, then, will serve as our guide in the following characterization of the mode of being (*Seinsweise*) of language.

## Ontic, Linguistic Heteronomy

In retrospect, the adumbrational aspects of linguistic acts discussed in the preceding chapters together constitute a phenomenological profile of natural language. Central to this profile is Husserl's opening gesture in the *Logical Investigations* where he frames his inquiry by declaring language as primarily a communicative system. As argued, this choice determines the expanded boundaries of the linguistic meaning chain. Viewed through the lens of phenomenology, natural language appears as a transformational meaning sequence from acts of meaning intention via symbolic *Bedeutung* to their *proximate* reconstruction in meaning fulfilment as an always *socially* overdetermined process. Nor does this transformation display a merely linear directionality. Rather, in actual speech, the meaning process typically appears as an *intersubjective, reciprocal* interaction generating indirectly public meaning events in the exchange of individual *instantiations* under communal *coercion*. Thus, the components that we can identify as necessary features making up language as a system all contribute to the *social mode* of the being of language. At the same time, the necessary combination of linguistic materiality (word sounds, writing, screen fonts), ideality (categorial relations, syntax, condition of the possibility of a shared plurality of meanings, social rules of *Abrichtung*), and the indispensable intentionality of imaginability together determine the ontic heteronomy of language as a form of communication.

## Linguistic Materiality

For its overall existence as an intentional set of relations, natural language requires a material base. It partakes of sound waves realized in word sound consciousness and as voice for the grasp of aboutness and implicit deixis. On its own, however, this material side of language cannot constitute language; it can only provide a platform for higher-order intentional acts. The same existential dependence relation applies to other material aspects of language, such as writing, print, and digital transmission. In this respect, the physical materiality of language is a necessary but insufficient condition of language. Likewise, without the material base of neurons, their synaptic networks, and brain chemistry, natural language could neither have evolved nor exist in its present forms. Yet again, as the slow progress of brain-language research confirms, the biomaterial base of language appears to amount to not much more than this: the necessary material condition without which linguistic complexities could not get off the ground. What can be agreed upon is that neurological research increasingly supports the thesis of the embodiment of language and the apparent interdependence of linguistic performance and perceptual, motor-sensory, and emotional activities of the human brain. Yet nowhere can a material *language faculty* be found in the brain. Rather, it would seem that linguistic neural activity is distributed across hundreds of billions of neurons rather than concentrated in an identifiable area within the cortex. In this limited sense, materiality makes up the first ontological stratum as a necessary condition of natural language.

## Ideality in Language

What is to count as ideality in language is not entirely self-evident. Husserl thought that meanings are an ideal species allowing for a multiplicity of empirical realizations. Likewise falling under ideality would be meaning identity, even in its reduced form of mere numerical identity as a result of exclusive directionality. If we accept that empirical meaning events are socially recognizable within a certain bandwidth of pronunciation and idiomatic use, one could hold that concepts such as "bandwidth" are idealizations in the form of social rules in contrast to their specific, empirical applications. Likewise, notions such as the Hallidayan *meaning potential* can be stipulated as a form of ideality in that it exists as a principle empirically realized in specific linguistic practices. We argued against Husserl's *Bedeutung* as an ideal species on the grounds that without at least a minimum of social intentionality, mere logical or verbal sense would confine us to a vicious circularity of mere word sounds. The all-important leap from word sound consciousness to word meaning consciousness, the book argued, cannot be made without at least a minimal form of nonverbal meaning fulfilment. That meaning fulfilment as *Sinn* cannot be an ideality follows from Husserl's own emphasis on its necessary multimodal, intentional ingredients. On the other hand, we can concede that ideality is present in language in such core forms as substantivity and adjectivity and the categorial relations that inform linguistic syntax. Ideality could likewise be said to characterize Husserl's coercion or linguistic *Abrichtung*, as long as it is conceived as a set of rules abstracted for such physical manifestations of dictionaries, grammar books, and pedagogy. Ideality in this sense is demonstratable for example by the linguistic linkage compulsion, conceived as community rules that are manifested in cultural praxis. Last, as social rules, our imaginability thesis and the definition of natural language as "a set of instructions for imagining, and acting in, a world" qualify as candidates of ideality. The vast bulk of linguistic ingredients, however, cannot be covered by the traditional ontological categories of either materiality or ideality. It is here that the phenomenological addition of intentionality proves indispensable.

## Language as Communal Intentionality

Language has been characterized as intersubjectively intentional in that it cannot be performed as a communicative sign system without a communally shared competence in the imaginative variation of the eidetically reduced system of linguistic expressions. Sharing in this sense was argued to involve reciprocal *introjection* by which language reveals itself as the dominant manner of the meeting of minds. Language has also been argued to be socially overdetermined, in its extrinsic features (instantiation), its intrinsic instructions (coercion, *Zumutung*), in its acquisition (ontogeny), and maintenance (continuity of linguistic coercion as tradition), as well as in its emergence from prelinguistic, categorial relations, core forms, and ordered *typifications* as quanta of experience (phylogeny). Above all, because the bulk of communication via language is about absent things rather than immediate, perceptual actuality, center stage has been granted to the ontological role played by imaginability as a precondition as well as a fundamental component of language. According to our initial theses, imaginability cannot be regarded as an incidental linguistic extra but must be acknowledged as a founding basis that continues to link language with perception. Shifting our gaze to the function of linguistic expressions, the profile of the meaning chain stretching from meaning intention to meaning fulfilment in experiential *Sinn* exhibits a series of specific ontological moments.

At the beginning of the phenomenological meaning chain we find meaning intentions, described as consisting in the projection of imaginable, categorially organized nonverbal, quasi-perceptual situations drawing on sedimented, *typified* experience. As typically practiced by members of a speech community, such nonverbal configurations appear as socially circumscribed intentional instantiations within a *culture*. In language, meaning intentions were shown to be displaced by symbolic, verbal signifiers, a process of transformation by intentional acts, and reconstituted via a reversal of displacement terminating in the corresponding intentional acts of meaning fulfilment within the horizon of communal expectations. *Displacement* was described as a special form of imaginability, understood once more as the replacement of perceptual and quasi-perceptual situations by word strings under communal guidance. As such, displacement is a transformation of acts of iconicity into symbolicity, the finding of the most appropriate words for what I intend to say. Here, verbal expressions viewed as strings of arbitrary, merely conventional signifiers function as *bounded symbolicity* since in their categorial relations they carry socially agreed upon, motivated, signified content. At the end of the meaning chain, we find meaning fulfilment as a transformation of expressions via intention-reading from verbal configurations to nonverbal, *imaginable states of affairs* realized in terms of the reconstruction of exclusive directionality, quantity, quality, and degree of schematization according to the requirements of speech situations. In this transformation, speakers and listeners are intentionally engaged in a form of not only being-with-one-another but more intricately in a kind of being-within-one-another, according to Husserl's theorization of intersubjectivity. On this point, Husserl's concepts of intimation and introjection were identified as early precursors of his later emphasis on degrees of *approximate reciprocity* in linguistic communication.

The ontic heteronomy of the components of language is especially striking when we turn our phenomenological gaze toward the uptake of the sound of linguistic expressions. It splits into two different intentional acts, word sound consciousness and word consciousness. The former permits recognition at the level of the *signifier*, the latter at the level of the signified. For example, homophones demand word identification beyond word sound consciousness. Once this intentional hurdle is taken, the listener (reader) faces the challenge of initial, exclusive directionality, a fleeting moment in the meaning chain identified by Husserl as *Leerintention*. It occurs dramatically when I do not understand an expression and ask for clarification. A second option of rough synonymy is then offered by a speaker (or dictionary), which may, or may not, facilitate the deferred semantic ascent. When it does happen, Husserl's exclusive directionality ushers us at high speed to the intentionality of meaning fulfilment, which we can wrap up in a minimal manner via rough nonverbal schematizations or explore at imaginative leisure in Husserl's acts of *Sinn*. The difference between the two responses has been treated under the concept of degrees of schematization.

We concurred with Husserl's critique of replicating, *mental images* in *Logical Investigations*, a position that, as we saw, he qualified later by introducing the idea of *approximation* in the vividly imaginable *Anschaulichkeit* of meaning fulfilment. So, on the one hand, Husserl rejected realist, representational, nonverbal representations in meaning constitution, yet on the other, he did not jettison the idea of degrees of abstraction to which mental materials are reduced in acts of linguistic comprehending. Contrary to empirical notions of image schemas in cognitive linguistics, this kind of *schematization* was traced to Kant's schematism as the transcendental condition of our image producing faculty. The schematization of nonverbal materials in meaning fulfilment was meant to fulfil a range of functions, such as allowing for a spectrum from a mere nonverbal indication of aboutness to elaborate vividness of meaning exploration in all semiotic modalities. In habitual speech, it is likely that high-speed, coarse-grain schematization is the communal, intentional norm, while in exploratory, interpretive contexts fine-grain schematizations can be entertained. In this sense we encounter a spectrum from economizing "passive ego-participation" to the "important activity of explicating our meaning," that is, from the constitution of a "passive meaning-pattern" to "active production."[51] In linguistic habituality, the substitution of acts of meaning intention for material signifiers is drilled into its members by the speech community during language acquisition and lifelong monitoring as a transformation of nonverbal typifications into appropriate linguistic expressions in which categorial relations are transformed into *syntax* to carry indicated, categorially arranged lexical information (aboutness) and judgments and their intended, *intimated* mode of presentation (explicit deixis; sentence-specific prosodic contour; voice as implicit deixis). In these relations, the transformation from linguistic materiality and ideality to social intentionality once more underscores both the ontic heteronomy of language as a compound social phenomenon and the subordination in language of materiality and ideality to intentionality.

The solution that emerged to the Lockean paradox of not being able to reconcile semantic privacy and public discourse was the demonstration of linguistic meaning as an always indirectly public event. Indirect, because it requires individual instantiation and public, because it presupposes interactive social training. Natural language here revealed itself as an ontically compound and heteronomous process, as it does in yet another crucial component, which I called the *linguistic linkage compulsion*. A specification under Husserl's notion of linguistic coercion and Wittgenstein's *Abrichtung*, the linkage compulsion indicates the mechanism by which we forge the conventionally accepted connection between sound and meaning. We found that it is the speech community that trains and monitors its members as to how to associate the sounds of linguistic expressions with vividly imaginable, quasi-perceptual situations, schematized to appropriate degrees, depending on intersubjective need. If I succeed in performing the expected connection between sound and meaning, I have mastered an instance of the reversal of displacement, understood as the necessary process of substituting nonverbal intentionality for merely verbal grasp, resulting in a broad spectrum of possible meaning fulfilment by motivated signifieds.

Two components of meaning fulfilment that were argued to deserve special attention in an ontology of natural language are aboutness (Husserl's *Worüber*) and voice (Husserl's *Ton*). Although what Husserl has to say on tone does not occupy much space in the *Nachlass*, it is nevertheless elemental, in the sense that voice qualifies aboutness, sometimes to the point of reversing the propositional content of an expression. What, then, is the mode of being of aboutness? As a schematized, mental iconic projection of a portion of the actual world, aboutness is a *derived intentional object*. In the case of merely imagined aboutness we are dealing with *purely intentional objectivity*, though both derived and pure intentionality are subject to the rules of the speech community. In this context, it does not matter for semantic value whether aboutness directs us to an actual state of affairs or to a merely imaginable scenario. The very same words in the same order serve to satisfy both meaning events. For the ontological identification of language what is vital is not *existence*, as it is in truth-conditional semantics, but eidetic aboutness modified by voice.

Voice, as implicit deixis, is likewise a decisive existential moment in the ontological profile of natural language. As argued, voice functions as the all-pervasive *modal shadow* of all components of a linguistic expression. In terms of its *Seinsweise*, voice, or the *manner* of utterance, has a dual mode of existence: it exists materially as sound waves and intentionally as utterance intention, the combination of which furbishes voice with further ontic heteronomy. The existential moments of voice can be summed up as partly *original* and partly *derivative* in the sense that voice always carries a personal expression and at the same time the typical manner by which to sound doubtful, assertive, sarcastic, ironical, soothing, or encouraging. Voice can be said to be existentially *associative* in that a certain tone is produced as well as comprehended in relation to a social scale of standard intonation. Voice could be said to be existentially *dependent* in its specificity on emotional interpretants, as much as on the speaker's intentionality of purpose and judgment of occasion. In light of these observations, the elimination of voice from the *semantic* description of language is a violation of its fundamental, ontological make-up. As a consequence of insisting on the intentionality of reconstructing voice as the carrier of implicit deixis the customary abstraction of sentences from utterance events likewise violates the social reality of natural language. So, the book argued for *the primacy of utterance* over the distillation of sentences as tokens and types. This is in agreement with Husserl's view that "the origin of language" and "its existence in the real world" are "grounded in *utterance* and documentation."[52] The very notion of sentence meaning is a transformation that fatally undermines the actuality of language as social negotiation of intersubjective reciprocity. Utterance, then, rather than the sentence should be accepted as the *natural*, ontological baseline of linguistic meaning.

As a result of taking on board Husserl's communicative conception of language as part of intersubjective intentionality, a significant emphasis has been the shift away from an externalist description of language as a set of observable features. We highlighted this accent by the slogan *language is the world in absentia*, drawing attention to the fact that the vast bulk of actual language use is about things that are not there in front of us. Wittgenstein's often-cited *slab* is typically out of sight. This is why a holistic description of language must focus on imaginable forms of aboutness, voice, and categorial relations. This warrants the clarification and specification of the schematic nature of the replacement of symbolic linguistic sounds by vividly imaginable slices of world, on a scale from mere fleeting recognition to the possibility of the most detailed imaginative elaboration as *intersubjective, empathetic apperception*. Empathetic, because the reconstruction of meaning intentions is always a case of intentional appresentation, which further adds to the ontic heteronomy of language. As communally circumscribed system of fuzzy *eide*, language is the dominant means of guaranteeing the kind of successful reading of minds that produces and is produced by intersubjectivity as a being-within-one-another. The eidetic fuzziness of language facilitates this form of interaction by levelling the peaks and troughs of merely subjective meaning intention and its fulfilment.

However advantageous the symbolic signifiers of language have proved in the communication of absent things, we should not therefore jump to the conclusion that the arbitrariness of natural language can be reduced to formal symbolicity. An important difference, it was argued, is that the symbolicity of language is balanced by its motivated signifieds that speakers of a language must activate in order to reconstruct mental material content. We looked at the very different roles symbolicity plays when we operate with formal signs in comparison with the sort of acts demanded by linguistic expressions. In formal systems our acts are exhausted by the performance of categorial relations. What is missing are the sedimented constitution of aboutness and voice, two vital ingredients of natural language. In *applied calculus*, acts of aboutness do reenter as typified quanta, yet they differ from linguistic intentionality in that they are predetermined by strictly defined, stipulated, extrinsic measuring units, that is, units of formal ideality. This, together with the absence of voice, distances applied calculus decisively from language and so it is wrongheaded to regard natural language as a kind of *interpreted calculus*.[53] Instead, symbolicity plays a strictly limited role in linguistic expressions. While in formal signification symbolicity is all there is, language is characterized by *bounded symbolicity* in that each signifier is immediately and of necessity transformed into a motivated signified. Which once more places imaginability squarely at the center of what makes language *natural*. We can also say that language is natural in the sense of having emerged from within communal intentionality rather than being axiomatically stipulated.

Communal intentionality reveals itself foremost in language as a set of social instructions. We found that this kind of coercion is present in the smallest linguistic unit. But instead of producing meaning identity, Husserl's "ought" functions as a regulatory mechanism within proximate boundaries, a principle I termed *intersubjective sufficiency*. What is lost here in terms of accuracy of ideal meaning transmission is made up for by more or less flexible, communal control. As such, Husserl's imposition (*Zumutung*) identified as the tendency of an "ought (*Sollenstendenz*)" revealed itself as a major component of all language. On the cue "red table" we are simply not able, during the split second of meaning realization, to imagine a green chair. The linguistic linkage compulsion prevents us from doing so. The ideality of Husserl's *Zumutung* reveals the social constraints under which individual linguistic performance is typically attuned to intersubjective intentionality. A convenient way of summing up this ontological characteristic of language was the introduction of the notion of *Abrichtung*. However, though the term was borrowed from Wittgenstein, it was used against his own externalist definition of meaning as use, which disavows intentional acts as foundational. And yet, intentional acts defy elimination. We cannot simply say that intentional states "do not play a role" in language.[54] How would we be able to imagine past situations mentioned in an utterance without drawing on intentionality? Linguistic coercion was also shown to go deeper than the surface of the observable performance of language games, down to the diverse acts of consciousness that we cannot but conduct in doing language. What then is the mode of being of *Abrichtung* in its social manifestations? It revealed itself as an ontically heteronomous, pedagogic process consisting of material, institutionalized signifiers, intersubjective rules, and their internalization by speakers of a language, informing individual competence and performance. As such, *Abrichtung* too reflects the Janus-faced character of language as a *public* and at the same time *indirectly public* phenomenon. Its existential moments can be characterized as ontically heteronomous, derivative as to community agreement, associative in the sense of belonging to a system of rules, and dependent on the contingencies of the historical period of a language. But language is not only dependent on the speech community, vice versa, without language as the main facilitator of communal being-within-one-another, society could not function as an ontically heteronomous complexity within a phenomenologically conceived "life-world ontology."[55]

A description of natural language in the footsteps of Husserl's *Nachlass* is identifiable from the outset by its comprehensive scope of viewing language as fundamentally *communicative*. It avoids the propositional path as a lessening of what occurs at the empirical level of language use and, more decisively, at the level of its deep ground addresses the intentional acts of speakers without which language could not exist. As the book has argued, at the level of intentionality, all phases of the linguistic meaning process, meaning intention, verbal displacement, and its reversal in meaning fulfilment, of necessity draw on imaginability, the variation and multiplication of perception performed under communal constraints. We saw that across the analytic-phenomenological divide, imaginability confronts propositional pathways as a reductive levelling of the *heterosemiotic* and ontically *heteronomic* components of language. Instead, by choosing as its starting point Husserl's comprehensive, communicative conception of language, the book aimed to show that a description of individual linguistic acts and their distillation into general principles will inevitably reveal the salient components of the linguistic, ontic heteronomy of natural language. A decisive finding was the regulatory presence of the speech community as an intrinsic feature of linguistic expressions. To define natural language from the perspective of phenomenological ontology, we could say that it displays itself through its necessary linguistic intentionality as an ontically heteronomous process revealing *a set of social instructions for imagining, and communicatively acting in, a world.*

# Notes

1 Noam Chomsky, *Language and Mind* (New York: Hartcourt, Brace, 1972), p. 169n.
2 Willard van Orman Quine, "On What There Is," in *From a Logical Point of View* (New York: Harper and Row, 1963), pp. 1–19 (1).
3 In *Speaking and Meaning: The Phenomenology of Language* (Bloomington: Indiana University Press, 1976), James M. Edie argues the necessary ontological status of language in terms of the ideality of language and its actual manifestations as speech acts, resulting in a portrayal in which metaphor plays a central role.
4 Jitendra N. Mohanty, *Phenomenology and Ontology* (The Hague: Martinus Nijhoff, 1970); for Ingarden's ontology, see below.
5 Roman Ingarden, *The Literary Work of Art: An Investigation on the Borderlines of Ontology, Logic, and Theory of Literature*, trans. G. G. Grabowicz (Evanston: Northwestern University Press, 1973); *The Cognition of the Literary Work of Art*, trans. R. A. Cowley and K. R. Olson (Evanston: Northwestern University Press, 1973).
6 Horst Ruthrof, "Knowing a Language—What Sort of Knowing Is It?" *Analysis and Metaphysics* 19 (2020), 7–30. Cf. Stephen Stich, "What Every Speaker Knows," *Philosophical Review* 80 (1971), 476–96; David E. Cooper, *Knowledge of Language* (New York: Humanities Press, 1975); Noam Chomsky, *Knowledge of Language: Its Nature, Origin, and Use* (New York: Praeger, 1986); Crispin Wright, "Theories of Meaning and Speakers' Knowledge," in *Realism, Meaning and Truth* (Oxford: Blackwell, 1987), pp. 204–38; Michael Dummett, "What Do I Know When I Know a Language?," in *The Seas of Language* (Oxford: Oxford University Press, 1993b), pp. 94–105; James Higginbotham, "On Knowing One's Own Language," in *Knowing Our Own Mind*, ed. C. Wright, B. C. Smith, and C. Macdonald (Oxford: Oxford University Press, 1998), pp. 429–41; Barry C. Smith, "On Knowing One's Own Language1," in *Knowing Our Own Minds*, ed. C. Wright, B. C. Smith, and C. Macdonald (Oxford: Clarendon Press, 1998), pp. 391–428; Robert Matthews, "Does Linguistic Competence Require Knowledge of Language?" in *Epistemology of Language*, ed. A. Barber

(Oxford and New York: Oxford University Press, 2003), pp. 187–213; Barry C. Smith, "What I Know When I Know a Language," in *The Oxford Handbook of Philosophy of Language*, ed. E. LePore and B. C. Smith (Oxford: Clarendon Press, 2006), pp. 941–82; John Collins, "Linguistic Competence Without Knowledge of Language," *Philosophy Compass* 2, 6 (2007), 880–95.
7  Martin Heidegger, *Poetry, Language, Thought*, trans. A. Hofstadter (New York: Perennial Classics, 2001), pp. 188f.
8  Martin Heidegger, *Unterwegs zur Sprache* (Pfullingen: Neske, 1959), pp. 176, 254, 266.
9  Heidegger, *Poetry, Language, Thought*, pp. 197, 199.
10  Ibid., p. 205.
11  Heidegger, *Unterwegs zur Sprache*, p. 267.
12  Cf. Hua XIII, pp. 42, 55ff., 66f., 68, 113f., 229, 236, 249, 321; XIV, pp. 3ff., 57fff., 66ff., 75f., 88f. 234ff., 281ff., 374f., 410, 453f.; XV, pp. 245–315, 490, 661; cf. also Hua IV, §§ 18, 36, 38f.
13  Edmund Husserl, *The Crisis of European Sciences and Transcendental Phenomenology*, trans. D. Carr (Evanston: Northwestern University Press, 1970), p. 108.
14  Maurice Merleau-Ponty, "On the Phenomenology of Language," in *Signs*, trans. R. C. McCleary, 84–97 (Evanston: Northwestern University Press, 1964), pp. 84–97 (90).
15  Maurice Merleau-Ponty, *The Visible and the Invisible*, trans. A. Lingis (Evanston: Northwestern University Press, 1968), p. 31.
16  Maurice Merleau-Ponty, *Phenomenology of Perception*, trans. C. Smith (London: Routledge, 1962), p. 184.
17  Merleau-Ponty, *The Visible and the Invisible*, pp. 135f.
18  Merleau-Ponty, *Phenomenology of Perception*, p. 51.
19  Maurice Merleau-Ponty, *Signs*, trans. R. C. McCleary (Evanston: Northwestern University Press, 1964), pp. 88f.
20  Merleau-Ponty, *Phenomenology of Perception*, pp. 179, 193, 403.
21  Horst Ruthrof, *The Body in Language*, pp. 10ff.
22  Merleau-Ponty, "On the Phenomenology of Language," p. 10; my emphasis.
23  Merleau-Ponty, *Signs*, pp. 87f.; my emphasis.
24  Merleau-Ponty, *The Visible and the Invisible*, p. 118.
25  Jacques Derrida, "The Question of Style," in *The New Nietzsche: Contemporary Styles of Interpretation*, ed. D. B. Allison (New York: Dell Publishing, 1979), pp. 176–89 (185).
26  Kant, CPR A728/B756.
27  'Was ist also Wahrheit? Ein bewegliches Heer von Metaphern, Metonymien, Anthropomorphismen, kurz eine Summe von menschlichen Relationen, die, poetisch und rhetorisch gesteigert, übertragen, geschmückt wurden und die nach langem Gebrauch einem Volke fest, kanonisch und verbindlich dünken . . . die Wahrheiten sind Illusionen, von denen man vergessen hat, daß sie welche sind, Metaphern, die abgenutzt und sinnlich kraftlos geworden sind.' Friedrich Nietzsche, "Ueber Wahrheit und Lüge im aussermoralischen Sinn," pt. 1 (dated 1873). *The Complete Works of Friedrich Nietzsche*, v.2, ed. O. Levy, trans. M. A. Mügge (London: Allen and Unwin, 1911), pp. 171–92 (180).
28  Eric Blondel, "Nietzsche: Life as Metaphor," in *The New Nietzsche: Contemporary Styles of Interpretation*, ed. D. B. Allison (New York: Dell Publishing, 1979), pp. 150–75 (168).
29  Jacques Derrida, "Letter to a Japanese Friend," trans. David Wood and Andrew Benjamin, in *A Derrida Reader: Between the Blinds*, ed. Peggy Kamuf (New York: Columbia University Press, 1991), pp. 270–6 (275).

30 Jacques Derrida, *Limited Inc*, ed. Gerald Graff (Evanston: Northwestern University Press, 1988), p. 116.
31 Jacques Derrida, "Différance," in *Speech and Phenomena and Other Essays on Husserl's Theory of Signs*, trans. David Allison (Evanston: Northwestern University Press, 1973), pp. 129–60.
32 Jacques Derrida, *Writing and Difference*, trans. Alan Bass (London: Routledge and Kegan Paul, 1978), pp. 212f.
33 Jacques Derrida, *Of Grammatology*, trans. Gyatri Chakravorti Spivak (Baltimore and London: Johns Hopkins University Press, 1976), pp. 145, 154.
34 Derrida, *Limited Inc*.
35 Jacques Derrida, "The Retreat of Metaphor," *Enclitic* 2, 2 (1978), 5–33.
36 Cf. David Wood, "Différance and the Problem of Strategy," in *Derrida and Différance*, ed. D. Wood and R. Bernasconi (Evanston: Northwestern University Press, 1988), pp. 63–70 (64f.).
37 Derrida, *Speech and Phenomena*, p. 104.
38 Note here the standard rendering of Kant's *Ding an sich* as "thing in itself," which invites an essentialist reading. What Kant clearly has in mind is something like the "thing without perspective," or the "thing on its own" or perhaps the "thing deep down," or more literally even if unidiomatically, "the thing-*at*-itself." Cf. Horst Ruthrof, "A Translation Problem: The Thing-*at*-Itself in Light of Kant's Pragmatism," *Analysis and Metaphysics* 12 (2013), 47–67.
39 Ingarden, *The Literary Work of Art; The Cognition of the Literary Work of Art*.
40 Arkadiusz Chrudzimski, "Are Meanings in the Head? Ingarden's Theory of Meaning," *Journal of the British Society for Phenomenology* 30 (1999), 306–26; "Von Brentano zu Ingarden: Die phänomenologische Bedeutungslehre," *Husserl Studies* 18, 3 (2002), 185–208; "Roman Ingarden: Ontology from a Phenomenological Point of View," *Reports on Philosophy* 22 (2004), 121–42; (ed.), *Existence, Culture, Persons: The Ontology of Roman Ingarden* (Frankfurt: Ontos, 2005); "Varieties of Intentional Objects," *Semiotica* 194 (2013), 189–206; "Intentional Objects and Mental Contents," in *Brentano's Concept of Intentionality: New Assessments*, ed. G. Fréchette, 81–119; *Brentano Studien* (Dettelbach: J.H. Röll Verlag, 2015), p. 13; Liselotte Gumpel, "Language as Bearer of Meaning: The Phenomenology of Roman Ingarden," in *Kunst und Ontologie: Für Roman Ingarden zum 100. Geburtstag* (Amsterdam: Rodopi, 1994); Knut Hanneborg, "New Concepts in Ontology. A Review Discussion of Roman Ingarden: Der Streit um die Existenz der Welt," *Inquiry* 9 (1996), 401–109; Gregor Haeflinger and Guido Küng, "Substances, States, Processes, Events: Ingarden and the Analytic Theory of Objects," in *Existence, Culture, and Persons: The Ontology of Roman Ingarden*, ed. A. Chrudzimski (Frankfurt: Ontos, 2005), pp. 9–31; Jacek Jadacki, "On Roman Ingarden's Semiotic Views: A Contribution to the History of Polish Semiotics," *Analecta Husserliana* 27 (1989), 523–40; Ingvar Johansson, "Proof of the Existence of Universals and Roman Ingarden's Ontology," *Metaphysica* 10, 1 (2009), 65–87; 'The Basic Distinctions in Der Streit," *Semiotica* 194 (2013), 137–57; "The Ideal as Real and as Purely Intentional: Ingarden-based Reflections," *Semiotica* 194 (2013), 21–37; Joseph Keeping, "The Ontology of Roman Ingarden," *Symposium* 2, 2 (1998), 246–9; Guido Küng, "The Role of Language in Phenomenological Analysis," *American Philosophical Quarterly* 6 (1969), 330–4; 'Ingarden on Language and Ontology," *Analecta Husserliana* 2 (1972), 204–17; Jeff Mitcherling, *Roman Ingarden's Ontology and Aesthetics* (Ottawa: University of Ottawa Press, 1997); Edward Swiderski, "Some Salient Features of Ingarden's Ontology," *Journal of the British*

*Society of Phenomenology* 6 (1975), 81–90; Daniel von Wachter, "Roman Ingarden's Ontology: Existential Dependence, Substances, Ideas, and Other Things Empiricists Do Not Like," in *Existence, Culture, and Persons: The Ontology of Roman Ingarden* (Frankfurt: Ontos, 2005), pp. 55–82.
41  Ingarden, *The Literary Work of Art*, p. 364.
42  Roman Ingarden, *Der Streit um die Existenz der Welt: II/2 Formalontologie 2* (Tübingen: Max Niemeyer, 1965), pp. 219f.
43  Roman Ingarden, *Ontology of the Work of Art*, trans. R. Meyer and J. T. Goldthwait (Athens, OH: Ohio University Press, 1989).
44  Roman Ingarden, *Der Streit um die Existenz der Welt*: I Existentialontologie (Tübingen: Max Niemeyer, 1964); *Der Streit um die Existenz der Welt*: II/1 Formalontologie (Tübingen: Max Niemeyer, 1965a); *Der Streit um die Existenz der Welt*: II/2 Formalontologie 2 (Tübingen: Max Niemeyer, 1965b); *Über die Kausalstruktur der Realen Welt: Der Streit um die Existenz der Welt III* (Tübingen: Max Niemeyer, 1974).
45  Ingarden, *Der Streit II/1*, pp. 174ff.
46  Ingarden, *Der Streit I*, pp. 65–129.
47  Ibid., p. 257 n9.
48  Ingarden, *Der Streit II/1*, pp. 199; 218ff.
49  I leave aside here Ingarden's detailed analyses of the role of language in the literary work of art as a special case of the Husserlian linguistic meaning chain.
50  Hua XIII, IV, XV.
51  Edmund Husserl, "The Origin of Geometry," in *Crisis*, p. 364.
52  Ibid., p. 358; my emphasis.
53  Grewendorf, Günther, Fritz Hamm, and Wolfgang Sternefeld, *Sprachliches Wissen: Eine Einführung in moderne Theorien der grammatischen Beschreibung* (Frankfurt: Suhrkamp, 1987).
54  Dagfinn Føllesdal, "In What Sense Is Language Public?" in *On Quine: New Essays*, ed. P. Leonardi and M. Santambrogio (Cambridge: Cambridge University Press, 1995), pp. 53–67 (66); cf. likewise his "Husserl's Notion of Noema," *The Journal of Philosophy* 66 (1969), 680–7; and "Noema and Meaning in Husserl," *Philosophy and Phenomenological Research* 50 (1990), 263–71.
55  Husserl, *Crisis*, p. 142; cf. also his phrasing "ontology of the life-world," Ibid., p. 173.

# References

Ackrill, J.L. (1963). *Aristotle: Categories and De Interpretatione*. Oxford: Clarendon Press.
Agha, A. (1996). "Schema and Superimposition in Spatial Deixis." *Anthropological Linguistics* 38, 4, 643–82.
Apostolopoulos, D. (2019). *Merleau-Ponty's Phenomenology of Language*. London: Roman and Littlefield International.
Aristotle. (2002). *De Interpretatione*. Trans. J.L. Ackrill. Oxford: Oxford University Press.
Aristotle. (2013). *Categories*. Trans. E.M. Edghill. Adelaide: Adelaide University.
Austin, J.L. (1962). *How to Do Things with Words*. Oxford: Oxford University Press.
Bach, K. and R.M. Harnish. (1979). *Linguistic Communication and Speech Acts*. Cambridge, MA: MIT Press.
Balle, J.D. (2008). "Husserl's typisierende Apperzeption und die Phänomenologie dynamischer Intentionalität." In *Meaning and Language: Phenomenological Perspectives*. Ed. F. Mattens, 89–104. Phaenomenologica 187. Dordrecht: Springer.
Barber, A. (2003). *Epistemology of Language*. Oxford and New York: Oxford University Press.
Bar-Hillel, Y. (1954). "Indexical Expressions." *Mind* 63, 359–79.
Bar-Hillel, Y. (1970). *Aspects of Language: Essays in Philosophy of Language, Linguistic Philosophy, and Methodology of Linguistics*. Amsterdam: North Holland.
Barthes, R. (1968). *Elements of Semiology*. New York: Hill and Wang.
Barwick, L., B. Birch, and N. Evans. (2007). "Iwaidja Jurtbirrk Songs: Bringing Language and Music Together." *Australian Aboriginal Studies* 2, 6–34.
Bell, D. (1991). *Husserl*. London: Routledge.
Benoist, J. (2002). "Non-Objectifying Acts." In *One Hundred Years of Phenomenology: Husserl's* Logical Investigations *Revisited*. Eds. D. Zahavi and F. Stjernfelt, 41–49. Dordrecht: Kluwer.
Benoist, J. (2008). "Linguistic Phenomenology?" In *Meaning and Language: Phenomenological Perspectives*. Ed. F. Mattens, 215–35. Dordrecht: Springer.
Bernet, R. (1990). "Husserl's Begriff des Noema." In *Husserl-Ausgabe und Husserl-Forschung*. Ed. S. Ijselling, 61–80. Dordrecht: Kluwer.
Bickerton, D. (1981). *Roots of Language*. Ann Arbor, MI: Karoma.
Bickerton, D. (1987). "The Supremacy of Syntax." *Behavioral and Brain Sciences* 10, 658–9.
Bickerton, D. (1990). *Language and Species*. Chicago: University of Chicago Press.
Bickerton, D. (1995) *Language and Human Behaviour*. Seattle: University of Washington Press.
Bickerton, D (2000). "How Proto-Language Became Language." In *The Evolutionary Emergence of Language: Social Function and the Origins of Symbolic Form*. Eds. C. Knight, J.R. Hurford, and M. Studdert-Kennedy, 264–84 (p. 217). Cambridge: Cambridge University Press, 2000.
Bickerton, D. (2007). "Language Evolution: A Brief Guide for Linguists." *Lingua* 117, 510–26.
Bickerton, D. (2008). "Two Neglected Factors in Language Evolution." In *The Evolution of Language*: *Proceedings of the 7th International Conference* (EVOLANG7). Eds. A.D.M. Smith, K. Smith, and R.F.I. Cancho, 26–33. Barcelona.

Biemel, W. and H. Saner (Eds.) (2003). *Martin Heidegger, Karl Jaspers: Correspondence (1920–1963)*. Trans. G.E. Aylesworth. Amherst, NY: Humanities Books.
Blondel, E. (1979). "Nietzsche: Life as Metaphor." In *The New Nietzsche: Contemporary Styles of Interpretation*. Ed. D.B. Allison, 150–75. New York: Dell Publishing.
Boghossian, P.A. (1999). "Analyticity." In *A Companion to the Philosophy of Language*. Eds. B. Hale and C. Wright, 331–68. Oxford: Blackwell.
Borg, E. (1984). *Minimal Semantics*. Cambridge: Cambridge University Press.
Borg, E. (2004). *Minimal Semantics*. Oxford: Clarendon Press.
Braund, M. (2008). "The Structures of Perception: An Ecological Perspective." *Kritike* 2, 2, 123–44.
Brown, S. (2000). "The Musilanguage Model of Music Evolution." In *The Origins of Music*. Eds. N.L. Wallin, B. Merker, and S. Brown, 271–300. Cambridge, MA: MIT Press.
Bühler, K. (1982 [1934]). *Sprachtheorie*. Stuttgart: Fischer.
Bühler, K. (1990). *Theory of Language*. Trans. T.F. Goodwin. Amsterdam: John Benjamins.
Burks, A.W. (1949). "Icon, Index, and Symbol." *Philosophical and Phenomenological Research* 9, 673–89.
Burling, R. (2005). *The Talking Ape: How Language Evolved*. Oxford: Oxford University Press.
Cairns, D. (1941). "The Ideality of Verbal Expressions." *Philosophy and Phenomenological Research* 1, 453–62.
Cairns, D. (2013). *The Philosophy of Edmund Husserl*. Ed. Lester Embree. Dordrecht: Springer.
Cappelen, H. and E. Lepore. (2005). *Insensitive Semantics: A Defence of Semantic Minimalism and Speech-Act Pluralism*. Oxford: Blackwell.
Carnap, R. (1975). *Introduction to Semantics and the Formalisation of Logic*. Cambridge, MA: Harvard University Press.
Cartwright, R. (1962). "Propositions." In *Analytical Philosophy*. Ed. R. J. Butler, 81–103. Oxford: Basil Blackwell.
Casey, E.S. (2000). *Imagining: A Phenomenological Study*. Bloomington: Indiana University Press.
Casey, E.S. (2003). "Imagination, Fantasy, Hallucination, and Memory." In *Imagination and Its Pathologies*. Eds. J. Philips and J. Morley, 65–87. Cambridge, MA: MIT Press.
Cassirer, E. (1944). "The Concept of Group and the Theory of Perception." *Philosophy and Phenomenological Research* 5, 1, 1–36.
Cassirer, E. (1957). *The Philosophy of Symbolic Forms*, v.3, *The Phenomenology of Knowledge*. Trans. R. Manheim. New Haven: Yale University Press.
Chalmers, D. (1996). *The Conscious Mind: In Search of a Fundamental Theory*. Oxford: Oxford University Press.
Chang, F., G.S. Dell, and K. Bock. (2006). "Becoming Syntactic." *Psychological Review* 113, 2, 234–72.
Chomsky, N. (1957). *Syntactic Structures*. The Hague: Mouton.
Chomsky, N. (1965). *Aspects of the Theory of Syntax*. Cambridge, MA: MIT Press.
Chomsky, N. (1967). "Recent Contributions to the Theory of Innate Ideas." *Synthese* 17, 1, 2–11.
Chomsky, N. (1968). *Language and Mind*. New York: Hartcourt, Brace.
Chomsky, N. (1972). *Language and Mind*. Enlarged edition. New York: Hartcourt, Brace.
Chomsky, N. (1975a). *The Logical Structure of Linguistic Form*. New York: Plenum.
Chomsky, N. (1975b). *Reflections on Language*. New York: Pantheon.

Chomsky, N. (1986). *Knowledge of Language: Its Nature, Origin, and Use.* New York: Praeger.
Chomsky, N. (1987). *The Chomsky Reader.* Ed. J. Peck. New York: Pantheon.
Chomsky, N. (2002). *On Nature and Language.* Eds. A. Belletti and L Rizzi. Cambridge: Cambridge University Press.
Chomsky, N. (2006). *Language and Mind.* Cambridge: Cambridge University Press.
Christensen, C.B. (2008). *Self and World: From Analytic Philosophy to Phenomenology.* Berlin: Walter de Gruyter.
Chrudzimski, A. (1999). "Are Meanings in the Head? Ingarden's Theory of Meaning." *Journal of the British Society for Phenomenology* 30, 306–26.
Chrudzimski, A. (2002). "Von Brentano zu Ingarden: Die phänomenologische Bedeutungslehre." *Husserl Studies* 18, 3, 185–208.
Chrudzimski, A. (2004). "Roman Ingarden: Ontology from a Phenomenological Point of View." *Reports on Philosophy* 22, 121–42.
Chrudzimski, A. (Ed.) (2005). *Existence, Culture, Persons: The Ontology of Roman Ingarden.* Frankfurt: Ontos.
Chrudzimski, A. (2013). "Varieties of Intentional Objects." *Semiotica* 194, 189–206.
Chrudzimski, A. (2015). "Intentional Objects and Mental Contents." In *Brentano's Concept of Intentionality: New Assessments.* Ed. G. Fréchette, 81–119. Brentano Studien 13. Dettelbach: J.H. Röll Verlag.
Chu, Y. and H. Ruthrof. (2012). "Cultural Obstacles to Political Dialogue in China." *Culture and Dialogue* 2, 2, 31–50.
Chu, Y. and H. Ruthrof. (2017). "The Social Semiotic of Homophone Phrase Substitution in Chinese Netizen Discourse." *Social Semiotics* 27, 5, 640–55.
Collins, J. (2007). "Linguistic Competence Without Knowledge of Language." *Philosophy Compass* 2, 6, 880–95.
Cook, V.J. (1988). *Chomsky's Universal Grammar.* Oxford: Basil Blackwell.
Cooper, D. E. (1975). *Knowledge of Language.* New York: Humanities Press.
Corballis, M. (2002). *From Hand to Mouth: The Origins of Laanguage.* Princeton: Princeton University Press.
Corballis, M. (2010). "The Gestural Origins of Language." *WIREs Cognitive Science* 1, 2–7.
Corballis, M. (2013a). "Wandering Tales: Evolutionary Origins of Mental Time Travel and Language." *Frontiers in Psychology* 4, 485.
Corballis, M. (2013b). "Mental Time Travel: A Case for Evolutionary Continuity." *Trends in Cognitive Science* 17 (2013b), 5–6.
Corballis, M. (2016). "The Evolution of Language: Sharing Our Mental Lives." *Journal of Neurolinguistics* 30 (2016), 1–13.
Crimmins, M. (1997). "Propositions." In *Concise Encyclopedia of Philosophy of Language.* Ed. P. Lamarque, 287–91. Oxford: Pergamon.
Crowell, T.G. (2001). *Husserl, Heidegger and the Space of Meaning: Paths Towards Transcendental Phenomenology.* Evanston: Northwestern University Press.
Crystal, D. (2008). *How Language Works.* London: Penguin Books.
Cunningham, S. (1976). *Language and the Phenomenological Reductions of Edmund Husserl.* The Hague: Martinus Nijhoff.
Davidson, D. (1981). "What Metaphors Mean." In *On Metaphor.* Ed. S. Sacks, 29–45. Chicago: The University of Chicago Press.
Davidson, D. (2004). "Truth and Meaning." In *Semantics: A Reader.* Eds. S. Davis and B.S. Gillon, 222–33. Oxford: Oxford University Press.

Davidson, D. (2005). *Truth and Predication*. Cambridge, MA: Harvard University Press.
Davies, M. (2006). "Foundational Issues in the Philosophy of Language." In *The Blackwell Guide to the Philosophy of Language*. Eds. M. Devitt and R. Hanley, 19–40. Oxford: Blackwell.
Davis, S. and B.S. Gillon. (Eds.) (2004). *Semantics: A Reader*. Oxford: Oxford University Press.
Deleuze, G. (1986). *Cinema 1: The Movement Image*. Trans. H. Tomlinson and B. Habberjam. Minneapolis: Minnesota University Press.
Deleuze, G. (1989). *Cinema 2: The Time Image*. Trans. H. Tomlinson and R. Galeta. Minneapolis: Minnesota University Press.
Deleuze, G. and F. Guattari. (1987). *A Thousand Plateaus: Capitalism and Schizophrenia*. Trans. B. Massumi. Minneapolis: Minnesota University Press.
Derrida, J. (1973a). *Speech and Phenomena and Other Essays on Husserl's Theory of Signs*. Trans. D. Allison. Evanston: Northwestern University Press.
Derrida, J. (1973b). "Differance." In *Speech and Phenomena and Other Essays on Husserl's Theory of Signs*. Trans. D. Allison, pp. 129–160. Evanston: Northwestern University Press.
Derrida, J. (1974). *Of Grammatology*. Trans. G.C. Spivak. Baltimore: The Johns Hopkins University Press.
Derrida, J. (1977). "Limited Inc. abc …." In *Glyph: Johns Hopkins Textual Studies*. Eds S. Weber and H. Sussman, 162–254. Baltimore: Johns Hopkins University Press.
Derrida, J. (1978a). *Writing and Difference*, trans. A. Bass. London: Routledge and Kegan Paul.
Derrida, J. (1978b). "The *Retreat* of Metaphor." *Enclitic*, 2, 2 5–33.
Derrida, J. (1979). "The Question of Style." In *The New Nietzsche: Contemporary Styles of Interpretation*. Ed. D.B. Allison, 176–89. New York: Dell Publishing, 1979.
Derrida, J. (1988). *Limited Inc*. Ed. Gerald Graff. Evanston: Northwestern University Press.
Derrida, J. (1991). "Letter to a Japanese Friend." Trans. D. Wood and A. Benjamin. In *A Derrida Reader: Between the Blinds*. Ed. P. Kamuf, 270–6. New York: Columbia University Press.
Dever, J. (1999). "Compositionality as Methodology." *Linguistics and Philosophy* 22, 311–26.
Dever, J. (2006). "Compositionality." In *The Oxford Handbook of Philosophy of Language*. Eds. E. Lepore and B.C. Smith, 633–66. Oxford: Clarendon.
Devitt, M. (1996). *Coming to Our Senses*. Cambridge: Cambridge University Press.
Devitt, M. and R. Hanley (Eds.) (2006). *The Blackwell Guide to the Philosophy of Language*. Oxford: Blackwell.
Devitt, M. and K. Sterelny. (1990). *Language and Reality: An Introduction to the Philosophy of Language*. Oxford: Basil Blackwell.
Dilworth, J. (2005). "The Twofold Orientational Structure of Perception." *Philosophical Psychology* 18, 2, 187–203.
Drummond, J. and L. Embree (Eds.) (1992). *The Phenomenology of the Noema*. Dordrecht: Kluwer.
Dummett, M. (1973). *Frege: Philosophy of Language*. London: Duckworth.
Dummett, M. (1993a). "What Is a Theory of Meaning?" In *The Seas of Language*, 1–33. Oxford: Oxford University Press.
Dummett, M. (1993b). "What Do I Know When I Know a Language?" In *The Seas of Language*, 94–105. Oxford: Oxford University Press.

Duzi, M., B. Jespersen and P. Materna. (2010). *Procedural Semantics for Hyperintensional Logic: Foundations and Applications of Transparent Intensional Logic*. Dordrecht: Springer.

Edie, J.M. (1976). *Speaking and Meaning: The Phenomenology of Language*. Bloomington: Indiana University Press.

Elliot, B. (2005). *Phenomenology and Imagination in Husserl and Heidegger*. New York: Routledge.

Ely, L. (1997). "Afterword." In Husserl, E. *Experience and Judgement: Investigations in a Genealogy of Logic*. Trans. J.S. Churchill and K. Ameriks, 399–429. Evanston: Northwestern University Press.

Embree, L. (2013). "Dorion Cairns, Empirical Types, and the Field of Consciousness." In *Husserl's* Ideen. Eds. L.Embree and T. Nenon, 225–39. Contributions to Phenomenology 66. Dordrecht: Springer.

Enfield, N.J. (2010). "Language Evolution Without Social Context?" *Science* 24, 329, 5999, 1600–601.

Engelenhoven, A. van. (2010). "Deixis." In *The Cambridge Encyclopedia of the Language Sciences*. Ed. P.C. Hogan, 247–8. Cambridge: Cambridge University Press.

Erickson, S.A. (1970). *Language and Being: An Analytic Phenomenology*. New Haven: Yale University Press.

Evans, G. (1982). *The Varieties of Reference*. Ed. J. MacDowell. Oxford: Clarendon Press.

Evans, N. (2012). "Anything Can Happen: The Verb Lexicon and Interdisciplinary Fieldwork." In *The Oxford Handbook of Linguistic Fieldwork*. Ed. N. Thieberger, 183–208. Oxford: Oxford University Press.

Evans, V. (2003). *The Structure of Time: Language, Meaning, and Temporal Cognition*. Amsterdam: John Benjamins.

Evans, V. (2009). *How Words Mean: Lexical Concepts, Cognitive Models, and Meaning Construction*. Oxford: Oxford University Press.

Everett, D.L. (2016). "Grammar Came Later: Triality of Patterning and the Gradual Evolution of Language." *The Journal of Neurolinguistics* 43, 133–65.

Fauconnier, G. (1997). *Mappings in Thought's Language*. Cambridge: Cambridge University Press.

Fauconnier, G. and M. Turner. (2002). *The Way We Think: Conceptual Blending and the Mind's Hidden Complexities*. New York: Basic Books.

Favareau, D. (2002). "Beyond Self and Other: On the Neurosemiotic Emergence of Intersubjectivity." *Sign System Studies* 30, 1, 57–100.

Feldman, C.F. (1971). "The Interaction of Sentence Characteristics and Mode of Presentation in Recall." *Language and Speech* 14, 1, 18–25.

Fillmore, C.J. (1975 [1971]). *Santa Cruz Lectures on Deixis*. Bloomington: Indiana University Linguistics Club.

Finke, R. (1989). *Principles of Mental Imagery*. Cambridge, MA: MIT Press.

Fitch, T. (2008). "Nano-Intentionality: A Defense of Intrinsic Intentionality." *Biology and Philosophy* 23, 157–77.

Fitch, T. (2009). "Prolegomena to a Future Science of Biolinguistics." *Biolinguistics* 3, 4, 283–320.

Fitch, T. (2010). *The Evolution of Language*. Cambridge: Cambridge University Press.

Fitch, T. (2011). "The Evolution of Syntax: An Exaptationist Perspective." *Frontiers in Evolutionary Neuroscience* 3, 1–46.

Fodor, J.A. (1975). *The Language of Thought*. Cambridge, MA.: Harvard University Press.

Fodor, J.A. (1998). *Concepts: Where Cognitive Science Went Wrong*. Oxford: Clarendon Press.
Fodor, J.A. (2008). *Lot 2: The Language of Thought Revisited*. Oxford: Oxford University Press.
Føllesdal, D. (1969). "Husserl's Notion of *Noema*." *The Journal of Philosophy* 66, 680–7.
Føllesdal, D. (1990). "Noema and Meaning in Husserl." *Philosophy and Phenomenological Research* 50, 263–71.
Føllesdal, D. (1995). "In What Sense Is Language Public?" In *On Quine: New Essays*. Eds. P. Leonardi and M. Santambrogio, 53–67. Cambridge: Cambridge University Press.
Føllesdal, D. (2004). "Husserl on Evidence and Justification." In *Phenomenology: Critical Concepts in Philosophy*, v. 1. Eds. D. Moran and L.E. Embree, 207–30. London: Routledge.
Foster, J. (2003). *The Nature of Perception*. Oxford: Oxford University Press.
Foucault, M. (1986). *The Archaeology of Knowledge*. Trans. A.M.S. Smith. London: Tavistock.
Frege, G. (1893). *Grundgesetze der Arithmetik*. Jena: Pohle.
Frege, G. (1963). "Compound Thoughts." *Mind* 72, 1–17.
Frege, G. (1967 [1892]). "Über Sinn und Bedeutung." In *Kleine Schriften*. Ed. I. Angelelli, 143–62. Hildesheim: Olms.
Frege, G. (1970). "On Sense and Reference." In *Translations from the Philosophical Writings of Gottlob Frege*. Eds. P. Geach and M. Black, 56–78. Oxford: Basil Blackwell.
Frege, G. (1997). "Der Gedanke: Eine logische Untersuchung." In *The Frege Reader*. Ed. M. Beaney, 325–45. Oxford: Blackwell.
Fricke, E. (2007). *Origo, Geste und Raum: Lokaldeixis im Deutschen*. Berlin: De Gruyter.
Gärdenfors, P. and M. Osvath. (2010). "Prospection as a Cognitive Precursor to Symbolic Communication." In *Evolution of Language: Biolinguistic Approaches*. Ed. R. Larson, 103–14. Cambridge: Cambridge University Press.
Gallagher, S. and D. Schmicking. (Eds.) (2010) *Handbook of Phenomenology and Cognitive Science*. Dordrecht: Springer.
Gallagher, S. and D. Zahavi. (2012). *The Phenomenological Mind*. London: Routledge.
Gallese, V. (2006) "Embodied Simulation: Mirror Neurons, Neurophysiological Bases of Intersubjectivity, and Some Implications for Psychoanalysis." *Psicoterapia e Scienze Umane* 40, 3, 543–80.
Gans, E. (1981) *The Origin of Language: A Formal Theory of Representation*. Berkeley: University of California Press.
Gans, S. (1982) "Schematism and Embodiment." *Journal of the British Society of Phenomenology* 13, 237–45.
Gillon, B.S. (2004). "Ambiguity, Indeterminacy, Deixis, and Vagueness." In *Semantics: A Reader*. Eds. S. Davis and B.S. Gillon, 157–87. Oxford: Oxford University Press.
Golebiewska, M. (2019). "Edmund Husserl's Semantics and the Critical Theses of Late Structuralism." *Eidos: A Journal for Philosophy of Culture*, 3, 1, 30–50.
Grandy, R. (1990). "Understanding and Compositionality." *Philosophical Perspectives* 4, 557–72.
Greenfield, P.M. and S.E. Savage-Rumbaugh. (1991). "Imitation, Grammatical Development, and the Invention of Protogrammar." In *Biological and Behavioral Determinants of Language Development*. Eds. N.A. Krasnegor, D.M. Rumbaugh, M. Studdert-Kennedy, and R. Schiefelbusch, 235–58. Hillsdale, NJ: Erlbaum.
Grewendorf, G., F. Hamm, and W. Sternefeld. (1987). *Sprachliches Wissen: Eine Einführung in moderne Theorien der grammatischen Beschreibung*. Frankfurt: Suhrkamp.

Gumpel, L. (1994). "Language as Bearer of Meaning: The Phenomenology of Roman Ingarden." In *Kunst und Ontologie: Für Roman Ingarden zum 100. Geburtstag*, 21–58. Amsterdam: Rodopi.

Gurwitch, A. (1977). "Outline of a Theory of Essentially Occasional Expressions." In *Readings on Edmund Husserl's* Logical Investigations. Ed. N.J. Mohanty, 112–27. The Hague: Martinus Nijhoff.

Habermas, J. (1979). "Universal Pragmatics." In *Communication and the Evolution of Society*, 1–68. London: Heinemann.

Haeflinger, G. and G. Küng. (2005). "Substances, States, Processes, Events: Ingarden and the Analytic Theory of Objects." In *Existence, Culture and Persons: The Ontology of Roman Ingarden*. Ed. A. Chrudzimski, 9–34. Frankfurt: Ontos.

Halliday, M. (1975). *Learning How to Mean: Explorations in the Development of Language*. London: Edward Arnold.

Halliday, M. (1978). *Language as Social Semiotic*. London: Edward Arnold.

Halliday, M. (1985). *An Introduction to Functional Grammar*. London: Edward Arnold.

Hanneborg, K. (1996). "New Concepts in Ontology. A Review Discussion of Roman Ingarden: *Der Streit um die Existenz der Welt*." *Inquiry* 9, 401–9.

Haugland, J. (1987). *Artificial Intelligence: The Very Idea*. Cambridge, MA: MIT Press.

Hauser, M.D., N. Chomsky, and T. Fitch. (2002). "The Faculty of Language: What Is It? Who Has It? And How Did It Evolve?" *Science* 298, 5598, 1569–79.

Heck, R. (2013). "Is Compositionality a Trivial Principle?" *Frontiers of Philosophy in China* 8, 1, 140–55.

Heidegger, M. (1959). *Unterwegs zur Sprache*. Pfullingen: Neske.

Heidegger, M. (1962 [1927]). *Being and Time*. Trans. J. Macquarrie and E. Robinson. London: SCM.

Heidegger, M. (1993). *Sein und Zeit*. Tübingen: Max Niemeyer.

Heidegger, M. (2001). *Poetry, Language, Thought*. Trans. A. Hofstadter. New York: Perennial Classics.

Held, K. (2003). "Husserl's Phenomenology of the Life-World." Trans. L.Rodemeyer. In *The New Husserl*. Ed. D. Welton, 32–62. Bloomington: Indiana University Press.

Herbermann, C.-P. (1988). *Modi Referentiae: Studien zum sprachlichen Bezug zur Wirklichkeit*. Heidelberg: Winter.

Higginbotham, J. (1998). "On Knowing One's Own Language." In *Knowing Our Own Mind*. Eds. C. Wright, B.C. Smith, and C. Macdonald, 429–41. Oxford: Oxford University Press.

Hill, C.O., G. Haddock, and E. Rosado. (2003). *Husserl or Frege: Meaning, Objectivity, and Mathematics*. Chicago: Open Court.

Hintikka, J. (2003). "The Notion of Intuition in Husserl." *Revue Internationale de Philosophie* 224 (2003), 57–79.

Hirst, G. (1987). *Semantic Interpretation and the Resolution of Ambiguity*. Cambridge: Cambridge University Press.

Hockett, C.F. (1960). "The Origin of Speech." *Scientific American* 203, 88–96.

Hockett, C.F. (1966). "The Problems of Universals in Language." In *Universals of Language*. Ed. J.H. Greenberg, 1–29. Cambridge, MA: MIT Press.

Hodges, W. (2001). "Formal Features of Compositionality." *Journal of Logic, Language, and Information* 10, 7–28.

Hookway, C.J. (1997). "Occasion Sentences and Eternal Sentences." In *Concise Encyclopedia of Philosophy of Language*. Eds. P. Lamarque and R.E. Asher, 286–7. Oxford: Pergamon.

Hopkins, B.C. (2008). "On the Origin of the 'Language' of Formal Mathematics: An Intentional-Historical Investigation of the Discovery of the Formal." In *Meaning and Language: Phenomenological Perspectives*. Ed. F. Mattens, 149–69. Phaenomenologica 187. Dordrecht: Springer.

Hopkins, B.C. (2011). *The Origin of the Logic of Symbolic Mathematics: Edmund Husserl and Jacob Klein*. Bloomington: Indiana University Press.

Hopkins, B.C. (2016). "Husserl and Jacob Klein." *The European Legacy* 21, 5–6, 535–55.

Horváth, L. C. Szummer, and A. Szabo. (2018). "Weak Phantasy and Visionary Phantasy: The Phenomenological Significance of Altered States of Consciousness." *Phenomenology and the Cognitive Sciences* 17, 1. 117–29.

Hurford, J.R. (2003). "The Language Mosaic and Its Evolution." In *Language Evolution*. Eds. M.H. Christiansen and S. Kirby, 38–57. Oxford: Oxford University Press.

Hurford, J.R. (2007). *The Origins of Meaning: Language in the Light of Evolution*. Oxford: Oxford University Press.

Husserl, E. (1950). *Cartesianische Meditationen und Pariser Vorträge*. Ed. S. Strasser. The Hague: Martinus Nijhoff. (Hua I)

Husserl, E. (1965). *Erste Philosophie. (1923/4)*. Erster Teil: Kritische Ideengeschichte. Ed. R. Boehm. The Hague: Martinus Nijhoff. (Hua VII)

Husserl, E. (1968). *Phänomenologische Psychologie. Vorlesungen Sommersemester 1925*. Ed. W. Biemel. The Hague: Martinus Nijhoff. (Hua IX)

Husserl, E. (1969a). *Ideas: General Introduction to Pure Phenomenology*. Trans. W.R. Boyce Gibson. London: Collier-Macmillan.

Husserl, E. (1969b). *Formal and Transcendental Logic*. Trans. Dorion Cairns. The Hague: Martinus Nijhoff.

Husserl, E. (1970a). *The Crisis of European Siences and Transcendental Phenomenology*. Trans. D. Carr. Evanston: Northwestern University Press.

Husserl, E. (1970b). "The Origin of Geometry." In *The Crisis*, 353–78.

Husserl, E. (1970c). *Philosophie der Arithmetik. Mit ergänzenden Texten (1890–1901)*. Ed. L. Eley. The Hague: Martinus Nijhoff. (Hua XII)

Husserl, E. (1972). *Erfahrung und Urteil: Untersuchungen zur Genealogie der Logik*. Hamburg: Felix Meiner.

Husserl, E. (1973a). *Cartesianische Meditationen und Pariser Vorträge*. Ed. S. Strasser. The Hague: Martinus Nijhoff. (Hua I)

Husserl, E. (1973b). *Cartesian Meditations*. Trans. Dorion Cairns. The Hague: Martinus Nijhoff.

Husserl, E. (1973c). *Zur Phänomenologie der Intersubjektivität. Texte aus dem Nachlass. Erster Teil: 1905–1920*. Ed. I. Kern. The Hague: Martinus Nijhoff. (Hua XIII)

Husserl, E. (1973d). *Zur Phänomenologie der Intersubjektivität. Texte aus dem Nachlass. Zweiter Teil: 1921–1928*. Ed. I. Kern. The Hague: Martinus Nijhoff. (Hua XIV)

Husserl, E. (1973e). *Zur Phänomenologie der Intersubjektivität. Texte aus dem Nachlass. Dritter Teil: 1929–1935*. Ed. I. Kern. The Hague: Martinus Nijhoff. (Hua XV)

Husserl, E. (1974). *Formale und transzendentale Logik: Versuch einer Kritik der logischen Vernunft*. Mit ergänzenden Texten. Ed. P. Janssen. The Hague: Martinus Nijhoff. (Hua XVII)

Husserl, E. (1977). *Ideen zu einer reinen Phänomenologie und phänomenologischen Philosophie*. Erstes Buch: Allgemeine Einführung in die reine Phänomenologie. Erster Halbband. Text der 1–3. Auflage. Ed. K. Schuhmann. The Hague: Martinus Nijhoff. (Hua III/1)

Husserl, E. (1984). *Logische Untersuchungen. Zweiter Band. Untersuchungen zur Phänomenologie und Theorie der Erkenntnis.* Ed. U. Panzer. Dordrecht: Kluwer. (Hua XIX/2)

Husserl, E. (1985). *Einleitung in die Logik und Erkenntnistheorie. Vorlesungen 1906/7.* Ed. U. Melle. Dordrecht: Kluwer. (Hua XXIV)

Husserl, E. (1987). *Vorlesungen über Bedeutungslehre, Sommersemester 1908.* Ed. U. Panzer. The Hague: Martinus Nijhoff. (Hua XXVI)

Husserl, E. (1991). *Ideen zu einer reinen Phänomenologie und phänomenologischen Philosophie. Zweites Buch. Phänomenologische Untersuchungen zur Konstitution.* Ed. M. Biemel. The Hague: Martinus Nijhoff. (Hua IV)

Husserl, E. (1994a). "On the Logic of Signs (Semiotic)." In *Early Writings in the Philosophy of Logic and Arithmetic*, 20–51. Trans. D. Willard. New York: Springer.

Husserl, E. (1994b). *Early Writings in the Philosophy of Logic and Mathematics.* Trans. D. Willard. Dordrecht: Kluwer.

Husserl, E. (1997a). *Experience and Judgment: Investigations in a Genealogy of Logic.* Rev. and ed. L. Landgrebe. Trans. J.S. Churchill and K. Ameriks. Evanston: Northwestern University Press.

Husserl, E. (1997b). *Psychological and Transcendental Phenomenology and the Confrontation with Heidegger (1927–1931).* Eds. and trans. T. Shehan and R.E. Palmer. Dordrecht: Kluwer.

Husserl, E. (2000). *Logical Investigations.* Trans. J.N. Findlay, v.1 and 2. Amherst, NY: Humanity Books.

Husserl, E. (2002). *Logische Untersuchungen. Ergänzungsband. Erster Teil. Entwürfe zur Umarbeitung der VI. Untersuchung und zur Vorrede für die Neuauflage der Logischen Untersuchungen (Sommer 1913).* Ed. U. Melle. Dordrecht: Kluwer. (Hua XX/1)

Husserl, E. (2005a). *Logische Untersuchungen. Ergänzungsband. Zweiter Teil. Texte für die Neufassung der VI. Untersuchung. Zur Phänomenologie des Ausdrucks und der Erkenntnis (1893–1921).* Ed. U. Melle. Dordrecht: Springer. (Hua XX/2)

Husserl, E. (2005b). *Phantasy, Image Consciousness, and Memory (1898–1925).* Trans. J.B. Brough. Collected Works. Ed. R. Bernet, XI. Dordrecht: Springer.

Husserl, E. (2008). *Die Lebenswelt: Auslegungen der vorgegebenen Welt und ihre Konstitution.* Ed. R. Sowa. Dordrecht: Springer. (Hua XXXIX)

Husserl, E. (2011). *Zur Lehre vom Wesen und zur Methode der eidetischen Variation: Texte aus dem Nachlass.* Ed. D. Fonfara. Dordrecht: Springer. (Hua XLI)

Husserl, E. (2012). *Zur Lehre vom Wesen und zur Methode der eidetischen Variation: Texte aus dem Nachlass (1891–1935).* Ed. D. Fonfara. Dordrecht: Springer. (Hua XLI)

Ingarden, R. (1964). *Der Streit um die Existenz der Welt: I Existentialontologie.* Tübingen: Max Niemeyer.

Ingarden, R. (1965a). *Der Streit um die Existenz der Welt: II/1 Formalontologie.* Tübingen: Max Niemeyer.

Ingarden, R. (1965b). *Der Streit um die Existenz der Welt: II/2 Formalontologie 2.* Tübingen: Max Niemeyer.

Ingarden, R. (1973a). *The Literary Work of Art: An Investigation on the Borderlines of Ontology, Logic, and Theory of Literature.* Trans. G.G. Grabowicz. Evanston, IL: Northwestern University Press.

Ingarden, R. (1973b). *The Cognition of the Literary Work of Art.* Trans. R.A. Crowley and K.R. Olson. Evanston, IL: Northwestern University Press.

Ingarden, R. (1974). *Über die Kausalstruktur der Realen Welt: Der Streit um die Existenz der Welt III.* Tübingen: Max Niemeyer.

Ingarden, R. (1989). *Ontology of the Work of Art*. Trans. R. Meyer and J.T. Goldthwait. Athens, Ohio: Ohio University Press.

Inkpin, A. (2016). *Disclosing the World: On the Phenomenology of Language*. Cambridge, MA: MIT Press.

Jackendoff, R. (1994). "Word Meanings and What It Takes to Learn Them: Reflections on the Piaget-Chomsky Debate." In *The Nature and Ontogenesis of Meaning*. Ed. W.F. Overton, 129–44. Hillsdale, NJ: Lawrence Erlbaum.

Jackendoff, R. (1999). "Possible Stages in the Evolution of the Language Capacity." *Trends in Cognitive Science* 3, 272–9.

Jackendoff, R. (2002). *Foundations of Language: Brain, Meaning, Grammar, Evolution*. Oxford: Oxford University Press.

Jackendoff, R. (2004). "What Is a Concept, That a Person May Grasp It?" In *Semantics: A Reader*. Eds. S. Davis and B.S. Gillon, 322–45. Oxford: Oxford University Press.

Jackendoff, R and E. Wittenberg. (2017). "Linear Grammar as a Possible Stepping-Stone in the Evolution of Language." *Psychonomic Bulletin Review* 20, 219–24.

Jadacki, J. (1989). "On Roman Ingarden's Semiotic Views: A Contribution to the History of Polish Semiotics." *Analecta Husserliana* 27, 523–40.

Jakobson, R. (1971). *Selected Writings*, v. 2. The Hague: Mouton.

Jakobson, R. (1981). *Selected Writings*, v. 3. The Hague: Mouton.

Janssen, T.M.V. (1997a). "Compositionality." In *Handbook of Logic and Language*. Eds. J. van Bentham and A. ter Meulen, 417–73. Amsterdam: Elsevier.

Janssen, T.M.V. (1997b). "Compositionality of Meaning." In *Concise Encyclopedia of Philosophy of Language*. Eds. P. Lamarque and R.E. Asher, 102–7. Oxford: Pergamon.

Janssen, T.M.V. (2001). "Frege, Contextuality and Compositionality." *Journal of Logic, Language and Information* 10, 115–36.

Johansson, I. (2009). "Proof of the Existence of Universals and Roman Ingarden's Ontology." *Metaphysica* 10, 1, 65–87.

Johansson, I. (2013a). "The Basic Distinctions in *Der Streit*." *Semiotica* 194, 137–57.

Johansson, I. (2013b). "The Ideal as Real and as Purely Intentional: Ingarden-based Reflections." *Semiotica* 194, 21–37.

Johansson, S. (2005). *Origins of Language – Constraints on Hypotheses*. Amsterdam: Benjamins.

Johansson, S. (2016). "Working Backwards from Modern Language to Proto-Grammar." Jönköping: School of Education and Communication University.

Johnson, M. (1987). *The Body in the Mind: The Bodily Basis of Meaning, Imagination, and Reason*. Chicago: University of Chicago Press.

Johnson, M. (2005). "The Philosophical Significance of Image Schemas." In *From Perception to Meaning: Image Schemas in Cognitive Linguistics*. Ed. B. Hampe, 15–34. Berlin: Mouton de Gruyter.

Johnson, M. and G. Lakoff. (1999). *Philosophy in the Flesh: The Embodied Mind and Its Challenge to Western Thought*. New York: Basic Books.

Kamp, H. and B. Partee. (1995). "Prototype Theory and Compositionality." *Cognition* 57, 129–91.

Kamuf, P. (Ed.) (1991). *A Derrida Reader: Between the Blinds*. New York: Columbia University Press.

Kandel, E., J.H. Schwartz, and T.M. Jessell. (1991). *Principles of Neural Science*. New York: McGraw Hill.

Kant, I. (1965). *Critique of Pure Reason*. Trans. L.W. Beck. New York: Liberal Arts Press. (CPR)

Kant, I. (1966). *Kritik der reinen Vernunft.* Darmstadt: Wissenschaftliche Buchgesellschaft. (CPR)
Kant, I. (2007). *Critique of Judgment.* Trans. J.C. Meredith. Oxford: Oxford University Press.
Kazmi, A. and F.J. Pelletier. (1998). "Is Compositionality Formally Vacuous?" *Linguistics and Philosophy* 21, 629–33.
Keefe, R. (2004). "The Phenomena of Vagueness." In *Fuzzy Grammar.* Eds. B. Aarts, D. Denison, E. Keizer, and G. Popova, 45–64. Oxford: Oxford University Press.
Keeping, J. (1998). "The Ontology of Roman Ingarden." *Symposium* 2, 2, 246–49.
Kendon, A. (2004). *Gesture: Visible Action as Utterance.* Cambridge: Cambridge University Press.
Kendon, A. (2009). "Kinesic Components of Multimodal Utterances." Berkeley Linguistics Society Proceedings. Berkeley: Linguistics Society.
Kersten, F. (2013). "Thoughts on the Translation of Husserl's *Ideen, Erstes Buch*." In *Husserl's Ideen.* Eds. L. Embree and T. Nenon, 467–75. Dordrecht: Springer.
Kinsella, A.R. (2009). *Language Evolution and Syntactic Theory.* Cambridge: Cambridge University Press.
Kita, S. (2000). "How Representational Gestures Help Speaking." In *Language and Gesture.* Ed. D. McNeill, 162–85. Cambridge: Cambridge University Press.
Kita, S. (Ed.) (2003). *Pointing: Where Language, Culture, and Cognition Meet.* Amsterdam: John Benjamins.
Korta, K and J. Perry. (2011). *Critical Pragmatics: An Inquiry into Reference and Communication* Cambridge: Cambridge University Press.
Kosslyn, S.M., W.L. Thompson, and G. Ganis. (2006). *The Case of Mental Imagery.* Oxford: Oxford University Press.
Koukal, D.R. (2008). "The Necessity of Communicating: Phenomenological Insights – and Its Difficulties." In *Meaning and Language: Phenomenological Perspectives.* Ed. F. Mattens, 257–79. Phaenomenologica 187. Dordrecht: Springer.
Kripke, S.A. (1982). *Wittgenstein on Rules and Private Language: An Elementary Exposition.* Oxford: Basil Blackwell.
Kristeva, J. (1989). *Language the Unknown: An Introduction into Linguistics.* Trans. A.M. Menke. London: Harvester.
Küng, G. (1969). "The Role of Language in Phenomenological Analysis." *American Philosophical Quarterly* 6, 330–4.
Küng, G. (1972a). "The World as Noema and as Referent." *Journal of the British Society of Phenomenology* 3, 15–26.
Küng, G. (1972b). "Ingarden on Language and Ontology." *Analecta Husserliana* 2, 204–17.
Küng, G. (1973). "Husserl on Pictures and Intentional Objects." *The Review of Metaphysics* 26, 4, 670–80.
Küng, G. (1975). "Zum Lebenswerk von Roman Ingarden: Ontologie, Erkenntnistheorie und Metaphysik." In *Die Münchener Phänomenologie.* Eds. H. Kuhn, E. Avé-Lallemant, and R. Gladiator, 158–73. The Hague: Martinus Nijhoff.
Kung, P. (2010). "Imagination as a Guide to Possibility." *Philosophy and Phenomenological Research* 81, 620–63.
Kung, P. (2016). "You Really Do Imagine It: Against Error Theories of Imagination." *Noûs* 50, 1, 90–120.
Kusch, M. (1988). "Husserl and Heidegger on Meaning." *Synthese* 77, 99–127.
Kusch, M. (1989). *Language as Calculus and Universal Medium.* Dordrecht: Kluwer.
Kwant, R.C. (1965). *Phenomenology of Language.* Pittsburgh: Dusquenne University Press.

Labov, W. (2004). "The Boundaries of Words and their Meanings." In *Fuzzy Grammar*. Eds. B. Aarts, D. Denison, E. Keizer, and G. Popova, 67–90. Oxford: Oxford University Press.

Lacan, J. (1985). "Sign, Symbol, Imaginary." In *On Signs*. Ed. M. Blonsky, 203–9. Oxford: Basil Blackwell.

Lakoff, G. (1990). "The Invariance Hypothesis: Is Abstract Reasoning Based on Image-Schemas?." *Cognitive Linguistics* 1, 39–74.

Lakoff, G. (1994). "What Is a Conceptual System?" In *The Nature and Ontogenesis of Meaning*. Eds. W.F. Overton and D.S. Palermo, 41–90. Hilldale, NJ: Lawrence Erlbaum.

Lakoff, R.T. (1974). "Remarks on *This* and *That*." In *Berkeley Studies in Syntax and Semantics 1*. Eds. C. Fillmore, G. Lakoff, G. and R. Lakoff. Berkeley: Department of Linguistics. Berkeley University.

Lamarque, P.V. (Ed.) (1997). *Concise Encyclopedia of Philosophy of Language*. Oxford: Pergamon.

Land, M. and B.W. Tatler. (2009). *Looking and Acting: Vision and Eye Movement in Natural Behaviour*. Oxford: Oxford University Press.

Langacker, R.W. (1999). *Foundations of Cognitive Grammar*, v.1: *Theoretical Linguistics*. Stanford: Stanford University Press.

Langacker, R.W. (2004). "Discreteness." In *Fuzzy Grammar*. Eds. B. Aarts, D. Denison, E. Keizer, and G. Popova, 131–8. Oxford: Oxford University Press.

Langacker, R.W. (2008). *Cognitive Grammar: A Basic Introduction*. New York: Oxford University Press.

Langsdorf, L. (1984). "The Noema as Intentional Entity: A Critique of Føllesdal." *The Review of Metaphysics* 37, 757–84.

Lanigan, R. (1977). *Speech Act Phenomenology*. The Hague: Martinus Nijhoff.

Leavens, D. (2004). "Review of Sotaro Kita (2003) *Where Language, Culture, and Cognition Meet*." *Cognitive Systems Research* 5, 157–65.

Lecercle, J.-J. (1990). *The Violence of Language*. London and New York: Routledge.

Leech, G. (1975). *Semantics*. Harmondsworth: Penguin.

Leibniz, G.W. (1968). *The Nonadology and Other Philosophical Writings*. Trans. R. Latta. Oxford: Oxford University Press.

Lepore, E. and B.C. Smith (Eds.) (2006). *The Oxford Handbook of Philosophy of Language*. Oxford: Clarendon Press.

Levinson, S.C. (1983). *Pragmatics*. Cambridge: Cambridge University Press.

Levinson, S.C. (1997). "Deixis." In *Concise Encyclopedia of Philosophy of Language*. Eds. P. Lamarque and R.E. Asher, 214–19. Oxford: Pergamon.

Levinson, S.C. (2004). "Deixis." In *The Handbook of Pragmatics*. Eds. L.R. Horn and G. Ward, 97–121. Oxford: Blackwell.

Levinson, S.C. (2013). "Recursion in Pragmatics." *Language* 89, 149–62.

Locke, J. (1993). *An Essay Concerning Human Understanding*. Eds. J.W. Yolton. London: Dent.

Löwith, K. (2013). *Das Individuum in der Rolle des Mitmenschen*. Freiburg and Munich: Karl Alber.

Lohmar D. (2002). "Husserl's Concept of Categorial Intuition." In *Hundred Years of Phenomenology: Husserl's Logical Investigations Revisited*. Eds. D. Zahavi and F. Stjernfelt, 125–45. Dordrecht: Springer.

Lohmar, D. (2003). "Husserl's Type and Kant's Schemata: Systematic Reasons for their Correlation or Identity." In *The New Husserl: A Critical Reader*. Ed. D. Welton, 93–124. Bloomington: Indiana University Press.

Lohmar, D. (2005). "Die phänomenologische Methode der Wesensschau und ihre Präzisierung als eidetische Variation." *Phänomenologische Forschungen*. Eds. T. Breyer, J. Jansen, and I. Römer, 65–91. Hamburg: Felix Meiner.
Lohmar, D. (2006). "Mirror Neurons and the Phenomenology of Intersubjectivity." *Phenomenology and Cognitive Science* 5, 5–16;
Lohmar, D. (2008). "Denken ohne Sprache? Zur Phänomenologie alternativer Repräsentations-Systeme kognitiver Inhalte beim Menschen und anderen Primaten." In *Meaning and Language: Phenomenological Perspectives*. Ed. F. Mattens, 169–94. Phaenomenologica 187. Dordrecht: Springer.
Lohmar, D. (2010). "The Function of Weak Phantasy in Perception and Thinking." In *The Handbook of Phenomenology and Cognitive Science*. Eds. S. Gallagher and D. Schmicking, 159–77. Dordrecht: Spinger.
Lohmar, D. (2012). "Zur Vorgeschichte der transzentalen Reduktion in den *Logischen Untersuchungen*: Die unbekannte Reduktion auf den reellen Bestand." *Husserl Studies* 28, 1, 1–24.
Lohmar, D. (2015). "Language and Non-Linguistic Thinking." In *The Oxford Handbook of Contemporary Phenomenology*. Ed. D. Zahavi, 377–98. Oxford: Oxford University Press.
Lyons, J. (1968). *Introduction to Theoretical Linguistics*. Cambridge: Cambridge University Press.
Lyons, J. (1995). *Linguistic Semantics: An Introduction*. Cambridge: Cambridge University Press.
MacKay, D.G. (1987). "Perceptual Sequencing and Higher-Level Activation." In *The Organization of Perception and Action: A Theory of Language and Other Cognitive Skills*. Ed. D.G. McKay, 62–89. Berlin: Springer.
McDowell, J. (1998). *Meaning, Knowledge, and Reality*. Cambridge, MA: Harvard University Press.
McGregor, W.B. (2009). *Linguistics: An Introduction*. London: Continuum.
McNeill, D. (1992). *Hand and Mind: What Gestures Reveal About Thought*. Chicago: University of Chicago Press, 1992.
McNeill, D. (Ed.) (2000). *Language and Gesture*. Cambridge: Cambridge University Press.
McNeill, D. (2005). *Gesture and Thought*. Chicago: University of Chicago Press.
McNeill, D. (2012). *How Language Began: Gesture and Speech in Human Communication*. Cambridge: Cambridge University Press.
McNeill, D., B. Bertenthal, J. Cole, and S. Gallagher (2005). "Gesture-First – But No Gesture." *Behavioral and Brain Sciences* 28, 138–9.
Manning, H.P. (2001). "On Social Deixis." *Anthropological Linguistics* 43, 1, 54–100.
Margolis, E. and S. Laurence (Eds.) (1999). *Concepts: Core Readings*. Cambridge, MA: MIT Press.
Mattens, F. (Ed.). (2008a). *Meaning and Language: Phenomenological Perspectives*. Phaenomenologica 187. Dordrecht: Springer.
Mattens, F. (2008b). "Introducing Terms: Philosophical Vocabulary, Neologisms and the Temporal Aspects of Meaning." In *Meaning and Language: Phenomenological Perspectives*. Ed. F. Mattens, 281–326. Dordrecht: Springer.
Matthews, R. (2003). "Does Linguistic Competence Require Knowledge of Language?" In *Epistemology of Language*. Ed. A. Barber, 187–213. Oxford and New York: Oxford University Press.
Mayberry, R. (2000). "Gesture Reflects Language Development: Evidence for Bilingual Children." *Current Directions in Psychological Science* 9, 6, 192–6.

Mazzone, M. (2018). *Cognitive Pragmatics: Mindreading, Inferences, Consciousness*. New York: de Gruyter Mouton.

Meillassoux, Q. (2013). *After Finitude: An Essay on the Necessity of Contingency*. Trans. R. Brassier. London: Bloomsbury.

Melle, U. (2002). "Husserl's Revision of the Sixth Logical Investigation." In *One Hundred Years of Phenomenology: Husserl's* Logical Investigations *Revisited*. Eds. D. Zahavi and F. Stjernfelt, 111–23. Dordrecht: Kluwer.

Melle, U. (2008). "Das Rätsel des Ausdrucks: Husserls Zeichen- und Ausdruckslehre in den Manuskripten für die Neufassung der VI. Logischen Untersuchung." In *Meaning and Language: Phenomenological Perspectives*. Ed. F. Mattens, 3–26. Phaenomenologica 187. Dordrecht: Springer.

Mendelsohn, R. (2005). *The Philosophy of Gottlob Frege*. Cambridge: Cambridge University Press.

Mensch, J. (2001). "Derrida-Husserl: Towards a Phenomenology of Language." *New Yearbook for Phenomenology and Phenomenological Philosophy* 1, 1–66.

Merleau-Ponty, M. (1962). *Phenomenology of Perception*. Trans. C. Smith. London: Routledge.

Merleau-Ponty, M. (1964a). "On the Phenomenology of Language." In *Signs*. Trans. R.C. McCleary, 84–97. Evanston: Northwestern University Press.

Merleau-Ponty, M. (1964b). *Sense and Non-Sense*. Trans. H.L. Dreyfus and P.A. Dreyfus. Evanston: Northwestern University Press.

Merleau-Ponty, M. (1964c). *Signs*. Trans. R.C. McCleary. Evanston: Northwestern University Press.

Merleau-Ponty, M. (1968). *The Visible and the Invisible*. Trans. A. Lingis. Evanston: Northwestern University Press.

Merleau-Ponty, M. (1974). *The Prose of the World*. Ed. C. Lefort. Trans. J. O'Neill. London: Heinemann.

Metz, C. (1974). *Film Language: A Semiotics of the Cinema*. New York: Oxford University Press.

Michaelian, K. (2016). *Mental Time Travel: Episodic Memory and Our Knowledge of the Personal Past*. Cambridge, MA: MIT Press.

Millikan, R. (1990). "The Myth of the Essential Indexical." *Noûs* 24, 723–34.

Mitcherling, J. (1997). *Roman Ingarden's Ontology and Aesthetics*. Ottawa: University of Ottawa Press.

Mitcherling, J. (2012). "Roman Ingarden: Aesthetics." *Philosophy Compass* 7, 436–7.

Mithen, S. (2005). *The Singing Neanderthals: The Origins of Music, Language, Mind, and Body*. London: Weidenfeld and Nicholson.

Mithen, S. (2012). "Musicality and Language." In *The Oxford Handbook of Language Evolution*. Eds. M.M. Tallerman and K.R. Gibson, 296–98. Oxford: Oxford University Press.

Mohanty, J.N. (1970). *Phenomenology and Ontology*. The Hague: Martinus Nijhoff.

Mohanty, J.N. (2008a). *The Philosophy of Edmund Husserl: A Historical Development*. New Haven: Yale University Press.

Mohanty, J.N. (2008b). "On Husserl's 'Lectures on Theory of Meaning (1908)." In *The Philosophy of Edmund Husserl*, 224–41. New Haven: Yale University Press.

Moran, D. (2011). "Edmund Husserl's Phenomenology of Habituality and Habitus." *Journal of the British Society for Phenomenology* 42, 2, 53–77.

Moran, D. (2013). "From the Natural Attitude to the Life-World." In *Husserl's* Ideen. Eds. L. Embree and T. Nenon, 105–24. Dordrecht: Springer.

Moran, D. (2016). "Ineinandersein and L'interlacs: The Constitution of the Social World or 'We-World' (*Wir-Welt*) in Edmund Husserl and Maurice Merleau- Ponty." In *Phenomenology of Sociality: Discovering the 'We.'* Eds. T. Szanto and D. Moran, 107–26. New York and London: Routledge.
Moran, D. and J. Cohen. (2012). *The Husserl Dictionary*. London: Continuum.
Moran, D. and L. Embree (Eds.) (2004). *Phenomenology: Critical Concepts in Philosophy*, v.1. London: Routledge.
Moran, D. and T. Szanto (Eds.) (2016). *Phenomenology of Sociality: Discovering the 'We.'* Research in Phenomenology v. 3. New York and London: Routledge.
Mulligan, K. (1987). *Speech Act and Sachverhalt: Reinach and the Foundations of Realist Phenomenology*. Dordrecht: Martin Nijhoff.
Münch, D. (2002). "The Relation of Husserl's *Logical Investigations* to Descriptive Psychology and Cognitive Science." In *One Hundred Years of Phenomenology: Husserl's Logical Investigations Revisited*. Eds. D. Zahavi and F. Stjernfelt, 199–215. Dordrecht: Kluwer.
Muskens, R.A. (1997). "Propositional Attitudes." In *Concise Encyclopedia of Philosophy of Language*. Eds. P. Lamarque and R.E. Asher, 291–4. Oxford: Pergamon.
Nagel, T. (1969). "Linguistics and Epistemology." In *Language and Philosophy*. Ed. S. Hook, 171–81. New York: New York University Press.
Natanson, M. (1973). *Edmund Husserl: Philosopher of Infinite Tasks*. Evanston: Northwestern University Press.
Natanson, M. (1998). *The Erotic Bird: Phenomenology in Literature*. Foreword by Judith Butler. Princeton: Princeton University Press.
Nietzsche, F. (1911 [1873]). "Ueber Wahrheit und Lüge im aussermoralischen Sinn." In *The Complete Works of Friedrich Nietzsche*, v.2. Eds. O. Levy. Trans. M.A. Mügge, 171–92. London: Allen and Unwin.
Novak, A. and L. Sosnowski (Eds.) (2001). *Dictionary of Roman Ingarden's Philosophical Concepts*. Krakao: Jagellonian University Institute of Philosophy.
Nunberg, G. (1993). "Indexicality and Deixis." *Linguistics and Philosophy* 16, 1–43.
Overgaard, S. (2010). "The Problem of Other Minds." In *Handbook of Phenomenology and Cognitive Science*. Eds. S. Gallagher and D. Schmicking, 254–68. Dordrecht: Springer.
Palma, V. de. (2014). "Die Fakta leiten alle Eidetik: Zu Husserls Begriff des materialen Apriori." *Husserl Studies* 30, 3, 195–223.
Palmer, F.R. (1982). *Semantics*. Cambridge: Cambridge University Press.
Partee, B.H. (1984). "Compositionality." In *Varieties of Formal Semantics*. Eds. F. Landman and F. Veltman, 281–312. Dordrecht: Foris.
Partee, B.H., A. ter Meulen and R.E. Wall. (1990). *Mathematical Methods in Linguistics*. Dordrecht: Kluwer.
Patočka, J. (1998). *Body, Community, Language*. Chicago: Open Court.
Peirce, C.S. (1974). *Collected Papers of Charles Sanders Peirce 1931–1966*. 8 vols. Eds. C. Hartsworth, P. Weiss, and A.W. Burks. Cambridge, MA: Belknap Press. (CP)
Peirce, C.S. (1984). *Writings of Charles S. Peirce: A Chronological Edition*, v.2. 1867–71. Peirce Edition Project. Bloomington: Indiana University Press. (EP)
Pelletier, F.J. (1994). "The Principle of Semantic Compositionality." In *Semantics*: A Reader. Eds. S. Davis and B.S. Gillon, 133–56. Oxford: Oxford University Press.
Pelletier, F.J. (2001). "Did Frege Believe Frege's Principle?" *Journal of Logic, Language and Information* 10, 87–114.
Peregrin, J. (2003). "Is Compositionality an Empirical Matter?" *Journal of Logic, Language and Information* 10, 115–36.

Perry, J. (2006). "Using Indexicals." In *The Blackwell Guide to the Philosophy of Language*. Eds. M. Devitt and R. Hanley, 314–34. Oxford: Blackwell.
Philipse, H. (1982). "The Problem of Occasional Expressions in Edmund Husserl's *Logical Investigations*." *Journal of the British Society for Phenomenology* 13, 168–85.
Popova, Y. (2005). "Image Schemas and Verbal Synesthesia." In *From Perception to Meaning: Image Schemas in Cognitive Linguistics*. Ed. B. Hampe, 421–42. Berlin: Mouton de Gruyter.
Praetorius, N. (2010). "Intersubjectivity, Cognition, and Language." In *Handbook of Phenomenology and Cognitive Science*. Eds. S. Gallagher and D. Schmicking, 301–16. Dordrecht: Springer.
Pulvermüller, F., Y. Shtyrov, and O. Hauk. (2009). "Understanding in an Instant: Neurophysiological Evidence for Mechanistic Language Circuits in the Brain." *Brain and Language* 110, 2, 81–94.
Putnam, H. (1989). *Mind, Language and Reality: Philosophical Papers*. 2 vols. London: Cambridge University Press.
Pylyshyn, Z.W. (2002). "Mental Imagery: In Search of a Theory." *Behavioral and Brain Sciences* 25, 157–82.
Pylyshyn, Z.W. (2003). *Seeing and Visualizing*. Cambridge, MA: MIT Press.
Quine, W. van O. (1960). *Word and Object*. Cambridge, MA: MIT Press.
Quine, W. van O. (1963). "On What There Is." In *From a Logical Point of View*, 1–19. New York: Harper and Row.
Quine, W. van O. (1981). *Theories and Things*. Cambridge, MA: Belknap of Harvard University Press.
Quine, W. van O. (1993). *Pursuit of Truth*. Cambridge, MA: Harvard University Press.
Reinach, A. (1989). "Zur Theorie des negativen Urteils." In *Sämtliche Werke, v*.1. Eds. K. Schuhmann and B. Smith, 95–140. Munich: Philosophia.
Richard, M. (1990). *Propositional Attitudes*. Cambridge: Cambridge University Press.
Richard, M. (1999). "Propositional Attitudes." In *A Companion to the Philosophy of Language*. Eds. B. Hale and C. Wright, 197–226. Oxford; Blackwell.
Richard, M. (2005). "Compositionality." In *The Shorter Routledge Encyclopedia of Philosophy*. Ed. E. Craig, 133. London: Routledge.
Richard, M. (2008). *When Truth Gives Out*. Oxford: Oxford University Press.
Riska, A. (1974). "The A Priori in Ingarden's Theory of Meaning." In *Analecta Husserliana* 3, 138–58.
Riska, A. (1976). "Language and Logic in the Work of Roman Ingarden." *Analecta Husserliana* 4, 187–217.
Risser, J. (2003). "Interpreting Tradition." *Journal of the British Society for Phenomenology* 34, 3, 297–308.
Risser, J. (2009) "The Incapacity of Language." *Journal of the British Society for Phenomenology* 40, 300–311.
Rodemeyer, L.M. (2008). "I Don't Have the Words: Considering Language (and the lack thereof) through the Phenomenological Paradigms of Temporality and Corporeality." In *Meaning and Language: Phenomenological Perspectives*. Ed. F. Mattens, 195–212. Phaenomenologica 187. Dordrecht: Springer.
Rosch, E. (1999). "Principles of Categorization." In *Concepts: Core Readings*. Eds. E. Margolis and S. Laurence, 189–206. Cambridge, MA: MIT Press.
Russell, B. (1923). "Vagueness." *The Australian Journal of Psychology and Philosophy* 1, 84–92.

Russell, B. (1961). *An Inquiry into Meaning and Truth*. London: George Allen and Unwin.
Russell, B. (1973 [1905]). "On Denoting." In *Essays in Analysis*. Ed. D. Lackey, 103–19. New York: George Braziller.
Ruthrof, H. (1992). *Pandora and Occam: On the Limits of Language and Literature*. Bloomington: Indiana University Press.
Ruthrof, H. (1997). *Semantics and the Body: Meaning from Frege to the Postmodern*. Toronto: University of Toronto Press.
Ruthrof, H. (2011a). "From Kant's Monogram to Conceptual Blending." *Philosophy Today* 55, 2, 111–26.
Ruthrof, H. (2011b). "Semantics of Imaginability –13 Theses." *Review of Contemporary Philosophy* 10, 165–83.
Ruthrof, H. (2013a). "Recycling Locke: Linguistic Meaning as Indirectly Public." *Philosophy Today*, 57, 1, 3–27.
Ruthrof, H. (2013b). "Metasemantics and Imaginability." *Language Sciences* 35, 20–31.
Ruthrof, H. (2013c). "A Translation Problem: The Thing-*at*-Itself in Light of Kant's Pragmatism." *Analysis and Metaphysics* 12, 47–67.
Ruthrof, H. (2014a). *Language and Imaginability*. Newcastle upon Tyne: Cambridge Scholars Publishing.
Ruthrof, H. (2014b). "Shutter-Speed Meaning, Normativity, and Wittgenstein's Abrichtung." *Linguistic and Philosophical Investigations* 13, 33–54.
Ruthrof, H. (2015a). "Implicit Deixis." *Language Sciences* 47, 107–16.
Ruthrof, H. (2015b). "Sufficient Semiosis." *The American Journal of Semiotics* 31, 1–2, 117–46.
Ruthrof, H. (2015c). *The Body in Language*. London: Bloomsbury.
Ruthrof, H. (2016). "Speculations on the Origins of Language." *Linguistic and Philosophical Investigations* 15, 90–107.
Ruthrof, H. (2017). "Heidegger: *Wahrnehmungsvergessenheit*." *Analysis and Metaphysics* 16, 84–102.
Ruthrof, H. (2020a). "Phenomenology." *Oxford Encyclopedia of Literary Theory*. Ed. J. Frow. Oxford: Oxford University Press. doi:10.1093/acrefore/9780190201098.013.998
Ruthrof, H. (2020b). "Knowing a Language – What Sort of Knowing Is It?" *Analysis and Metaphysics* 19, 7–30.
Sacks, H. (1995). *Lectures on Conversation: Volumes I and II*. Ed. G. Jefferson. Oxford: Blackwell.
Sainsbury, R.M. (2006). "The Essence of Reference." In *The Oxford Handbook of Philosophy of Language*. Ed. B.C. Smith, 393–421. Oxford: Oxford University Press.
Sainsbury, R.M. and T. Williamson. (1999). "Sorites." In *A Companion to the Philosophy of Language*. Eds. B. Hale and C. Wright, 458–84. Oxford: Blackwell.
Salice, A. and B. Schmid (Eds.). (2016). *The Phenomenological Approach to Social Reality: History, Concepts, Problems*. Dordrecht: Springer.
Salmon, W.C. (2001). *Zeno's Paradoxes*, 2nd ed. Indianapolis: Hackett Publishing.
Saussure, F. de. (2005). *Cours de linguistique générale*. Eds. C. Bally, A. Séchehaye, A. Riedlinger, and T. de Mauro. Paris: Payot.
Scheler, M. (2004). "The Perception of Other Minds." In *Phenomenology: Critical Concepts in Philosophy*, v.2, Phenomenology: Themes and Issues. Eds. D. Moran and L.E. Embree, 119–42. London and New York: Routledge.
Schiffer, S. (2006a). "Propositional Content." In *The Oxford Handbook of Philosophy of Language*. Ed. B.C. Smith, 267–94. Oxford: Oxford University Press.

Schiffer, S. (2006b). "Vagueness." In *The Blackwell Guide to the Philosophy of Language*. Eds. M. Devitt and R. Hanley, 225–43. Oxford: Blackwell.

Schlick, M. (1936). "Meaning and Verification." *Philosophical Review* 45, 339–68.

Schlossberger, M. (2016). "The Varieties of Togetherness: Scheler on Collective Affective Intentionality." In *The Phenomenological Approach to Social Reality*. Eds. A. Salice and H.B. Schmid, 173–95. Dordrecht: Springer.

Schütz, A. (1959). "Type and Eidos in Husserl's Late Philosophy." *Philosophy and Phenomenological Research* 20, 147 –65.

Schütz, A. (1970). *Reflections on the Problem of Relevance*. New Haven: Yale University Press.

Schütz, A. (2004). "The Problem of Transcendental Intersubjectivity in Husserl." In *Phenomenology: Critical Concepts*, v.2, Themes and Issues. Eds. D. Moran and L.E. Embree, 143–78. London and New York: Routledge.

Searle, J.R. (1975). "The Logical Status of Fictional Discourse." *New Literary History* 6, 319–32.

Sheets-Johnstone, M. (2012). "Movement and Mirror Neurons: A Challenging and Choice Conversation." *Phenomenology and the Cognitive Sciences* 11, 385–401.

Simons, P. (1995). "Meaning and Language." In *The Cambridge Companion to Husserl*. Eds. B. Smith and D.W. Smith, 106–37. Cambridge: Cambridge University Press.

Slater, P. (2012). "Bird Song and Language." In *The Oxford Handbook of Language Evolution*. Eds. de Tallerman, M. and K.R. Gibson, 96–101. Oxford: Oxford University Press.

Smith, B.C. (1980). "Ingarden Versus Meinong on the Logic of Fiction." *Philosophy and Phenomenological Research* 41, 93–105.

Smith, B.C. (1987). "Husserl, Language, and the Ontology of the Act." In *Speculative Grammar, Universal Grammar, and Philosophical Analysis of Language*. Eds. D. Buzetti and M. Ferriani, 205–27. Amsterdam: John Benjamins.

Smith, B.C. (1994). "Husserl's Theory of Meaning and Reference." In *Mind, Meaning and Mathematics: Essays on the Philosophy of Husserl and Frege*. Ed. L. Haaparanta, 163–83. Dordrecht: Kluwer.

Smith, B.C. (1998). "On Knowing One's Own Language1." In *Knowing Our Own Minds*. Eds. C. Wright, B.C. Smith, and C. Macdonald, 391–428. Oxford: Clarendon Press.

Smith, B.C. (2006). "What I Know When I Know a Language." In *The Oxford Handbook of Philosophy of Language*. Eds. E. LePore and B.C. Smith, 941–82. Oxford: Clarendon Press.

Smith, D.W. and R. McIntyre. (1982). *Husserl on Intentionality*. Dordrecht: Reidel.

Smith, Q. (1989). "The Multiple Uses of Indexicals." *Synthese* 78, 167–91.

Soames, S. (2010). *Philosophy of Language*. Princeton: Princeton University Press.

Sokolowski, R. (1977). "The Logic of Parts and Wholes in Husserl's *Investigations*." In *Readings on Edmund Husserl's Logical Investigations*. Ed. J.N. Mohanty, 94–111. The Hague: Martinus Nijhoff.

Sokolowski, R. (2000). *Introduction to Phenomenology*. Cambridge: Cambridge University Press.

Sokolowski, R. (2002). "Semiotics in Husserl's *Logical Investigations*." In *One Hundred Years of Phenomenology: Husserl's* Logical Investigations *Revisited*. Eds. D. Zahavi and F. Stjernfelt, 171–83. Dordrecht: Kluwer.

Sokolowski, R. (2006). *The Formation of Husserl's Concept of Constitution*. Washington, DC: The Catholic University of America Press.

Sokolowski, R. (2008). *Phenomenology of the Human Person*. Cambridge: Cambridge University Press.

Sowa, R. (2008). "Deiktische Ideationen: Ueber die mit den Wörtern ‚dies' und ‚so' vollziehbaren okkasionellen Bezugnahmen auf ideale Gegenständlichkeiten." In *Meaning and Language: Phenomenological Perspectives.* Ed. F. Mattens, 105–23. Phaenomenologica 187. Dordrecht: Springer.
Staiti, A. (2013). "The *Ideen* and Neo-Kantianism." In *Husserl's Ideen.* Eds. L. Embree and T. Nenon, 71–90. Dordrecht: Springer.
Starobinsky, J. (1970). "Jalons pour une histoire du concept d'imagination." In *La relation critique,* 174–95. Paris: Gallimard, 1970.
Stawarska, B. (2015). *Saussure's Philosophy of Language as Phenomenology: Undoing the Doctrine of the Course in General Linguistics.* Oxford: Oxford University Press.
Stawarska, B. (2020). *Saussure's Linguistics, Structuralism, and Phenomenology.* London: Palgrave Macmillan.
Steinbock, A. (2017). *Limit-Phenomena and Phenomenology in Husserl.* London and New York: Rowman and Littlefield.
Stich, S. (1971). "What Every Speaker Knows." *Philosophical Review* 80, 476–96.
Strawson, P.F. (1950). "On Referring." *Mind* 59, 320–44.
Suddendorf, T. and M. Corballis. (1997). "Mental Time Travel and the Evolution of the Human Mind." *Genetic Social and General Psychology Monographs* 123, 133–67.
Suddendorf, T. and M. Corballis. (2007). "The Evolution of Foresight: What Is Mental Time Travel and Is It Unique to Humans?" *Behavioural and Brain Sciences* 30, 3, 299–313.
Sweetser, E. (1990). *From Etymology to Pragmatics: Metaphorical and Cultural Aspects of Semantic Structure.* Cambridge: Cambridge University Press.
Swiderski, E. (1975). "Some Salient Features of Ingarden's Ontology." *Journal of the British Society of Phenomenology* 6, 81–90.
Szabo, Z.G. (2000). "Compositionality as Supervenience." *Linguistics and Philosophy* 23, 5, 475–505.
Szabo, Z.G. (2006). "The Distinction between Semantics and Pragmatics." In *The Handbook of Philosophy of Language.* Eds. E. LePore and B.C. Smith, 361–89. Oxford: Clarendon Press.
Szanto, T. (2016). "Husserl on Collective Intentionality." In *The Phenomenological Approach to Social Reality.* Eds. A. Salice and H.B. Schmid, 145–72. New York: Springer.
Talmy, L. (2000). *Towards a Cognitive Semantics.* Cambridge, MA: MIT Press.
Tanz, C. (1980). *Studies in the Acquisition of Deictic Terms.* Cambridge: Cambridge University Press.
Tarski, A. (1956). *Logic, Semantics, Metamathematics.* Trans. J.H. Woodger. Oxford: Clarendon Press.
Tatler, B.W., M. Hayhoe, M.F. Land, and D.H. Ballard. (2011). "Eye Guidance in Natural Vision: Reinterpreting Salience." *Journal of Vision* 11, 5, 1–23.
Tellier, M. (2009). "The Development of Gesture." In *Language Development Over a Lifespan.* Ed. K. de Bot, 191–216. London: Routledge.
Tomasello, M. (1999). *The Cultural Origins of Human Cognition.* Cambridge, MA: Harvard University Press.
Tomasello, M. (2003). *Constructing a Language: A Usage-Based Theory of Language Acquisition.* Cambridge, MA: Harvard University Press.
Tomasello, M. (2006). "Why Don't Apes Point?" In *Roots of Human Sociality, Culture, Cognition and Interaction.* Eds. N.J. Enfield and S.C. Levinson, 506–24. Oxford and New York: Berg.
Tomasello, M. (2014). *Origins of Human Communication.* Cambridge, MA: MIT Press.

Tomasello, M., and H. Moll. (2013). "Why Don't Apes Understand False Beliefs?" In *Navigating the Social World: What Infants, Children, and Other Species Can Teach Us*. Eds. M. R. Banaji and S. A. Gelman, 81–7. Oxford Series in Social Cognition and Social Neuroscience. Oxford: Oxford University Press.

Tsai, C.-H. (2006). "On the Epistemology of Language." *The Southern Journal of Philosophy* 44, 677–96.

Tugendhat, E. (1970). "Phänomenologie und Sprachanalyse." In *Hermeneutik und Dialektik*. Ed. R. Bubner, 3–33. Tübingen: J.C.B. Mohr.

Tugendhat, E. (1976). *Vorlesungen zur Einführung in die sprachanalytische Philosophie*. Frankfurt: Suhrkamp.

Tulving, E. (1972). "Episodic and Semantic Memory." In *Organization of Memory*. Eds. E. Tulving and W. Donaldson, 381–402. New York: Academic Press.

Tulving, E. (2002). "Chronesthesia: Awareness of Subjective Time." In *Principles of Frontal Lobe Functions*. Eds. D.T. Stuss and R.C. Knight, 311–25. New York: Oxford University Press.

Tulving, E. (2005). "Episodic Memory and Autopoiesis: Uniquely Human?" In *The Missing Link in Cognition*. Eds. H.S. Terrace and J. Metcalfe, 4–56. Oxford: Oxford University Press.

Tversky, B., J.M. Zacks, and B.M. Hart. (2008). "The Structure of Experience." In *Understanding Events: From Perception to Action*. Eds. T.F. Shipley and J.M. Zacks, 436–64. New York and Oxford: Oxford University Press.

Twardowski, K. (1977). *On the Content and Object of Presentations*. Trans. R. Grossmann. The Hague: Martinus Nijhoff.

Tye, M. (2000). *The Imagery Debate*. Cambridge, MA: MIT Press.

Uehlein, F. (1992). "Eidos and Eidetic Variation in Husserl's Phenomenology." In *Phenomenology, Language and Schizophrenia*. Eds. M.Spitzer, F. Uehlein, M.A. Schwartz and C. Mundt, 88–102. New York: Springer.

Vandervelde, P. (2008). "An Unpleasant but Felicitous Ambiguity: *Sinn* and *Bedeutung* in Husserl's Revisions of the *Logical Investigations*." In *Meaning and Language: Phenomenological Perspectives*. Ed. F. Mattens, 29–48. Phaenomenologica 187. Dordrecht: Springer.

Villanueva, E. (1998). *Concepts*. Atascadero, CA: Ridgeview.

Vygotsky, L.S. (1987). *The Collected Works of L.S. Vygotsky*, v.1, *Problems of General Psychology*. Eds. R.W. Rieber and A.S. Carton. New York and London: Plenum Press.

Wachter, D. von. (2005). "Roman Ingarden's Ontology: Existential Dependence, Substances, Ideas, and Other Things Empiricists Do Not Like." In *Existence, Culture and Persons: The Ontology of Roman Ingarden*, 55–82. Frankfurt: Ontos.

Warren, N. de. (2013). "Emmanuel Levinas and a Soliloquy of Light and Reason." In *Husserl's Ideen*. Eds. L. Embree and T. Nenon, 265–82. Dordrecht: Springer.

Welton, D. (1973). "Intentionality and Language in Husserl's Phenomenology." *The Review of Metaphysics* 27, 2, 260–97.

Welton, D. (1983). *The Origins of Meaning*. The Hague: Martinus Nijhoff.

Welton, D. (Ed.) (2003). *The New Husserl: A Critical Reader*. Bloomington: Indiana University Press.

Werning, M. (2004). "Compositionality, Context, Categories, and the Indeterminacy of Tradition." *Erkenntnis* 60, 145–78.

Wettstein, H. (1986). "Has Semantics Rested on a Mistake?" *Journal of Philosophy* 83, 185–209.

Wiggins, D. (1997). "Languages as a Social Objects." *Philosophy* 72, 282, 499–524.

Willard, D. (1972). "The Paradox of Logical Psychologism: Husserl's Way Out." *American Philosophical Quarterly* 9, 94-100.
Willard, D. (1984). *Logic and Objectivity of Knowledge*. Athens, Ohio: Ohio University Press.
Willard, D. (1988). "A Critical Study of Husserl and Intentionality." *The Journal of the British Society of Phenomenology* 19, 186-98, 311-22.
Willard, D. (1995). "Knowledge." In *The Cambridge Companion to Husserl*. Eds. B. Smith and D.W. Smith, 138-67. Cambridge: Cambridge University Press.
Willems, R.M. and P. Hagoort. (2007). "Neural Evidence for the Interplay Between Language, Gesture, and Action: A Review." *Brain and Language* 101, 3, 1, 4-6.
Wittgenstein, L. (2009). *Philosophical Investigations*. Trans. G.E.M. Anscombe, P.M.S. Hacker, and J. Schulte. Oxford: Blackwell. (*PI*)
Wood, D. (1988). "Differance and the Problem of Strategy." In *Derrida and Difference*. Eds. D. Wood and R. Bernasconi, 63-70. Evanston: Northwestern University Press.
Woodfield, A. (1997). "Intentionality." In *Concise Encyclopedia of Philosophy of Language*. Ed. P. Lamarque, 55-59. Oxford: Pergamon.
Wright, C. (1987). "Theories of Meaning and Speakers' Knowledge." In *Realism, Meaning and Truth*, 204-38. Oxford: Blackwell.
Zahavi, D. and F. Stjernfelt (Eds.). (2002). *One Hundred Years of Phenomenology: Husserl's Logical Investigations Revisited*. Dordrecht: Springer.
Zentall, T. (2006). "Mental Time Travel in Animals: A Challenging Question." *Behavioral Processes* 72, 173-83.
Zlatev, J. (1997). *Situated Embodiment: Studies in the Emergence of Spatial Meaning*. Stockholm: Gotab Press.
Zlatev, J. (2007). "Embodiment, Language, and Mimesis." In *Body, Language and Mind*, v. 1. Eds. T. Ziemke, J. Zlatev, and R. Frank, 297-338. Berlin: Mouton de Gruyter.
Zlatev, J., T. Persson, and P. Gärdenfors. (2005). "Bodily Mimesis as the Missing Link." *Lund University Cognitive Studies* 121, 1-43.
Zweig, A. (Ed.). (1967). *Kant: Philosophical Correspondence 1759-1799*. Trans. A. Zweig. Chicago: University of Chicago Press.

# Index

aboutness (*Worüber*)   21, 25, 49, 51, 86, 118, 124, 140, 189
   always modified   97
   perceptual   124
   quasi-perceptual   9
*Achilles and the Tortoise*   153
acoustic words   82
   as vehicles of comprehension   143
act-matter   25
act-quality   128–30
acts
   of cognition   39, 142
   of communal life (*Akte des Gemeinschaftslebens*)   29
   of comprehending   75
   of consciousness
      heterologous   66
      mandatory   162
   eidetically reduced   39, 54, 187
   epistemic   179
   formal   139
   habitual   112
   identifying   89, 128, 140
   intentional   1–4, 7, 10, 12, 13, 21, 25, 27, 33, 45, 49, 51, 61, 65–7, 71–3, 75, 83, 84, 86, 88, 90, 92, 94, 97, 101, 106, 110, 112, 114, 118–19, 121, 124, 126, 128, 131, 143, 152, 153, 169, 170, 178–9, 184, 186–8, 191–2
   linguistic   2, 31, 33, 42, 50, 163, 185, 192
   logical   21
   meaning-conferring   24, 119
   meaning-fulfilling   24
   non-linguistic   53
   non-verbal   3, 27, 39
   ontically heteronomous   185
   sense-conferring   23, 24
   sense-giving   23, 24, 53, 128
   sensuous (*sinnliche*)   141, 154
   of social reciprocity (*soziale Wechselbeziehung*)   162
   symbolic   107, 139
adequation   107, 144
   as *Erfüllungseinheit*   108
adjectival qualifications   140
adjectivity   31, 50, 94, 125, 140, 160, 168, 172, 186
adumbrational   2, 27, 43, 63, 129, 170, 185
advent of language   171
adverbiality   94, 125
advocacy   68
affections of the soul (*Affektionen der Seele*)   21
affective attitudes   147
Agha, Asif   99 n.48
algorithmic systems   144
alien world (*Fremdwelt*)   96
analytic language philosophy   83
anticipated as fulfillable   9
apodictic   3, 28, 49, 61, 65, 74
*apophantic*   118, 148
apperception   23, 55, 61, 67, 73, 87, 120, 127, 160
   empathetic   61, 64, 66, 73–5, 190
   windows of   66, 73
   typifying   120, 121
   vivid (*anschauliche Vergegenwärtigung*)   61, 67, 75
appresentation (co-presentation)   6, 23, 27–9, 49, 61, 67, 73, 75, 85, 170, 180, 190
   reciprocal   180
approximation   39, 40, 101, 102, 104, 106, 114, 122, 123, 126, 128, 145, 163, 188
   practice of (*Praxis der Approximation*)   55
   towards the target of cognition   145
arbitrariness   93, 161, 166, 190
   radical   8

# Index

Aristotle
    *homoiomata*   8, 10, 21–2, 33, 68, 123, 147
    *pathemata*   21, 147
    *pragmata*   22
attention   1, 7
    steering of   24
Austin, John L.   25, 78 n.55, 94, 96, 126, 130
authentic (*eigentlich*)   32

Ballard, Dana H.   177 n.79
Balle, Johannes   104, 115 n.35, 120, 132 n.14
bandwidth   109, 186
Bar-Hillel, Yehoshua   92, 95, 99 n.57
Barwick, Linda   76 n.11
*Bedeutung*   6, 21, 50, 51, 63, 97, 101, 103–7, 114, 127, 131, 139, 143, 151, 163, 180, 185
    in Frege   8, 10, 22, 32
    in Husserl   6, 9, 12, 23, 31, 32, 52, 68, 81, 104, 106, 107, 119, 130, 186
    merely verbal   xiii
being
    ideal   53
    intentional   184
    material   13
    purely intentional   184
being apart from one another (*Auseinandersein*)   64
being-for-one-another (*Füreinandersein*)   107, 171
being-in-congruence (*in-Deckung-Sein*)   107
being-within-one-another (*Ineinandersein*)   31, 64, 68, 72, 107, 154
being-with-one-another (*Miteinandersein*)   31, 64, 107
Benoist, Jocelyn   14 n.10, 132 n.1
Bernet, Rudolf   36 n.67, 111
Bertenthal, Bennett   177 n.78
*Bezugnahme*   115 n.36, 131
Bickerton, Derek   156 n.66, 161, 162, 167, 173 n.6, 173 n.10, 173 n.11, 176 n.53
Birch, Bruce   76 n.11
Bock, Katryn   173 n.8

body
    *Körper*   181
    *Leib*
        apperceptive   181
    lived   182
    living   4, 65, 182
Borg, Emma   14 n.18
Braund, Michael   170, 176 n.73
Bühler, Karl   88, 89, 98 n.39
Burks, Arthur   99 n.60

Cairns, Dorion   3, 124, 125
camera-shutter speed   67, 109, 110, 126, 129
Cappelen, Herman   14 n.18
Casey, Edward S.   15 n.24
Cassirer, Ernst   64, 170, 175 n.41, 176 n.74
catastrophe theories   143, 161
categorial   54, 93
    contingency   138
    core forms   42
    intuition   9, 40, 143, 165
    relations   12, 13, 21, 31, 49, 52, 70, 72, 94, 103, 124–6, 128, 138–44, 160, 164–9, 172, 179, 185–8, 190
        post-verbal   144
        pre-linguistic   170
        pre-verbal   163
chains of past experiences   146
Chalmers, David   71
Chang, Franklin   173 n.8
chess   10
    analogy   10
Chomsky, Noam   4, 51, 152, 156 n.66, 164, 168, 173 n.7, 174 n.28
chronesthesia   167
Chrudzimski, Arkadiusz   194 n.40
Chu, Yingchi   100 n.62, 158 n.127
circles of resemblance   27
circumlocution   149–51
clearness   26
    grades of   47
co-belief (*Mitglauben*)   3
coercion   6, 31, 69, 102, 109, 110, 144, 187
    degree of   106
cognition   119–21, 145
cognitive   119, 131

arms race 167
equivalence 146
grammar 165
linguistics 9, 165, 178
maps 9
mimesis 9
semantics 9, 165
Cole, Jonathan 177 n.78
commonality 50, 54, 74
    grades of 55
communal 61–76
    coercion 68, 106, 107, 113, 185
    experience (*Erfahrung der Gemeinschaft*) 3, 69, 161
    guidance 5, 13, 187
    instructions 12, 66, 127
        eidetically coded 187
        embedded 63, 69
        implicit 113
    spirit (*Gemeingeist*) 74
communalization (*Vergemeinschaftung*) 63
communalized life (*vergemeinschaftetes Leben*) 63
communicability (*Mitteilbarkeit*) 4, 103, 172
    linguistic 24, 97, 102, 107, 109, 114
communication 2–4, 21, 22, 65, 73, 95, 103, 107, 112, 164
    imagined (*Phantasiekommunikation*) 144, 184
communicative 3, 87, 161, 180, 191
    consciousness
        as addressing and comprehending 86
community 6, 69
    cohesion of 32–3
    controlled pedagogy
        as necessary component 185
    empathetic (*Einfühlungsgemeinschaft*) 71
    experience (*Erfahrung der Gemeinschaft*) 63
    interpretive 84
    of monads (*Monadengemeinschaft as Ineinander der Monaden*) 6, 8, 72
    pre-predicative 168
completeness 69
    degrees of 130
compositionality 13, 146, 148–51
    heuristic 151
comprehension 4, 27, 51, 109, 110
    adequate 105, 126
    deepening of 191
    flash of 112
    iconic 101
    linguistic 12, 24, 52, 71, 108, 180, 188
    logical 101
    merely symbolic 154
    merely verbal 101
    reciprocal 71
    reconstructive acts of 24
    verbal 40
    vividly imaginable (*anschaulich*) 40, 101, 130, 145, 154
compulsion tendency 110
concept (*Begriff*)
    empirical 46, 120, 183
        ever-to-be-corrected (*unter Korrektur*) 46, 53
    formal 46, 139
    formalized 147
    neural 9, 10, 122, 165
    non-linguistic 53
conceptual
    blending 9, 122, 165
    boundaries 46, 138
concrete contingencies 169
condition 43, 105
    of cognition 62
    of subjective acts 31
    sufficient 186
conflation 92
    of spatial and temporal aspects 160
congruence (*Deckung*) 104, 107, 108
    proximate 180
    of similarities 40
    static 28, 50
    unity of (*Deckungseinheit*) 108, 142
consciousness (*Bewusstsein*) 3, 27, 32
    autonoetic 167
    embodied 113
    empty (*Leerbewusstsein*) 64, 119, 130
    encompassing communal (*übergreifendes Gemeinschaftsbewusstsein*) 123

interrogative (*Fragebewusstsein*)  81
intimately unified (*innig einiges Bewusstsein*)  86
meaning (*Bedeutungsbewusstsein*)  31
presumptive (*Vermutungsbewusstsein*)  53
reproductive  6, 29
sense-giving  53
supra-personal (*überpersonales Bewusstsein*)  122
teleological structure of  5, 145
transitional (*Durchgangsbewusstsein*)  95, 112, 151, 163
word (*Wortbewusstsein*)  12, 51, 119, 131, 139, 142, 162, 180, 188
word sound (*Wortlautbewusstsein*)  47, 51, 66, 86, 110, 112–14, 119, 131, 163, 186, 188
constraint(s)  39, 43, 44, 46, 97, 108
  methodological  3, 4
construction  75, 85, 95
  stepped (*Stufenbau*)  28
content  7, 127
  aspectual  170
  iconic  121
  intrinsic  170
  mental material  12, 93, 108, 114, 120, 121, 123, 128, 130, 190
  quasi-perceptual  63, 121, 128, 141
context(s)  54, 63
  complex  67
  independent  81, 103
  linguistic  67, 89, 93
  meaning-,  32, 122
  semiotic  9
  social  9, 89, 182
  of utterance  81, 89, 92
control mechanisms  127
convenient replacements  137
Convention-T  147
Cook, Vivian J.  173 n.7
Corballis, Michael  166, 170, 175 n.41, 175 n.44, 175 n.49
core forms  9, 140, 160, 186, 187
  pre-predicative  42, 125
corporeality  73, 146, 182
correctness (*Richtigkeit*)  144

COSS (communicative sign system)  101, 187
counter subjects (*Gegensubjekte*)  65
cross-domain mapping  165
Crowell, Teven Galt  14 n.21
Crystal, David  4, 9
cultural  93
  life (*Kulturleben*)  74
  practice (*Praxis*)  xii, 187
culture specific  46
Cunningham, Suzanne  55 n.8

Davidson, Donald  32, 83, 146
Davies, Martin  159 n.133
Davis, Steven  17 n.80
declarative sentences  118
deep
  ground  2, 39, 182, 191
  structure  91
deeply ingrained habits  3
definition
  extensional  25
  formal  44
  intensional  92
definitional
  backup  47
  certitude  105
deictic  90
  anchorage  89
  ideation  129
  markers  86, 90, 91, 94
  modification  86, 100 n.64
deixis  81
  alio-centric  90
  anaphoric  89
  exophoric  89
  explicit  12, 67, 85–93, 171, 189
  general  12, 85
  as grammaticalization  88
  implicit  12, 31, 68, 81–97, 113, 126, 127, 143, 144, 171, 186, 189, 190
  marked  82, 90–3
  spatial  90
  temporal  89
  unmarked  91
Deleuze, Gilles  69, 78 n.61, 109, 110
Dell, Gary S.  173 n.8
dependence relations  1, 140

Derrida, Jacques   11, 130, 134 n.63, 182, 183
desedimentation   12, 28, 96, 137–46, 153
determinability   172
*deus ex machina* solution   168
Dever, Josh   148, 149
Devitt, Michael   17 n.80, 34 n.4, 99 n.57, 148, 158 n.122
differences in vitality   27
Dilworth, John   176, 177 n.79
direction   128
   of gaze (*Blickrichtung*)   128, 141
directional factor (*Richtungsfaktor*)
directionality   12
   exclusive   24, 25, 40, 48, 102, 104, 105, 128, 131, 180, 183, 186, 188
discourse   89
   public   2, 74, 113, 178, 189
displacement   6, 50, 90, 160–72
   as communal achievement (*Gemeinschaftsleistung*)   163
   competence   168
   dual   161-4
   linguistic   5, 11, 13, 123, 138, 160, 165, 166, 171
   reversal of
     from word to thing   180
dispositional phenomena   84, 85, 142
distillation   192
   Eidetic   2, 97, 184
drilled (*abgerichtet*)   111
Drummond, John   36 n.67
Dummett, Michael   17 n.79
Duzi, Marie   17 n.80, 34 n.7

Edie, James M.   192 n.3
egocentric particulars   25
ego-life of the other   61
eidetic   11, 51
   fuzziness   40, 49, 50, 54, 190
   generality   51, 125
   reduction   4, 5, 39–55
     Husserl's blueprint of   41
   schemata   52
   system   11, 39, 52, 53, 75, 113
   truths
     as valid   149
   variation   41, 43, 46, 69

viewing   89
*eidos*   39–41, 52
   feature (*Merkmalswesen*)   45
   fuzzy   11, 39–55, 123
   as prior to all concepts   42, 44
   species (*Gattungswesen*)   45
elimination   43, 72, 120, 127, 190, 191
   of *Vorstellung*   5, 10
Eliot, T.S.   4
Ely, Lothar   176 n.56
embodiment   186
Embree, Lester   42
emotional phenomena (*Gemütsphänomene*)   85, 145
empathetic   190
   apperception   61, 64, 66, 73–5, 190
empirical   2
   belief   53
   induction   44, 53
emptiness   139
   formal   26, 154
empty intention (*Leerintention*)   12, 67, 75, 118, 119, 130, 139–40, 163
Enfield, Nick J.   165
Engelenhoven, Aone van   98 n.38
entanglement   66, 70, 73, 74, 142
   in contingencies   140
enunciative modalities   85
environment   9, 73
   generally shared (*allgemeinsame Umwelt*)   65
epistemic   90
   act analysis   179
   analyses   84, 179
   essence   7, 23, 31, 53, 83, 101, 137
essence   41, 42, 102, 123
   abstraction of an (*Wesensabstraktion*)   54
   epistemic   7, 23, 31, 53, 83, 101, 137
   experiential   47
   formal   47
   semantic   22, 23, 31, 53, 83, 101, 106, 137
   typical (*typisches Wesen*)   40
   without existence   123
*essentia*   52, 148
essential   5
   *Anschauung*   42

content 121
essentially occasional expressions 25, 84, 85
Evans, Gareth 25, 35 n.49
Evans, Nicholas 76 n.11
Evans, Vyvian 177 n.82
Everett, Daniel L. 173 n.8, 177 n.87
evidence 5
   apodictic 49, 65, 74
   grades of 28
evolutionary trajectory 161
evolving mental projections (*erwachsende Vorstellungen*) 145
exactitude 53
   formal 180
exhibiting congruence (*in-Deckung-sein*) 107
existential moments 27, 184, 189, 191
expectation(s) 24
   horizon of 187
experience 2
   circle of 3
   pre-verbal structure of 163
   quanta of 12, 119–23
experiential 75, 105
   character 104
   openness (*Erfahrungsoffenheit*) 121, 127
explicit naming 86
   qualified by a certain tone 85, 86
expressions 2, 4, 10, 12, 68, 75, 84
   context insensitive 96
   extension of 164
   as inherently rhetorical 68
   objective correlative of
      as meant by a meaning 25
   saturated 67
   as superficial phenomenon 163
extensional 25
externalism 22, 26, 62, 75, 83, 110, 113
externalist 10, 71, 72, 110, 118, 178, 190, 191
exteroception 164
extra-linguistic 22, 95

factualness 53
familiarity 30
   horizon of (*Bekanntheitshorizont*) 46
family resemblance 54

Fauconnier, Gilles 9, 133 n.25, 165, 174 n.36
Favareau, Donald 79 n.81
Feldman, Carol F. 94, 100 n.63
fellow human beings (*Nebenmenschen*) 65
fiction 124
   transforming 6, 29
filling 52
   partial 130
Fillmore, Charles 88–91, 98 n.39
Finke, Ronald 17 n.69
Fitch, Tecumseh 156 n.66, 164, 174 n.28
fluid 26
   relations 26
   type concepts (*fliessende Typenbegriffe*) 28, 40, 55
   types 52, 53, 137
Fodor, Jerry A. 18 n.88, 132 n.13
Føllesdal, Dagfinn 26, 36 n.64, 36 n.66, 195 n.54
forgetting of being (*Seinsvergessenheit*) 46
formal 27, 28, 41, 46
   approaches 10
   fallacy 10
   relations 22, 83
   signs 12, 137–8, 140, 142–4, 154, 190
formalization 26, 28, 30, 50, 129, 137–9, 153
formula world 30
Foucault, Michel 85, 98 n.18
Frege, Gottlob 5, 10, 17 n.78, 21, 34 n.6, 98 n.36
Fregean 31
   *Färbungen* 88
   reference 25, 32, 53, 82
   sense 25
Frege's law 148, 150
Fricke, Ellen 88
fulfilment 8, 64, 107
   conceptual 104
   graded series of 5, 27
   proximate 31
   quasi-perceptual 9
   unity of (*Erfüllungseinheit*) 108
fullness 26
   gradation of 130, 131
*Fundamentalontologie* 181, 183

fuzziness (*Ungefähres*)  52, 70

Gallagher, Shaun  13 n.1, 16 n.60, 77 n.27, 78 n.70
Gallese, Vittorio  76 n.8
Ganis, Giorgio  36 n.62
Gans, Eric  161, 173 n.5
Gans, Steven  134 n.69
Gärdenfors, Peter  166, 176 n.51
gaze  4, 187
    direction of (*Blickrichtung*)  128, 141
generality  28, 40, 154
    sphere of (*Sphäre der Allgemeinheit*)  39
    typical (*typische Allgemeinheit*)  46
    of word  23
generalization  30, 43, 120, 123
    degrees of  26
genesis  29, 46, 49, 52, 137, 143, 145
genetic fallacy  10
geometry of experiences  47
gesticulation  171
gestures  168, 170
    grammar of  171
Gibson, Helen  vii
Gillon, Brendan S.  17 n.80, 34 n.4, 81, 97 n.7
gradation of liveliness  27
gradations  126
    of clarity  130
    of fullness  130
graded
    conception  106, 161
    fulfilment  27
    series of fulfilment  5, 27
gradualism, radical  168
grammaticality  88
Grandy, Richard  158 n.117
grasp
    merely symbolic  112
Greenfield, Patricia M.  165, 175 n.39
Grewendorf, Günther  18 n.84, 159 n.151, 195 n.53
Guattari, Felix  69, 78 n.61, 109, 110, 116 n.59
Gumpel, Liselotte  194 n.40
Gurwitch, Aaron  84, 85, 98 n.14

habit (*Gewohnheit*)

communal  30
habitual  68
    familiarity  30
    speech (*Sprachüblichkeit*)  6, 69, 107
habituality (*Habitualität*)
    of the *Lebenswelt*  29
    linguistic  188
    social  74
habitualization  67
Haeflinger, Gregor  194 n.40
Hagoort, Peter  177 n.85
half-measures (*Halbheiten*)  21
Halliday, Michael A.K.  9, 17 n.66, 17 n.67
Hamm, Fritz  18 n.84, 159 n.151, 195 n.53
Hanley, Richard  17 n.80, 34 n.4, 99 n.57, 148
Hanneborg, Knut  194
Hard, Bridgette Martin  175 n.41
Haugland, John  158 n.121
Hauk, Olaf  116 n.64
Hauser, Marc D.  57 n.67, 156 n.66, 159 n.147, 164, 174 n.28
Hayhoe, May M.  177 n.79
haziness  26
Heck, Richard  158 n.123
Heidegger, Martin  xii, 179, 181-3, 193 n.7
Held, Klaus  37 n.101
Herbermann, Clemes-Peter  90, 99 n.50
here-now-I-system  89
Herz, Marcus  5
heterosemiotic  11, 25, 27, 63, 124
    components  192
    process  25, 164
Hirst, Graeme  148, 158 n.120
Hockett, Charles, F.  15 n.29, 35 n.36, 56 n.55, 160-3, 173 n.1
Hockett's catalogue  161
Hodges, Wilfrid  158 n.123
holistic  22, 31, 33, 53, 64, 83, 85, 88, 190
home world (*Heimwelt*)  3, 75
hominid  160
    Communities  164
*homoiomata* (resemblance relations)  8, 10, 22, 33, 68
homophone phrase substitution  149, 150

Hopkins, Burt    137, 155 n.7
horizon    146
    empty (*Leerhorizont*)    139
    of recollection    146
Humboldt's law    161
Hurford, James R.    92, 99 n.57, 168, 173 n.8
hypoiconic    8
hypoiconicity    92
    diagrammatic    8, 93
hypotaxis    168

icon    8, 92, 93
iconicity    92, 125, 160
    diagrammatical    125
    direct    123
    displaced    160
    indirect    93
    pre-predicative    121
    primacy of    92
icons of qualities    8
idealistic isolation    72
ideality    7, 13, 43, 103, 178, 179, 183–7
    subservient to intentionality    13
idealization    30, 46, 53, 120
    gradual    53, 106
idealized world    106
    an ideal infinity of things    106
ideation    42, 46, 53
    non-empirical, essential insight    42
identifying synthesis    140
identity    22, 23, 103, 106
    as absolute and ideal unity    104
    as counterpart of the individual    104
    formal    31
    numerical    101, 104, 128, 130, 180, 186
    qualitative    128
    of thematic object    104
    as universal    104
    as wholly indefinable    104
idiomatic expressions    147, 149, 150, 161
idiomaticity    152, 153
images    28, 29, 118
image schemas    188
    cross-modal nature of    165
imaginability (*Vorstellbarkeit*)    1, 5–6
    in the concept (*Anschauung im Begriff*)    1

    conditions    68
    linguistic    5
    nonverbal    26, 52
    as precondition of *displacement*    5
    social    5
    supplementing    142
    tangible    43
    thesis    xiii, 2, 6, 32, 91, 111, 129, 187
    vivid (*lebendige Vorstellbarkeit*)    xiii, 11, 101, 118, 130, 146, 152, 180, 182
imaginable (*vorstellbar*)    22, 43
    scenarios    112, 114, 144, 179
imaginative    21, 23, 71
    reconstruction    44
    specification    54
    variations    25, 41–3, 47, 151, 187
imaginatively objective (*anschaulich gegenständlich*)    154
imagined apple    117 n.81, 166
immanence of expressions    148, 149
implicit deixis    12, 31, 81–97, 113, 126, 127, 143, 171, 186, 189
    as broad principle    82
    as fundamental    95
    as manner of presentation    84, 86, 94
    as modal shadow    12, 68, 86, 88, 91, 97
imposition (*Zumutung*)    1, 6, 69, 97, 109–11, 191
    social    69
    by the speaker    69, 130
inauthentic (*uneigentlich*)    32
incarnate logic    182
incommensurate    124
indeterminacy of tradition    158 n.123
index    8, 92
    as indirectly iconic    93
    indexical    144
    communicative precursors    137
indexicality    92–3, 97, 160
indicating function (*Hinweisfunktion*)    122
indication    12, 23, 61, 85, 89, 93, 106, 142
indicative
    function (*Hinweisfunktion*)    31, 127, 142
    tendency (*Hinweistendenz*)    104, 142
    towards the thing meant    104

indices of reactions   8
indirect resemblance   93
indirect speech act   90, 126, 149
induction, empirical   44, 53
inference   29, 39, 89, 149, 150
infinite
   mirroring   74
   regress   10, 130, 145, 153
infinity of imperfection   53, 106
Ingarden, Roman   13, 27, 179, 183, 184, 192 n.5, 194 n.40
inhabit   67
   a physical sign   110
inner
   life (*Innenleben*)   73
instantiation   49, 187
   individual   4, 11, 12, 49, 61, 66, 113, 119, 131, 185, 189
intension   25, 92
intensional   141
intention
   of acquaintance   43
   directional   64, 107, 139
   elementary (*Elementarintentionen*)   141
   *erfüllungsbedürftig*   63, 141
intentional   88, 129, 179
   acts   xiii, 1–4, 7, 10, 12, 13, 21, 24, 25, 27, 33, 45, 49, 51, 61, 65, 66, 71–5, 83, 84, 86, 88, 90, 92, 94, 97, 101, 106, 110, 112–14, 118, 119, 121, 124, 126, 128, 131, 138, 143, 152, 153, 169, 170, 178, 179, 184, 186–8, 191, 192
   essence   22, 108, 145
   intertwining (*intentionale Verflechtung*)   67
   medium   33
   objects (*Objekt-Vorstellungen*)   194 n.40
   within-one-another (*intentionales Ineinander*)   64, 68, 154
intentionality   2, 43, 172, 178, 179
   collective   75, 80 n.129, 122, 124
   communal   75, 160, 187–92
   formal   8, 138
   as foundation   xiii, 191
   higher level of   67
   individual   2, 27, 42

intersubjective   1–13, 72, 76, 119, 147, 178, 185, 190, 191
   of intersubjective reciprocity   6, 24, 62, 64, 73, 85, 180, 190
   social   31, 113, 186, 189
intention-reading   67, 167, 187
intergrammaticality   9
internalism   27
interpretant   8
   emotional   8, 190
   hypoiconic   8
   iconic   8, 93
   logical   8
interpreted calculus   22, 191
inter-sensuous   124
   organism-phantom   124
   syntheses   124, 125
intersubjective   74
   mentalism   22, 71, 75, 84, 91
   reciprocity   6, 24, 62, 64, 73, 85, 180, 190
   sharability   103
   sufficiency   12, 55, 91, 102, 106–9, 111, 114, 143, 145, 152, 154, 191
intersubjectivity   2, 4, 21, 49
   as adequate agreement   45, 145
   linguistic   6, 12, 66, 72, 191
   sufficient   109, 123
intimating function   23
intimation   12, 23, 31
   of mental states   23
introject   23
introjection   12, 23, 33, 70–2
   empathetic   8
   as intention-reading   67
   as necessary condition   61
   reciprocal   185, 187
introspection   110
   as inner perception   110
   as perception of intentional experience   110
intuition   1, 24
   empirical   42, 44, 53
   illustrative   118
   individual   42
   more or less corresponding   107, 145
   of the thing   44
intuitive   40, 144
   fulfilment   24

grasp 30, 53, 70
intuitively empty (*unanschaulich*) 40
invariable form 44
invariant 11, 41, 47, 48, 50

Jackendoff, Ray 134 n.54, 173 n.8, 176 n.52
Jadacki, Jacek 194
Jakobson, Roman 88, 89, 98 n.39
Janssen, Theo M.V. 158 n.123, 158 n.131
Jespersen, Bjorn 17 n.80, 34 n.7
Johannson, Sverker 173 n.8
Johansson, Ingvar 194 n.40
Johnson, Mark 17 n.69, 122, 133 n.25
joint attention frame 171
judgments 104, 189
Juluwarly Aboriginal Corporation 62

Kamp, Hans 158 n.123
Kant, Immanuel 15 n.26, 78 n.75
Kazmi, Ali 158 n.123
Keeping, Joseph 194 n.40
Kendon, Adam 171, 176 n.62, 177 n.80
Kersten, Fred 24, 42
Kinsella, Anna R. 173 n.8
Kita, Sotaro 177 n.79, 177 n.84
Kosslyn, Steven M. 36 n.62
Koukal, David R. 31, 68
Kripke, Saul 15 n.27
Kristeva, Julia 173 n.4
Küng, Guido 194 n.40
Kung, P. 132 n.2
Kusch, Martin xii, xiii n.1, 7, 13 n.2, 33, 34 n.11, 65, 77 n.36, 154 n.1

Lacan, Jacques 137, 155 n.5
lacunae of indeterminacy 94
Lakoff, George 17, 122, 133 n.25, 134 n.54, 174 n.31
Lamarque, Peter V. 17 n.80, 34 n.4, 99 n.56, 158 n.123
Land, Michael F. 176 n.65, 177 n.79
Langacker, Ronald 9, 17 n.73, 99 n.55, 165, 174 n.33
Langsdorf, Lenore 26, 36 n.65
language 1
    drill (*Abrichtung*) 31, 84, 91, 97, 102, 109
    as economizing matrix 69, 125
    as eidetic system 11, 39, 52, 53, 75, 113
    formal 10, 145
    as idealization of the world 53
    natural 1, 2, 4, 6, 10–12, 13 n.2, 18, 22, 23, 26, 27, 29–33, 39–43, 47–8, 50, 52–5, 61, 68–72, 81–5, 88, 89, 91–6, 101, 102, 105, 106, 108, 109, 112–14, 120, 127, 129–32, 137–45, 147–54, 165, 171, 172, 179, 180, 184–7, 189–92
    perception-driven 161, 162
    seduction of 68
    as a symbolic system 12, 137
    as system of essences of essences 54, 181
    as system of invariants 4
    as universal medium 33, 102
    as world *in absentia* 12, 54, 118, 190
*langue* 16 n.44
Laurence, Steven 134 n.54
Leavens, David 177 n.79
*Lebenswelt* 22, 28
    as *a priori* 27, 29, 30
    as ground 30
    historicity of 122
    as transcendental ground 30, 65
Lecercle, Jean-Jacques 109, 116 n.60
Leibniz, Gottfried Wilhelm 115 n.38
Lepore, Ernest 14 n.18
Levinson, Stephen C. 89, 91, 92, 99 n.56, 152
Lévi-Strauss, Claude 173 n.4
lexico-grammatical level 9
lexicographer 50–2
likeness 53, 54
    complete 28
    as limit of similarity 29
    degrees of 28
limit phenomenon 64, 139, 140
linear grammar 176 n.52, 177 n.87
linguistic 1
    communication 2, 4, 12, 66, 84, 102, 106, 109, 110, 126, 128, 140, 164, 178, 188
    comprehension 12, 24, 52, 71, 108, 180
    content 127, 171

expressions
  double intentionality of 85
externalism 22, 62, 83, 110
iconicity 94
idealism 8
immanence 148
instantiations 63
internalism 27
meaning 1, 5, 6, 8, 9, 11, 13 n.2, 22, 23, 26, 27, 29, 30, 32, 44, 50, 52, 56 n.51, 62–4, 66, 72, 75–6, 81, 84, 94, 96, 101–3, 105–7, 112–14, 118–32, 137, 139, 141, 146, 148, 149, 152, 163, 166, 180, 182, 185, 189, 190, 192
  modality 25
  ontogenesis 162, 171, 172
  phylogenesis 162, 171, 187
  refinement 125, 169
  self-referentiality 90
  signs 44, 112, 142
    adapted to the *eidos* 44
  symbols 190
linguistic linkage compulsion 6, 49–51, 85, 109, 111, 112, 114, 121, 123, 164, 187, 189, 191
literal 82
  tone 66
little-by-little arguments 152
living body 4
  as *leibliche Ichlichkeit* 182
Locke, John 116 n.57
logic 10, 29, 169
logical 8
  equivalence 125, 143
Lohmar, Dieter 8, 10, 14 n.21, 16 n.60, 16 n.65, 17 n.82, 28, 36 n.79, 40, 55 n.7, 55 n.16, 76 n.8, 105, 115 n.37, 133 n.26, 143, 169, 175 n.38
Löwith, Karl 79 n.85
Luckmann, Thomas 122, 133 n.32
Lyons, John 88, 90, 92, 98 n.39

McGregor, William B. 99 n.47
McIntyre, Ronald xii, xiii n.1, 36 n.64, 154 n.1
MacKay, Donald G. 174 n.26, 176 n.65
McNeill, David 170, 177 n.76

manner of presentation 49, 67, 82, 84–6, 95, 126, 129
manner of speaking 83, 127
Manning, Paul H. 88, 90, 98 n.39
Margolis, Eric 134 n.54
materiality 13, 43, 178, 179, 184, 185
  subservient to intentionality 13
Materna, Pavel 17 n.80, 34 n.7
mathematization 30
Mattens, Filip 33 n.1, 66, 77 n.24, 106, 110, 111, 116 n.70
Mazzone, Marco 78 n.70
meaning(s)
  act 4, 25, 30, 52, 69, 84, 85, 107, 112, 114, 119, 131, 163
  bestowing 84, 118
  chain xiii, 3, 7, 8, 12, 107, 110, 142, 147, 180, 182, 185, 187, 188
  cognitive 63
  communal 39, 63
  as communal cognitive event 11, 56 n.51, 61–76
  components 104
    extensional (imaginable) 8
    intensional (logical) 8
  congruence 50, 108
  constitution 6, 8, 29, 72, 114, 130, 143, 145, 151, 188
  as definition 1
  empty 64, 107
  endowing (*bedeutungsverleihend*) 31, 84, 119
  endowment 31, 39, 66, 104, 111, 119, 123, 124, 130
  experiential 75, 103
  fulfillment 4, 5, 9, 11, 24, 52, 62–6, 71, 92–4, 97, 101–4, 121, 123, 126–9, 146, 147, 149, 151, 152, 154, 163–5, 179, 180, 183, 185–9
    approximate character of 24, 51, 96, 130, 145
  gestural 182
  gradation of 165
  grasp 118
  identity 12, 22, 23, 26, 32, 97, 101, 103–9, 122
    as object meant in the meaning 102
  incarnated 103

indicated (*angezeigte*) Bedeutung   25
indicating (*anzeigende*)
    Bedeutung   25
indirectly public   12, 75, 113–14, 119, 131, 185, 189
intentions
    (*Bedeutungsintentionen*)   141
intimated   25
logical   103
    as ideally closed set   103
modification   26
negotiation   41, 71, 109
    as teleological   5, 145
*phansische*   103
pointing ray of   103
postverbal   144
potential   9, 12, 95, 97, 186
preverbal   168
public   185
saturation   107, 119, 130, 154
    degree of   101
    -specifying   84
sufficiency   12, 97, 101–14
transfer   24
    accuracy of   24
ultimate (*Zielmeinen*)   143
uptake   24, 49
    without recognition   28
meaning bestowal   94
meaningful (*bedeutsam*)   31
meaning fulfilment
    (*Bedeutungserfüllung*)   4, 5, 9, 11, 24, 52, 62–6, 71, 92–4, 97, 101–4, 121, 123, 126–9, 146, 147, 149, 151, 152, 154, 163–5, 179, 180, 183, 185–9
    heterosemiotic   11
    imaginable   112, 151, 163, 179
    as imaginable reconstruction   53
    minimal   186
    as a more or less   12
    proximate   31
    saturated   96
    schematized   27
    as special form of cognition   123
    standard   127
meaning intention
    (*Bedeutungsintention*)   4, 7, 12, 23, 24, 28, 32, 40, 50, 51, 53, 70, 71, 101, 102, 104, 108, 110, 113, 121, 124, 126–8, 130, 141, 145, 147, 160, 162, 179, 180
    nonverbal   3, 21, 50–2, 131
    nonverbal reconstitution of   21, 23
Melle, Ullrich   21, 30, 32, 33 n.2, 87, 132 n.18, 156 n.38, 162
memorial, as-if   6, 29
memory   107
    episodic   167, 175 n.45
    semantic   175 n.45
mental   160–72
    acts   23, 24, 85, 86, 102, 146
    iconicity   93
    imagery   5, 9, 23, 29
    mapping   9
    materiality   128
    material scenarios   97
    projection   31, 40, 67, 72, 86, 91, 93, 140, 145, 146, 167
    scenarios   50
    spaces   9, 122, 165
    time travel   166–7
        spatial and temporal aspects of   160
mentalism
    inevitable   113
    intermonadic   119
    intersubjective   22, 71, 75, 84, 91
Merleau-Ponty, Maurice   xii, xiii n.2, 179, 181–2
meta
    -deixis   90
    language   7, 147
    -linguistic   162
metaphor   92, 124, 149, 150, 165
    literal meaning of   83
metasemantic principles   4
methodological
    choices   3
    commitment   23, 71, 92, 180
Meulen, Alice ter   158 n.123, 159 n.135
Michaelian, Kourken   175 n.49
Milikan, Ruth   99 n.56
mimesis   165–6
    dyadic   166
    post   166
    proto   166
    triadic   166

mimetic schemas  165
Mitcherling, Jeff  194
Mithen, Steven  164, 174 n.28
modal shadow  12, 68, 86, 88, 91
modalities
    nondominant  165
    nonverbal  30, 124
modality of certitude  87
mode
    of act (*Aktweise*)  142
    of being (*Seinsweise*)  185
        actual  185
        possible  185
    of saturation (*Modus der Sättigung*)  142
modes of similarity  106
modification
    as-if  29
    inactuality  29
Mohanty, Jitendra N.  103, 168, 179
moments  27
    existential  27, 184, 189, 191
monadic
    multitude  72, 74
    plurality  52
monads
    community of  6, 8, 12, 30
    linguistic  72-5, 180
monogram  28
Moran, Dermot  14 n.19
more or less  12, 40, 55, 101, 102, 106-8, 114, 137, 145
most-primed-wins-principle  164, 170
motility of the body  182
motivated signified  127, 128, 166, 187, 191
    as carrier of resemblance  137, 144
Mulligan, Kevin  35 n.52, 100 n.69, 117 n.73
multiplicity  41, 103, 109
    of acts  146
    dispersed  105
    ideally limited  141
musilanguage  164, 174 n.28

*Nachlass*  1, 3, 5-7, 11, 12, 21, 24, 26, 27, 30-3, 40, 45, 50, 53, 55, 64, 68, 73, 75, 81, 82, 84-6, 96, 101-4, 106-8, 110, 111, 114, 118, 123, 125, 128, 130, 141, 142, 145, 154, 163, 165, 180, 185, 189, 191
naming
    explicit (*explizite Nennung*)  86
    identically  39, 142
natural attitude, critique of  2, 3, 64
neural
    concept  9, 10, 122, 165
    speed  186
neutrality modification
    of tone  51
noema
    nonformal  26, 27
noematic
    correlates  30
    essential stock  23
    nucleus  25
non-formal
    idealization  106
    noemata  27
nonidentical meaning components  104
non-verbal
    context  129, 148, 152
    practices  62
    precursors  30, 125, 127, 161
    reality  63
    semiosis  11, 172
    signification  8, 160
    signs  124
    sign systems  124
Nunberg, Geoffrey  88, 92, 98 n.39, 99 n.57

object
    actual  25
    categorial  141, 172
        sedimented  190
    -determination  168
    ideal  22, 43
    sensuous  141
    as species  103
objective sense, transmission of  145
observables  10, 83, 88, 110, 178
olfactory  9, 63, 120, 124, 125, 131, 165
ontic
    heteronomy  185, 188-90, 192
ontically
    compound phenomena  179
    heteronomous (*seinsheteronom*)  185

ontogenesis
  community based 172
ontogeny 162, 171, 187
ontological
  commitment 29, 30, 119, 121
ontology
  dualist 13, 43, 178, 179
  existential 184
  material 184
  phenomenological 172, 178, 181, 183, 184, 192
  of sets and particles 179
  tripartite 13, 43, 179–85
openness
  experiential (*Erfahrungsoffenheit*) 121, 127
  multirayed 126
order words 69, 109
originary *Anschauungen* 40
origo of the now 89
Osvath, Mathias 176 n.51
the Other 3, 6, 65, 69, 74, 75
  as analogon 73

Palma, Vittorio de 14 n.20, 174 n.21, 175 n.41
paradigms 10
parallelism 105
  picture-analogical 105, 124
parallel phantasies 52
Partee, Barbara 150, 158 n.123, 159 n.135
*pathemata* (affections of the soul) 21, 147
Patocka, Jan 71, 79 n.78
patterns of wholeness 64
pedagogy 12, 44, 67, 84, 91, 111, 114, 130, 153, 164, 187
Peirce, Charles Sanders 8, 16 n.47, 71, 88, 99 n.40, 159 n.140
Peircean semiotics 2
Pelletier, Francis Jeffry 148, 149, 158 n.119, 158 n.123
percept
  bound 162
  empirical 41, 103, 162
perception 1, 23, 27, 29, 30, 49, 52, 54, 72, 140, 141, 164, 169–71, 182, 187

perceptual
  acts 138
  multimodal 162
  actuality 187
  faith 123
  modification 72, 164
  proto-syntax 172
  sequencing 170
  world (*Wahrnehmungswelt*) 9, 53, 84, 152, 153, 169, 182
perceptually given (*wahrnehmungsmässig gegeben*) 61, 69, 163
Peregrin, Jaroslav 158 n.123
performance 1, 7, 41, 49, 71, 75, 83, 92, 109, 110, 114, 127, 140, 143, 178, 190, 191
Perry, John 92, 99 n.57, 157 n.107
perspective
  first-person 29
  third-person 29
Persson, Tomas 166, 175 n.40
phantasy
  as re-presentation 6, 29
phenomena
  dispositional 84, 85, 142
  of emotions (*Gemütsphänomene*) 145
phenomenological
  approach 113, 153, 182
  first-person vantage point 120
  gaze 3, 69, 76, 127, 188
  method 3
  stretching 3
Philipse, Herman 35 n.56
philosophy of being 180
phylogeny 162, 171, 187
Picasso, Pablo 2
picture-analogical parallelism 105, 124
placeholders 137, 138, 140
Platonic
  ideal species 27
pointing
  for another 171
  declarative 166, 171
  field (*Zeigfeld*) 88–9
  as a form of collaboration 172
  through-the-word-towards-the-thing 142
polythetic 119

Popova, Yanna   165, 174 n.36
postverbal   144
*pragmata* (actual things)   22
pragmatic   2, 4, 21, 81–4, 150, 152, 180
    parameters   108
    satisfaction   109
    scope   109
pre-constituted
    passively   4
precursor
    of syntax   125
predicability   109, 151–3
predicates
    ensemble of   44, 45, 48
predication   50, 94
    adjectival   50
pre-linguistic   170
presentation   67
    fullness of   27
presuppositions
    absence of
        (*Voraussetzungslosigkeit*)   3
pre-syntactic   168
pre-verbal   163
principle of all principles   148
profile
    phenomenological   185
    as thing-synthesis   27
pronunciation   85, 110, 143, 150, 186
    as social act   112
propositional
    content   67, 189
        reversal of   68, 126
propositions   7, 10, 21, 33, 92, 102, 146, 168
proprioception   164
prosodic contour   67, 83, 95, 127, 142
    literal   82
    neutral   82
    standard   143
prospection   176 n.51
protentions   27
protogrammar   165
protomimesis   166
proto-syntactic   125
protosyntax   13, 160–72
    gestural   13, 169–72
    perceptual   54, 169–70
proximate (*das Ungefähre*)   33

psychologism   4, 21, 65
    Locke's   27
Pulvermüller, Friedemann   116 n.64
pure morphology of significations
    (*reine Formenlehre der Bedeutungen*)   102
purpose
    illocutionary   126
Putnam, Hilary   62, 76 n.10, 117 n.76
Pylyshyn, Zenon   36 n.62

quasi-
    acts   29, 165
    appearance   43
    judging   29
    life   74
    perceiving   29
    perception   43, 45
    wishing   29
Quine, Willard van Orman   10, 50, 51, 57 n.60, 179, 192 n.2

radical multiplier   127
reality content (*Realitätsgehalt*)   27
receptivity   147, 168
reciprocal
    interaction (*Wechselverkehr*)   65
reciprocity   70–2
    intersubjective   6, 24, 62, 64, 73, 85, 180, 190
    introjective   11, 12, 61–76
    linguistic   24
    non-verbal   65
    as presupposition of discourse   71
    of standpoints   71, 109
reconstruction   67
    imaginative   44
    proximate   4, 5, 21, 102, 185, 188
recursion   151–3
recursivity   44, 51, 109, 152
reference   22
    Fregean   25, 32, 53
regress
    infinite   10, 130, 145, 153
    vicious   186
Reinach, Adolf   25, 100 n.69, 112, 117 n.73
representation
    analogical   27

diagrammatical   125
nonverbal   188
verbal   188
resemblance   21
    direct   93, 160
    limiting cases of   28–9, 54
    non-verbal   26
    relations (*homoiomata*)   8, 10, 22, 33, 68
resolution   72, 113
retentions   27
reversal of displacement   7, 131, 180, 187, 189
reverse engineering   172
Ricavec, Frank   62
Richard, Mark   157 n.104, 158 n.118
Risser, James   78 n.52
Russell, Bertrand   25, 35 n.58
Ruthrof, Horst   15 n.38, 34 n.10, 36 n.82, 77 n.43, 97 n.5, 98 n.17, 99 n.55, 116 n.72, 192 n.6

Sainsbury, Mark   152, 159 n.143
Salmon, Wesley C.   159 n.149
sameness   54, 101, 103
    approximate   109
saturation (*Sättigung*)   154
    *anschauliche*   53, 107, 130
Saussure, Ferdinand de   7, 15 n.43, 18 n.87
Savage-Rumbaugh, Sue E.   165, 175 n.39
scenarios
    iconic   50
    imaginable   72, 91, 112, 114, 144, 147, 179, 189
    quasi-perceptual   123
Scheler, Max   64, 77 n.26
schema
    cognitive   9
    empirical   9
    meta-semantic   24
    transcendental   28
schematism
    Kantian   8, 122, 188
schematization   28
    degrees of   6, 26, 52, 121, 131, 145, 188
    graded   129, 131
Schlick, Moritz   146, 157

Schlossberger, Matthias   77 n.27
Schütz, Alfred   36 n.79, 42, 53, 64, 65, 71, 77 n.29, 120, 122, 133 n.28, 133 n.32, 170
Searle, John R.   25, 78 n.55, 126, 134 n.49, 158 n.115
sedimentation   45, 48, 65, 121
seeing
    as analogy   42
    essences (*Wesensschau*)   40
    universals   41
semantic   7
    ascent   95, 112–13, 188
    closure   148
    dissemination   183
    drift   46, 65, 161
    essence   22, 23, 31, 53, 83, 101, 106, 137
    exactitude   53, 180
    fuzziness   101
    grasp   28
    holism   21, 30
    identity   22, 23, 28, 29, 102, 106
    immanence   148, 149
    latitude   102, 108
    privacy   27, 91, 103, 113, 189
    scope   41, 109, 127, 145, 149
    sufficiency   7, 145
semantics
    analytical   162
    *a posteriori*   84
    *a priori*   84
    cognitive   9, 165
    formal   92
    hyperintensional   10, 22
    minimal   14 n.18, 153
    minimalist   4
    reductive   85
semiology   2, 7–8
semiotic   xiii, 3, 140
semiotically
    heterogeneous   25
    homogeneous   25
semiotics   7–8, 48, 92
sense (Frege's *Sinn*; Husserl's *Bedeutung*)   26
sensorimotor   165
*sensus communis*   71
sentence

declarative (*apophantic*)  87, 118
  meaning  12, 83, 96, 190
  stripped of voice  85
  -tokens  xiii, 12, 96, 97, 147, 152, 190
  -types  12, 97, 143, 190
sentence-token potential  12, 97
sequential isomorphism  169
Shtyrov, Yuri  116 n.64
sign
  formal  32, 52, 68, 94, 122, 137, 139–45, 148, 154, 182
  systems  6, 39, 48, 122, 131
signification (*Signifikation*)  108, 110
  verbal (*Wortbedeutung*)  42, 66
signified  8, 13, 102
  content  166, 187
  motivated  119, 121
signifiers  11, 84
  arbitrary  7, 119, 127, 128, 130, 131, 137, 140
  formal  10, 53, 96, 132, 141–3, 191
  symbolic  113, 140, 144, 151, 190
similarity  28, 39–41, 54, 55, 121
  circle of (*Ähnlichkeitskreis*)  40
  divergencies in  40, 54
  gradations of  130
  grades of  40
  milieu of (*Ähnlichkeitsmilieu*)  40
  partial  40, 106
  series of increasing (*Steigerungsreihe in Ähnlichkeit*)  40
  total  40
Simons, Peter  35 n.56
singing the world  182
*Sinn* (Husserlian)  8, 9, 11, 12, 24, 26, 32, 68, 75, 95, 119, 121, 123, 128, 152
  as cashed out *Bedeutung*  32
  as non-verbal placement  131
  quasi-material  48
  sedimented (*Sinnsedimentierung*)  168
situation of affairs (*Sachlage*)  125, 141, 144
Slater, Peter  164, 174 n.28
Smith, Barry C.  13 n.2, 17 n.80, 34 n.4, 35 n.49
Smith, David W.  xii, xiii n.1, 154 n.1
Smith, Quentin  99 n.57
Soames, Scott  18 n.83, 100 n.67

social
  coercion  49, 69, 110, 111, 164
  compulsion  112
  mentalism (*Geistigkeit*)  31, 146
  reciprocity  162
sociality (*soziale Geistigkeit*)  27, 31, 61, 65, 70, 101, 165
  as being-within-one-another  31
socially overdetermined  131, 185, 187
Sokolowski, Robert  16 n.59, 26, 27, 35 n.33, 36 n.80, 40, 44, 55 n.9
soliloquy  3, 31, 75
solipsism  4, 65
sorites puzzles  129, 152
Sowa, Rochus  98 n.38, 104, 115 n.36, 129, 130
space  28, 42, 153
  of variation (*Variationsspielraum*)  129
speech
  -act  25, 68
    phenomenology  25
    theories  25, 78 n.55
  analysis (*Sprachanalyse*)  4
  community  xiii, 5–7
    as invariant  11, 50
    as loosely compacted person  8
    as *Monadengemeinschaft*  6, 8, 72–5, 180
  habituality (*Sprachüblichkeit*)  6, 69, 107
  partner (*gemeinsames Gegenüber*)  70
  partners (*Mitunterredner*)  146
Staiti, Andrea  43, 55 n.6, 56 n.29
Starobinsky, Jean  15 n.24
state of affairs (*Sachverhalt*)  68, 81, 86, 95, 111, 119, 144, 164, 189
  meant  125, 137
Stawarska, Beata  8, 15 n.44
*Steigerungsreihe* (increasing trajectory)  54
Steinbock, Anthony  58 n.96, 77 n.22
Sternefeld, Wolfgang  18 n.84, 159 n.151, 195 n.53
stimulus  164
  distal  169
  proximal  169
Stjernfelt, Frederik  33 n.1, 55 n.7, 132 n.1, 175 n.38
Strawson, P.F.  25, 35 n.49

structure
    deep  91
structure of the world
    as precondition  169
subjectivism  4, 45
substantivity  31, 50, 94, 125, 140, 160, 168, 172, 186
such-consciousness (*so-Bewusstsein*)  129
Suddendorf, Thomas  166, 167, 175 n.44
sufficiency  105, 106, 108, 109, 139
sufficient
    intersubjectivity  49
    meaning negotiation  41, 71, 109
    mental materials  6, 109
    reason  12, 53, 105, 114, 127
Sweetser, Ann  100 n.64, 165, 175 n.37
Swiderski, Edward  194 n.40
symbol
    field (*Symbolfeld*)  88
symbolic
    algorithms  141
    calculus  138, 141, 144
    signifier  113, 140, 144, 151, 190
syntax  xii, 4, 9, 13, 51, 62, 113
    as mutation  161
    presupposes semantics  10
    as refinement  161, 169
systems
    of pure deduction  143
Szabo, Zoltan Gendler  81, 97 n.6, 158 n.123
Szanto, Thomas  14 n.19, 80 n.129

Talmy, Leonard  9, 17 n.72, 145, 157 n.81, 165, 174 n.34
Tanz, Christine  95, 99 n.58
Tarski, Alfred  96, 100 n.68, 147, 157 n.105
Tatler, Benjamin W.  176 n.65, 177 n.79
Tellier, Marion  171, 177 n.81
tendency
    aiming at clarity  139
    of the ought (*Sollenstendenz*)  109-11, 191
thematic  40, 74, 170
theories
    externalist  118
thinking  5, 32, 44, 46, 52, 63, 106, 145, 165, 168, 170-2

as speechless (*sprachlos*)  32
Thompson, William L.  36 n.62
thought
    analysis (*Denkanalyse*)  4
    Fregean  10
threshold variations
        (*Schwellenunterschiede*)  145
Tomasello, Michael  171, 172, 175 n.41, 177 n.86
tone  1, 30, 33, 68, 81-97
    a component of all linguistic expressions  xiii, 12
    a component of the word  87
    as a critical tool  87
    as deviation  81
    as implicit deixis  81-97
    as indication of kinds of sentences  87
    as indispensable intentional component  86
    as modification of aboutness  86
    as public  83
    two strata of  83, 85, 88
    ubiquity of  84-8
    as voice  85, 108
total typicality (*Totalitätstypik*)  29
transcendental  7, 9, 30, 50, 65, 172
transitional consciousness
        (*Durchgangsbewusstsein*)  31, 112, 151, 163
translation  183
    indeterminacy of  158 n.123
truth
    truth-conditional  146, 147
    truth value (*Wahrheitswert*)  21
truth-conditional semantics  68, 146-8, 189
Tugendhat, Ernst  34 n.8
Tulving, Endel  167, 175 n.45, 175 n.50
Turner, Mark  17 n.77, 122, 133 n.25, 165, 174 n.36
Tversky, Barbara  175 n.41
Twardowski, Kasimir  34 n.29, 72
twin-system theory  170
Tye, Michael  36 n.62
types
    fluid  52, 53, 137
typifications
    gustatory  120

non-essential   30
olfactory   124
as quanta of experience   12, 119–23, 187
typified
    experience   53, 120, 121, 131, 187
    knowledge   145, 154
    percepts   154, 162

Uehlein, Friedrich   52, 55 n.17, 56 n.33, 57 n.74
*Umwelt*   75, 141
underdetermination   105
unuttered sentences   95–7, 148
utterance   66, 68, 81–4
    as carrier of intentionality   12
    competence   152
    literal   83
    primacy of   6, 12, 122, 190

vagueness   26, 120, 129, 151, 152
validity (*Geltung*)   30
Vandervelde, Pol   32, 37 n.125, 112, 117 n.78, 127, 134 n.51
variability
    limits of   129
variants   4, 41, 46, 123, 182
variation
    imaginative   25, 41–3, 47, 123, 151, 187
verbal
    meanings   3, 9, 64
    pointing   51, 171
    substitution   50, 51, 63, 106, 107, 130
verbality   140
verification principle   146
visual bias   165
vitality   27
vivid imaginability (*Anschaulichkeit*)   118
vividness   1, 40, 130, 188
vivid presentation (*anschauliche Vorstellung*)   145
voice   1, 10
    as implicit deixis   31, 84, 127, 189
    necessary presence of   71
    primacy of   82
    within social constraints   75
*Vorstellung*   5, 6, 9, 10, 23, 24, 27–30, 40, 51, 67, 71, 72, 84, 87, 93, 104, 107, 119, 127, 128, 130, 140, 145, 165, 166, 172
    empty   40
    schematized   111
    underdetermined   152
*Vorstellungsklavier*   5
*Vorstellungswelten*   166
*vouloir dire*   51, 131
Vygotsky, Lev S.   117 n.81, 166, 175 n.43

Wachter, Daniel von   194 n.40
Wall, Robert E.   159 n.135
Warren, Nicholas de   48, 56 n.34, 56 n.50
we-community (*Wir-Gemeinschaft*)   65
Werning, Markus   158 n.123
Willems, Roel M.   177 n.85
Williams, Timothy   159 n.143
Wittenberg, Eva   176 n.52, 177 n.87
Wittgenstein, Ludwig   5, 8, 10, 15 n.27, 24, 25, 29, 44, 54, 55 n.15, 72, 77 n.42, 109, 110, 116 n.58, 144, 158 n.113, 161, 191
Woodfield, Andrew   35
word
    acoustic   82, 143
    evocative power of   68
    meaning consciousness (*Wortbedeutungsbewusssein*)   66, 86, 110, 112, 113, 119, 141, 186
    as ought (*Sollenstendenz*)   109–11, 191
    sound consciousness (*Wortlautbewusstsein*)   47, 51, 66, 86, 110, 112–13, 119, 131, 163, 186, 188
world
    *in absentia*   12, 118, 190
    coherent   65
    imperfect contingency of   106
    perceptual   9, 53, 84, 152, 153, 182
    prephantomic   124
    schematic   124
    shared spiritual (*gemeingeistliche Welt*)   31
    as *tertium comparationis*   74, 75

Zacks, Jeffrey M.   175 n.41
Zahavi, Dan   33 n.1, 132 n.1
Zeno's paradox   13, 153, 159 n.149

Zentall, Thomas   175 n.49
Zlatev, Jordan   9, 17 n.68, 17 n.74, 165, 166, 174 n.36, 175 n.40

*Zumutung*   1, 6, 69, 97, 109–11, 144, 187, 191
Zweig, Arnulf   15 n.30

www.ingramcontent.com/pod-product-compliance
Lightning Source LLC
Chambersburg PA
CBHW062138300426
44115CB00012BA/1977